D0031845

# CLINICAL AND NEUROPSYCHOLOGICAL ASPECTS OF CLOSED HEAD INJURY

# Clinical and neuropsychological aspects of closed head injury

*Second Edition*

John T.E. Richardson
*Brunel University, Uxbridge, UK*

First published 2000 by Psychology Press Ltd
27 Church Road, Hove, East Sussex, BN3 2FA

http://www.psypress.co.uk

Simultaneously published in the USA and Canada
by Taylor & Francis Inc
325 Chestnut Street, Suite 800, Philadelphia, PA 19106

Psychology Press is part of the Taylor & Francis Group



*British Library Cataloguing in Publication Data*
A catalogue record for this book is available from the British Library

ISBN 0-86377-751-1 (Hbk)
ISSN 0967 9944

Cover design by Joyce Chester
Typeset in Times by Facing Pages, Southwick, West Sussex
Printed and bound in the United Kingdom by Biddles Ltd, Guildford and King's Lynn

# Contents

# Acknowledgements

I began the task of rewriting this book whilst I was on study leave from Brunel University and working as a Visiting Research Professor in the Institute of Educational Technology at the Open University. I am most grateful to both these institutions for their support. I am also grateful to Doreen Baxter of the National Centre for Brain Injury Rehabilitation, Northampton, Graham Beaumont of the Royal Hospital for Neuro-Disability, London, and Bryan Jennett of the University of Glasgow for their helpful comments on the draft manuscript of this book; and to Chris Code of the University of Sydney, Duane Haines of the University of Mississippi, Narinder Kapur of the University of Southampton, and Donald Stein of Emory University, Atlanta, for their additional advice. Finally, I am grateful to Ibrar Ahmad of the UK Department of Health, to David Murphy and Jennifer Weir of the Information and Statistics Division of the Common Services Agency for the National Health Service in Scotland, and to Jim Plunkett of the Welsh Health Common Services Authority for providing the data on the epidemiology of head injuries presented in Chapter 1.

John T.E. Richardson
July 1999

*Brain Damage, Behaviour and Cognition: Developments in Clinical Neuropsychology Titles in Series*

---

*Series Editors*
**Chris Code,** University of Sydney, Australia
**Dave Miller,** University of College, Suffolk, UK

**Cognitive Retraining Using Microcomputers**
*Veronica A. Bradley, John L. Welch, and Clive E. Skilbeck*
**The Characteristics of Aphasia**
*Chris Code (Ed.)*
**Classic Cases in Neuropsychology**
*Chris Code, Claus-W. Wallesch, Yves Joanettte, and André Roch Lecours (Eds.)*
**The Neuropsychology of Schizophrenia**
*Anthony S. David and John C. Cutting (Eds.)*
**Neuropsychology and the Dementias**
*Siobhan Hart and James M. Semple*
**Clinical Neuropsychology of Alcoholism**
*Robert G. Knight and Barry E. Longmore*
**Neuropsychology of the Amnesic Syndrome**
*Alan J. Parkin and Nicholas R.C. Leng*
**Unilateral Neglect: Clinical and Experimental Studies**
*Ian H. Robertson and John C. Marshall (Eds.)*
**Cognitive Rehabilitation in Perspective**
*Rodger Wood and Ian Fussey (Eds.)*

---

*Series Editors*
**Chris Code,** University of Sydney, Australia
**Glyn Humphreys,** University of Birmingham, UK

**Transcortical Aphasias**
*Marcelo L. Berthier*
**Communication Disorders following Traumatic Brain Injury**
*Skye McDonald, Leanne Togher, and Chris Code (Eds)*
**Clinical and Neuropsychological Aspects of Closed Head Injury (2nd ed.)**
*John T.E. Richardson*
**Spatial Neglect: A Clinical Handbook for Diagnosis and Treatment**
*Ian H. Robertson and Peter W. Halligan*
**Apraxia: The Neuropsychology of Action**
*Leslie J. Gonzalez Rothi and Kenneth Heilman*
**Developmental Cognitive Neuropsychology**
*Christine Temple*

# Series preface

From being an area primarily on the periphery of mainstream behavioural and cognitive science, neuropsychology has developed in recent years into an area of central concern for a range of disciplines. We are witnessing not only a revolution in the way in which brain–behaviour–cognition relationships are viewed, but a widening of interest concerning developments in neuropsychology on the part of a range of workers in a variety of fields. Major advances in brain-imaging techniques and the cognitive modelling of the impairments following brain damage promise a wider understanding of the nature of the representation of cognition and behaviour in the damaged and undamaged brain.

Neuropsychology is now centrally important for those working with brain-damaged people, but the very rate of expansion in the area makes it difficult to keep up with findings from current research. The aim of the *Brain Damage, Behaviour and Cognition* series is to publish a wide range of books that present comprehensive and up-to-date overviews of current developments in specific areas of interest.

These books will be of particular interest to those working with the brain-damaged. It is the editors' intention that undergraduates, postgraduates, clinicians and researchers in psychology, speech pathology and medicine will find this series a useful source of information on important current developments. The authors and editors of the books in this series are experts in their respective fields, working at the forefront of contemporary research. They have produced texts that are accessible and scholarly. We thank them for their contribution and their hard work in fulfilling the aims of the series.

CC and GH
Sydney, Australia and Birmingham, UK
Series Editors

# Abbreviations

| | |
|---|---|
| CT | Computerised tomography |
| DSM | *Diagnostic and Statistical Manual of Mental Disorders* |
| DSM-III | DSM, 3rd edition |
| DSM-IV | DSM, 4th edition |
| GAS | Glasgow Assessment Schedule |
| GCS | Glasgow Coma Scale |
| GOAT | Galveston Orientation and Amnesia Test |
| GOS | Glasgow Outcome Scale |
| ICD | *International Classification of Diseases* |
| ICD-8 | ICD, 8th revision |
| ICD-9 | ICD, 9th revision |
| ICD-9-CM | ICD-9, clinical modification |
| ICD-10 | ICD, 10th revision |
| IQ | Intelligence Quotient |
| MAE | Multilingual Aphasia Examination |
| MMPI | Minnesota Multiphasic Personality Inventory |
| MQ | Memory Quotient |
| MRI | Magnetic resonance imaging |
| NART | National Adult Reading Test |
| NCCEA | Neurosensory Center Comprehensive Examination for Aphasia |
| PASAT | Paced auditory serial addition task |
| PET | Positron emission tomography |
| PICA | Porch Index of Communicative Ability |
| PTA | Post-traumatic amnesia |
| RA | Retrograde amnesia |
| SPECT | Single photon emission computed tomography |
| WAIS | Wechsler Adult Intelligence Scale |
| WAIS-R | Wechsler Adult Intelligence Scale—Revised |
| WAIS-III | Wechsler Adult Intelligence Scale—3rd Edition |
| WISC | Wechsler Intelligence Scale for Children |
| WMS | Wechsler Memory Scale |
| WMS-R | Wechsler Memory Scale—revised |
| WMS-III | Wechsler Memory Scale—3rd edition |

CHAPTER ONE

# Definitions, epidemiology, and causes

In all industrialised countries, closed head injuries are responsible for vast numbers of hospital admissions and days of work lost. For instance, over 120,000 patients are admitted to hospital in the United Kingdom each year with a diagnosis that reflects closed head injury. Such injuries are a major cause of deaths following accidents, especially those that involve children and young people, and they are also a major cause of disablement and morbidity among the survivors. The population of individuals who have sustained head injuries is a substantial one and one that is not likely to decrease in the foreseeable future. However, the clinical problem of treating these vast numbers of patients is not going to be solved by any dramatic medical breakthrough. Rather, it must be tackled by seeking a better appreciation of the condition that these people present.

This clinical condition is intrinsically a neurological one, but its proper evaluation demands an understanding of the associated psychology and psychopathology. At the same time, a major neurological condition with such a high incidence ought to be extremely informative about the functioning of the human brain and hence provide a major focus for neuropsychological investigation. In this book, I have tried to integrate these two different perspectives by reviewing the clinical and neuropsychological aspects of closed head injury in a manner that is equally intelligible to researchers who are interested in the effects of brain damage upon human behaviour and to practitioners who are responsible for the assessment, the management, and the rehabilitation of head-injured patients.

An initial remark is necessary concerning my terminology. Nowadays, it is generally recommended that clinical descriptors should follow rather than precede the nouns that they qualify to avoid labelling people by their clinical conditions or disabilities: thus, one should talk of "people who have a disability" rather than of "disabled people", and certainly not of "the disabled" (see American Psychological Association, 1994, pp. 59–60). For the same reason, one should talk of "people who have sustained a head injury" rather than "head-injured people". Nevertheless, the exclusive use of the former expression in a publication of this sort would soon become cumbersome and repetitive, and so I shall use these expressions interchangeably in this book.

# DEFINITIONS

## Closed and open head injuries

Strictly speaking, a *closed head injury* is an injury to the head that does not expose the contents of the skull. Such an injury can be distinguished from an *open* head injury in which the dura mater (the membrane that lines the interior of the skull) is torn and consequently the contents of the skull are exposed. This distinction is important in connection with the patient's immediate clinical management because of the risk of infection. However, it is of only limited value for present purposes, because head injuries of both sorts can occur that are otherwise relatively similar in terms of their clinical and neuropsychological consequences.

It is more useful, if rather less precise, to use the term "closed head injury" to denote an injury in which the primary mechanism of damage is one of *blunt* impact to the head (Levin, Grossman, & Kelly, 1976a). This usually arises either as the result of rapid acceleration of the head due to a physical blow from a relatively blunt object or as the result of rapid deceleration of the head due to contact with a blunt and relatively immovable object or surface (although compression injuries resulting from crushing of the head may occasionally be encountered). A blunt impact may cause an open head injury by inducing a fracture of the vault or the base of the skull. Indeed, some authorities nowadays prefer to talk in terms of "blunt head injury" rather than "closed head injury".

In this sense, closed head injuries are conventionally distinguished from *penetrating* head injuries of the sort produced by sharp instruments, such as knives or umbrellas, or by explosively propelled missiles, such as bullets or fragments of shells. The latter account for most cases of head injury sustained in military conflicts (Dresser et al., 1973; Russell, 1951). During peace-time, the incidence of penetrating head injury is much less common, though in some parts of the United States gunshot wounds (self-inflicted or otherwise) are the most common cause of fatal head injury (Frankowski, 1986).

Closed and penetrating head injuries differ not merely in terms of their likely external causes, but also in the patterns of neurological deficit to which they tend to give rise. In particular, penetrating head injuries produced by low-velocity missiles may well give rise to severe focal brain lesions but they often cause little or no disturbance of consciousness (Russell, 1951; Salazar et al., 1986). In contrast, closed head injuries are much more likely to produce disturbances of consciousness and diffuse cerebral damage. In this book I shall be concerned solely with the clinical and neuropsychological aspects of closed head injuries as just defined; that is, *a closed head injury is an injury to the head in which the primary mechanism of damage is one of blunt impact.*

The *International Classification of Diseases* (ICD) was originally developed by the World Health Organisation for the classification and comparison of morbidity and mortality data and for the indexing of hospital records. In terms of the ninth revision, ICD-9 (World Health Organisation, 1977, chap. XVII), cases of head injury are classified as follows (cf. Jennett, 1996; Jennett & Teasdale, 1981, pp. 1–2):

800 Fracture of vault of skull
801 Fracture of base of skull
802 Fracture of face bones
803 Other and unqualified skull fractures
804 Multiple fractures involving skull or face with other bones
850 Concussion
851 Cerebral laceration and contusion
852 Subarachnoid, subdural and extradural haemorrhage, following injury
853 Other and unspecified intracranial haemorrhage following injury
854 Intracranial injury of other and unspecified nature.

The practical utility of this classification is rather limited, as Jennett (1996) remarked, because it is based on pathological rather than clinical criteria, because the categories are not mutually exclusive, and because they are not explicitly related to clinical criteria of the severity of the injury.

Some authors have excluded ICD-9 category 802 ("Fracture of face bones") from consideration (e.g. Caveness, 1979; Jennett & MacMillan, 1981; Sosin, Sniezek, & Waxweiler, 1995; cf. also Brookes et al., 1990), apparently on the assumption that injuries of this sort are unlikely to give rise to serious brain damage. To be sure, the facial skeleton consists of compressible, energy-absorbing bones that cushion and protect the intracranial structures in the event of a frontal impact. Nevertheless, many patients with major facial injuries, especially those involving the forehead, show clear deficits on neurological examination, and in such cases computerised tomography (CT) reveals a variety of intracranial lesions (Lee, Wagner, & Kopaniky, 1987).

The US Department of Health and Human Services developed a clinical modification of ICD-9 (ICD-9-CM) "to serve as a useful tool in the area of classification of morbidity data for indexing of medical records, medical care review, and ambulatory and other medical care programs, as well as for basic health statistics" (Public Health Service, Health Care Financing Administration, 1980, p. xvii). The disease classification of the original three-digit categories relating to a fracture of the skull (i.e. 800, 801, 803, and 804) was expanded along the following lines (chap. 17):

800.0 Closed without mention of intracranial injury
800.1 Closed with cerebral laceration and contusion
800.2 Closed with subarachnoid, subdural, and extradural haemorrhage
800.3 Closed with other and unspecified intracranial haemorrhage
800.4 Closed with intracranial injury of other and unspecified nature
800.5 Open without mention of intracranial injury
800.6 Open with cerebral laceration and contusion
800.7 Open with subarachnoid, subdural, and extradural haemorrhage
800.8 Open with other and unspecified intracranial haemorrhage
800.9 Open with intracranial injury of other and unspecified nature

The preamble to the relevant section of ICD-9-CM explained that in this context "open" subsumed the following descriptions: "compound", "infected", "missile", "puncture", and "with foreign body". All other cases of nonpathological skull fracture (including those described as "comminuted", "depressed", "elevated", "fissured", "linear", and "simple") were classified as "closed" fractures. A somewhat different subclassification was applied to the original three-digit categories relating to intracranial injury without a fracture of the skull (i.e. 851, 852, 853, and 854), based on whether there was mention of an open intracranial wound.

The tenth revision, ICD-10, introduced a different coding scheme for "injuries to the head" (World Health Organisation, 1992, chap. XIX). Only certain headings within this scheme are relevant to closed head injuries as they were defined earlier:

S02.0 Fracture of vault of skull
S02.1 Fracture of base of skull
S02.2 Fracture of nasal bones
S02.3 Fracture of orbital floor
S02.4 Fracture of malar and maxillary bones
S02.6 Fracture of mandible
S02.7 Multiple fractures involving skull and facial bones
S02.8 Fractures of other skull and facial bones
S02.9 Fracture of skull and facial bones, part unspecified
S06.0 Concussion
S06.1 Traumatic cerebral oedema
S06.2 Diffuse brain injury
S06.3 Focal brain injury
S06.4 Epidural haemorrhage
S06.5 Traumatic subdural haemorrhage
S06.6 Traumatic subarachnoid haemorrhage

S06.7 Intracranial injury with prolonged coma
S06.8 Other intracranial injuries
S06.9 Intracranial injury, unspecified
S07.0 Crushing injury of face
S07.1 Crushing injury of skull
S07.8 Crushing injury of other parts of head
S07.9 Crushing injury of head, part unspecified
S09.7 Multiple injuries of head
S09.8 Other specified injuries of head
S09.9 Unspecified injury of head

At the time of writing, ICD-10 is gradually superseding ICD-9 as the system adopted by national epidemiological sources. It should however be emphasised that ICD codes are intended for epidemiological purposes (and relevant data on the incidence of head injury will be discussed later in this chapter).

ICD codes are of limited practical relevance because they are hardly ever used by themselves to characterise individual head-injured patients for clinical purposes, as opposed to the purposes of keeping medical records (see also Jennett, 1996). However, they are used by psychologists and psychiatrists in connection with the *Diagnostic and Statistical Manual of Mental Disorders* (DSM). This was devised in response to the clinical limitations of earlier editions of the ICD. The third edition (DSM-III) was developed in coordination with ICD-9; the fourth edition (DSM-IV) was devised in coordination with ICD-9-CM and ICD-10 (American Psychiatric Association, 1994, pp. xvi–xxi).

DSM-IV promotes the use in clinical assessment of a system based on five axes. Axis I is concerned with clinical disorders and other conditions that may be a focus of clinical attention, and Axis II is concerned with personality disorders and mental retardation. These subsume the conditions classified as "mental disorders" in ICD-9-CM or ICD-10, for which detailed diagnostic criteria are provided. Axis IV is for reporting psychosocial or environmental factors that may affect the diagnosis, treatment, or prognosis of the mental disorders classified on Axes I and II, whereas Axis V is for reporting the clinician's judgement of the patient's overall level of functioning.

Axis III is for reporting general medical conditions that may be relevant for the understanding or the management of the mental disorders classified on Axes I and II. These subsume all conditions not classified as "mental disorders" in ICD-9-CM and ICD-10. This axis simply uses the extended classifications from ICD-9-CM that were listed earlier (with no additional diagnostic criteria); for example, dementia due to head trauma is coded as 294.1 on Axis I and 854.00 on Axis III. However, it is possible to use a different coding if there is insufficient evidence for a causal relationship; for instance, dementia in a head-injured patient could be coded as 294.8 on Axis I (that is, "Dementia not Otherwise Specified") and 854.00 on Axis III (see American Psychiatric Association, 1994, pp. 25–31, 148, 152, 155).

## Concepts and measures of severity

Jennett (1976a) pointed out that the severity of a head injury could be measured in terms of the occurrence or duration of its initial features, the incidence of complications and its long-term consequences or *sequelae*. Most clinicians attempt to determine the severity of a closed head injury in terms of the degree of neurological or neuropsychological impairment during the immediate post-traumatic period. In particular, closed head injuries tend to produce an immediate loss or impairment of consciousness, and Symonds (1928) suggested that the duration of this impairment could be used as an indication of the degree of cerebral damage.

The notion of an immediate loss of consciousness is included in the traditional concept of cerebral *concussion*. The clinical usage of this term has been influenced by assumptions about the underlying pathophysiology and the wider effects of closed head injury upon neurological function. Concussion (or *commotio cerebri*) was traditionally defined as the transient loss of consiousness without permanent damage to the brain (e.g. Denny-Brown & Russell, 1941; Symonds, 1928; Ward, 1966). In this sense, it was to be contrasted with "contusion" (*contusio cerebri*), the physical bruising of the brain with or without a loss of consciousness (e.g. Eden & Turner, 1941).

Nowadays, the latter is reflected in the use in the United States of the expression "(traumatic) brain injury" to refer to actual physical damage to the brain, as opposed to the more generic expression "head injury" (e.g. Kraus et al., 1984; Waxweiler, Thurman, Sniezek, Sosin, & O'Neil, 1995). (In Europe, in contrast, the expression "brain injury" often subsumes all kinds of neurological damage and disease.) This does beg the question of how to classify individuals who have sustained a blow to the head and who show the characteristic symptoms of brain injury but who do not ascribe those symptoms to the injury. Gordon et al. (1998) suggested that these should be described as cases of "hidden" traumatic brain injury.

However, this sort of distinction has long been recognised to be problematic (Symonds, 1962). As Ommaya and Gennarelli (1974) pointed out, the modern concept of cerebral concussion includes at least the possibility of permanent brain damage (see Chapter 2). It is recognised that such damage is not an inevitable result of a single concussive blow. Indeed, studies using magnetic resonance imaging (MRI) have shown that lesions to the grey and white matter of the brain may well resolve within three months following a minor closed head injury; any residual lesions are likely to be extraparenchymal abnormalities, such as chronic subdural haematomas (Levin, Amparo, et al., 1987). Nevertheless, there is barely any difference between the force necessary to cause a purely transient functional impairment and that sufficient to produce irreversible structural change (Shetter & Demakas, 1979). In addition, many authorities stress the cumulative effect of episodes of minor but permanent damage in people exposed to repeated mild head trauma, such as boxers, footballers, or horse riders.

As a separate issue, it is sometimes assumed that closed head injury gives rise *both* to an impairment of consciousness *and* to an amnesia for episodes immediately preceding the injury, and the latter condition of *retrograde amnesia* has sometimes been incorporated into the concept of cerebral concussion. However, it is important to distinguish carefully between a loss of consciousness and retrograde amnesia, since these may be produced by different sorts of cerebral dysfunction, and retrograde amnesia is not an inevitable concomitant of a loss of consciousness. Moreover, research findings to be discussed in Chapter 3 suggest that the duration of retrograde amnesia has little value as an index of the severity of injury.

It is generally agreed that the duration and extent of the patient's impairment of consciousness is likely to be a factor of major importance in evaluating the severity of a closed head injury and in predicting the eventual outcome (e.g. Evans et al., 1976). It has been suggested that a *severe* head injury can be defined as one that produces a state of unconsciousness or *coma* lasting longer than six hours (e.g. Jennett, Teasdale, & Knill-Jones, 1975a; Medical Disability Society, 1988). However, the duration of coma is difficult to estimate in less severely injured patients, who often have recovered consciousness by the time they are admitted to hospital (Gronwall & Wrightson, 1980).

Wilson, Teasdale, Hadley, Wiedmann, and Lang (1994) found that the duration of coma was correlated with the amount of damage to central brain structures (the corpus callosum, the brainstem, and the cerebellum) that was apparent in magnetic resonance imaging carried out within the first week after head injury. However, it showed no correlation with the amount of damage to hemispheric regions. This suggested that disturbances of consciousness were related to disruption of the function of subcortical activating mechanisms (Ommaya & Gennarelli, 1974).

Moreover, even the concept of coma or unconsciousness is not immune to definitional problems. Many definitions that have been offered emphasise the inability to establish intellectual contact with the patient (Bond, 1979; Overgaard et al., 1973; Roberts, 1979, p. 30; Stover & Zeiger, 1976; Thomsen, 1975, 1976): the patient's consciousness is impaired to the extent that he or she cannot be aroused by spoken commands, understand questions, or provide coherent responses. Nevertheless, other aspects of the patient's behaviour may be important.

Recently, a committee set up by the American Congress of Rehabilitation Medicine (1995, p. 206) recommended that the following neurobehavioural criteria should be adopted for defining coma:

1. The patient's eyes do not open either spontaneously *or* to external stimulation; and
2. The patient does not follow any commands; and
3. The patient does not mouth or utter recognizable words; and
4. The patient does not demonstrate intentional movement (may show reflexive movement such as posturing, withdrawal from pain, or involuntary smiling); and
5. The patient cannot *sustain* visual pursuit movements of the eyes through a 45° arc in any direction when the eyes are held open manually; and
6. The above criteria are not secondary to use of paralytic agents. (p. 206)

## The Glasgow Coma Scale

To try to resolve such problems of definition and to facilitate communication among different medical units and among different hospital staff, Teasdale and Jennett (1974) devised the Glasgow Coma Scale (GCS). This involved a separate assessment of motor responses, verbal responses, and eye opening on an ordered set of criteria indicating the degree of cerebral dysfunction:

Motor responses:
- Obeying commands
- A localising response
- A flexor response
- Extensor posturing
- No response

Verbal responses:
- Orientation
- Confused conversation
- Inappropriate speech
- Incomprehensible speech
- No response

Eye opening:
- Spontaneous eye opening
- Eye opening in response to speech
- Eye opening in response to pain
- No response

In the absence of an appropriate motor response to command, the first element of this Scale was assessed by observing the responses to painful pressure applied to the fingernail bed with a pencil; if flexion of the relevant limb was observed, stimulation was applied to the head, neck and trunk to test for localisation. "Orientation" referred to an awareness of the self and one's environment: "The patient should know who he is, where he is, and why he is there; know the year, the season, and the month" (Teasdale & Jennett, 1974, p. 82).

Preliminary applications of this Scale suggested that it could be readily and routinely used by relatively inexperienced junior doctors or nursing staff to assess a patient's level of consciousness (Teasdale, 1975). High rates of consistency were demonstrated among different raters, whether the Scale was being used by nurses, neurosurgeons, or general surgical trainees, and it also seemed to be fairly insensitive to linguistic and cultural variations among different observers (see Braakman, Avezaat, Maas, Roel, & Schouten, 1977; Teasdale, Knill-Jones, & Jennett, 1974; Teasdale, Knill-Jones, & Van der Sande, 1978).

In their original presentation of the GCS, Teasdale and Jennett (1974) emphasised that for any particular patient one or other element of the Scale might prove to be untestable. For example, the limbs might be immobilised by splints for fractures, speech might be precluded by intubation or a tracheostomy, and swollen eyelids or bilateral lesions of the third nerve might make eye opening impossible (cf. Marshall, Becker, et al., 1983). For this reason, as Jennett (1976a) noted, a patient's state was simply described in terms of his or her place on each individual element, and any attempt to define a series of levels of coma was deliberately avoided. Nevertheless, Jennett, Teasdale, and Knill-Jones (1975a, 1975b) suggested that the criteria appropriate to each element of the Scale could be rank-ordered from the poorest to the best possible response, and that a patient's overall level of consciousness could be quantified by summing the ranks of the best observed response across the three elements. This yielded a total score between 3 and 14, reflecting various levels of impairment extending from deep coma through mild confusion to normal consciousness.

Subsequently, Teasdale and Jennett (1976) amended the motor-response element by distinguishing between a normal flexor response (i.e. a rapid withdrawal of the stimulated arm by lateral movement at the shoulder away from the body and often by external rotation of the arm) and abnormal or stereotyped responses (such as the hemiplegic or decorticate posture with the shoulder drawn in towards the body and the elbow and fingers flexed). It has been suggested that this can be a difficult distinction for nurses, nonspecialist doctors, and even experienced observers to make (Braakman et al., 1977; Jennett & Teasdale, 1981, p. 78). Nevertheless, this extended version of the GCS is the one that is now in general use (see Table 1.1).

TABLE 1.1

Extended Glasgow Coma Scale

| | |
|---|---|
| Eye opening (E) | |
| spontaneous | 4 |
| to speech | 3 |
| to pain | 2 |
| nil | 1 |
| Best motor response (M) | |
| obeys | 6 |
| localises | 5 |
| withdraws | 4 |
| abnormal flexion | 3 |
| extensor response | 2 |
| nil | 1 |
| Verbal response (V) | |
| orientated | 5 |
| confused conversation | 4 |
| inappropriate words | 3 |
| incomprehensible sound | 2 |
| nil | 1 |
| Coma score (E + M + V) = 3 to 15 | |

From Management of head injuries, by B. Jennett & G. Teasdale (1981) p. 78). Philadelphia: Davis. Copyright © 1981 Oxford University Press Inc. Used by permission of Oxford University Press.

Using the standard scoring method, this version yields a total score between 3 and 15.

Teasdale and Jennett (1976, p. 50) defined "coma" clinically as "a patient who showed no eye opening, who did not obey commands, nor give any comprehensible verbal response"; this corresponds to a total score on the original GCS of 7 or less (cf. Winogron, Knights, & Bawden, 1984) and to a total score on the amended GCS of 8 or less. The latter has been widely used as an operational definition of "coma" by researchers in the United States, Western Europe, and Australia.

Wilson et al. (1994) showed that the duration of coma on the above definition showed a very high correlation (–.83) with the total GCS score on admission. They found that both measures were correlated with the amount of damage to central brain structures (the corpus callosum, the brainstem, and the cerebellum) that was apparent in magnetic resonance imaging carried out within the first week after head injury. However, they showed no correlation with the amount of damage to hemispheric regions. As mentioned earlier, this suggested that disturbances of consciousness were related to disruption of the function of subcortical activating mechanisms.

Nevertheless, the committee of the American Congress of Rehabilitation Medicine (1995) argued that GCS scores of 8 or less did not always correspond to the clinical definition of coma: "For example, brain-injured patients with concomitant high cervical lesions may present with spontaneous eye opening (E4), flaccid limbs (M1), and inappropriate words (V3) yielding a total GCS score of 8." Although the committee recognised that a numerical grading system could be a practical way of tracking a patient's progress for prognostic or research purposes, its members insisted that it was "not sufficient for determining an accurate clinical diagnosis nor should it be used in isolation to establish return of consciousness"(p. 206).

The apparent consistency with which the GCS could be used by observers in different centres encouraged its use in an international collaborative study, initially between units in Scotland and the Netherlands (Jennett, Teasdale, Braakman, Minderhoud, & Knill-Jones, 1976) and subsequently involving also units in the United States (Heiden, Small, Caton, Weiss, & Kurze, 1983; Jennett, Teasdale, et al., 1977, 1979). This eventually encompassed 1000 patients and demonstrated that the total score on the GCS was highly predictive of the eventual clinical outcome following head injury. The same conclusion emerged from other investigations (e.g. Alexandre, Colombo, Nertempi, & Benedetti, 1983; Bowers & Marshall, 1980; Gennarelli, Champion, Copes, & Sacco, 1994; Marshall et al., 1991; Marshall, Becker, et al., 1983; Marshall & Bowers, 1985).

Some researchers have classified the severity of patients' head injuries in terms of their total score on the extended GCS on their admission to hospital. Commonly used categories are:

13–15: "mild" or "minor"
9–12: "moderate" or "moderately severe"
3–8: "severe".

In many research studies, the vast majority of patients who are admitted to hospital have "mild" head injuries in terms of this classification (Jennett, 1989). However, there are merely three possible scores on the GCS in this range, and this has led some researchers to suggest that a more sensitive and differentiated instrument would be more appropriate than the GCS for assessing patients with mild head injuries (Kraus & Nourjah, 1989; see also Esselman & Uomoto, 1995).

During the immediate phase of recovery from severe closed head injury, the total score on the GCS is largely a function of the patient's motor responses (Braakman et al., 1977; Jennett, 1976b, 1979; Levin & Eisenberg, 1979b; Levin, Grossman, Rose, & Teasdale, 1979; Teasdale, Murray, Parker, & Jennett, 1979). In contrast, during the later phase of recovery from minor closed head injury, it is largely a function of the patient's verbal responses (Rimel, Giordani, Barth, Boll, & Jane, 1981). Indeed, Jennett and Teasdale (1981, p. 89) suggested that, once head-injured patients were speaking, the distinction between expletive language, confused conversation and normal orientation provided a useful means of grading their brain dysfunction. Others have suggested that the prognostic capacity of the GCS could be enhanced by including radiological findings (see Levin et al., 1993; Williams, Levin, & Eisenberg, 1990).

The GCS has also been incorporated into more general systems for measuring the severity of physiological injury (e.g. Champion et al., 1989, 1990). These scales appear to be useful in deciding upon the management of patients with severe multiple injuries and in predicting the likelihood of survival. However, it has been argued that they are inappropriate for the specific purpose of assessing the severity of head injuries (Jennett, 1996).

## Problems with the Glasgow Coma Scale

*Time of administration.* There has been some controversy concerning the appropriate time after injury when the GCS should first be administered. Reilly, Adams, Graham, and Jennett (1975) noted that roughly one-third of all fatally injured patients were known to have had a "lucid interval" in which they had talked at some time after their accidents. They suggested that a lucid interval occurred in a similar proportion of severely injured but nonfatal cases, and this was borne out by subsequent research (Jennett et al., 1976, Jennett, Teasdale, et al., 1977; cf. Bruce, Schut, Bruno, Wood, & Sutton, 1978). Teasdale and Jennett (1976) noted that in such patients the development of coma would be delayed. In this situation, they made an initial assessment using the GCS after the development of coma, but also noted the patient's clinical state during the interim period. In considering the prognostic value of the GCS, they suggested the use of a patient's best level of clinical function during the first 24 hours after the onset of coma, and they restricted their attention to those patients who remained in coma for at least six hours (see also Jennett et al., 1976).

Jennett, Teasdale, et al. (1977) sought to justify the latter decision by arguing that a patient's clinical state during the first few hours following a head injury could be contaminated by extracranial injuries and their associated complications (such as shock and respiratory insufficiency). They suggested that other researchers might well have overestimated the extent of brain damage in their patients by taking as a baseline their clinical state during the immediate post-traumatic phase. Bruce et al. (1978) considered that such problems were especially likely to arise in studies of the effects of head injury in children. In their study of coma due to nontraumatic causes, Levy et al. (1981, p. 293) also confined their attention to those patients whose coma had lasted at least six hours "to eliminate from consideration the transient unresponsiveness of syncope (or the unresponsiveness of imminent death)". The impact of head injury in the acute phase may, of course, also be confounded by the effects of sedation or general anaesthetic in patients who require immediate treatment for other injuries.

Jennett and Teasdale (1977) and Jennett, Teasdale, et al. (1979) reinforced these arguments by observing that in adult patients alcohol intoxication would affect brain function during this period. Galbraith, Murray, Patel, and Knill-Jones (1976) had indeed shown that the influence of alcohol would contaminate the assessment of a head-injured patient's conscious level on admission to hospital and lead to lower scores on the GCS (see also Rimel et al., 1981). This would in turn mean that impaired consciousness among head-injured patients might be incorrectly attributed to the consumption of alcohol, or that the development of complications such as intracranial haematoma might be disguised. Nevertheless, provided that a head-injured patient's blood alcohol level was less than 200mg per 100ml, Galbraith et al. recommended that alterations in the patient's conscious state should be ascribed to the head injury itself rather than to intoxication.

In the United States, the researchers who instituted a National Traumatic Coma Data Bank involving a number of urban and regional neurosurgical centres resolved to administer the amended GCS both on the patients' admission and following their noncranial resuscitation (that is, after the stabilisation of fluid volume and the treatment of hypoxia), which was typically between 30 minutes and 1 hour later. Patients were to be included in the Data Bank as cases of acute severe head injury either if they had a total GCS score of 8 or less on admission or if they deteriorated to a score of 8 or less during the first 48 hours after injury (Marshall, Becker, et al., 1983). Having surveyed patients admitted over a four-year period, Marshall et al. (1991) concluded that the postresuscitation GCS score was more accurate from the prognostic point of view, partly because the different centres appeared to be inconsistent in judging scores on admission.

In other studies carried out in North America, the GCS has been applied retrospectively to case notes produced by the medical and nursing staff at the time of a patient's admission to hospital. Levin and Eisenberg (1979a, 1979b) found that the best verbal and motor responses of head-injured children could usually be classified in this manner, although the case notes were often equivocal with regard to eye opening. They found that the best verbal response and the best motor response on admission were both closely related to the duration of coma, defined as the period during which the patient failed to respond verbally or motorically to simple verbal commands.

*The role of language.* A further problem that subsequently came to light concerns the involvement of linguistic skills in the various elements of the GCS. When "consciousness" and "coma" were defined in terms of the ability or the inability to establish intellectual contact, Overgaard et al. (1973) observed that in most cases this meant intelligent *verbal* contact. Similarly, Jennett (1976a) noted that both doctors and relatives tended to characterise the end of coma as the point when a head-injured patient began to talk.

Teasdale and Jennett (1974) remarked that intelligible speech had figured in nearly all previous attempts to describe impairments of consciousness, and they explicitly identified the patients' verbal responses as one of the defining elements of the GCS. However, they added an important qualification (p. 82): "Certainly the return of speech indicates the restoration of a high degree of integration within the nervous system, but continued speechlessness may be due to causes other than depressed consciousness (e.g. tracheostomy or dysphasia)" (see also Teasdale, Murray, et al., 1979). Because the majority of their patients with severe head injuries exhibited problems of communication, Gilchrist and Wilkinson (1979) defined "unconsciousness" simply as the inability to respond purposefully to the environment. However, one of the advantages of the GCS is that it specifically excludes the subjective judgement of whether a patient's responses are "purposeful".

The role of verbal *comprehension* received little attention in applications of the GCS, apparently because intelligible speech is totally abolished following severe closed head injury and (as mentioned earlier) the total coma score is largely determined by the patient's motor responses. Nevertheless, obeying simple commands is the highest level of response on the latter element of the Scale, and Levin, Grossman, et al. (1979) used this rudimentary level of comprehension to define the termination of coma (see also Levin & Eisenberg, 1979a, 1979b; Temkin, Holubkov, Machamer, Winn, & Dikmen, 1995). Similarly, Lewin, Marshall, and Roberts (1979, p. 1534) defined "unconsciousness" as "persisting until there was comprehension of the spoken word as demonstrated by obeying a verbal request" (see also Roberts, 1969, p. 30). Bricolo, Turazzi, and Feriotti (1980) argued that obeying simple commands was an important "milestone" in recovery from coma: "By far the most important step in the evolution of prolonged coma patients is the return of the capacity to execute simple commands: this constitutes unambiguous evidence of resumed mental activity, marks the end of unconsciousness, and is the necessary premise to all further recuperation" (p. 628). Obeying simple commands is also used in surgical practice as a criterion of "waking up" from general anaesthesia (Russell, 1986).

Research on the sequelae of cerebrovascular accidents suggested that lesions of the left cerebral hemisphere produce greater disturbances of consciousness than comparable lesions of the right hemisphere (e.g. Albert, Silverberg, Reches, & Berman, 1976; Schwartz, 1967). Similar results were obtained following both penetrating brain wounds (Salazar et al., 1986) and closed head injury (Levin & Eisenberg, 1986). Levin, Gary, and Eisenberg (1989) suggested that these latter results might be artefacts due to the verbal demands imposed by the GCS. They examined the recovery from coma of 43 severely head-injured patients from the National Traumatic Coma Data Bank who had developed a unilateral intracerebral haematoma. When recovery was defined in terms of the highest level of motor response (obeying simple commands), the patients with lesions of the left hemisphere showed a much longer period of impaired consciousness than those with lesions of the right hemisphere. However, this was no longer true when the criterion of recovery was the next lower motor response (a localising response to pain). Levin et al. concluded that the purported relation between language and consciousness was attributable to the verbal methods used to assess consciousness level, and that it would be necessary to devise alternative, nonverbal indicators of consciousness level in order adequately to assess the recovery of patients with left-hemisphere lesions.

Another consideration is that the linguistic demands of the GCS render it inappropriate for children in the first few years of life. There have been several attempts to make it more relevant for infants or young children. These proposals were reviewed by Simpson, Cockington, Hanieh, Raftos, and Reilly (1991), who concluded that a simplified paediatric version of the original (14-point) GCS based on age-related normal responses could be used in routine practice. In this, the best verbal response was classified as follows (p. 186):

> In testing best verbal response (levels 1-5), we classed as orientation (level 5) any spoken awareness of personal identity, e.g. "what's your name?" or "is that your mummy?" Orientation in place was not routinely tested, though it could sometimes be demonstrated. Words (level 4) were identified only if appropriate and clearly verbal: thus mum-mum and dad-dad were only accepted as words if applied to a person, being otherwise classified as vocal sounds. Vocal sounds (level 3) were taken to include preverbal babbling and inappropriate words (as in the comparable level 3 in the adult verbal scale). Crying (level 2), the normal response of the neonate, was equated with other incomprehensible noises (e.g. groans).

Simpson et al. showed that the level of coma on this instrument was highly correlated with the neurological outcome at one month.

## Other measures of severity

An additional problem is that recovery from coma is typically marked, not by the restoration of full consciousness, but by a period of confusion known as *post-traumatic amnesia* (PTA). The latter expression refers to the characteristic inability of head-injured patients to form new memories during this period; this phenomenon will be discussed in more detail in Chapter 3. A different basis for categorising cases of closed head injury in terms of the severity of their injuries is the duration of PTA. Of course, this provides merely a retrospective means of assessing the severity of a head injury, and so it does not constitute an alternative to assessment during the acute stage.

Following an original suggestion by Russell and Smith (1961), many clinicians regard as a "severe" head injury (as opposed to a "minor" head injury) one which gives rise to a period of PTA extending for more than 24 hours after the injury. Jennett et al. (1975a) mentioned that this corresponded to a period of coma of at least six hours' duration. A more detailed classification based on the duration of PTA was proposed by Jennett and Teasdale (1981, p. 90):

Less than 5 minutes—very mild
5 to 60 minutes—mild
1 to 24 hours—moderate
1 to 7 days—severe
1 to 4 weeks—very severe
More than 4 weeks—extremely severe

A working party set up by the Medical Disability Society (1988, p. 3) proposed a slightly different classification, and this is nowadays widely used in the United Kingdom. In this scheme, "post-traumatic amnesia" refers to the time interval between the head injury and the reinstatement of continuous day-to-day memory (as assessed clinically) and "unconsciousness" refers to a state of unconsciousness scoring 9 points or less on the GCS:

*Minor brain injury:* An injury causing unconsciousness for 15 minutes or less.
*Moderate brain injury:* An injury causing unconsciousness for more than 15 minutes but less than 6 hours, and a PTA (post-traumatic amnesia) of less than 24 hours.
*Severe brain injury:* An injury causing unconsciousness for 6 hours or more, or a post-traumatic amnesia (PTA) of 24 hours or more. (This category includes very severe head injury.)
*Very severe brain injury:* An injury causing unconsciousness for 48 hours or more or a post-traumatic amnesia of 7 days or more.

Except in the case of minor injuries, this scheme places equal weight upon the duration of unconsciousness and the duration of PTA. Note that either criterion can warrant a classification of "severe" or "very severe". In fact, Wilson et al. (1994) found a group of patients who had been in coma for less than six hours but in whom PTA had lasted for more than seven days. The results of magnetic resonance imaging suggested that the duration of PTA provided a better assessment of brain damage in these patients than either the depth or duration of coma (see Chapter 3).

A different definition of the severity of a closed head injury might be given in terms of whether or not the patient was admitted to hospital or the duration of in-patient care. For instance, London (1967, p. 462) characterised a severe head injury as "one that either killed the patient or enforced a stay in hospital of at least seven days". Conversely, Rimel et al. (1981, p. 222) defined a minor head injury as "cranial trauma resulting in a loss of consciousness of 20 minutes or less, an admission GCS score of 13 or better, and the need for 48 hours or less of hospitalization." The latter criterion "excluded patients with severe extracranial associated injuries or medical complications and, in general, reflected the neurosurgeons' assessment that the included patients had sustained minor head injuries not requiring treatment or additional observation". Wrightson and Gronwall (1998) similarly proposed that a "mild" head injury should be defined as one where the patient could be managed out of hospital or needed no more than 48 hours of hospital care.

Finally, the severity of a head injury can be defined retrospectively in terms of the extent or duration of recovery. Indeed, Jennett (1976a) observed that it was implicit in the traditional concept of cerebral concussion that no structural damage had occurred to the brain and hence that the injury had no persisting sequelae. Nevertheless, as will be explained in Chapter 2, it is nowadays generally recognised that even a brief period of traumatic unconsciousness may well be associated with permanent structural damage, and indeed that a "concussional" head injury is not necessarily a "minor" one with regard to its consequences.

The idea that the severity of a head injury might be defined with regard to the quality of the eventual outcome is well motivated and is especially relevant to those concerned with the social and economic impact of head injuries and with the provision and evaluation of rehabilitation services. This is particularly important since the assessment of the severity of the initial injury may need to be differentiated from the impact of secondary brain damage. For instance, a clinically minor head injury might lead to life-threatening complications (such as an intracranial haematoma) that result in permanent brain damage and severe disability.

## EPIDEMIOLOGY

### Britain

The most convenient source of information on the epidemiology of head injuries in England is the Hospital Episode Statistics system. This was introduced in 1987 and constitutes a national database relating to finished consultant episodes within the National Health Service. Summary tables have been published by the UK Department of Health for each financial year (running from April 1 to March 31) since 1988–89. These tables contain estimates of the corresponding totals which are grossed up to allow for missing records and missing data within records.

At the time of writing, the most recent published tables are those relating to the financial year 1994–95. Up to and including that year, episodes were classified using ICD-9-CM. From 1995–96, however, episodes are classified using ICD-10. Table 1.2 shows the estimated number of finished consultant episodes for each of the ICD-10 categories identified in the previous section for the year 1995–96. Strictly speaking, this is not identical to the number of head-injured patients, since a person may have more than one episode of care within a year. Nevertheless, Table 1.2 implies that the annual incidence rate in 1995–96 (based on a national population of 48,903,000: see Church, 1997, p. 28) was 1.99 cases per 1000 population.

Similar information is collected by the National Health Service in Scotland and Wales but is not routinely published. In Scotland, episodes were classified using ICD-9-CM up to and including the financial year 1995–96; from 1996–97, however, they will be classified using ICD-10. Table 1.3 summarises the estimated number of episodes for each of the ICD-9 categories identified in the previous section for the year 1995–96. This implies that the annual incidence rate (based on a national population of 5,137,000) was 3.63 cases per 1000 population, which is nearly double the incidence rate obtained in England.

TABLE 1.2

Completed episodes at public hospitals in England for the year ending 31 March 1996, for selected primary diagnoses

| *Nature of injury* | *ICD-10 code* | *Number* |
|---|---|---|
| Fracture of vault of skull | S02.0 | 2,333 |
| Fracture of base of skull | S02.1 | 2,621 |
| Fracture of nasal bones | S02.2 | 12,432 |
| Fracture of orbital floor | S02.3 | 574 |
| Fracture of malar and maxillary bones | S02.4 | 5,358 |
| Fracture of mandible | S02.6 | 4,829 |
| Multiple fractures involving skull and facial bones | S02.7 | 234 |
| Fractures of other skull and facial bones | S02.8 | 601 |
| Fractures of skull and facial bones, unspecified | S02.9 | 1,478 |
| Concussion | S06.0 | 6,285 |
| Traumatic cerebral oedema | S06.1 | 219 |
| Diffuse brain injury | S06.2 | 1,197 |
| Focal brain injury | S06.3 | 458 |
| Epidural haemorrhage | S06.4 | 570 |
| Traumatic subdural haemorrhage | S06.5 | 2,132 |
| Traumatic subarachnoid haemorrhage | S06.6 | 265 |
| Intracranial injury with prolonged coma | S06.7 | 161 |
| Other intracranial injuries | S06.8 | 467 |
| Intracranial injury, unspecified | S06.9 | 8,708 |
| Crushing injury of face | S07.0 | 4,326 |
| Crushing injury of skull | S07.1 | 11 |
| Crushing injury of other parts of head | S07.8 | 11 |
| Crushing injury of head, part unspecified | S07.9 | 4 |
| Multiple injuries of head | S09.7 | 118 |
| Other specified injuries of head | S09.8 | 465 |
| Unspecified injury of head | S09.9 | 41,352 |
| Total | | 97,209 |

From unpublished Hospital Episode Statistics supplied by the UK Department of Health.

TABLE 1.3
Completed episodes at public hospitals in Scotland for the year ending 31 March 1996, for selected primary diagnoses

| *Nature of injury* | *ICD-9 code* | *Number* |
|---|---|---|
| Fracture of vault of skull | 800 | 378 |
| Fracture of base of skull | 801 | 639 |
| Fracture of face bones | 802 | 3,862 |
| Other and unqualified skull fractures | 803 | 340 |
| Multiple fractures involving skull or face with other bones | 804 | 21 |
| Concussion | 850 | 1,147 |
| Cerebral laceration and contusion | 851 | 159 |
| Subarachnoid, subdural and extradural haemorrhage, following injury | 852 | 367 |
| Other and unspecified intracranial haemorrhage following injury | 853 | 71 |
| Intracranial injury of other and unspecified nature | 854 | 11,656 |
| Total | | 18,640 |

From unpublished Hospital Episode Statistics supplied by the Information and Statistics Division of the National Health Service in Scotland.

In Wales, as in England, episodes were classified using ICD-9-CM up to and including 1994–95; from 1995–96, however, they have been classified using ICD-10. In the year 1995–96, unpublished data provided by the Welsh Health Common Services Authority indicate that the total number of episodes for the ICD-10 categories identified in the previous section was 7653, implying that the annual incidence rate (based on a national population of 2,917,000) was 2.62 cases per 1000 population. If one combines the figures for England, Scotland, and Wales, the estimated incidence for Britain as a whole during 1995–96 was 123,502 episodes or 2.17 cases per 1000 population.

As Field (1976, p. 3) pointed out, hospital activity data "will exclude mild cases not admitted to hospital, as well as the most severe who die before admission. Admission will depend not only on the severity of the injury, but also the admission policy of the hospital, which in turn will reflect the facilities and skills available in that hospital" (see also Kraus, 1980). Jennett (1976a, p. 648) observed that "about a third of patients admitted to hospital with head injury have another injury, and it may be this rather than the head injury which leads to hospital admission, or which determines the length of stay". Subsequently, Jennett and MacMillan (1981) reported that patients with a minor head injury but a major extracranial injury accounted for 11% of admissions but for one-third of all occupied bed days attributed to head injuries.

Jennett (1975b, p. 267) suggested on the basis of experience in Scotland that "probably four or five times as many patients attend casualty departments as are admitted". Rather more specifically, Jennett and MacMillan (1981) reported an annual rate of attendance during 1974 at accident and emergency departments in an area in the North East of England of 16.20 cases of head injury per 1000 population, corresponding to 11% of all new patients attending such departments. Of the cases of head injury seen by the accident and emergency departments in the area, 22% were subsequently admitted to hospital for treatment. If taken together with the figures discussed earlier, these estimates imply that in Britain at least 600,000 people receive a head injury each year that is sufficiently serious to lead them to seek medical treatment at a hospital.

## United States

The National Health Interview Survey (Benson & Marano, 1994) is one source of national epidemiological data in the United States. This involves household interviews with samples drawn from the civilian, noninstitutionalised population in which the respondents are asked to report any acute conditions suffered over the previous two weeks. Head injuries are unfortunately not differentiated from other kinds of injury in the annual reports based on these interviews.

However, Caveness (1979) reported findings concerning head injuries reported during the period between 1970 and 1976, and a similar analysis was carried out on the results from the 1977 Survey. These accounts identified head injuries associated with "skull fracture and intracranial injury" (i.e. ICD-8 codes N800, N801, N803, and N850–854, equivalent to the corresponding numerical ICD-9 codes). The findings suggest that during 1977 roughly 2,211,000 persons suffered an injury of this kind that required medical attention or restricted their activity for at least one day. The total national population was approximately 212,153,000, yielding an annual incidence rate of 10.42 cases per 1000 population. Kraus (1993) derived a similar estimate for 1990 of 1,975,000 cases or 7.96 per 1000 population.

As Frankowski (1986, p. 154) noted, such results "are subject to a number of limitations. The data on injuries are self-reported and thus lack clinical confirmation. The data include self-treated injuries as well as medically-treated injuries; new injuries are not distinguished from previous injuries, and the extent of recall bias is unknown". In addition, Fife (1987) pointed out that the results may exclude fatal injuries.

These criticisms do not apply to the National Head and Spinal Cord Injury Survey, which was a multistage probability survey of relevant hospital discharges in the United States between 1970 and 1974 (Anderson, Kalsbeek, & Hartwell, 1980). For 1974, it was estimated that 422,000 persons were hospitalised following head injuries, corresponding to an incidence rate of 2.00 cases per 1000 population (Kalsbeek, McLaurin, Harris, & Miller, 1980). Similar figures have been reported in several local surveys within the United States (e.g. Annegers, Grabow, Kurland, & Laws, 1980; Cooper et al., 1983; Jagger, Levine, Jane, & Rimel, 1984; Klauber, Barrett-Connor, Marshall, & Bowers, 1978; Kraus et al., 1984; Waxweiler et al., 1995; cf. Whitman, Coonly-Hoganson, & Desai, 1984). A comparison between these figures and those produced by the National Health Interview Survey implies that, in line with the experience of the United Kingdom, only 20% of people who seek treatment following head injuries in the United States are actually admitted to hospital (cf. Jennett, 1975b). Fife (1987) observed that this proportion was much lower for patients from low-income families with relatively poor access to health care, and that many head-injured patients who were not hospitalised nevertheless sustained a relatively prolonged disability.

However, information about detailed diagnoses in hospital patients in the United States is available from the National Hospital Discharge Survey (Graves & Gillum, 1997). This covers an annual multistage sample of patients discharged from civilian, noninstitutional hospitals, and it provides estimates of the annual incidence of all diseases according to the ICD-9-CM classification. Table 1.4 shows the estimated incidence during 1995 of the 10 diagnostic categories described in the previous section. This indicates that approximately 400,000 people were admitted to hospital in the United States that year with a diagnosis reflecting a head injury. Since the total national population was 261,407,000, this figure corresponds to an incidence rate of 1.52 cases per 1000 population.

## Changes over time

During the 1960s and early 1970s, several commentators pointed out that there had been a steady rise in hospital admissions in England and Wales that were associated with closed head injury. In principle, epidemiological variation of this sort might have been produced by changes in environmental conditions, and some concern was expressed that existing hospital resources would be inadequate to accommodate the apparently increasing numbers of severely brain-damaged survivors (e.g. Jennett, 1976d; London, 1967). Nevertheless, Caveness (1979)

TABLE 1.4

Estimated total number of discharges following head injury from hospitals in the United States in 1995 by nature of injury

| *Nature of injury* | *ICD-9 code* | *Number (000s)* |
|---|---|---|
| Fracture of vault of skull | 800 | 17 |
| Fracture of base of skull | 801 | 39 |
| Fracture of face bones | 802 | 115 |
| Other and unqualified skull fractures | 803 | 6 |
| Multiple fractures involving skull or face with other bones | 804 | * |
| Concussion | 850 | 70 |
| Cerebral laceration and contusion | 851 | 18 |
| Subarachnoid, subdural and extradural haemorrhage, following injury | 852 | 40 |
| Other and unspecified intracranial haemorrhage following injury | 853 | 7 |
| Intracranial injury of other and unspecified nature | 854 | 86 |
| Total | | 398 |

From Graves and Gillam (1997).

*Less than 5000.

reported a decline in the number of head injuries in the United States associated with skull fracture or intracranial injury between 1970 and 1976, and he ascribed this to improvements in occupational safety.

In fact, Field (1976, pp. 18–21) argued that the steady rise in hospital admissions during this period had been largely the result of more liberal admission policies and the increased availability of resources (see also Jennett & MacMillan, 1981). He presented three kinds of data to support such a conclusion. First, the overall increase in hospital admissions was largely attributable to the less serious ICD-9 categories 802, 850, and 854, and especially to the last of these, "intracranial injury of other and unspecified nature". Second, the increase was also largely attributable to patients who had stayed in hospital for seven days or less. Third, there was no sign of any corresponding increase in the number of deaths caused by head injury. Indeed, Jennett and MacMillan (1981) suggested that there had actually been a fall in the number of fatal and serious head injuries in the United Kingdom during the relevant period.

In many countries, patients who have sustained minor head injuries are admitted to hospital purely for observation in case of the development of complications such as intracranial haematoma, intracranial infection, or post-traumatic epilepsy (see Chapter 2). In fact, comparatively few go on to develop such complications: in the United Kingdom, fewer than 5% have sustained injuries that are serious enough for them to be transferred to specialist neurosurgical units for investigation or treatment (Jennett, Murray, et al., 1979). As a result, most are discharged from hospital within a few days: Jennett (1996) reported that about 60–70% of all patients with head injuries admitted to hospitals in the United Kingdom were discharged within 48 hours. However, given the difficulty of predicting exactly *which* patients might develop complications, the criteria for admission remain vague, and vast numbers are apparently admitted unnecessarily and at considerable cost to health services (Jennett, 1975b, 1976b; Jennett et al., 1975a).

To try to tackle this problem, guidelines for the initial management of head injuries in adult patients were published in the United Kingdom in 1984 (Group of Neurosurgeons, 1984). It was subsequently argued that these were equally appropriate for the management of head injuries in children (Teasdale et al., 1990). It was anticipated that the adoption of these guidelines would lead to a reduction in the overall proportion of patients attending accident and emergency departments who were admitted to hospital, and some early data were interpreted in just this manner (Jennett, 1989, 1996).

Table 1.5 shows the estimated incidence of the diagnostic categories described in the previous section in England since the introduction of the Health Episode Statistics system. This indicates that hospital admissions attributable to closed head injury have actually fallen by about 25% in less than a decade. However, this decline is almost wholly attributable to the less serious ICD-9 categories 850 and 854. This result is consistent with the expectation that adopting formal guidelines would lead to fewer patients with more minor head injuries being admitted. Nevertheless,

TABLE 1.5

Completed episodes at public hospitals in England for the years 1989–90 to 1994–95, by selected primary diagnoses

| *ICD-9 codes* | *1988–89* | *1989–90* | *1990–91* | *1991–92* | *1992–93* | *1993–94* | *1994–95* |
|---|---|---|---|---|---|---|---|
| 800 | 2,662 | 3,137 | 3,142 | 3,332 | 2,872 | 2,760 | 2,716 |
| 801 | 2,878 | 2,949 | 3,051 | 3,228 | 3,186 | 3,207 | 3,096 |
| 802 | 21,380 | 20,590 | 21,303 | 22,599 | 23,079 | 22,573 | 22,701 |
| 803 | 2,071 | 2,019 | 2,097 | 2,181 | 1,799 | 2,018 | 1,877 |
| 804 | 195 | 151 | 141 | 94 | 122 | 81 | 86 |
| 850 | 11,629 | 11,951 | 12,123 | 10,780 | 9,418 | 7,870 | 6,927 |
| 851 | 602 | 684 | 794 | 809 | 874 | 629 | 830 |
| 852 | 1,584 | 1,874 | 1,835 | 2,150 | 2,107 | 2,496 | 2,728 |
| 853 | 510 | 534 | 559 | 424 | 520 | 696 | 578 |
| 854 | 85,100 | 77,756 | 68,483 | 63,214 | 61,401 | 57,630 | 55,720 |
| Totals | 128,611 | 121,645 | 113,528 | 108,811 | 105,378 | 99,960 | 97,259 |

From Deparment of Health (1993, 1994a, 1994b, 1994c, 1994d, 1995, 1996. (See Table 1.4 for the meanings of the various diagnostic categories.)

following Field's (1976) argument, it is equally consistent with the idea that hospitals simply introduced less liberal admissions policies at a time of financial stringency.

Table 1.6 shows the estimated incidence of the relevant diagnostic categories over the same period in Scotland. Here, it would appear that hospital admissions attributable to head injury have remained between 18,000 and 19,000, except for a slight fall during 1992–93 that was maintained during 1993–94. However, the latter variation is almost wholly attributable to the less serious ICD-9 category 854. This pattern is not really consistent with the expectation that adopting formal

TABLE 1.6

Completed episodes at public hospitals in Scotland for the years 1989–90 to 1994–95, by selected primary diagnoses

| *ICD-9 codes* | *1988–89* | *1989–90* | *1990–91* | *1991–92* | *1992–93* | *1993–94* | *1994–95* |
|---|---|---|---|---|---|---|---|
| 800 | 487 | 451 | 454 | 500 | 490 | 504 | 451 |
| 801 | 554 | 597 | 657 | 616 | 625 | 572 | 573 |
| 802 | 3,624 | 3,803 | 3,529 | 3,532 | 3,556 | 3,585 | 3,600 |
| 803 | 469 | 462 | 463 | 458 | 386 | 346 | 363 |
| 804 | 30 | 37 | 32 | 43 | 61 | 56 | 28 |
| 850 | 398 | 731 | 1,326 | 1,612 | 1,698 | 1,615 | 1,442 |
| 851 | 92 | 123 | 129 | 112 | 162 | 183 | 135 |
| 852 | 278 | 334 | 357 | 342 | 314 | 382 | 362 |
| 853 | 110 | 99 | 133 | 105 | 86 | 90 | 76 |
| 854 | 12,942 | 11,708 | 11,688 | 11,264 | 10,395 | 10,199 | 11,876 |
| Totals | 18,984 | 18,345 | 18,768 | 18,584 | 17,773 | 17,532 | 18,906 |

From unpublished Hospital Episode Statistics supplied by the Information and Statistics Division of the National Health Service in Scotland. (See Table 1.4 for the meanings of the various diagnostic categories.)

guidelines would lead to fewer patients being admitted; rather, it implies that hospitals temporarily constrained the level of admissions.

Similarly, Table 1.7 shows the incidence of the relevant diagnostic categories in the United States from 1988 to 1995. There was a decline in the absolute number of patients from 460,000 to 400,000 and in the incidence of head injury from 1.88 cases to 1.50 cases per 1000 population. The decline is associated mainly with the less serious ICD-9 categories 802 and 850, and it, too, can therefore be attributed mainly to changes in hospital admissions policies.

## Age and gender

Table 1.8 shows the number of finished consultant episodes for hospitals in England, Scotland, and Wales classified separately by the patients' age and gender. It is apparent that there were more than twice as many male patients as female patients, but that this discrepancy was most pronounced in young adults. Very similar ratios have been obtained in previous research on the incidence of head injury in the United Kingdom (Jennett , Murray, et al., 1977; Rowbotham, Maciver, Dickson, & Bousfield, 1954; Steadman & Graham, 1970) and the United States (Annegers et al., 1980; Cooper et al., 1983; Graves & Gillum, 1997; Kalsbeek et al., 1980; Kraus, 1993; Kraus et al., 1984; Marshall, Becker, et al., 1983). Not only are men more likely to sustain closed head injuries than women, they are also likely to suffer more severe injuries as evidenced by their scores on the GCS on admission and by the subsequent duration of coma (see Levin, Grossman, et al., 1979).

Although the agebands used are, unfortunately, of varying widths, Table 1.8 does in fact also confirm the findings of previous studies that in males the incidence of closed head injury increases progressively during childhood and early adulthood,

TABLE 1.7

Estimated total number of discharges following head injury from hospitals in the United States in 1988–1995, by nature of injury (in 000s)

| *ICD-9 codes* | *1988* | *1989* | *1990* | *1991* | *1992* | *1993* | *1994* | *1995* |
|---|---|---|---|---|---|---|---|---|
| 800 | 17 | 21 | 17 | 18 | 15 | 15 | 14 | 17 |
| 801 | 29 | 27 | 30 | 33 | 35 | 28 | 34 | 39 |
| 802 | 141 | 129 | 139 | 117 | 115 | 116 | 103 | 115 |
| 803 | 12 | 11 | 8 | 6 | 8 | 7 | 8 | 6 |
| 804 | * | * | * | * | * | * | * | * |
| 850 | 148 | 125 | 122 | 101 | 95 | 85 | 80 | 70 |
| 851 | 16 | 15 | 19 | 22 | 19 | 26 | 17 | 18 |
| 852 | 22 | 27 | 28 | 30 | 31 | 30 | 33 | 40 |
| 853 | 7 | 9 | 8 | 10 | 9 | 9 | 9 | 7 |
| 854 | 97 | 85 | 87 | 91 | 67 | 69 | 66 | 86 |
| Totals | 459 | 449 | 458 | 429 | 394 | 385 | 364 | 398 |

From Graves, 1991a, 1991b, 1992, 1994a, 1994b, 1995; Graves & Gillum, 1997a, 1997b. (See Table 1.4 for the meanings of the various diagnostic categories.)

*Less than 5000.

TABLE 1.8

Completed episodes at public hospitals in England, Scotland, and Wales for the year ending 31 March 1996, for selected primary diagnoses by age and gender of patient

| | *England* | | *Scotland* | | *Wales* | |
|---|---|---|---|---|---|---|
| *Age* | *Males* | *Females* | *Males* | *Females* | *Males* | *Females* |
| 0–4 years | 5,904 | 4,536 | 890 | 673 | 419 | 261 |
| 5–14 years | 11,263 | 5,088 | 2,153 | 903 | 945 | 430 |
| 15–44 years | 37,612 | 9,629 | 7,425 | 1,735 | 2,763 | 796 |
| 45–64 years | 7,243 | 2,884 | 2,020 | 601 | 561 | 237 |
| 65–74 years | 2,304 | 1,662 | 701 | 266 | 172 | 158 |
| 75–84 years | 1,924 | 2,914 | 393 | 429 | 160 | 264 |
| 85 years and over | 942 | 2,501 | 118 | 333 | 105 | 186 |

From unpublished Hospital Episode Statistics supplied by the UK Department of Health, the Information and Statistics Division of the National Health Service in Scotland, and the Welsh Health Common Services Authority; 999 episodes in which either the age or the gender of the patient was not recorded (803 in England and 196 in Wales) have been omitted.

reaching a peak around 20 years of age; but that in females it tends to decline gradually with age (Annegers et al., 1980; Jennett & MacMillan, 1981; Kraus, 1993; Kraus et al., 1984). The result of these trends is that more than half of all head-injured patients seen in accident and emergency departments and more than half of all head-injured patients subsequently admitted to hospital are children or young adults (Field, 1976, p. 8; Jennett, Murray, et al., 1977; Kalsbeek et al., 1980). Klonoff (1971) found that a particularly high proportion of patients seen in a Canadian general hospital but not admitted were young children.

## Social class

Another personal characteristic which might be expected to influence the likelihood of closed head injury is the patient's social class. Whereas Steadman and Graham (1970) found no clear differences between a sample of 390 head-injured patients and the general population in the distribution of social class, other studies have found a higher incidence of closed head injury both among members of the lower social classes (Kerr, Kay, & Lassman, 1971; Kraus, 1993; Rimel et al., 1981; Selecki, Hoy, & Ness, 1968) and among their children (Klonoff, 1971; Rutter, Chadwick, Shaffer, & Brown, 1980).

Field (1976, pp. 10–11) presented unpublished material that suggested that male patients in unskilled manual occupations were over-represented among the total number of admissions to hospital, especially those between 35 and 54 years of age. Similarly, there is a negative correlation between the incidence of head injury and the number of years of full-time education (Kraus, 1978). The effect of social class is, however, confounded with the increased incidence of closed head injuries among the inner-city population (Whitman et al., 1984). In a survey of fatal childhood accidents involving head injury in the North of England, Sharples, Storey,

Aynsley-Green, and Eyre (1990) found that the mortality rate was more than 14 times higher in the most socially deprived areas than in the least socially deprived areas.

## Alcohol consumption

It is generally assumed that a major predisposing factor in cases of traumatic injury is the use and abuse of alcohol (e.g. Reilly, Kelley, & Faillace, 1986), although, as Field (1976, p. 12) pointed out, comparable data are not available as to the proportion of the population at risk who have consumed alcohol but not had accidents. As a result, in most cases it is simply not known whether the recent consumption of alcohol is more likely in head-injured patients than in the general public within the same geographical area. Indeed, in some urban areas, chronic alcoholism may be endemic: in one particular study, it was suggested that approximately 20% of the entire patient population of the hospital in question were known alcoholics, and that amongst head-injured patients the proportion was even higher (Heilman, Safran, & Geschwind, 1971).

It would seem that between 20% and 40% of all head-injured patients have consumed alcohol shortly before their accidents (Brookes et al., 1990; Jennett, Murray, et al., 1977; Kerr et al., 1971; Selecki et al., 1968). However, research carried out in Scotland has suggested that this proportion may be 50% or greater among patients attending the accident departments of inner-city hospitals and patients subsequently admitted to such hospitals (Galbraith, Murray, et al., 1976; Livingston, 1986; Strang, MacMillan, & Jennett, 1978; Swann, MacMillan, & Strang, 1981).

The importance of alcohol as a contributory cause of head injuries was confirmed in a study by Rimel et al. (1981), which involved 538 patients with minor head injury (defined by a GCS score on admission of 13–15) and 260 patients with severe head injury (defined by a GCS score on admission of 8 or less). In this study, alcohol was detected on admission in the blood of 43% of the former and 84% of the latter; the mean level of blood alcohol across all patients tested was 80mg per 100ml in those with minor head injuries and 190mg per 100ml in those with severe head injuries. As noted earlier, this obviously makes it more difficult to assess the patient's clinical state. Moreover, as McMillan and Glucksman (1987) pointed out, excessive alcohol consumption can mimic PTA and thus can make estimations of the duration of PTA inaccurate, especially in the case of patients who have sustained minor head injuries. On subsequent psychometric testing, it can be hard to discriminate the consequences of head injuries from deficits induced by alcohol abuse (Mearns & Lees-Haley, 1993).

## Other predisposing factors

There has been somewhat less investigation of other predisposing or constitutional factors in the incidence of closed head injuries. There have been some suggestions that certain victims are "accident-prone" because of being psychiatrically disturbed or socially maladjusted (Ruesch, Harris, & Bowman, 1945; Sims, 1985), and Dencker (1958, p. 119) concluded a study of closed head injuries in twins by commenting that "the head injured persons seemed to differ in pretraumatic mental make-up from the average subject".

Based upon their enquiries into the family backgrounds of 162 children admitted to hospital following head injury, Hjern and Nylander (1964, p. 35) concluded as follows:

> A remarkably large number came from homes with mentally ill or asocial parents, a remarkably large number had parents with anxious and grossly exaggerated fears of the sequelae of head injuries, a remarkably large number had already had head injuries previously or had been involved in other accidents and a remarkably large number had already manifested pronounced symptoms of mental illness before the head injury.

The absence of any comparison group in this study makes it difficult to evaluate how "remarkable" the findings really were, but Jennett (1972, p. 143) concurred that "socially deprived and mildly backward children are more frequently encountered than in the general population". There is some evidence that this is especially true of those children who sustain only mild or moderate head injuries (Rutter et al., 1980; but cf. Klonoff, 1971).

Moreover, one study in the United States found a history of poor premorbid academic performance in 42% of a sample of adult patients with severe closed head injuries and in 50% of those who had been born after the concept of learning disability had been legally recognised (Haas, Cope, & Hall, 1987). It is interesting in this context to note that figures of 33–35% have been reported in the case of patients suffering from spinal injuries (Hall, Cope, & Wilmot, 1987; Wilmot, Cope, Hall, & Acker, 1985). The role of constitutional "risk" factors is also shown by the relatively high incidence of subsequent accidents in those who have received an initial head injury (Klonoff, 1971; and cf. Rimel et al., 1981). Among adults the most important characteristic mediating this effect is probably persistent alcohol abuse (Annegers et al., 1980).

## MORTALITY

The World Health Organisation (1977, p. xvi) recommends that deaths due to injury should be classified according to the external cause of the injury rather than according to its nature. As a consequence, in the mortality statistics of many countries, deaths resulting from closed head injuries are subsumed with other accidents and are not shown as a distinct category. This is true, for example, of the Annual Reports produced by the Registrar General for Scotland (1996) and of the annual mortality data published by the National Center for Health Statistics (1996) in the United States.

In such cases, information about the incidence of fatal head injuries has to come from studies conducted in particular regions or centres. Jennett (1996) reviewed a number of such studies and noted that there were considerable differences in the death rates from head injury found in different countries. The latter varied between 10 per 100,000 in the United Kingdom and 80 per 100,000 in South Africa. The case fatality rates showed a very similar pattern, varying between 3–4% of hospital admissions in Britain and 25% of hospital admissions in South Africa.

Gennarelli, Champion, Sacco, Copes, and Alves (1989) described the results of a survey of 49,143 patients admitted to trauma centres in the United States over a four-year period, of whom 4982 had subsequently died. Those with head injuries accounted for 34% of admissions but for 60% of deaths. More than 80% of all patients with head injuries also had extracranial injuries (which in nearly half of such cases were judged as severe). The mortality rate was actually lower in these patients (17%) than in those with head injuries alone (23%), but this was because the latter included a disproportionate number of highly lethal penetrating gunshot wounds. In other respects, the presence of extracranial injury had little impact on the mortality rate of head-injured patients unless it was of maximal severity.

Sosin et al. (1995) analysed records of all deaths of US residents between 1979 and 1992. During this period, they found that an average of 51,832 people each year had sustained a head injury which contributed to their deaths. The annual mortality rate fell from 24.6 to 19.3 per 100,000 population, chiefly as a result of a 42% decline in the mortality rate associated with motor vehicle accidents. However, this was substantially offset by an increase in the mortality rate associated with firearms. Indeed, by 1992, 44% of all deaths following head injury could be attributed to firearms, compared with 34% to motor vehicles.

In England and Wales, deaths due to an external cause are also classified in terms of the nature of the injury (regarded as a secondary cause) in the Registrar General's annual review of deaths, published by the Office of National Statistics. In cases of multiple injury, the guidelines provided by the World Health Organisation (1977, p. 730) are used to determine which injury is regarded as having caused the victim's death. Table 1.9 shows the number of deaths during 1996 in each of the 10 diagnostic categories from ICD-9, described earlier. This indicates that there were 2815 fatal head injuries in England and Wales that year, which corresponds to a mortality rate of 5.41 deaths per 100,000 population.

It is however likely that this is a serious underestimate. Table 1.10 shows the number of deaths in England and Wales in each of the 10 diagnostic categories according to the Registrar General's annual review of deaths between 1987 and 1996. There is a major discontinuity in 1993, when a number of changes were implemented in the procedures for reporting and classifying the causes of deaths. In particular, coroners were provided with a revised form for certificating cause of death, which no longer included specific questions about the locus and type of injury. At the same time, the Government department responsible for the compilation of such statistics suspended the procedure whereby further enquiries

TABLE 1.9

Total number of deaths following head injury in England and Wales in 1996 by nature of injury and gender of patient

| *Nature of injury* | *ICD-9 code* | *Males* | *Females* |
|---|---|---|---|
| Fracture of vault of skull | 800 | 6 | 0 |
| Fracture of base of skull | 801 | 67 | 35 |
| Fracture of face bones | 802 | 5 | 5 |
| Other and unqualified skull fractures | 803 | 471 | 185 |
| Multiple fractures involving skull or face with other bones | 804 | 32 | 17 |
| Concussion | 850 | 4 | 2 |
| Cerebral laceration and contusion | 851 | 104 | 48 |
| Subarachnoid, subdural and extradural haemorrhage, following injury | 852 | 300 | 214 |
| Other and unspecified intracranial haemorrhage following injury | 853 | 79 | 56 |
| Intracranial injury of other and unspecified nature | 854 | 868 | 317 |
| Totals | | 1936 | 879 |

From Office for National Statistics (1998, pp. 65–66).

TABLE 1.10

Total number of deaths following head injury in England and Wales in 1987–1996 by selected diagnoses

| *ICD code* | *1987* | *1988* | *1989* | *1990* | *1991* | *1992* | *1993* | *1994* | *1995* | *1996* |
|---|---|---|---|---|---|---|---|---|---|---|
| 800 | 30 | 21 | 22 | 28 | 20 | 13 | 10 | 9 | 12 | 6 |
| 801 | 256 | 265 | 243 | 237 | 213 | 219 | 101 | 114 | 101 | 102 |
| 802 | 23 | 19 | 22 | 18 | 16 | 21 | 21 | 12 | 12 | 10 |
| 803 | 1995 | 1827 | 1874 | 1971 | 1689 | 1510 | 922 | 764 | 712 | 656 |
| 804 | 476 | 390 | 485 | 521 | 515 | 405 | 47 | 37 | 42 | 49 |
| 850 | 11 | 11 | 8 | 10 | 1 | 2 | 5 | 7 | 3 | 6 |
| 851 | 241 | 238 | 259 | 203 | 222 | 168 | 156 | 170 | 179 | 152 |
| 852 | 355 | 339 | 365 | 330 | 347 | 385 | 433 | 483 | 483 | 514 |
| 853 | 132 | 119 | 97 | 99 | 84 | 90 | 105 | 116 | 116 | 135 |
| 854 | 572 | 627 | 619 | 739 | 647 | 689 | 1032 | 1009 | 1109 | 1185 |
| Totals | 4091 | 3856 | 3994 | 4156 | 3754 | 3502 | 2832 | 2708 | 2769 | 2815 |

From Office for National Statistics, 1996, 1997, 1998; Office of Population Censuses and Surveys, 1989, 1990, 1991a, 1991b, 1993a, 1993b.

were made when insufficient information had been provided by the certifier to classify the cause of death.

As a result of these changes, proportionately more deaths are nowadays assigned to residual (or nonspecific) categories. For instance, there was a major decline in the number of deaths that were attributed to fracture of the skull (800–804), with a somewhat less pronounced increase in the number of deaths that were attributed to intracranial injury without skull fracture (850–854). With specific regard to these trends, the Office for National Statistics (1998, p. viii) counselled that "such changes are considered more likely to arise from using a less well-defined set of categories, rather than from secular change". Indeed, comparison with the mortality statistics prior to 1993 suggests that the current procedures underestimate the numbers of deaths due to head injury by between 500 and 1000 per year.

Apart from such artefacts, Field (1976, pp. 29–31, Fig. 10) elegantly showed how fluctuations in the annual mortality rate associated with closed head injuries were attributable almost entirely to variations in the number of such deaths caused by motor vehicle accidents (though cf. Kalsbeek et al., 1980). In this context it is interesting that the total number of deaths following closed head injury in England and Wales was consistently around 4500 per year throughout the 1960s and 1970s (corresponding to a rate of 9–10 deaths per 100,000 population) and reached a peak of 5053 in 1978. However, it then fell to around 4000 per year, apparently in response to official Government campaigns to promote the wearing of seat belts by drivers and front-seat passengers in road vehicles.

The latter was made compulsory on 31 January 1983, and Rutherford, Greenfield, Hayes, and Nelson (1985) showed that the total number of fatal head injuries among front-seat occupants declined by one-third over the 12 months before and after this date. In the United States, the introduction of laws to compel the use of seat belts in cars and the use of helmets by motorcyclists had a similar effect (Cooper, 1982a; Frazee, 1986). Indeed, Jennett (1996) pointed out that a reduction in the number of deaths caused by road accidents following the introduction of preventative measures was apparent in national statistics from many industrialised countries, but that the mortality rates remained high in most developing countries.

During the early 1970s, researchers in several European countries consistently found that the mortality rate following severe head injury (defined in terms of a period of coma of six hours or more) was about 50% (Teasdale & Jennett, 1976), and similar rates were yielded by the international collaborative study involving patients in Scotland, the Netherlands, and the United States (Heiden et al., 1983; Jennett, Teasdale, et al., 1977, 1979). However, Jennett and his colleagues (Jennett & Carlin, 1978; Rose, Valtonen, & Jennett, 1977) identified a number of avoidable factors in the management of head-injured patients which might contribute to mortality, of which the most common was delayed treatment of intracranial haematoma in primary surgical wards. They went on to suggest that 50% of all deaths in neurosurgical units exhibited one or more of these factors, and that the the development of more effective policies for the early management of head-injured patients would make a significant impact upon both mortality and morbidity.

Indeed, in a study of 53 head-injured children that used precisely the same selection criteria as the international collaborative study, Bruce et al. (1978) recorded a mortality rate of just 6%. These researchers acknowledged that there were probably differences in the pathophysiology of head injury in children and adults (see Chapter 7), but they suggested that the particularly good outcome obtained in their study resulted also from the introduction of computerised tomography as a routine diagnostic tool permitting early surgical intervention and from the aggressive control of intracranial hypertension. Similarly, Bowers and Marshall (1980, p. 241) suggested that mortality rates could be markedly improved by "the skillful management of patients at the scene of the accident by well-trained paramedical and police personnel, the availability of rapid diagnostic scanning techniques, and the rapid response and aggressive treatment by the community's neurosurgeons". In accordance with this notion, Clifton et al. (1980) achieved a mortality rate of 29% in a series of 124 severely injured patients, which they ascribed to the early evacuation of haematomas and efficient control of intracranial pressure.

Subsequent studies carried out in the United States during the 1980s did indeed produce lower mortality rates (Eisenberg & Weiner, 1987). For example, Marshall et al. (1991) reviewed 746 patients admitted to four neurosurgical centres during a four-year period who had a GCS score of 8 or less at some time within the first 48 hours of admission. The mortality rate for this series was just 36%, which Marshall et al. ascribed to the routine use of CT and monitoring of intracranial pressure. It might also be noted, with regard to England and Wales, that Table 1.10 shows a fall in the number of deaths linked to skull fracture in 1992 that cannot be attributed to any changes in the data-collection procedures. Nevertheless, to what extent these trends were due to improvements in clinical management rather than to changes in public behaviour on the roads and elsewhere is not clear (see Jennett, 1996).

Table 1.11 shows the mortality statistics in England and Wales for 1996 with regard to both the age and the gender of the victim. Bearing in mind the strong possibility that these figures underestimate the total numbers of patients, there are three major features of interest here. First, the overall proportion of males to females is comparable to that apparent in the estimated incidence of closed head injury in Table 1.8. Second, the prognosis appears to be rather poorer in the case of older patients. Thus, more than 60% of all deaths following head injury occur in victims aged 40 years or older. Carlsson, von Essen, and Löfgren (1968) also observed a marked increase in mortality among patients over 40 years old, but they showed that this was solely the result of extracranial complications such as pneumonia, thromboembolism, or myocardial infarction: as complications of fatal head injuries, these occurred almost exclusively and increasingly among the higher age groups, and the likelihood of mortality due to primary cerebral injury was essentially constant across all age groups over 10 years. Third, there is however also a marked increase in the number of deaths in adolescent boys and young men. Indeed, among young people aged between 15 and 19, closed head injuries account for 26% of deaths in males and 17% of deaths in females. Similar trends have been noted in other studies (Annegers et al., 1980; Jennett & MacMillan, 1981; Kraus et al., 1984; National Center for Health Statistics, 1984; Sosin et al., 1995).

## CAUSES

In most countries, detailed information concerning the precise causes of closed head injuries and the circumstances in which they occur is not routinely collected.

TABLE 1.11

Total number of deaths following head injury in England and Wales in 1996 age and gender of patients

| *Age* | *Males* | *Females* | *Total* |
|---|---|---|---|
| Under 1 year | 12 | 10 | 22 |
| 1–4 years | 25 | 16 | 41 |
| 5–9 years | 25 | 13 | 38 |
| 10–14 years | 49 | 23 | 72 |
| 15–19 years | 156 | 48 | 204 |
| 20–24 years | 164 | 35 | 199 |
| 25–29 years | 146 | 30 | 176 |
| 30–34 years | 144 | 28 | 172 |
| 35–39 years | 114 | 31 | 145 |
| 40–44 years | 104 | 26 | 130 |
| 45–49 years | 102 | 34 | 136 |
| 50–54 years | 132 | 32 | 164 |
| 55–59 years | 101 | 35 | 136 |
| 60–64 years | 94 | 39 | 133 |
| 65–69 years | 113 | 48 | 161 |
| 70–74 years | 126 | 74 | 200 |
| 75–79 years | 97 | 98 | 195 |
| 80–84 years | 124 | 102 | 226 |
| 85–89 years | 78 | 96 | 174 |
| 90–94 years | 26 | 53 | 79 |
| 95 years and over | 4 | 8 | 12 |
| Totals | 1936 | 879 | 2815 |

Compiled from Office for National Statistics (1998, pp. 156–159).

In England, however, the Hospital Episode Statistics database includes estimates of the incidence of broad diagnostic categories classified by a short list of external causes. For the relevant categories in ICD-10, S02 ("Fracture of skull and facial bones"), S06 ("Intracranial injury"), S07 ("Crushing injury of head"), and S09 ("Other and unspecified injuries of head"), external causes were identified for 82.0% of all episodes in 1995–96. The most common causes were falls (37.2% of known causes), assault (19.7% of known causes), and land transport accidents (19.1% of known causes).

In the United States, the National Head and Spinal Cord Injury Survey used three broad categories of external cause of injury taken from ICD-8: motor vehicle accidents, falls, and all other causes. The proportions of cases falling into these three categories who had received head injuries during 1974 were 49%, 28%, and 23%, respectively (Kalsbeek et al., 1980). The National Health Interview Survey classifies all incidents into motor vehicle injuries, work injuries, home injuries, and injuries at play, in school, or in the public domain. In the analysis of head injuries in the 1977 Survey, the estimated numbers of cases in these categories were: motor vehicle, 536,000; work, 301,000; home, 1,058,000; and other, 472,000. The corresponding proportions are 24%, 14%, 48%, and 21%, respectively (the four categories are not mutually exclusive). Finally, Gennarelli et al. (1994) reviewed 59,713 patients who had been admitted to 165 hospitals in the United States with a head injury, of whom 98.5% had sustained a blunt head injury. Of the latter, 69.7% had been caused by vehicular accidents, 15.3% by falls, and 15.0% by assaults and other mechanisms.

On the basis of the limited number of special studies that had then been carried out on the circumstances of closed head injury, Field (1976, pp. 13–17, 26) concluded that road traffic accidents were the major cause of injuries amongst adults, that falls were the major cause of injuries amongst children, and that domestic accidents and falls were the major cause of injuries amongst the elderly. Subsequent research confirmed and elaborated Field's conclusions (see also Kraus, 1993).

## Road traffic accidents

As a general point, it is quite clear that road traffic accidents represent the major cause of closed head injuries amongst adults up to the age of 65 (Annegers et al., 1980; Frankowski, 1986; Gennarelli et al., 1994; Gennarelli, Champion, et al., 1989; Hawthorne, 1978; Jennett, Murray, et al., 1977; Kalsbeek et al., 1980; Kerr et al., 1971; Klonoff & Thompson, 1969; Kraus et al., 1984; Rowbotham et al., 1954; Waxweiler et al., 1995). However, Jennett (1996) noted considerable variation in the proportion of head injuries due to road traffic accidents across different countries, varying from 24% in Scotland to 90% in Taiwan.

In more precise terms, Jennett and MacMillan (1981) noted that road accidents accounted for only a small minority of patients attending accident and emergency departments who were not subsequently admitted to hospital, but that they accounted for more than half of all fatal and severe head injuries. Bowers and Marshall (1980), Jennett, Teasdale, et al. (1979), Kalsbeek et al. (1980), Marshall, Becker, et al. (1983), Marshall et al. (1991), and Rutter et al. (1980) all found that vehicular accidents were responsible for over 70% of severe closed head injuries. Such accidents also seem to be chiefly responsible for the rise in the incidence of head injuries between the ages of 15 and 24 years among males (Annegers et al., 1980; Kalsbeek et al., 1980; Marshall, Becker, et al., 1983). Nevertheless, road traffic accidents are also the second most likely cause of closed head injuries among both children and the elderly (Annegers et al., 1980; Hjern & Nylander, 1964; Kalsbeek et al., 1980; Klonoff, 1971; Marshall, Becker, et al., 1983; Rowbotham et al., 1954; Rune, 1970).

The converse relationship also holds: closed head injuries are the most common cause of death and serious permanent disability following road traffic accidents (Gennarelli, Champion, et al., 1989, 1994; Grattan & Hobbs, 1980; Jennett & MacMillan, 1981; Perrone, 1972). In particular, injuries to the head and face are the most likely outcome of accidents among the occupants of cars (Elia, 1974; Hobbs, 1981; Perrone, 1972; Rutherford et al., 1985, p. 48). They are less likely in the case of occupants of larger vehicles but are still a frequent outcome of serious accidents (Grattan & Hobbs, 1978).

Closed head injury is also the most common form of life-threatening injury involving pedestrians and users of two-wheeled vehicles (Grattan, Hobbs, & Keigan, 1976). Motorcycle accidents tend to be the cause of the most severe closed head injuries (Annegers et al., 1980; Grattan & Hobbs, 1980). Conversely, closed head injuries account for approximately one-third of all moderate injuries and for most fatal injuries following motorcycle accidents. Among pedal cyclists, head injury is again a common outcome of falls and collisions with other vehicles, and it is a frequent cause of death following such accidents (Thorson, 1974). Most bicycle accidents leading to head injuries appear to occur in the 5–14 age group (Kraus et al., 1984; Steadman & Graham, 1970). However, Brookes et al. (1990) noted that many accidents of this sort actually occur when the children are off the road, and it is probably more appropriate to regard these as recreational accidents (see later).

Among pedestrians, closed head injury is a common outcome of severe road accidents, as well as the most frequent cause of accidental death (Ashton, Pedder, & Mackay, 1977). Field (1976, p. 13) commented that it was as pedestrians that children were mainly at risk of being involved in road accidents leading to closed head injuries, rather than as cyclists or as vehicle passengers; this was confirmed in subsequent surveys involving a number of European countries (Brookes et al., 1990; Jennett, Teasdale, et al., 1977). In their survey of fatal childhood accidents involving head injuries, Sharples et al. (1990) found that most victims had been pedestrians who had become involved in road traffic accidents, often whilst playing unsupervised near their homes.

## Domestic accidents

Domestic accidents and especially falls represent another significant cause of closed head injuries. Steadman and Graham (1970) found that more than half of their cases of head injury resulted from falls, but they had included falls from bicycles, motorcycles, and other vehicles, which together constituted roughly half of these cases. A more realistic impression was given by Kerr et al. (1971), who found that domestic accidents accounted for 16% of admissions following head injury (see also Gennarelli, Champion, et al., 1989, 1994); these tended to be falls from a height (usually down stairs) or onto a level surface. Such falls appear to be the major cause of head injuries among children under 15 years and among the elderly (Annegers et al., 1980; Brookes et al., 1990; Hjern & Nylander, 1964; Kalsbeek et al., 1980; Klonoff, 1971; Kraus et al., 1984; Marshall, Becker, et al., 1983; Strang et al., 1978). Falls among adults up to the age of 65 are relatively uncommon and tend to give rise to milder forms of injury (Annegers et al., 1980), although they may be seen more often at inner-city hospitals because of assault or alcohol consumption (Swann et al., 1981). Head injuries due to falls are also more likely in people with epilepsy (Zwimpfer, Brown, Sullivan, & Moulton, 1997).

## Assault

Cases of assault account for up to 20% of adult head injuries (Bowers & Marshall, 1980; Gennarelli, Champion, et al., 1989, 1994; Hawthorne, 1978; Jennett, Murray, et al., 1977; Jennett, Teasdale, et al., 1979; Kerr et al., 1971; Klonoff & Thompson, 1969; Kraus et al., 1984; Marshall, Becker, et al., 1983; Steadman & Graham, 1970; Waxweiler et al., 1995). Jennett (1996) once again noted that different countries varied considerably in the proportion of head injuries due to assault, from 1% of males in France to 45% of males in South Africa.

In their multinational study, Jennett, Teasdale, et al. (1977, p. 293) noted that "assaults and 'falls under the influence of alcohol' were common in Glasgow and Los Angeles, accounting between them for almost a third of all injuries over the age of 10 years; these kinds of accident were rare in the Netherlands". In general, the proportion of head injuries due to assault is increased and may be as high as 40% in depressed urban areas such as inner-city Glasgow (Swann et al., 1981), the Bronx (Cooper et al., 1983), and inner-city Chicago (Whitman et al., 1984). However, in the United States these are often penetrating head injuries resulting from gunshot wounds (Frankowski, 1986); Gennarelli, Champion, et al. (1989) found that such injuries accounted for 25% of all head injuries by assault and were associated with a mortality rate of 68%.

There seems to be an increased incidence of head injuries by assault in 15–24 year old males but not in females (Annegers et al., 1980; Kraus et al., 1984). Indeed, Jennett and MacMillan (1981) stated that assaults were twice as common as road accidents as causes of head injuries in men of between 15 and 24 years of age who were treated in Scottish accident and emergency departments. However, Marshall, Becker, et al. (1983) found a relatively high incidence of closed head injuries resulting from assaults in all adult age-groups, and they noted that in patients aged 60 and over falls and assaults caused more than half as many head injuries again than motor-vehicle accidents.

Klonoff (1971) found that cases of assault accounted for 4% of head injuries among children, in whom they were frequently associated with battering by a parent. It has even been suggested that child abuse is the most common cause of severe head injuries during the first year of life (Chadwick, 1985). Jennett (1972) advised that the possibility of head injury should be considered whenever child abuse was suspected, regardless of whether there was any direct evidence of head trauma. One potential source of injury among so-called battered children is concussion induced by repeated severe shaking. Caffey (1972, 1974) observed that infants were highly vulnerable to many kinds of whiplash stresses because their heads were relatively heavier and their neck muscles relatively weaker than at any other age. He described children who had suffered subdural haematomas in the absence of obvious external signs of head impact and concluded that many so-called "battered babies" were really cases of a "whiplash shaken infant syndrome". However, he also noted that whiplash shaking was regarded as a socially acceptable means of disciplining young children in both the United Kingdom and the United States, and that it was involved in a number of activities habitually engaged in by adults playing with young children.

One problem in interpreting such findings, however, as Leventhal and Midelfort (1986) pointed out, is that neurological problems may have preceded (and perhaps even precipitated) child abuse rather than being caused by it. Moreover, Duhaime et al. (1987) pointed out that any history of documented occurrences of shaking was typically lacking in such children. These researchers noted that evidence of blunt head impact had been apparent in only 7 out of 13 fatal cases of the syndrome, but was found in every single case at post-mortem; in particular, all had cerebral contusions as well as diffuse and usually massive brain swelling. Duhaime et al. then demonstrated that the measurements of angular acceleration and velocity obtained in shaking inanimate models of infants were considerably below the range associated with significant brain injury in experiments on primates, whereas similar measurements obtained with impact against a hard object or surface fell well within that range. They inferred that shaking alone in an otherwise normal baby was unlikely to cause the syndrome. Although the notion of a "shaken infant syndrome" is nowadays accepted by paediatricians (e.g. Carty & Ratcliffe, 1995), it remains likely that the more severe brain injuries result from actual head impact (see Lancon, Haines, & Parent, 1998).

## Occupational accidents

Kerr et al. (1971) found that industrial accidents reflected 14% of admissions following head injury; half of these were caused by falls at work, a quarter were caused by falling objects, while a fifth were the result of mining accidents. In the survey of Scottish hospitals during 1974, Jennett, Murray, et al. (1977) found that 10% of all patients with head injury who attended accident and emergency departments and 8% of all those who were admitted to hospital had sustained their head injuries at work. However, more recent research (e.g. Annegers et al., 1980) has suggested that occupation-related head injuries are relatively infrequent and relatively constant between the ages of 15 and 64; they occur predominantly among men in manual occupations such as farming and the construction industry.

## Recreational accidents

Accidents relating to recreational activities also account for up to 14% of head injuries (Annegers et al., 1980; Jennett, Murray, et al., 1977; Kraus et al., 1984; Whitman et al., 1984), especially among patients in middle-class occupations (Kerr et al., 1971). However, they constitute only 7% of serious cases admitted for treatment to neurosurgical units (Lindsay, McLatchie, & Jennett, 1980). Contact sports such as football are often implicated in such injuries, and Gurdjian and

Gurdjian (1978) pointed to subdural haematomas as an important cause of deaths in American college football, even among players wearing protective helmets. The most common sort of injury is helmet-to-helmet collision in the course of tackling or blocking manoeuvres (Barth et al., 1989).

In soccer, it has been claimed that heading footballs is a cause of significant neurological damage in players at college, professional, or national level, as evidenced according to EEG abnormalities or neuropsychological impairment (Tysvaer, 1992; Witol & Webbe, 1994). A study using magnetic resonance imaging found that soccer players were more likely to show white-matter foci than were American football players (Autti, Sipilä, Autti, & Salonen, 1997). However, damage of this nature might result instead from minor collisions with goalposts or other players or, indeed, from head injuries sustained off the field of play (Jordan, Green, Galanty, Mandelbaum, & Jabour, 1996).

Kraus et al. (1984) suggested that many head injuries in children were the result of accidents involving pedal cycles, roller skates, and skateboards, and a more recent study added playground equipment and children's play vehicles to this list (Baker, Fowler, Li, Warner, & Dannenberg, 1994). Barber (1973) observed that head injuries were also a common outcome of horse-riding accidents; he concluded that such injuries were more common and more severe than was generally appreciated and comparable to those sustained by motorcyclists. Foster, Leiguarda, and Tilley (1976) found that professional National Hunt jockeys in particular were exposed to frequent and often severe concussive head injuries; these could lead to permanent brain damage and intellectual deterioration but often went unreported.

Finally, although it is perhaps not strictly a recreational activity, closed head injuries obviously arise in the course of boxing. There are some serious methodological problems involved in the neuropsychological assessment of boxers (see Stewart et al., 1989). However, these injuries seem to be the cause of significant neurological damage, not only in the case of professional boxers (Roberts, 1969), but even among amateurs (McLatchie et al., 1987).

## OVERVIEW

For the purposes of this book, a "closed head injury" is an injury to the head in which the primary mechanism of damage is one of blunt impact. Such injuries are a major cause of deaths following accidents, especially those that involve children and young people, and they are also a major cause of disablement and morbidity among the survivors.

The severity of a head injury can be measured in terms of its initial effects, the incidence of complications, or its long-term consequences. In particular, the extent and the duration of the patient's impairment of consciousness are of major importance in evaluating the severity of a closed head injury. The GCS provides a standard set of criteria for quantifying the depth of unconsciousness in terms of motor responses, verbal responses and eye opening. However, there are certain problems in its use concerning the time after injury when it should be administered and the involvement of linguistic skills in the different elements of the Scale.

The number of people who receive a head injury each year that is sufficiently serious to lead them to seek treatment at a hospital is more than 600,000 in the United Kingdom and roughly 2,000,000 in the United States. These figures correspond to 12 and 8 cases per 100,000 population, respectively. However, only 20% of these patients are subsequently admitted to hospital, and in the United Kingdom fewer than 5% of the latter are transferred to specialist neurosurgical units for investigation and treatment.

The incidence of head injury is higher in males than in females, in young adults than in children or the elderly, and in the working classes than in the middle classes, and it is higher following the consumption of alcohol. Each year, roughly 4000 individuals die following a head injury in England and Wales, corresponding to 8 cases per 100,000 population. The death rate appears to be similar in Scotland, but about two to three times higher in the United States and even higher in some other countries (Jennett, 1996). The major causes of closed head injury are road traffic accidents, domestic falls, assaults, occupational injuries, and recreational accidents.

CHAPTER TWO

# Mechanisms of structural pathology

To obtain a proper understanding of the clinical and neuropsychological effects of a closed head injury, it is important to appreciate the physical and physiological mechanisms by which these effects have come about. This chapter describes the different types of damage which occur at the time of injury and are directly attributable to the trauma itself, as well as the various complications that may result.

Figure 2.1 shows a simplified view of the left side of the human brain. The cerebrum consists of two hemispheres that are connected by the three cerebral commissures, of which the most important is the great commissure or corpus callosum. Each of the two hemispheres consists of an inner core of white matter, surrounded by a covering of grey matter (the cerebral cortex). The cortex of each cerebral hemisphere is described in terms of four regions: the frontal lobe, the temporal lobe, the parietal lobe, and the occipital lobe. Areas within each of these lobes are identified by reference to different directions:

anterior (at or towards the front) versus posterior (at or towards the back);
superior (above) versus inferior (below);
lateral (at or towards the side) versus medial (at or towards the midline).

In humans and other upright species, "anterior" means the same as "ventral" (literally, "towards the belly"), and "posterior" means the same as "dorsal" (literally, "towards the back").

In the previous chapter, it was noted that the concept of concussion, as traditionally conceived, represented a transient disturbance of cerebral function without any associated permanent structural damage to the brain. However, an early investigation by English (1904) suggested that bruising (or *contusions*) and tearing

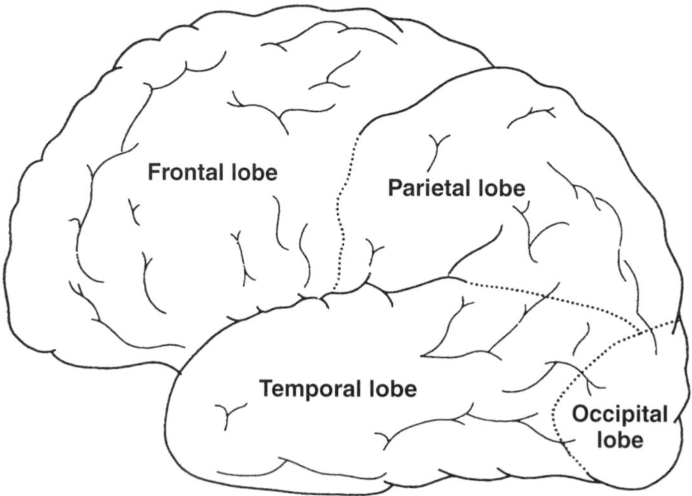


FIG. 2.1. Exterior view of the left side of the brain. From *Brain Damage, Behaviour, and the Mind* by M. Williams (1979), p.4: Chichester, UK. Wiley. Copyright 1979 by John Wiley & Sons Ltd. Reprinted with permission.

(or *lacerations*) might be identified even in patients who sustained a relatively slight head trauma but who then died of unrelated causes, such as thoracic or abdominal injuries. He found macroscopic damage in the brains of eight out of 10 such patients for whom there was an unambiguous history of loss of consciousness lasting less than five minutes. In addition, an examination of the brains of a number of patients who had died a substantial time after sustaining a minor head injury revealed in most cases residual structural changes such as meningeal thickening and a discoloration of the cerebral cortex from old extravasated blood.

Microscopic changes to the brain as the result of minor closed head injury were demonstrated by Windle, Groat, and Fox (1944) in the course of an experimental investigation using both anaesthetised and unanaesthetised guinea pigs. Progressive degeneration of nerve cells was observed over the course of one week following a closed head injury sufficient to induce concussion (defined as the abolition of the corneal reflex). Moreover, subtle intraneuronal disorganisation was observed in animals killed by vascular perfusion with formalin within 30 seconds of the injury. These changes were confined (in this species, at least) to interneurones within the brainstem and spinal cord, and they occurred despite the absence of any significant intracranial bleeding or brain swelling (see later). It was concluded that concussive injury gave rise to immediate cell changes within the brain. Degeneration of nerve cells was also shown in a study by Jane et al. (1982) of two monkeys killed seven days after sustaining a minor head injury.

In research on fatal injuries among human patients, Oppenheimer (1968) reported abnormal clusters of microglial cells in the brains of patients who had sustained only mild concussion but had subsequently died from other causes. As he himself concluded (p. 306), "permanent damage, in the form of microscopic destructive foci, can be inflicted on the brain by what are regarded as trivial head injuries". It was subsequently shown that minor head injuries give rise to persistent changes in cerebral blood flow (Taylor, 1969), in physiological activity according to electroencephalographic indices and evoked potentials (Binder, 1986; MacFlynn, Montgomery, Fenton, & Rutherford, 1984; Montgomery, Fenton, & McClelland, 1984; Noseworthy, Miller, Murray, & Regan, 1981), and (as will be described in later chapters) in performance in neuropsychological tests. Moreover, the cumulative effects in both pathological and clinical terms of repeated mild head injuries in boxers are well recognised (Roberts, 1969).

The contemporary position, as summarised for example by Jennett and Galbraith (1983, p. 216), is that a blow to the head that is sufficient to cause even a brief disturbance of consciousness may produce detectable structural damage. This is also the implication of studies using computerised tomography (see Hardman, 1979) and magnetic resonance imaging (e.g. Jenkins, Teasdale, Hadley, Macpherson, & Rowan, 1986; Levin, Amparo, et al., 1987). In considering neuropathological evidence obtained from patients who have sustained severe or even fatal head injuries, therefore, it should be borne in mind that nowadays the difference between these patients and those who have sustained relatively mild or minor closed head injuries is conceived of as a quantitative rather than a qualitative one.

## CEREBRAL CONTUSIONS

As explained earlier, closed head injuries typically give rise to contusions and lacerations on or within the surface of the brain. Strictly speaking, lacerations are lesions that breach the membrane that encloses the brain itself (the pia mater), whereas contusions leave the latter intact. This distinction is however difficult to make in practice, and the distributions of the two sorts of damage are essentially identical (Adams, 1988). These lesions are usually found on the crests of the convolutions (or *gyri*) on the surfaces of the cerebral hemispheres, but they may penetrate the whole thickness of the cortex and extend into the subcortical white matter (see Adams, Scott, Parker, Graham, & Doyle, 1980; Adams et al., 1985). They are haemorrhagic lesions (that is, they involve the loss of blood) and lead to the accumulation of fluid (oedema) and the death of nerve cells (necrosis) within the brain. They usually heal within a few weeks and leave yellow-brown atrophic scars that are easily recognised at post-mortem.

Clinicians have traditionally distinguished among several different potential sites of cerebral contusions following closed head injury (e.g. Jamieson, 1971, pp. 32–33). First, contusions and lacerations may arise at the site of impact; this is normally referred to as the "coup" injury. Second, local changes in intracranial pressure may give rise to damage in cerebral regions that are diametrically opposite to the site of impact; this is usually described as the "contrecoup" injury. Third, movement of the brain within the skull gives rise to lacerations and contusions in the region of the sphenoidal ridge, which produces damage to the frontal and temporal lobes. Finally, movement of the brain is also likely to produce a variety of surface lesions, especially by causing tearing (or *avulsion*) of the veins that leave the upper borders of the cerebral hemispheres. These four possible types of physical damage are illustrated in Fig. 2.2.

## Coup injury

It would be intuitively reasonable to expect contusions and lacerations to occur beneath the site of impact following a closed head injury. In most cases, the latter will obviously be marked by contusions and lacerations on the scalp. Indeed, 40% of all head-injured patients who attend an accident and emergency department have scalp lacerations that require closure by suture or other means (Jennett, Murray, et al., 1977). Nevertheless, provided that the skull remains intact, only a superficial bruising occurs in the region of the point of application of the blow as a result of local deformation of the skull (Holbourn, 1943, 1945). Of course, as Adams and Graham (1972) noted, a fatal brain injury may occur without discernible damage

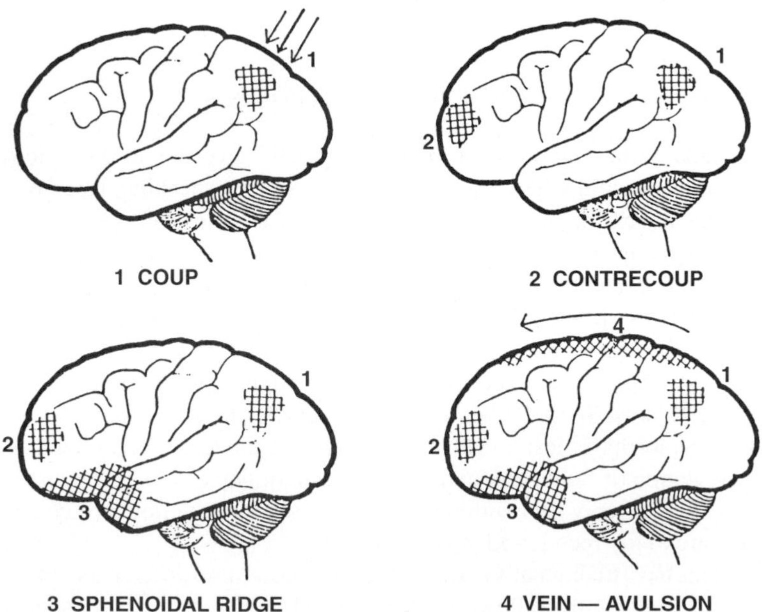


FIG. 2.2. Mechanisms of injury to the brain surface in closed head injury. From *A First Notebook of Head Injury* (2nd ed.), by K.G. Jamieson (1971), p.33. London: Butterworths. Copyright 1971 by Butterworths. Reprinted with permission.

to the scalp or the skull, but it follows that in such cases the critical lesions are to be found elsewhere in the brain (see later). In contrast to the sorts of head injuries that are associated with missile wounds, where the principal damage occurs beneath the point of impact even when the skull has been left intact (Russell, 1951), serious neurological damage at the site of impact tends to result from closed head injury only when the skull has been fractured.

Tables 1.2–1.7 indicate that the proportion of patients admitted to hospital with a diagnosis reflecting closed head injury who have sustained a fractured skull is roughly 30% in the United Kingdom but more than 40% in the United States. Nevertheless, at least two-thirds of all *severe* head injuries are associated with a fractured skull (Jennett, Murray, et al., 1977; Jennett, Teasdale, et al., 1977, 1979). The likelihood of a skull fracture obviously depends on the mass, the velocity, and the shape of the object that causes the head injury. Courville (1942) suggested that the location of a fracture tended to indicate the point at which the blow was applied, and that its direction tended to indicate the direction of the relevant force. However, Adams, Graham, Scott, Parker, and Doyle (1980) found that in 69 out of 120 cases of fatal head injury with skull fracture the latter was centred on the midline of the vault of the skull or restricted to the base of the skull, and hence it gave no indication as to the site of injury. Only 30 of these cases exhibited a predominantly unilateral fracture with a corresponding laceration or bruising of the scalp.

The presence of a fracture indicates that the skull has absorbed some of the kinetic energy of the object causing the head injury, but it also increases the probability of complications, both because of damage to the underlying tissue and because of the possibility of infection. *Linear* fractures constitute roughly 70–80% of all skull fractures and result from the deformation of the skull inwards at the point of impact and outwards further away. Fractures of the base of the skull are of particular significance: they are associated with a major physical impact to the head and are common among the most severely injured patients who do not survive to reach hospital. Such fractures carry an appreciable risk of intracranial infection derived from the sinuses or the middle ear, and they may lead to a leakage of cerebrospinal fluid from either the nose (rhinorrhoea) or the ear (otorrhoea).

A *depressed* fracture is one where a piece of bone is displaced by at least the thickness of the skull; this is of prognostic importance because damage to the underlying cerebral cortex may lead to post-traumatic epilepsy (see later). In a *closed* or *simple* fracture, the scalp is intact; in an *open* or *compound* fracture, the overlying scalp is lacerated or torn, and this carries the risk of intracranial infection. In a *comminuted* depressed fracture, the fractured portion of bone is broken into several fragments, and these may lacerate the brain surface. In roughly half of all depressed fractures, the scalp is lacerated and the dura mater is penetrated, and this allows infection to enter the subdural region.

The important characteristic of most cases of closed head injury is that substantial pressure gradients are temporarily set up within the brain as a result of its motion relative to the skull. This inertial loading within the brain is the major cause of neurological damage following closed head injury (Ommaya & Gennarelli, 1976). Obviously, the extent of the damage depends once again upon the mass, the velocity, and the shape of the object which produces the injury. However, animal experiments have shown that even subconcussive blows to the head may lead to clear gliding movements of the brain relative to the skull, chiefly in the sagittal (that is, dorsoventral) and horizontal planes (e.g. Gosch, Gooding, & Schneider, 1970; Pudenz & Shelden, 1946); and blunt, heavy weapons may produce massive brain damage with only slight contusions to the scalp.

There are two important corollaries to the idea that neurological damage following closed head injury is produced by inertial loading of the cerebral tissues. First, significant widespread damage depends upon the free acceleration or deceleration of the cranium. Therefore, if the cranial vault is fixed at the time of impact, or if the injurious forces are applied in a static, compressive manner (as in crushing), diffuse injuries are less likely and consciousness may even be unimpaired (Ommaya & Gennarelli, 1976; Pudenz & Shelden, 1946).

Second, and conversely, injuries that produce inertial loading within the skull without actual head impact (such as "whiplash" injuries in road accidents or falling onto the buttocks) may nevertheless give rise to concussion and gross cerebral contusions (Ommaya & Gennarelli, 1976). This has been shown repeatedly in experiments with nonhuman primates in which inertial angular acceleration was administered without head impact (Adams, Graham, & Gennarelli, 1983; Gennarelli, 1983; Gennarelli, Thibault, et al., 1982b; Graham, Adams, & Gennarelli, 1988; Jane, Steward, & Gennarelli, 1985). In this connection, it is interesting that 15% of all patients admitted to one regional spinal injury centre showed neurological signs of significant brainstem or cortical damage (Hall et al., 1987).

Nevertheless, it would seem that cerebral lesions are an extremely unlikely cause of fatality in patients with whiplash injury, at least following road traffic accidents (see McLean, 1995). Fatally injured cases of whiplash injury are more likely to suffer from thrombotic obstruction as a result of damage to the vertebral artery in the vicinity of the upper two cervical vertebrae (see Viktrup, Knudsen, & Hansen, 1995). Finally, it might also be noted that closed head injuries can be associated with blast injury resulting from explosions transmitted through water (Hirsch & Ommaya, 1972) or air (Hill, 1979), although injuries of this sort are of course rare during peace-time.

## Contrecoup injury

Following a closed head injury, the dynamic impact produces an inertial stress propagation in the direction of the force applied (Gurdjian & Gurdjian, 1975), and this may give rise to lesions and contusions at points within the skill that are roughly opposite the original site of impact. Such "contrecoup" damage has been discussed for more than 200 years, but it was first described in detail by Russell (1932) and

Courville (1942). Unlike the superficial bruising that occurs at the point of impact, these lesions and contusions are not caused by local deformation of the skull or by local changes in cerebral circulation (Pudenz & Shelden, 1946). Rather, contrecoup injury results from the movement of the brain against the interior surfaces of the skull.

In the past, the results of post-mortem investigations tended to encourage the idea that contrecoup lesions were typically more serious than those arising under the site of impact itself, although Russell (1932) commented that this impression was merely the result of the fact that the contrecoup injury was often marked by subarachnoid haemorrhage. However, this idea was called into question by more rigorous work on fatal head injuries. Adams, Scott, et al. (1980b) devised a "contusion index" in order to quantify the depth and extent of contusions in various parts of the brain in a systematic way. In cases of fatal head injury where the principal site of skull impact could be established with reasonable confidence, these researchers concluded that there was no tendency for contusions to be more severe in contrecoup locations than elsewhere.

In particular, among 30 patients who had suffered a unilateral fracture of the vault of the skull and an overlying scalp injury, there was no sign of any difference in the severity of contusions between the hemisphere contralateral to the fracture and the ipsilateral hemisphere. Moreover, there was no sign of any difference in the relative severity of frontal and occipital contusions between 23 patients with predominantly frontal fractures and 44 patients with predominantly occipital fractures. The former result was confirmed by Adams et al. (1985) in a much larger series of patients with fatal head injuries.

## Sphenoidal injury

Closed head injuries characteristically produce movements of the brain relative to the skull. Courville (1942) observed that the vault of the skull is relatively smooth, whereas the base of the skull contains major irregularities which restrict the movement of the cerebral tissues after a sudden impact: namely, the three cranial fossae on each side, separated by the sphenoidal and petrosal ridges. The latter bony projections tend to induce substantial shearing forces and give rise to contusions of the orbital surfaces of the frontal lobes, the areas of cortex above and below the Sylvian fissures, the temporal poles, and the inferior aspect of the temporal lobes. Most of this damage seems to occur in the vicinity of the sphenoidal ridge (see Fig. 2.3).

Courville's analysis was unequivocal in identifying frontotemporal contusions as the major source of contrecoup injury. Although chains of haemorrhages may occur along the line of maximal propagation of inertial stress, he pointed out that the most serious lesions were not necessarily produced along this line of force at all, but were dependent upon "local bony relations" (1942, p. 34). In fact, Courville showed that damage to both the frontal and temporal lobes was a likely outcome

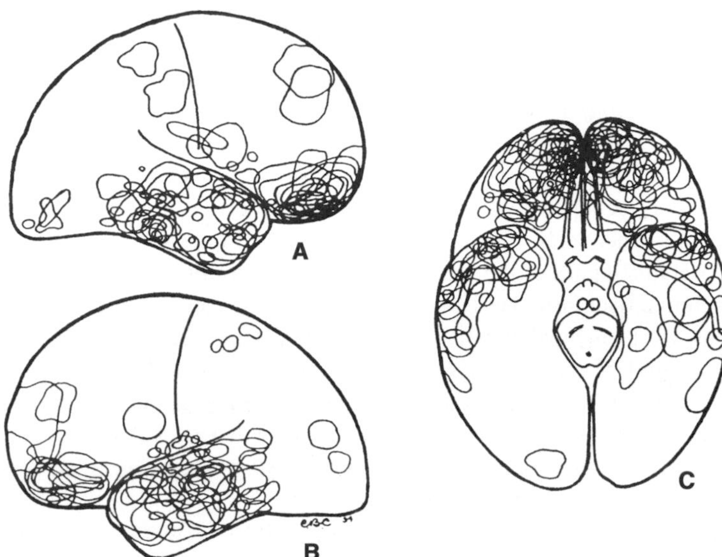


FIG. 2.3. Composite drawing showing the size and location of contusions found in a series of 40 consecutive cases of closed head injury. From *Pathology of the Central Nervous System* (3rd. ed.), C.B. Courville (1950), p.223. Nampa, ID: Pacific Press Publishing Association. Copyright 1950 by Pacific Press Publishing Association. Reprinted with permission.

of all closed head injuries. This might reflect ipsilateral, coup lesions following frontal or temporal impact; or it might reflect contralateral, contrecoup lesions following parietal or occipital impact. Coup lesions of the occipital regions only followed injuries that gave rise to depressed fractures, and contrecoup lesions of those areas were never found. Similar results were obtained in other autopsy studies of the relation between the site of head impact and the location of contusions in human beings, and also in experimental investigations using nonhuman primates (see Ommaya, Grubb, & Naumann, 1971).

In particular, Adams et al. (1985) applied their contusion index to a series of 434 fatal cases of head injury. The typical patient exhibited *no* contusions in the occipital lobes, the parietal lobes, the Sylvian fissures, or the cerebellum, but bilateral contusions of either moderate extent or moderate depth in the frontal and temporal lobes. Patients with fractured skulls exhibited contusions of greater severity, but those with unilateral fractures and a corresponding scalp injury showed essentially the same pattern regardless of the presumed side of impact. Moreover, a broadly similar distribution of contusions across the different cerebral regions was obtained in nonhuman primates subjected to inertial angular acceleration of the head that did not involve any actual impact. There was, in short, no evidence that cerebral contusions were produced by any "contrecoup" mechanism in the sense that they were systematically more severe diametrically opposite the point of impact, nor even that they were dependent upon the occurrence of any "coup" at all.

Research using computerised tomography (CT) and magnetic resonance imaging (MRI) has confirmed this distribution of cerebral lesions among the survivors of closed head injuries and has also demonstrated that it generalises to patients who have sustained less severe brain damage. For instance, Levin, Amparo, et al. (1987) reported findings from CT and MRI carried out upon 20 cases of mild or moderate head injury. MRI disclosed nearly five times as many lesions as CT and, in the case of lesions detected by both techniques, MRI generally indicated that they were larger in volume than CT; these disparities were especially pronounced in lesions within the grey and white matter of the brain (*parenchymal* lesions). (Similar assessments of the relative sensitivity of CT and MRI in cases of closed head injury were given by other researchers: see Gandy, Snow, Zimmerman, & Deck, 1984; Han et al., 1984; Jenkins et al., 1986; Kalisky, Goldman, Morrison, & Von Laufen, 1987; Wilson et al., 1988; and see Newberg & Alavi, 1996, for a recent review.) Lesions were detected in 17 of the 20 patients, and the vast majority of these were situated in the frontal and temporal lobes (see also Jenkins et al., 1986; B.C.M. Macpherson, Macpherson, & Jennett, 1990). None of the additional lesions disclosed by MRI required surgical intervention, however, and most resolved within a period of three months.

In short, the findings of autopsy studies following severe, fatal head injury and those of brain imaging research following nonfatal (and even minor) head injury are totally consistent with each other in implying that the notion of sphenoidal damage is rather more useful than that of contrecoup damage in evaluating the neurological damage consequent upon closed head injury. *A fortiori*, since the fronto-temporal region is a primary location of surface contusions, irrespective of the point of impact (Ommaya, Grubb, & Naumann, 1971), it follows that the locus of impact is relatively uninformative in establishing a likely prognosis unless the injury has produced a depressed fracture. Moreover, even though patients with a fractured skull reveal a much wider incidence of cerebral contusions, these are usually distributed across the surface of the brain and are not particularly associated with the principal site of skull impact (Adams, 1985; Adams, Scott, et al., 1980; Macpherson, Macpherson, & Jennett, 1990).

## Gliding contusions

The free movement of the brain within the skull is also constrained by the falx cerebri, which is a sickle-shaped fold of dura mater that descends vertically into the longitudinal fissure dividing the two cerebral hemispheres. This restricts any rotation of the brain within the coronal plane and thus gives rise to contusions of the medial surfaces of the cerebral hemispheres and also along the upper surface of the corpus callosum. Conversely, the falx cerebri also ensures that movement of the brain is mostly within the sagittal and horizontal planes (Pudenz & Shelden, 1946). Indeed, precisely because there is relatively little restraint to this movement between the superior surfaces of the cerebral hemispheres and the vault of the skull, there may be considerable avulsion of nerve fibres and blood vessels, with the consequent risk of subdural haematoma (see pp. 60–61).

Much attention has been directed towards the phenomenon of "gliding contusions", which are haemorrhagic lesions located in the dorsal paramedial regions of the cerebral hemispheres (Lindenberg & Freytag, 1960). Microscopic investigation often reveals that they extend into the deeper layers of the cerebral cortex and the adjacent white matter. Adams, Doyle, Graham, Lawrence, and McLellan (1986b) identified gliding contusions in over 30% of cases of fatal head injury, although they were less likely in patients who had sustained a fractured skull, more likely in the victims of road traffic accidents, and more likely in patients who exhibited evidence of diffuse brain damage. Adams et al. noted that similar lesions had been produced in experimental animals using inertial angular acceleration of the head, and they suggested that these contusions might result from the relative movement of the skull, the cortical surface, and subcortical structures. More specifically, they pointed out that the parasagittal bridging veins tethered the cortical surface to the superior sagittal sinus (which runs along the upper margin of the falx cerebri). They noted that the failure of a bridging vein itself would produce an acute subdural haematoma, and they hypothesised that gliding contusions were caused by a failure of the branching vessels of these veins that penetrate into the brain substance.

As was mentioned in Chapter 1, cerebral contusions were traditionally regarded as the hallmark of a clinically significant closed head injury. Nevertheless, it is clear from research on the neuropathology of fatal head injury that patients may die as a result of such an injury without having any contusions or lacerations of the brain (Adams, 1988). For instance, Adams et al. (1985) identified 27 cases of fatal head injury in whom cerebral contusions were entirely absent, plus another 28 cases in whom such lesions were minimal. Graham, Adams, and Gennarelli (1988) added that cases had also occurred in experimental research with primates where fatal brain damage had arisen in the absence of cerebral contusions.

Conversely, Adams, Graham, et al. (1980) identified only three out of 151 cases of fatal head injury where severe contusions seemed to be the principal cause of death insofar as they were the only evidence of severe brain damage. Indeed, Jennett and Teasdale (1981, p. 25) stated that a head injury could give rise to extensive cerebral contusions in the absence of any prolonged disturbance of consciousness. As they explained, the clinical significance of cerebral contusions usually lies in the fact that they can initiate brain swelling and intracranial haemorrhage, and that such processes can result in turn in the deterioration of the patient's level of consciousness or the prolongation of a coma that was caused initially by other mechanisms (see also Teasdale & Mendelow, 1984).

# DIFFUSE AXONAL INJURY

## Linear and rotatory components

Earlier in this chapter, it was emphasised that the neurological damage produced by a closed head injury is critically dependent upon whether or not the head is restrained at the time of impact. In addition, experimental research using inanimate models and laboratory animals showed that the dynamic effects of a head injury upon the movement of the brain relative to an unconstrained skull should be analysed in terms of an axial, linear translation together with a rotatory component (Holbourn, 1943, 1945; Ommaya & Gennarelli, 1974, 1976). These physical components produce quite different patterns of neurological damage.

The linear component of the head injury produces a translational acceleration or deceleration of the skull, and this gives rise to pressure gradients within the brain. However, the effects of these forces are both focal and relatively minor. There may be contusions at the site of impact and possibly also at points which are diametrically opposite to that site; but an axial translation by itself does not produce diffuse lesions throughout the brain. In particular, while linear blows that are severe or are applied repeatedly may interfere with consciousness by producing profound circulatory disturbances, they rarely give rise to cerebral concussion.

The nonlinear component of a closed head injury produces a rotational acceleration of the skull, and this gives rise to a rotation of the skull relative to the brain. As was pointed out in the previous section, such movement may well produce contusions and lacerations at points where the cerebral tissues come into contact with major bony irregularities. Thus, the rotation of the skull will cause major damage in the region of the sphenoidal ridge and possibly also at the vertex, with consequent risk of intracranial haemorrhage. In short, as Holbourn (1943, 1945) argued, so-called "contrecoup" injuries are really neurological damage caused by the rotation of the frontal and temporal lobes against the sphenoidal ridge.

However, the rotation of the brain within the skull does not simply give rise to contusions at the point of contact between the cerebral hemispheres and the bony projections of the cranium. Depending upon the inertial loading to which the head is subjected, it also produces damaging shearing strains within the brain which decrease in magnitude from the surface of the brain to its centre. As Holbourn (1943, p. 438) explained, this is "the type of deformation which occurs in a pack of cards, when it is deformed from a neat rectangular pile into an oblique-angled pile". In the absence of any complications, these forces seem to be the major cause of the brain damage that follows closed head injury. In particular, the rotational component of a head injury is usually necessary for consciousness to be impaired and for diffuse damage to occur throughout the brain. Thus, the rotation of the brain following a closed head injury may give rise to both focal and diffuse lesions that are relatively independent of the original site of impact.

Ommaya and Gennarelli (1974, pp. 637–638) integrated the results of experimental research into a formal hypothesis, which defined cerebral concussion as:

> a graded set of clinical syndromes following head injury wherein increasing severity of disturbance in level and content of consciousness is caused by mechanically induced strains affecting the brain in a centripetal sequence of disruptive effect on function and structure. The effects of this sequence always begin at the surfaces of the brain in the mild cases and extend inwards to affect the diencephalic-mesencephalic core at the most severe levels of trauma.

This hypothesis was in turn elaborated into a proposed classification of the possible grades of cerebral concussion (see Fig. 2.4). According to this "centripetal" conception of the biomechanics of brain injury, the distribution of damaging strains induced by inertial loading decreases in magnitude from the surface of the brain to its centre. It follows that in less severe cases (Grades I–III in the model) the patient's conscious awareness is only partially impaired, and damage is confined to the cortex, subcortex, and diencephalon. However, more severe shearing forces disrupt the rostral brainstem and in particular the reticular activating system, thus producing traumatic unconsciousness or even death (Grades IV–VI).

In real life, of course, most closed head injuries will have both linear and rotatory components, and relatively pure linear or pure rotatory forces are rarely seen (Gurdjian & Gurdjian, 1978). Indeed, accidental closed head injuries may involve multiple blows, and it may prove very hard to disentangle their linear and rotatory

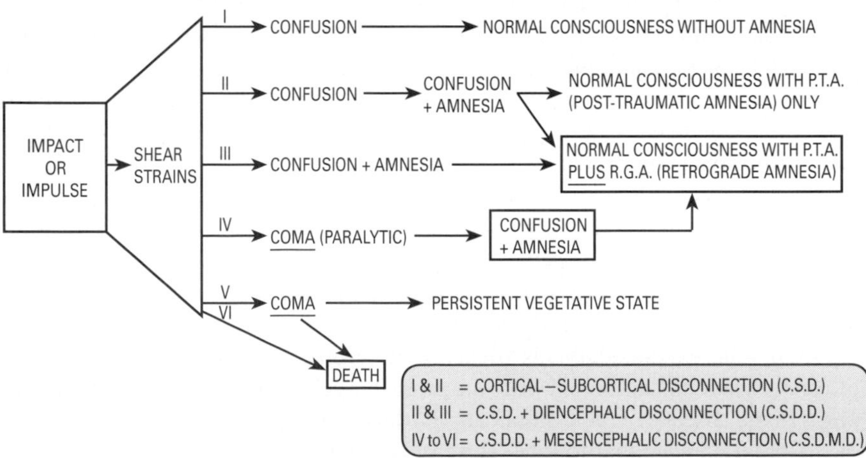


FIG. 2.4. Diagrammatic description of Ommaya and Gennarelli's (1974, 1976) hypothesis for the syndromes of cerebral concussion. From "Cerebral concussion and traumatic unconsciousness", by A.K. Ommaya and T.A. Gennarelli (1974), *Brain, 97,* p.638. Copyright 1974 by Oxford University Press. Reprinted with permission.

components after the event. The clinical value of this distinction may thus be limited; as Teasdale and Jennett (1976, p. 48) emphasised, "a complete description of the severity of brain injury requires the assessment of impaired consciousness to be complemented by eliciting signs of focal brain dysfunction". Moreover, it cannot be assumed that patterns of impaired consciousness seen in anaesthetised animals in the laboratory will inevitably mirror those observed following accidental injury in humans (Gurdjian & Gurdjian, 1975; Symonds, 1962).

Nevertheless, "whiplash" injuries in traffic accidents (Ommaya & Yarnell, 1969) and perhaps also in cases of child abuse (Caffey, 1974; but cf. Duhaime et al., 1987) constitute examples of fairly pure rotatory movements of the brain within the cranial cavity in the absence of linear translation. Falls onto the buttocks have already been mentioned as examples of inertial loading without actual head impact. Finally, it is well known in boxing that an axial blow to the head is the least damaging, whereas the most devastating blow in effecting the opponent's loss of consciousness is one that induces major rotational forces within the brain (Lampert & Hardman, 1984; Parkinson, 1977). In other words, it is probably true, as Ommaya and Yarnell (1969, p. 239) commented, that "rotation of the head is the common denominator to the cerebral trauma of both head injury and whiplash injury".

## Diffuse damage in fatal head injury

It is now generally recognised that diffuse cerebral damage produced by shearing forces within the brain is the primary mechanism of brain lesions following closed head injury. However, the damage in question would not have been evident in the early work of Courville and others for at least two different reasons. First, the lesions in question are typically not visible to the naked eye and their identification depends on comprehensive histological analysis using microscopic inspection of carefully preserved brain tissue. However, this was often precluded in forensic examinations of the sort on which much of this early work was based (Jennett & Teasdale, 1981, pp. 19, 26). As Adams, Graham, et al. (1980) pointed out, this led to an inevitable tendency for pathologists in determining the cause of death to lay particular stress on readily identifiable macroscopic abnormalities such as skull fractures, intracranial haematomas, and cerebral contusions.

Second, these lesions take about 12–18 hours to develop and are difficult to diagnose in patients who survive for less time than this (Adams et al., 1989b). Although more than half of all patients with fatal head injury die before they reach hospital (see Chapter 1), post-mortem findings in such cases reflect the overwhelming nature of their injuries, including severe basal skull fracture, brainstem laceration, or even disruption of the whole brain, as well as fracture or dislocation of the cervical spine or serious chest injury (Jennett & Carlin, 1978). Lesions of this kind are quite different from the injuries found in those patients who survive long enough to reach a specialist neurosurgical unit, and this is reflected in differences between the reports of forensic pathologists and those of neuropathologists (Jennett, personal communication). As a result, our current understanding of structural pathology in survivors of closed head injury has been immeasurably enhanced by careful histological analysis of patients who have died in specialist units.

For instance, Strich (1956) originally described extensive degeneration in the white matter of five patients who had suffered apparently uncomplicated head injuries, but who had remained in a profoundly demented state with gross neurological deficits until their deaths some months later. Strich (1961) reported similar results in a larger series of cases whose survival had extended from as little as two days to as much as two years after trauma. A number of subsequent post-mortem investigations confirmed the existence of diffuse white-matter damage following closed head injuries (see Strich, 1969, for a review). To the naked eye, the brain may often have a rather shrunken appearance, and the ventricular system may be enlarged because of the reduction in the bulk of the white matter. This is especially likely in patients who have survived for many months or even years in a persistent vegetative state (Adams et al., 1989b; see Chapter 7). Among young infants, grossly visible tears in the cerebral white matter are a characteristic finding following a closed head injury (Lindenberg & Freytag, 1969). Among adult patients, the extent of the underlying damage may not be immediately obvious. Microscopically, however, there may well be axonal damage to the corpus callosum, the internal capsule, and the subcortical mechanisms of both cerebral hemispheres, to the cerebellum, and to a number of sites within the brainstem, including the pyramidal tracts, the medial lemnisci, the medial longitudinal bundles, and the superior cerebellar peduncles (e.g. Nevin, 1967).

As implied earlier, clinical signs of brainstem dysfunction are commonly seen at an early stage after major closed head injury. This led to the notion of "primary brainstem damage": that is, of severe focal damage to the brainstem. Over 80% of patients demonstrating such signs following closed head injury will not recover (Turazzi, Alexandre, & Bricolo, 1975). Neuropathological and electrophysiological studies have however challenged the notion that this clinical picture is specifically associated with isolated damage to the brainstem (e.g. Mitchell & Adams, 1973), and it would seem that selective "primary brainstem damage" does not, in fact, occur. In one major study, for instance, not one of the patients who fitted this clinical syndrome was found at post-mortem to have lesions confined to the brainstem (Adams, Mitchell, Graham, & Doyle, 1977). On the contrary, as is indeed predicted by Ommaya and Gennarelli's (1974, 1976) "centipetal" conception of the biomechanics of head injury, primary damage to the rostral brainstem represents just one aspect of the widespread and diffuse damage that occurs to the white matter (though cf. Jane et al., 1982).

Adams, Graham, et al. (1980) identified a total of 19 patients with diffuse lesions of the cerebral white matter in a consecutive series of 151 cases of fatal nonmissile head injury. Adams, Graham, Murray, and Scott (1982) added another 26 patients with diffuse white-matter damage to this series. Every one of these 45 patients displayed a characteristic pattern of focal lesions in the corpus callosum and in the dorsolateral quadrant or quadrants of the rostral brainstem, together with diffuse damage to axons. Although the latter could only be determined by microscopic scrutiny of appropriately stained neural tissue, Adams et al. described this condition as one of *diffuse axonal injury*. All of the patients had been unconscious from the time of impact and had remained in a coma or a persistent vegetative state with no lucid interval until they died. Adams et al. found that they were more likely to have been involved in road traffic accidents and less likely to have been involved in falls than other cases of fatal head injury. They suggested that rotational movements necessary to induce primary brainstem damage would be more likely to ensue from road traffic accidents than from falls. Subsequently, Adams, Doyle, Graham, Lawrence, and McLellan (1984) found that this pattern of brain damage only arose in injuries caused by falls when the patient had fallen a considerable distance (in other words, one greater than his or her own height). It may also arise as the result of an assault (see Graham, Clark, Adams, & Gennarelli, 1992).

Adams, Graham, et al. (1982) also demonstrated that the patients with diffuse axonal injury had a much lower incidence of skull fracture, cerebral contusions, intracranial haematoma, and raised intracranial pressure than the other head-injured patients, although the two groups showed no difference in the incidence of brain swelling or hypoxic damage. From these observations they argued that the degeneration of white matter seen in diffuse axonal injury did not occur secondary to hypoxia, brain swelling, or raised intracranial pressure. Instead, they supported the contention of Strich (1961, 1969) that the degeneration of white matter was a direct result of physical damage to nerve fibres at the moment of impact, and they inferred from this that such lesions could be neither prevented nor remedied. They concluded that diffuse axonal damage was probably the single most important factor influencing the outcome in cases of closed head injury.

Adams et al. (1989b) confirmed these basic observations with a much larger sample of patients with fatal head injuries, except that in this series 14% of the patients with diffuse axonal injury had in fact exhibited a lucid interval. Moreover, there was an increased incidence of both gliding contusions and deep intracerebral haematomas among patients with diffuse axonal injury. On the basis of their experience with these patients, Adams et al. suggested that the basic clinicopathological entity of diffuse axonal injury could be differentiated into three broad types, reflecting various grades of severity. Grade 1 could be identified only on the basis of histological evidence of axonal injury in the white matter of the cerebral hemispheres, the corpus callosum, the brainstem, and also occasionally in the cerebellum. Grade 2 was identified by an additional focal lesion in the corpus callosum; this was typically haemorrhagic and tended to lie to one side of the midline, although it might also extend to the midline and involve the interventricular septum and the pillars of the fornix. Finally, Grade 3 was defined by focal lesions in both the corpus callosum and the dorsolateral quadrant of the rostral brainstem. In many cases these focal lesions could only be identified microscopically.

Blumbergs et al. (1995) recently identified diffuse axonal injury in six patients who had died of other causes following mild head injury (defined by a Glasgow Coma Scale score between 13 and 15 on admission to hospital). The most common locations of damage were the corpus callosum and the fornix. However, the physical extent of diffuse axonal injury was significantly less than in six further patients who had died following severe head injuries (defined by a Glasgow Coma Scale score between 3 and 8 on admission to hospital), and only the latter patients showed axonal damage in the cerebellar peduncles.

## Diffuse axonal injury in survivors of head injury

Gennarelli, Thibault, et al. (1982b) showed that exactly the same lesions could be produced in nonhuman primates that were subjected to concussion through inertial angular acceleration of the head, although only when motion was in the coronal plane (that is, at right angles to the body midline). The extent of such damage was directly proportional to the duration of coma. Gennarelli et al. concluded that diffuse axonal injury produced by coronal head acceleration was a major cause of prolonged traumatic coma, and that in the absence of complications the outcome of head injury depends on the amount and distribution of axonal damage. It is also pertinent to remark that once again these lesions had been induced without actual head impact (see Adams et al., 1983). The precise mechanism of diffuse axonal injury in such cases has yet to be established, but recent research suggests that it involves subtle structural changes within the cell membrane enclosing the axon (the axolemma) and within the myelin sheath as well as the actual tearing of the axon itself (see Gennarelli, 1996; Maxwell, Kansagra, Graham, Adams, & Gennarelli, 1988; Maxwell, Watt, Graham, & Gennarelli, 1993).

In the case of survivors from head trauma, the earliest CT scans typically failed to provide direct evidence of damage to the cerebral white matter (Zimmerman, Bilaniuk, & Gennarelli, 1978), although they were useful for detecting damage to the skull. Indeed, Snoek, Jennett, Adams, Graham, and Doyle (1979) found normal CT scans in 23 (or 38%) out of 60 severely injured patients who did not have an acute intracranial haematoma, and in 5 (or 26%) out of 19 of these patients who subsequently died. In 15 of the latter cases post-mortem examinations were carried out; diffuse damage to the cerebral white matter was identified in six of these cases, despite the fact that no parenchymal lesions had been identified in their CT scans.

Snoek et al. (1979) pointed out that the pathological lesions typical of diffuse white-matter damage are either small or only recognisable at a microscopic level; it is therefore not particularly surprising that such lesions are not evident on CT scans, although there may be circumstantial evidence from CT scans to suspect their presence. Bruce et al. (1981) used this sort of evidence obtained from head-injured children to confirm the idea of a link between diffuse damage to the cerebral white matter and the absence of a lucid interval. However, the main point emphasised by Snoek et al. was that caution was called for in drawing conclusions based solely on CT scans, especially in regarding a normal or near normal scan as excluding severe brain damage. Indeed, Gennarelli (1983) used as an indicator of diffuse axonal injury prolonged traumatic coma in the absence of any mass lesions (intracranial haematomas) on CT scans, but in subsequent research, diffuse axonal injury was ascribed on the basis of gliding contusions and small haematomas within the corpus callosum or rostral brainstem, as visualised by means of CT (Macpherson, Jennett, & Anderson, 1990).

Intracerebral lesions can be readily detected in patients with either severe or minor closed head injury using MRI (Kalisky et al., 1987; Levin, Amparo, et al., 1987; Levin, Handel, Goldman, Eisenberg, & Guinto, 1985; Levin, Kalisky, et al., 1985; Mittl et al., 1994; Wilson et al., 1988). In agreement with Ommaya and Gennarelli's (1974, 1976) "centripetal" conception of the biomechanics of head injury, the depth of lesions visualised in this way is inversely related to the patient's total score on the Glasgow Coma Scale and directly related to the duration of impaired consciousness; these lesions tend to occur only in patients with cortical lesions and to be smaller in volume than lesions to the brain surface (Jenkins et al., 1986; Levin, Williams, et al., 1988; Wilson et al., 1988; but cf. Newberg & Alavi, 1996).

Unfortunately, it is not at present entirely clear whether these lesions reflect regional variations specifically in the extent of diffuse axonal injury, as opposed to subsequent complications such as a transient elevation of intracranial pressure or to degenerative changes during the post-injury interval. Levin, Williams, et al. (1988) found that the exclusion of patients who exhibited neurological deterioration and raised intracranial pressure did not affect the overall relationship between the depth of the lesion and the level of consciousness.

Nevertheless, even a normal MRI scan does not exclude the possibility of microscopic brain damage. Wilson et al. (1988) found discrepancies between MRI scans obtained within 21 days of an injury and again 5–12 months afterwards. In particular, two patients with early lesions confined to the cerebral cortex and five patients with early lesions confined to the cortex and to the subcortical white-matter had developed deep white matter lesions or ventricular enlargement consistent with atrophy by the second occasion that they underwent MRI. These results suggested that significant abnormalities may only become fully apparent some time after a closed head injury.

Two additional problems are that MRI is sensitive to pre-existing demyelinating conditions such as multiple sclerosis (Levin, Amparo, et al., 1987a), and hence their effects may be confused with those of a head injury; but that it is unable to visualise compact bone (Han et al., 1984; Hughes & Cohen, 1993), and thus CT is superior in detecting skull fracture (Newberg & Alavi, 1996). The latest MRI techniques seem to be very reliable in detecting tissue damage following head injury (Smith et al., 1995). However, as Newberg and

Alavi (1996) pointed out, CT is more widely available and more cost-effective than MRI, and the scanning can be completed within a shorter period of time. They summarised the situation as follows (p. 70):

> Today, MRI is still limited by its inability to evaluate skull fractures, degradation of MR images by motion artifact in agitated patients, and difficulty in monitoring patients during MRI owing to the unavailability of nonferromagnetic monitoring equipment. ... However, with the introduction of equipment that allows for better patient monitoring during MRI and short imaging times, MRI may become a more useful tool for the early evaluation of acute brain injury. ... However, for now, it appears that CT is still the imaging study of choice in the acute management of brain injury.

An increasing number of studies have used techniques for monitoring regional cerebral blood flow in patients with closed head injuries, such as positron emission tomography (PET) and single photon emission computed tomography (SPECT). Newberg and Alavi (1996) concluded that the main limitation of these forms of brain imaging was that the regions of functional abnormality that they detect do not necessarily correspond to the regions of structural damage. They therefore need to be complemented by existing anatomical imaging techniques such as CT and MRI. MRI itself has been extended to study various physiological changes in the brain, in the form of diffusion-weighted MRI, perfusion MRI, and functional MRI. Again, an increasing number of studies have used these new techniques in patients with head injuries, and they are likely to be of considerable clinical importance in the future (for reviews of these and other techniques, see Ashwal & Holshouser, 1997; Matz & Pitts, 1997).

A fairly common outcome of severe closed head injury is an enlargement of the Sylvian aqueduct and the lateral ventricles in the absence of communicating hydrocephalus. On the basis of pneumoencephalographic studies, Boller, Albert, LeMay, and Kertesz (1972) argued that this clinical condition was the result of degeneration of the periventricular white matter, a notion that is entirely consistent with the results of the post-mortem investigations cited previously. Levin, Meyers, Grossman, and Sarwar (1981) showed that the extent of ventricular enlargement according to CT was significantly related to the duration of coma, though only among patients who had been involved in motor vehicle accidents. Subsequently, Levin, Williams, et al. (1988) found that the extent of ventricular enlargement was correlated with the depth of lesions that had been visualised by means of MRI.

Nevertheless, shearing forces at the time of impact may give rise to lesions in a variety of other intracranial structures. For instance, the possibility of damage to the corpus callosum was mentioned earlier. Adams and Graham (1972) found some damage of this sort amongst 80% of a consecutive series of 400 fatal head injuries. In particular, there were gross lesions within the corpus callosum in every patient who demonstrated diffuse degeneration of the white matter or evidence of primary injury to the brain stem. These lesions may sometimes be visualised by means of CT (Macpherson, Jennett, & Anderson, 1990; Zimmerman, Bilaniuk, & Gennarelli, 1978) or more readily by means of MRI (Jenkins et al., 1986; Levin, Williams, et al., 1990), and they can lead to a hemispheric disconnection syndrome (Rubens, Geschwind, Mahowald, & Mastri, 1977). Kampfl et al. (1998) found that the presence or absence of lesions of the corpus callosum and the dorsolateral brainstem were important in predicting recovery from a post-traumatic vegetative state (see Chapter 7).

There may be additional damage to the cranial nerves, and the resulting sensory impairment can affect the quality of subsequent recovery. Neurological deficits of this sort are seen in between 2% and 8% of survivors of severe head injuries. The olfactory, optic, and auditory nerves seem to be the most vulnerable. A detailed (though now rather dated) account of cranial nerve problems after closed head injuries was given by Russell (1960), who attributed these to small vascular lesions within the brainstem, whereas Sumner (1964) provided an early but authoritative analysis of post-traumatic anosmia (loss of the sense of smell).

Damage to the hypothalamo-pituitary system is also well recognised. More than 40% of patients who die as the result of head injuries show some evidence of haemorrhagic or ischaemic damage to the hypothalamus (Crompton, 1971), and complete or partial necrosis of the anterior lobe of the pituitary gland and haemorrhage into the posterior lobe are other common findings at post-mortem. Among patients who survive severe head injury, disordered hypothalamic or pituitary function may be evident: for instance, diabetes insipidus, which involves the excretion of large volumes of urine of low concentration and thus reflects a failure of secretion of antidiuretic hormone, is sometimes seen after head injury.

## SECONDARY BRAIN DAMAGE

Jennett and Teasdale (1981, p. 23) pointed out that a crucial distinction needs to be drawn between immediate impact damage after closed head injury (that is, skull fractures, cerebral contusions, and diffuse axonal injury), and subsequent complications or secondary brain damage. The complications of closed head injury are the only treatable aspects of closed head injury, and it follows that the main objective of medical management is to prevent or at least to minimise the various forms of secondary brain damage. The primary complications are *intracranial haematomas* and *brain swelling* (see Adams, Graham, et al., 1980). These changes can usually be identified by means of CT (Clifton et al., 1980; Macpherson, Jennett, & Anderson, 1990; Tarlov, 1976; Weisberg, 1979), although they may only be evident on close inspection of relevant images (Zimmerman, Bilaniuk, Bruce, et al., 1978), and they can also be detected by means of MRI (Snow, Zimmerman, Gandy, & Deck, 1986).

## Intracranial haematoma

Intracranial haemorrhage tends to occur in all but the most minor head injuries, but it is only of clinical significance if it gives rise to a space-occupying clot or intracranial haematoma. This occurs in almost 50% of severely injured patients, more commonly in older patients, and it often accounts for the delayed development of coma after a lucid interval or for the deterioration of patients already in coma (Jennett, Murray, et al., 1979; Jennett, Teasdale, et al., 1976; Jennett et al., 1977, 1979; Reilly, Adams, Graham, & Jennett, 1975; Teasdale, Skene, Parker, & Jennett, 1979).

Macpherson, Jennett, and Anderson (1990) found that the likelihood of an intracranial haematoma varied inversely with the patients' scores on the Glasgow Coma Scale (GCS) on their admission to a regional neurosurgical unit. Similarly, Teasdale et al. (1990) pooled the results of a number of different surveys to estimate the risk of acute traumatic intracranial haematoma in different patient groups. Their results entail that the diagnosis of a skull fracture in adult patients increases the likelihood of an intracranial haematoma by 7.5 times in comatose patients (with GCS scores of 3–8) and by 175 times in conscious patients (with a GCS score of 15). In children, the corresponding proportions are 5 and 80, respectively.

Prompt surgical intervention is needed to deal with this condition (Marshall, Toole, & Bowers, 1983). Nevertheless, Bowers and Marshall (1980) suggested that the occurrence of an intracranial haematoma did not itself have any adverse effect upon prognosis once it had been surgically treated. These researchers as well as others (e.g. Gennarelli, 1983) have also noted that intracranial haematomas are about half as common in head injuries resulting from motor accidents than in those resulting from other causes. They seem to be particularly common when the head injury is sustained in a fall caused by an epileptic seizure, possibly because, unlike a conscious person, the victim is unable to reduce the impact of the fall by reflex movements (Zwimpfer et al., 1997).

Intracranial bleeding may be categorised in terms of its anatomical location with respect to the brain and to the three membranes or *meninges* by which it is enveloped: the dura mater, the arachnoid mater, and the pia mater. The layers of cells that constitute the meninges are illustrated in Fig. 2.5. Intracranial bleeding is accordingly classified as extradural, subdural, subarachnoid, intracerebral, or intraventricular, although more than one of these forms may be involved in one and the same patient (see Macpherson, Macpherson, & Jennett, 1990). In general, CT is superior to MRI in detecting these intracranial haematomas and in distinguishing intracranial haemorrhage from brain swelling, although MRI may be more sensitive in detecting subdural haematomas and in distinguishing brain swelling from haemorrhagic contusions (see Newberg & Alavi, 1996).

The arachnoid and the pia mater are separated by a layer of cerebrospinal fluid which occupies the subarachnoid space. It used to be thought that the dura mater was separated from the arachnoid by a film of serous fluid, and hence that there

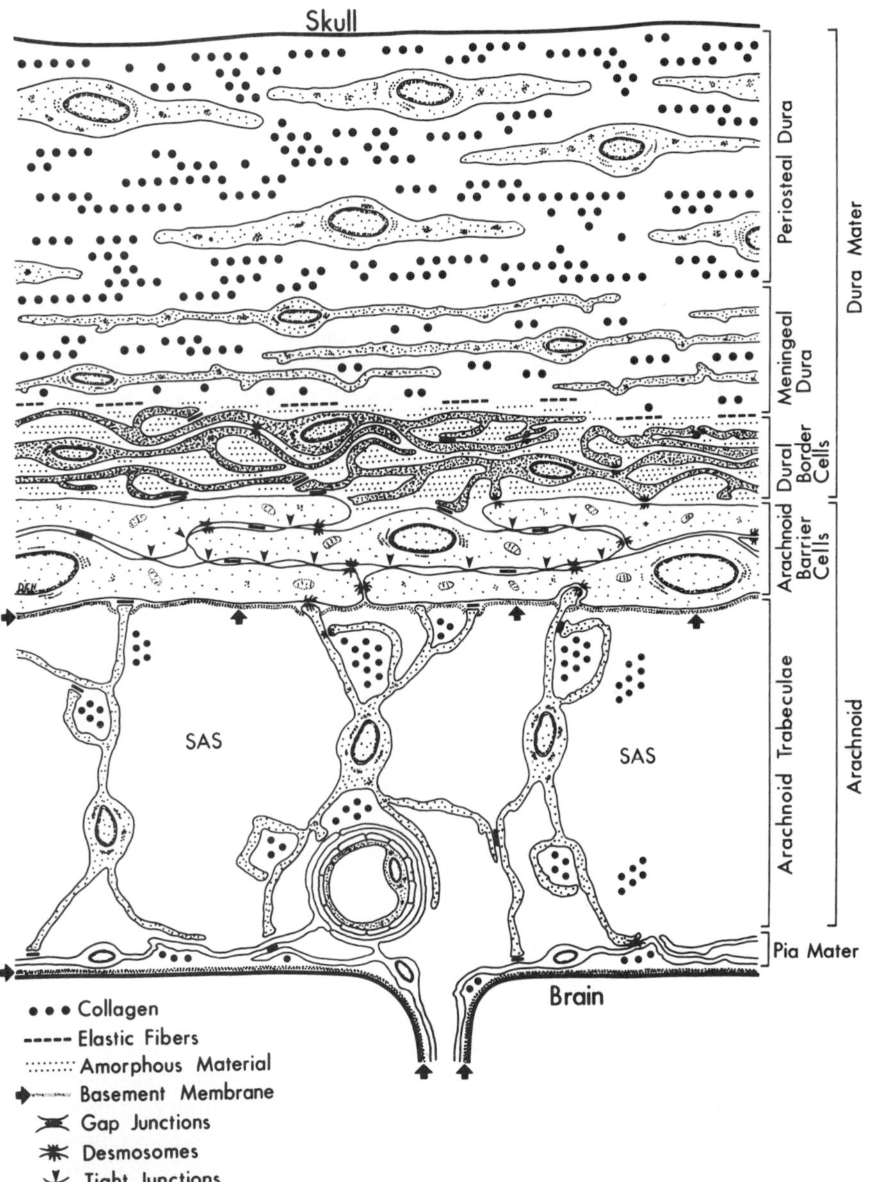


FIG. 2.5. Semidiagammatic representation of the structure of the meninges from the inner surface of the skull (at the top) to the external surface of the brain (at the bottom). Between the arachnoid and the pia, there is a subarachnoid space (SAS) containing cerebrospinal fluid. From "On the question of a subdural space", by D.E. Haines (1991), *Anatomical Record*, *230*, p.6. Copyright 1991 by Wiley-Liss Inc. Reprinted by permission of Wiley-Liss, Inc., a subsidiary of John Wiley & Sons, Inc.

was a potential "subdural space". It was similarly assumed that there was a potential "extradural space" (or "epidural space"). In fact, the dura adheres to the inner surface of the skull and is continuously attached to the arachnoid by a layer of tissue, the dural border cell layer. There is no evidence for a serous membrane in either case. Consequently, the "extradural space" and the "subdural space" do not exist in a normal anatomical state but arise only as the result of a pathological process. For instance, "subdural" haematomas occur when the infusion of blood cleaves open the dural border cell layer (Haines, 1991).

*Extradural haematoma.* An extradural haematoma (sometimes described as an *epidural* haematoma) forms when blood from torn meningeal vessels strips the dura away from the skull and produces a lens-shaped bulging mass within the extradural region. This mass of blood is well-defined, because the dura at the edges of the haematoma remains firmly attached to the inner table of the skull. Extradural haematomas are found in 1–2% of patients admitted to hospital with closed head injuries, and they are most common over the temporal and parietal regions, since it is the branches of the middle meningeal vessels that are most frequently damaged in cases of closed head injury (Jennett & Teasdale, 1981, p. 153).

Although haematomas at this site are not uncommonly seen after what clinically seems to have been only a slight trauma, a skull fracture is present in 85–90% of patients (Jamieson & Yelland, 1968; Macpherson, Macpherson, & Jennett, 1990). Indeed, Adams et al. (1983) concluded that extradural haematomas were essentially a complication of skull fracture, because neither extradural haematomas nor skull fractures were induced as the result of inertial angular acceleration of the head in experiments on nonhuman primates. The subsequent mortality rate may be high (between 15% and 30% in different series), despite the fact that there may often be no discernible brain damage other than that attributable to the space-occupying effects of the haematoma itself. However, it is these effects that make extradural haematoma such a dangerous complication, and death may supervene without prompt surgical intervention.

*Subdural haematoma.* A subdural haematoma most commonly results from the tearing of the bridging veins that run through the dural border cell layer to the dural venous sinuses, but the cause may also be direct injury to the sinuses themselves or bleeding from arteries and veins in areas of damaged cerebral cortex. Whereas the spread of extradural haematomas is circumscribed by dural attachments to the skull, subdural haematomas tend to be more widespread and often extend beneath and between the cerebral hemispheres (Adams, 1988, p. 11): indeed, they are commonly found over the convexities of the hemispheres, against the falx cerebri in the longitudinal fissure, or in the floor of the anterior, middle, or posterior cranial fossae. Cortical atrophy and ventricular enlargement have been well documented as sequelae of subdural haematomas (see Cullum & Bigler, 1985).

Subdural haematomas may be difficult to detect on CT images if they have the same density as brain tissue, but they can be readily identified using MRI (Han et al., 1984; Hughes & Cohen, 1993).

The expression "acute subdural haematoma" is often used to refer to those occurring within 48 hours of injury. A thin film of "subdural" blood is in fact commonly seen in cases of closed head injury and need not have any great clinical significance. However, in about 5% of cases the collection of blood is large, often as a result of haemorrhages from the capillaries in the outer membrane. In this situation prompt surgical intervention is certainly warranted, although the resulting mortality may still be relatively high (Bowers & Marshall, 1980; Gennarelli, 1983). Some authors describe as "subacute" a haematoma that occurs between three days and two to three weeks following a head injury, but Jennett and Teasdale (1981, p. 156) doubted whether this constituted a distinct diagnostic category. They suggested that any haematoma occurring within the first two weeks after injury should be described as "acute", whereas a haematoma diagnosed later than this should be described as "chronic" (see Cooper, 1982b).

In experimental research using nonhuman primates, Ommaya, Faas, and Yarnell (1968) demonstrated that rapid rotation of the head without direct impact could produce cerebral concussion, superficial cortical contusions, and subdural haematomas (see also Ommaya, Geller, & Parsons, 1971). It has subsequently been extensively confirmed that inertial angular acceleration of the head can induce subdural haematomas, but only when the acceleration is rapid and within the sagittal (that is, dorsoventral) plane (Adams et al., 1983; Gennarelli, 1983). Similarly, Ommaya and Yarnell (1969) described two cases of subdural haematoma in human patients which had apparently been produced by whiplash injury alone. Moreover, in his account of the "whiplash shaken infant syndrome", Caffey (1974) specifically noted the occurrence of bilateral subdural haematomas in the absence of external signs of trauma to the head and neck. More recently, Macpherson, Macpherson, and Jennett (1990) found that subdural haematoma occurred in 23% of head-injured patients without skull fracture who had been admitted to a regional neurosurgical unit.

*Subarachnoid haemorrhage.* A subarachnoid haemorrhage occurs when blood is released into the space between the arachnoid and the pia. Some degree of subarachnoid bleeding is almost universal after a closed head injury, particularly if there is an occipital fracture of the skull. A more substantial haematoma within the subarachnoid space is however somewhat rare, because the collection of blood tends to rupture into the brain or the subdural region. The presence of blood in the subarachnoid space seems to be involved in the genesis of arterial spasm, which may give rise to ischaemic brain damage (Macpherson & Graham, 1978). Moreover, the presence of blood and, in the longer term, the development of fibrous adhesions in the subarachnoid space may obstruct the flow of cerebrospinal fluid. This results in communicating high pressure hydrocephalus, which may arise even following a minor head injury in a patient with congenital narrowing (stenosis) of the Sylvian aqueduct (Jennett & Teasdale, 1981, p. 40; Teasdale & Mendelow, 1984).

*Intracerebral haematoma.* Intracerebral haematomas are characteristically associated with cerebral contusions and therefore tend to occur most frequently within the frontal and temporal lobes (see Fig. 2.6). They can also arise in other regions of the cerebral hemispheres and within the cerebellum and brainstem. They have been variously reported as occurring in 5–20% of serious head injuries (e.g. Levin et al., 1989), and, in over 50% of the latter, cases are associated with a fractured skull (Jamieson & Yelland, 1972; Macpherson, Macpherson, & Jennett, 1990). Nevertheless, they have also been reported in experimental research where inertial angular acceleration has been used to induce closed head injury in nonhuman primates without actual head impact, although like subdural haematomas they tend to arise only with rapid acceleration in the sagittal plane (Adams et al., 1983).

Three forms of intracerebral haematoma are associated with particularly severe head injuries. First, there may sometimes be a gross disruption of one lobe of the brain (usually the frontal or temporal pole) where severe contusions and lacerations are combined with an intracerebral haematoma in continuity with a related subdural haematoma at the same location. Such a phenomenon is described as a "burst lobe" (Jennett & Teasdale, 1981, p. 155). Second, an intracerebral haematoma may extend

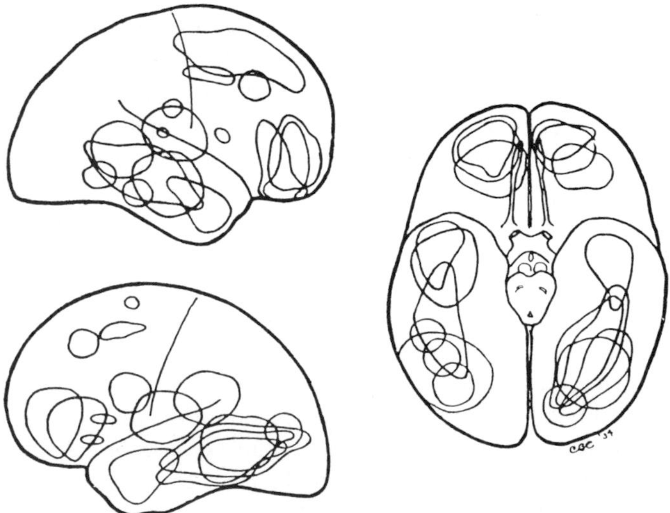

FIG. 2.6. Composite drawing showing the size and location of intracerebral haemorrhages found in a series of 27 cases of closed head injury. From *Pathology of the Central Nervous System* (3rd. ed.), C.B. Courville (1950), p. 231. Nampa, ID: Pacific Press Publishing Association. Copyright 1950 by Pacific Press Publishing Association. Reprinted with permission.

into the ventricular system and thus generate an intraventricular haemorrhage. This was formerly regarded as having an extremely poor prognosis, but the advent of CT has led to this view being revised. Third, intracerebral haematomas may also arise deep within the brain from vessels that have been torn by shearing forces at impact. Adams, Doyle, Graham, Lawrence, and McLellan (1986a) found such deep intracerebral haematomas (or "basal ganglia" haematomas) in the brains of 10% of patients with fatal head injuries. These patients showed more severe contusions and an increased incidence of diffuse axonal injury, and this led Adams et al. to conclude that a deep intracerebral haematoma was a primary event occurring at the moment of injury and not merely a form of secondary brain damage.

## Brain swelling

This type of brain damage may arise from the accumulation of excess water in brain tissue (i.e. cerebral oedema), but it can also arise following closed head injury as the result of the leakage of plasma from cerebral blood vessels because of vasodilation (see e.g. Adams, Graham, et al., 1980). Some local swelling is an almost invariable consequence of contusions and lacerations, from which plasma can spread to the underlying white matter by passing between the myelin sheaths. It may also occur in the vicinity of intracerebral haematomas or beneath extradural and subdural haematomas. However, Adams (1988) argued that the term "brain swelling" should be restricted to cases of diffuse swelling of one or both cerebral hemispheres.

Diffuse swelling of an entire cerebral hemisphere arises in about 10% of patients with severe head injury and often follows evacuation of an overlying acute subdural haematoma, although it is much more common in children (Adams et al., 1989a). Adams et al. (1983) found that diffuse swelling was also a frequent occurrence in nonhuman primates that had developed an acute subdural haematoma as the result of inertial angular acceleration of the head. However, they also noted that generalised brain swelling affecting both hemispheres was rare in human adults and could not be produced in nonhuman primates.

Nevertheless, this condition of generalised swelling is seen in children and adolescents, in whom it may develop after apparently minor injuries and in the absence of significant primary impact damage such as marked contusions or lacerations (see Bruce et al., 1981). Indeed, an early study by Hendrick, Harwood-Hash, and Hudson (1964) suggested that up to 50% of children who died following head injury had been conscious on admission to hospital but had deteriorated dramatically over the subsequent 48 hours. However, Graham, Ford, Adams, Doyle, et al. (1989) reported that only 16% of children with fatal head injuries had had a lucid interval of any kind, which was taken to mean that children died most often as a result of brain damage sustained at the moment of injury. In the latter series, 18% showed unilateral brain swelling and 52% showed bilateral swelling.

The findings that are typical of diffuse cerebral swelling from autopsy or CT are "slit-like" compressed ventricles and venous congestion (Bruce et al., 1978; Snoek et al., 1979; Zimmerman, Bilaniuk, Bruce, et al., 1978). In a study of 60 patients with severe head injury, Snoek et al. (1979) recorded findings of this sort in the CT scans of 15 cases and in the autopsies of 6 out of the 15 fatally injured cases, all of whom were under 20 years of age. Similarly, Levin and Eisenberg (1979a) reported that compressed ventricles were visualised in 8 out of 33 children and adolescents who had been referred for CT following closed head injury; 4 of these 8 patients had been awake and responsive to commands at the time of their admission to hospital. The pathophysiology of this phenomenon is probably cerebral vasodilation and increased cerebral blood volume secondary to disturbance of vasomotor tone (Adams, 1988; Bruce et al., 1981).

Finally, a similar though transient condition may be responsible for the so-called "fall-asleep syndrome" (*Einschlafsyndrom*), in which a child with a relatively mild head injury shows a delayed impairment of consciousness after a lucid interval, but improves within a matter of hours and exhibits little or no residual neurological impairment (Todorow & Heiss, 1978; cf. Bruce et al., 1981; Levin, Benton, & Grossman, 1982, pp. 195–196).

## Raised intracranial pressure

The cranial cavity is a relatively rigid container, but increases in the volume of blood (due to haematoma) or tissue (due to brain swelling) can be readily compensated for within certain limits by the displacement of cerebrospinal fluid. Nevertheless, there comes a point at which this buffering is exhausted, and the patient is then at risk from brain damage secondary to raised intracranial pressure. Although many of the classical features may even occur in patients whose intracranial pressure has never been significantly elevated, the neuropathology of this condition includes some or all of the following features: a compression and flattening of the cerebral convolutions; a herniation of the cingulate gyrus, the parahippocampal gyrus and uncus, and the cerebellar tonsils and medulla; infarction in the territory of the posterior cerebral artery; haemorrhage or infarction of the brainstem; and a shift of the interventricular septum across the midline, with a consequent distortion of the ventricles.

More than 80% of fatally injured cases show evidence of elevated intracranial pressure, usually as the result of diffuse brain swelling or an intracranial haematoma (Adams & Graham, 1976; Graham, Lawrence, Adams, Doyle, & McLellan, 1987; Jennett & Teasdale, 1981, pp. 31–34). Conversely, in fatally injured cases with no evidence of raised intracranial pressure, brain swelling is rare, intracranial haematomas are typically not found at all, and death usually results from extracranial complications such as bronchopneumonia, pulmonary embolism, sepsis, and renal failure (Graham, Lawrence, Adams, Doyle, & McLellan, 1988).

Adams and Graham (1976) established that the most common and consistent pathological marker of raised intracranial pressure between head injury and death was the presence of a wedge of pressure necrosis as the result of downward herniation within one or both parahippocampal gyri where they impinge against the free anterior border of the tentorium cerebelli (the arched layer of dura mater that separates the occipital lobes of the cerebral hemispheres from the cerebellum). In neuropathological studies of fatal head injury, the incidence of this phenomenon has proved to be consistently around 85–90% (see Graham, Ford, Adams, Doyle, Teasdale, et al., 1989). Results presented by Adams et al. (1983) showed that on this criterion raised intracranial pressure was a common outcome of head injury induced in nonhuman primates without head impact, but once again only when there was rapid acceleration within the sagittal plane.

Graham et al. (1987) identified pressure necrosis of either one or both parahippocampal gyri in 324 out of 434 cases of fatal nonmissile head injury, and in 42 of these patients there was no other brain damage attributable to raised intracranial pressure. However, they pointed out that a rapid increase in intracranial pressure might well prove fatal before internal herniation could appear, and this largely explained the apparently anomalous occurrence of other forms of brain damage conventionally ascribed to raised intracranial pressure among 16 patients with no evidence of pressure necrosis in the parahippocampal gyri.

Reilly et al. (1975) noted that raised intracranial pressure was a feature of 17 out of 22 head-injured patients who had died after a lucid interval but who had no intracranial haematoma. They suggested that the monitoring and treatment of elevated intracranial pressure would have a significant impact on mortality following severe head injury, and subsequent research has tended to confirm this (Bowers & Marshall, 1980). However, Graham et al. (1987) found no support at all for the specific proposition that death in head-injured patients after a lucid interval was associated with raised intracranial pressure as indicated by pressure necrosis in either one or both parahippocampal gyri. Moreover, Levin et al. (1991) found evidence of intracranial hypertension in more than half of all patients who had survived severe head injury, but this seemed to have little if any effect upon their subsequent level of cognitive functioning.

## Ischaemic brain damage

Uncontrolled intracranial pressure is an important factor determining mortality after severe closed head injury because it leads to vascular complications and is especially associated with ischaemic brain damage (that is, damage caused by an inadequate flow of blood). This tends to take the form of the death of nerve cells as the result of an inadequate blood supply (infarction), leading to a deficiency of oxygen in the brain tissues (hypoxia). For instance, tentorial herniation leads to infarction in the brainstem and in the territory supplied by the posterior cerebral artery, especially in the medial occipital cortex. The latter occurs in 30% of all cases of fatal head injury (Graham, Adams, & Doyle, 1978) and in 36% of those cases that show evidence of pressure necrosis (Graham et al., 1987). It was not identified by Adams et al. (1983) in nonhuman primates following inertial angular acceleration of the head, but this was attributed to the short period of survival before they were sacrificed.

Ischaemic brain damage can also take the form of focal infarction and necrosis in the vicinity of cerebral contusions as well as more widespread lesions associated with cardiorespiratory arrest, status epilepticus, and fat embolism (Graham et al., 1978). Hypoxic damage is particularly common in the boundary zones between the major cerebral arterial territories and especially in the parasagittal cortex between the regions supplied by the anterior and middle cerebral arteries (Adams, 1988); this occurs in up to 50% of patients with fatal head injuries, regardless of whether or not they have suffered diffuse axonal injury, but it occurs only rarely in nonhuman primates that are subjected to inertial angular acceleration and monitored for systemic hypoxia and hypotension (Adams et al., 1983). Adams, Graham, et al. (1980) noted that hypoxic brain damage had previously not been emphasised as a consequence of severe head injury, perhaps because it could often only be identified microscopically. For the same reason, the pathological lesions that are typical of recent hypoxic brain damage are unfortunately often not evident on CT scans (Snoek et al., 1979), although they are associated with angiographic evidence of post-traumatic arterial spasm (Macpherson & Graham, 1978).

Diffuse cortical damage of the sort seen after cardiac arrest or status epilepticus occurs in 30–40% of fatally injured patients (Graham, Ford, Adams, Doyle, Teasdale, et al., 1989). Lesions associated with fat embolism are more common in patients who have sustained multiple injuries. When there is a fracture of a long bone (or sometimes following the internal fixation of such a fracture), emboli of fat may be released into the circulation and be transported to the lungs and brain. This condition is heralded by an abrupt onset of confusion, drowsiness, and, in the more severely affected cases, coma. The characteristic features are fever, an increase in heart rate (tachycardia), and deficiency of oxygen in brain tissues (hypoxia); small haemorrhages may develop on the skin and conjunctivae, and epileptic seizures may occur. Cerebral fat embolism carries a high mortality risk, but it is fortunately a rare complication that normally does not produce additional deficits in those who survive. Emboli of brain tissue may also produce pulmonary insufficiency and are found at autopsy in the lungs of 2% of patients with fatal head injuries (Wacks & Bird, 1970).

Nevertheless, a more important mechanism of ischaemic brain damage is widespread cerebral infarction resulting from a generalised reduction in blood flow. Cerebral blood flow depends upon the pressure difference between the arteries and the veins (the cerebral perfusion pressure), and the latter is essentially the difference between the systematic arterial pressure and the intracranial pressure. In principle, then, either lower systemic arterial pressure or elevated intracranial pressure would reduce the cerebral perfusion pressure, resulting in reduced cerebral blood flow and therefore in diffuse ischaemic hypoxia (Bouma & Muizelaar, 1995; Graham, 1985).

Studies of fatal head injury produced evidence of small localised areas of dead tissue (infarcts) or widespread foci of ischaemic necrosis throughout the brain and especially in the areas that are known to be differentially sensitive to hypoxia, such as the hippocampus and the thalamus (Teasdale & Mendelow, 1984; cf. Brierley, 1976). In particular, hippocampal damage has been reported in more than 80% of all cases of fatal head injury (see e.g. Graham, Ford, Adams, Doyle, Teasdale, et al., 1989; Graham et al., 1987; Kotapka, Graham, Adams, & Gennarelli, 1992). There is also a high incidence of such lesions in nonhuman primates subjected to inertial angular acceleration of the head (Adams et al., 1983).

This type of ischaemic damage is more common in patients with a history of hypertension or hypoxia and in those whose head injuries have led to an elevation of intracranial pressure (see Graham et al., 1978; Price & Murray, 1972). Nevertheless, Adams and Graham (1976) found no correlation between pressure necrosis in the parahippocampal gyri and hypoxic necrosis in the hippocampus, whereas Graham, Lawrence et al. (1988) noted hippocampal damage in cases of fatal head injury with no evidence of high intracranial pressure (see also Kotapka et al., 1992; Kotapka, Graham, Adams, & Gennarelli, 1994). These findings suggest that raised intracranial pressure is not an important factor in the pathogenesis of hypoxic necrosis after severe head injury.

The effective causal mechanism might instead involve low arterial pressure (Graham et al., 1978) or else poor oxygen saturation (arterial hypoxaemia) as the result of obstruction of the airways (Adams, 1988), but the exact pathogenesis of diffuse hypoxic damage in head-injured patients has still to be established. Indeed, using nonhuman primates, Kotapka et al. (1991) found that hippocampal damage occurred in 46% of animals who had sustained relatively mild injuries, and that it was not associated with either raised intracranial pressure or lowered cerebral perfusion pressure. Other mechanisms must be involved in traumatic hippocampal damage (Kotapka et al., 1992, 1994).

It might be added that the findings of Graham et al. (1978) led many centres to attach more importance to the treatment of hypoxia and hypotension in head-injured patients at the accident scene, during transfer to and between hospitals, and during intensive care, and also to the detection and treatment of intracranial haematoma. However, there is no evidence that such endeavours in management and organisation of patient care have had any effect on the incidence of ischaemic damage following closed head injury, perhaps because they have been outweighed by the increasing numbers of very severely injured patients who are referred for specialist neurosurgical treatment that might otherwise have died in accident departments or primary surgical wards (Graham, Ford, Adams, Doyle, Teasdale, et al., 1989).

## Infection

Another source of complications following closed head injury is intracranial infection (see Landesman & Cooper, 1982, for a detailed review of this topic). Post-traumatic infection is seen especially in patients who have suffered skull fracture; conversely, it is not seen in nonhuman primates subjected to inertial angular acceleration of the head (Adams, Graham, & Gennarelli, 1982). Meningitis is a well-recognised problem that occurs in 2–3% of severely injured patients. The most common causative organism is pneumococcus. If the dura has been penetrated, then infection may enter, leading to the collection of pus in the subdural region (a subdural empyema). This is most frequently located over the convexity of the cerebral hemispheres or in the interhemispheric fissure. The condition of extradural empyema may also occur. A serious complication, which characteristically develops in the subacute phase after head injury, is a cerebral abscess. Despite the introduction of antibiotics, this is still associated with a 10% mortality. Among the survivors there may be additional residual neurological deficits, and epilepsy is especially frequent.

## Post-traumatic epilepsy

This is a condition that has received considerable discussion, although it is less common following closed head injury than following penetrating missile wounds. Indeed one study of 117 individuals with closed head injuries found just one instance where seizures had clearly started after the injury in question (Dencker, 1960). Jennett and Lewin (1960) identified a specific condition of *early* post-traumatic epilepsy, which occurred during the first week after a closed head injury. Jennett (1969, 1974) subsequently elaborated the logical basis for distinguishing a separate diagnostic entity thus: (a) that the first epileptic fit occurred many times more often in the first week after injury than in subsequent weeks; (b) that focal motor attacks were far more likely in the first week than in subsequent weeks; and (c) that fewer than one-third of the patients who have any seizures in the first week after injury have any further epileptic fits during the next four years (see Jennett, 1973). This condition appears to affect at most 5% of all patients admitted to hospital with closed head injuries, although it is more common in patients who have experienced severe head injuries and in children (see also Kollevold, 1976). Early epilepsy may indicate certain complications such as intracranial haematoma or infection, but it is not in itself a clinical hazard unless status epilepticus develops.

The prognostic importance of early epilepsy is that it increases the probability of *late* epilepsy, in which seizures begin at any time after the first week (and possibly not for many years after the original closed head injury). The incidence of this condition is also about 5% of all admissions, and it is related to the occurrence of early epilepsy, a depressed fracture of the skull, or an intracranial (and more especially an intradural) haematoma (Jennett, 1973, 1975a; Jennett & Lewin, 1960; Roberts, 1979, chap. 10; cf. Kollevold, 1978, 1979).

The conjoint influence of these different factors on the risk of late epilepsy is not strictly additive. Jennett (1973) found that neither depressed skull fracture nor intracranial haematoma increased the risk associated with early epilepsy, whereas early epilepsy doubled the risk associated with depressed fracture. In particular, after early epilepsy the incidence of late epilepsy was over 20% even following trivial injuries (with no post-traumatic amnesia, no depressed skull fracture, and no intracranial haematoma) and regardless of the patient's age. However, in patients with a compound depressed fracture of the skull, the incidence of both forms of epilepsy is increased overall, and that of late epilepsy can exceed 70%, depending on the occurrence of early epilepsy, the duration of post-traumatic amnesia, and whether the dura was torn (Jennett, Miller, & Braakman, 1974; Jennett, Teather, & Bennie, 1973).

Late post-traumatic epilepsy tends to be focal in nature, often implicating the temporal lobes, and, unlike early epilepsy, it can be a recurrent debilitating condition. Nevertheless, in most cases epileptic convulsions become progressively less frequent over a period of 10 years or so, and nearly half of all patients with late post-traumatic epilepsy eventually achieve complete remission (see Lewin et al., 1979; Roberts, 1979, p. 123).

## OVERVIEW

Any discussion of the effects of closed head injury must begin with the obvious but fundamental observation that the damage sustained by the brain is the most important factor determining the eventual outcome (Adams et al., 1983; Adams, Graham, et al., 1980). Even a blow to the head which causes merely a brief disturbance of consciousness may produce detectable structural damage to the brain. Some of this damage occurs at the moment of head injury (the primary brain damage), but some may be caused by subsequent complications (the secondary brain damage), of which the most important are intracranial haematoma, brain swelling, raised intracranial pressure, ischaemic brain damage, infection, and post-traumatic epilepsy.

The principal mechanism of brain damage following closed head injury is diffuse axonal injury as the result of shearing forces which decrease in magnitude from the surface of the brain to its centre. Nowadays, it is generally recognised that diffuse axonal injury is the single most important mechanism governing the outcome from closed head injury (Adams, 1988; Adams, Graham, et al., 1980). Indeed, one recent report claimed that axonal injury was almost universal in victims of fatal head injury (Gentleman et al., 1995). In practice, it appears to result from axonal swelling as well as from axonal shearing (Maxwell et al., 1988, 1993).

Closed head injury also gives rise to contusions and lacerations on the surface of the brain which may extend into the subcortical white matter. Such lesions are themselves neither necessary nor sufficient for a head injury to prove fatal; their clinical significance lies rather in the fact that they initiate brain swelling and intracranial haemorrhage. Contusions are predominantly the result of the rotational movement of the frontal and temporal lobes against the bony projections within the base of the skull. They do not occur principally at the site of original impact (coup injury), unless the skull has been fractured. Nor do they occur specifically at the point which is diametrically opposite the site of head impact (contrecoup injury). In fact, a similar distribution of cerebral contusions can be induced in nonhuman primates as a result of inertial angular acceleration that involves no impact at all (Adams et al., 1985).

The distinction between primary and secondary brain damage is obviously fundamental in the clinical management of head-injured patients, because in principle the complications are the only treatable aspects of a closed head injury. Nevertheless, a final point to be made is that in terms of understanding the consequences of head injury it may be more important to consider the resulting brain damage as being either *focal* or *diffuse*. As Adams et al. (1983, 1986a, 1986b) explained, the focal brain damage that results from closed head injury includes cerebral contusions, intracranial haematomas, and the damage that is characteristic of raised intracranial pressure and brain herniation. This can often be visualised by means of CT or MRI during life and is readily identified by the naked eye at post-mortem.

Although all of the broad types of brain damage that occur in human beings as the result of closed head injury can be induced in nonhuman primates by means of inertial angular acceleration (Adams, Graham, & Gennarelli, 1982; Adams et al., 1983; Gennarelli, 1983; Graham, Adams, & Gennarelli, 1988), the amount of focal brain damage is increased substantially by the occurrence of skull fracture, and to that extent it is associated with actual head impact of the sort encountered in assaults and falls (Adams et al., 1989; Gennarelli, 1983). In the extreme case, focal damage resulting from a compound depressed fracture of the skull may give rise to post-traumatic epilepsy or a localised deficit such as dysphasia or hemiparesis; yet, if there is no diffuse brain damage, there may be no history of loss of consciousness and no post-traumatic amnesia (Miller & Jennett, 1968).

The diffuse brain damage that results from closed head injury unless the patient fails to survive more than a few hours includes diffuse axonal injury, hypoxic damage, and brain swelling. The precise form that this damage takes in any particular patient is difficult to identify during life. However, the incidence of diffuse axonal injury is increased in those patients who have sustained either deep intracerebral haematomas (Adams et al., 1986a) or gliding contusions (Adams et al., 1986b), and Adams et al. (1989a) suggested that the visualisation of either of these lesions on a CT scan shortly after a head injury could be taken as evidence of diffuse axonal injury. However, MRI can detect signs of diffuse axonal injury in patients with minor head injury even when they have produced normal CT scans

(Mittl et al., 1994). The amount of diffuse brain damage is primarily dependent upon the rate of acceleration and deceleration, and to that extent it is associated with high inertial loading of the head of the sort that is encountered in vehicular accidents (Adams et al., 1989a; Gennarelli, 1983).

CHAPTER THREE

# Retrograde amnesia and post-traumatic amnesia

In the previous chapter, it was noted that a closed head injury tends to produce shearing forces within the brain that give rise to diffuse lesions and disturbance of function, and the most common effect of these forces is the immediate loss of consciousness known as coma or concussion. Russell (1971, p. 1) gave a vivid account of the course of recovery from this state:

> The immediate effects of concussion are usually that the individual drops to the ground motionless, often with an arrest of respiration, and at this stage basic reflexes such as the corneal response may be abolished. After respiration returns, restless movements appear and by very gradual stages the patient begins to speak, resist interference, make a noise, and becomes restless, talkative, abusive, and irritable in one way or another. Slowly his speech becomes more intelligible and then as the effect of the trauma wears off he looks around wondering where he is: the period of traumatic confusion is at an end, but he has no recollection of any event that occurred since the injury.

It was also pointed out in the previous chapter that the rotational motion of the brain within the skull gives rise to lacerations and contusions in the region of the sphenoidal ridge, producing damage to both the frontal and the temporal lobes. These frontotemporal lesions are not only a frequent outcome of closed head injury; they are also likely to constitute the area of greatest cortical damage wherever the site of impact. It is well established that the physiological integrity of the temporal lobes is a prerequisite for many of the important higher cognitive functions and especially for the normal functioning of human memory (Walsh, 1978, chap. 5). In addition, positron emission tomography (PET) during the acquisition and retrieval of memories by intact subjects reveals primary activation in regions of the frontal cortex (Shallice et al., 1994). Hence, it is unsurprising that disturbances of learning and remembering are a reliable outcome of closed head injury.

These characteristic disturbances of human memory are of considerable interest, both to the clinician and to the neuropsychologist. From the clinical point of view, the length of time over which remembering is impaired is broadly proportional to the duration of coma or concussion, and is relevant to both diagnosis and prognosis. It appears to be a reliable measure of the severity of the injury and a sensitive predictor of the eventual outcome. From the neuropsychological point of view, the study of head-injured patients offers a quasi-experimental model for testing theories of normal memory function. A variety of psychological theories of learning and remembering have been used in trying to give a useful analysis of the disorders shown by such patients, and the more important frameworks will be discussed in this chapter and the next.

The impairment of memory function that is characteristic of closed head injury takes three different forms. First, head-injured patients often manifest an inability to recall events experienced during a short period immediately prior to their injury. Second, head-injured patients manifest an inability to recall events experienced during a certain period immediately following the cessation of coma. Third, head-injured patients also manifest a measurable disturbance of memory function that persists beyond the latter period. The first and second type of memory deficit will be considered in this chapter; the third type will be considered in Chapter 4.

## RETROGRADE AMNESIA

Retrograde amnesia (RA) is a specific impairment of memory for events experienced immediately before a closed head injury. The duration of the period before the injury that is affected in this way normally varies with the severity of the head injury, as judged according to the duration of unconsciousness (Russell, 1932), and by implication with the later prognosis. Consequently, as Symonds (1940) noted, a long period of RA is generally an indication of severe or extensive brain damage.

RA is shown by most (but not all) patients who sustain a head injury sufficiently serious to cause loss of consciousness (Russell & Nathan, 1946). However, it is also shown in patients who have not suffered a loss of consciousness. In particular, Yarnell and Lynch (1970) described four patients who had received head injuries while playing American college football that resulted in transient confusion or motor incoordination; in three of the four cases, there seemed to have been no loss of consciousness. When these patients were examined immediately following their injuries, they all showed good recall of the events leading up to the relevant incidents. However, on repeated questioning between 3 and 20 minutes later, this information had been lost. Subsequently, Lynch and Yarnell (1973) increased their original sample to six patients, all of whom showed this pattern of findings (see also Yarnell and Lynch, 1973). These results suggest that RA is a condition which may develop within a few minutes of a closed head injury even when the victim has not lost consciousness.

Nevertheless, the measurement of RA in individual clinical cases presents a number of serious problems (Blomert & Sisler, 1974; Schacter & Crovitz, 1977). First, the precise timing of the most recent event that can be remembered before the head injury can often be determined only from the patients' own reconstructions of their previous activities; it may therefore be highly unreliable, especially in severely injured cases. Second, the period in question is not always characterised by a continuous amnesia; rather, patients may still be able to recollect isolated events or, as Russell and Nathan (1946) described them, "islands" of accessible memories. However, these are not necessarily memories of personally significant episodes or events; indeed, Williams (1969, p. 75) claimed that RA "tends to take little account of emotional bias. ... When islands of memory are retained, they are typically of trivial visual images". Third, RA does not seem to affect a fixed period immediately prior to the accident, but typically varies on repeated testing (Sisler & Penner, 1975). More specifically, a closed head injury often results in a retrograde amnesia that seems to "shrink" or gradually shorten during the course of the patient's recovery (Russell, 1935; Russell & Nathan, 1946), though this may leave persistent amnesic gaps or haziness within the otherwise continuous sequence of memories for events preceding the injury (Williams & Zangwill, 1952).

The latter process of shrinkage affects both the absolute interval of time over which the impairment extends and also the number of islands of memories occurring within that period. Much of this process occurs during the period of post-traumatic amnesia (Schilder, 1934), and it has been suggested that after that period any retrograde impairment of memory is relatively permanent (Teuber, 1969). However, Symonds (1940, p. 87) stated that "shrinkage of the retrograde amnesia may continue for some time after the patient has regained his orientation and memory for recent events, and may be taken as evidence of continued recovery of cerebral function". Similarly, Russell and Nathan (1946, p. 292) claimed that in cases of shrinking RA "the P.T.A. [post-traumatic amnesia] terminates long before the R.A. shrinks to its final duration", and Benson and Geschwind (1967) described a patient whose RA continued to shrink beyond the end of the period of post-traumatic amnesia.

By this point, more than half of all head-injured patients report a period of RA extending for less than one minute before their accidents, and a complete amnesia extending for more than two days is relatively rare (Eden & Turner, 1941; Russell, 1932, 1935; Russell & Nathan, 1946). It follows that the duration of persistent retrograde amnesia is normally too brief for it to be of any practical value as a reliable indication of the severity of injury or of the prognosis for recovery (Long & Webb, 1983). However, exceptions to this do arise: Kapur (1997) described three patients with extensive autobiographical memory loss following severe close head injuries, whereas Hunkin et al. (1995) described a patient who seemed to be unable to retrieve any memories at all prior to an accident at the age of 19.

Symonds (1962) likened the RA seen in cases of head injury to the memory disorders resulting from bilateral temporal lobectomy and herpes simplex encephalitis (which also produces damage to the temporal lobes). He argued that post-traumatic RA resulted from bilateral and symmetrical damage to the cerebral white matter. Symonds suggested that in more extreme cases the impairment resulted from lesions within the temporal lobes, and temporal-lobe damage was certainly a feature of the three cases described by Kapur (1997). However, Symonds suggested (p. 3) that "the ordinary retrograde amnesia of concussion" could follow lesions elsewhere in the brain.

Goldberg et al. (1981) described a patient with a dense and persistent RA extending back over nearly 20 years. On the basis of detailed findings from computerised tomography (CT), this was attributed to a lesion in the ventral tegmental region. Goldberg et al. concluded that the selective activation of limbic structures by the mesencephalic reticular formation was important in the retrieval of long-term memories. In contrast, from the results of magnetic resonance imaging (MRI) conducted 18 years after his accident, the patient described by Hunkin et al. (1995) had lesions confined to the parieto-occipital and occipital lobes and no damage at all to either temporal lobe.

## Encoding, storage, and retrieval

From a logical point of view, remembering can be characterised with reference to three consecutive processes or stages: an original event is witnessed or experienced; it is retained in memory over a period of time; and finally the relevant information is retrieved or otherwise put to use. The identification of these three distinct stages of *input* (or encoding or acquisition), of *storage* (or retention), and of *retrieval* goes back to the time of Plato and Aristotle. It is a purely conceptual device which in itself tells us very little about the structure and function of the cognitive system that makes learning and remembering possible. It has nevertheless formed the basis of theoretical discussions about the nature of RA following closed head injury.

The metaphorical notion of consolidation as a process whereby memory traces or representations are somehow rendered within a cerebral substance has an exceedingly long history in thought and discussion on the nature of remembering. It has a natural application to cases of disordered memory, according to which patients are assumed to lack the ability to develop consolidated memory traces. Various specific suggestions have been made as to why a closed head injury might disrupt such a consolidation process. One is that recent events are erased from memory by the interruption of protein synthesis (Dixon, 1962); another is that a concussive head injury stimulates the nervous system in a manner analogous to electroconvulsive shock, thus leading to the extinction of recent neural activity (Ommaya, Grubb, & Naumann, 1971). However, accounts of the initial duration of RA that are grounded upon deficits of storage or consolidation are inherently implausible, because it can extend over as much as a year or more into the past. In such cases, as Russell and Nathan (1946, p. 294) observed, "there is clear inability to recall important events which must previously have been well registered, retained and recalled before the injury" (see also Symonds, 1966).

Moreover, Benson and Geschwind (1967) argued that the phenomenon of shrinking RA was wholly incompatible with the idea that a closed head injury disrupted the process of memory consolidation, because remote memories that are not recalled in the early stages of recovery may well prove to be accessible when patients are retested at a later date. They inferred (p. 542) that "the disturbance is therefore a failure of retrieval rather than a loss of established memories", although Schilder (1934) pointed out that some apparent shrinkage of RA may be partially based on information provided by other people. Nevertheless, Benson and Geschwind did concede that a permanent, residual RA of only a few seconds' or a few minutes' duration might well reflect the true abolition of memories that had not yet been consolidated.

Wasterlain (1971) described 24 head-injured patients in whom the duration of RA had been confirmed by the testimony of eyewitnesses. Four patients showed electroencephalographic abnormalities, skull fractures, and persistent neurological sequelae; their RA, which originally extended over periods up to six months, was subject to progressive shrinking over subsequent months. In keeping with previous ideas, Wasterlain suggested that this pattern of forgetting was incompatible with any failure of storage or consolidation, but was strongly indicative of a failure of memory retrieval. In the remaining patients, however, the RA was of less than a minute's duration, was relatively constant on repeated testing, and showed no preserved islands within this period; Wasterlain considered this pattern of forgetting to be entirely consistent with an account of RA in terms of a failure of memory consolidation.

## Short-term and long-term memory

Such an account implies that experiences remain available in memory for a relatively brief period of time, but that they leave no permanent record. Contemporary thinking in psychology would regard such a pattern of results as manifesting a distinction between *short-term memory* and *long-term memory* as different structural components of the human memory system. During the 1950s and 1960s, these expressions were introduced to refer to different types of research paradigm: experiments in which the subjects were required to remember a relatively small amount of material for a relatively short period of time (of the order of several seconds) on the basis of a single presentation were characterised as investigations of short-term memory; experiments where the subjects were required to learn a relatively large amount of material over several presentations and to retain that material for a longer period of time were characterised as investigations of long-term memory.

This dichotomy bears no relation to the common clinical distinction between "recent" and "remote" memory, both of which would count as "long-term" memory in this sense. Moreover, it is in itself a purely operational description that carries no necessary theoretical implications. Nevertheless, it came to be used quite quickly by many researchers to demarcate different hypothetical components of the total memory system. Fortunately a large amount of subsequent evidence tended to support this notion of two separate components of human memory, and nowadays some such distinction between short-term storage (or *working memory*) and long-term storage (or *permanent memory*) is broadly accepted, at least as a first approximation, when discussing the architecture of human memory (see Baddeley, 1997, chap. 3).

Yarnell and Lynch (1970) noted that in the case of their head-injured football players information about events that had immediately preceded the injury was intact when the patients were examined shortly afterwards. It had therefore clearly been stored by some short-term memory process, contrary to the view put forward, for example, by Williams and Zangwill (1952), that RA was the result of a failure of initial registration. The fact that this information was subsequently lost suggested instead that the injury had damaged "the fixation into long-term traces" (p. 864). As Lynch and Yarnell (1973) elaborated this account, RA is best interpreted as the preserved storage of information within some relatively transient, short-term memory system, combined with the disruption of the considation or transformation of information into a relatively permanent, long-term memory system. Nevertheless, they also acknowledged that their findings could be handled equally well by the assumption of a single time-dependent and continuous consolidation process (see also Yarnell & Lynch, 1973).

A common finding in research into any retrograde memory disorder is that recently acquired information is impaired whereas remote memories are spared (Ribot, 1882). The fact that head-injured patients seem to have little or no difficulty in remembering events experienced in the remote past creates problems for the idea that RA results from defective retrieval processes. However, this temporal gradient might be caused by a number of confounded factors. First, biographical events from the remote past whose retention is assessed by clinicians may well have special personal significance for patients themselves. Second, because questions about the remote past tend to cover a broader time scale, they may well be cast in more general terms than questions about the more recent past (Squire, Slater, & Chace, 1975). Third, as Ribot (1882) himself noted, significant personal events from the remote past will have had more opportunity to be retrieved and rehearsed during the intervening years.

When 28 patients with neurological damage of a variety of aetiologies (including 12 patients with closed head injury) were tested on objective events that had little personal salience (the titles of old television programmes), Levin, Grossman, and Kelly (1977a) found that there was no selective sparing of the oldest memories. Levin, High, et al. (1985) used a similar task extended across a longer chronological interval with a sample consisting exclusively of head-injured patients. They also showed a persistent, partial RA extending back over more than a decade, which was entirely consistent with an explanation of RA as a dysfunction in the retrieval of established memories. When they were tested on personally salient life events, there was a significant temporal gradient indicating the preservation of older memories, but only among patients who were still exhibiting post-traumatic amnesia.

This relates to a feature of RA that has been relatively neglected by researchers: that memory for personal experiences is severely impaired, whereas general world knowledge is only partially disrupted, and skilled behaviour may not be affected at all. In particular, Russell (1971, p. 48) emphasised that "training experiences during the R.A. period may be preserved as a learned skill although the learning cannot be recalled". Current discussions of the functional architecture of long-term memory differentiate between *declarative memory* and *procedural memory*: the former contains knowledge about events and objects that can be consciously retrieved and described, whereas the latter is responsible for skills or capabilities that can only be manifested in overt behaviour.

Within the domain of declarative memory, Tulving (1972) distinguished between *episodic memory* and *semantic memory*: episodic memory was concerned with the retention of particular events and episodes in a person's life, whereas semantic memory was concerned with general knowledge about language and the world. Like the demonstration of skills or capacities held in procedural memory, the retrieval of declarative knowledge from semantic memory is an *implicit* expression of memory, insofar as it need not be accompanied by the conscious recollection of any biographical episode; in contrast, the retrieval of information from episodic memory is an *explicit* expression of memory that is characterised by just this sort of conscious recollection (Schacter, 1987).

Graf and Schacter (1985) made the specific claim that the amnesic syndrome was predominantly a disorder in the explicit expression of memory, and the same often seems to be true of RA following closed head injury. However, the patient described by Hunkin et al. (1995) seemed to have lost all knowledge about both personal and public figures and events before his accident and had had to relearn this from his family and from the media. In addition, one of the patients described by Kapur (1997) had persistent difficulties in recalling not only autobiographical facts and experiences, but also technical knowledge from his employment as a lift engineer. This would suggest that RA can constitute a more general disruption of autobiographical memory beyond the loss of memory for specific events and experiences.

The hypothesis that RA extending back beyond the immediate preinjury events is predominantly a problem of the retrieval of information from memory seems to be supported by evidence that it can be alleviated by the application of barbiturates (Russell & Nathan, 1946), neuropeptides such as vasopressin (Oliveros et al., 1978), or lithium (Kline, 1979). To some clinicians it even implies that extensive RA is an hysterical dissociative reaction (Russell, 1935; cf. Kline, 1979), although others have argued that this is not always the case (Symonds, 1966). Experimental research suggests that at least some of these preparations may influence memory performance by enhancing a person's general level of arousal rather than by affecting specific aspects of retention (e.g. Sahgal, 1984; Wolkowitz, Tinklenberg, & Weingartner, 1985).

A retrieval interpretation of RA is also consistent with suggestions that it can be alleviated by hypnosis (Milos, 1975; cf. Raginsky, 1969). In principle, this ought to be of great forensic importance, but there are serious methodological reservations about much of the work that has been carried out. The safest conclusion, according to one authoritative account, is that "hypnotically induced testimony is not reliable and ought not be permitted to form the basis of testimony in court" (Orne, Soskis, Dinges, & Orne, 1984, p. 211).

## POST-TRAUMATIC AMNESIA

Following concussion (in other words, following the return of normal somatic mobility and normal responsiveness to external stimuli), head-injured patients manifest a characteristic impairment of cognitive function. Symonds (1928, p. 829) emphasised that "it is important to distinguish between complete unconsciousness or coma and the condition of stupor or clouded consciousness", and he argued that the persistence of the latter state more than 24 hours after a head injury was the hallmark of "major cerebral contusion" rather than simple concussion. Symonds also noted (p. 829) of the head-injured patient that "on regaining his senses he is found to have an amnesia for the period of clouded consciousness".

Russell (1932, p. 552) subsequently gave a similar account of this state as the "loss of full consciousness", and he suggested (p. 554) that the return of normal consciousness was best estimated from the patient's subsequent memory of when he or she "woke up". Elsewhere, Russell (1934, p. 135) summarised this analysis:

> A fair indication of the severity of the cerebral injury can be obtained from the duration of the loss of full consciousness. This is a useful indication from the practical point of view, as it can be estimated at an interval after the injury from the duration of amnesia following the injury. This may be calculated by comparing the time of the injury with the time or date at which the patient again became fully orientated with regard to time and place.

Symonds (1937, p. 1081) made a similar proposal:

> The outstanding feature of mental disorder after head injury is loss of consciousness in some degree. ... For purposes of description in head injuries, if a man has no memory of what he has done, we assume that he was not at that time fully conscious. Therefore, the duration of unconsciousness may be measured by that of the traumatic amnesia following the accident.

Symonds (1940, p.77) subsequently used the phrase "post-traumatic amnesia" (PTA) to refer to this state, which he took to indicate "a general defect of cerebral function after consciousness has been regained". Symonds and Russell (1943, p. 7) added that it was "taken to end at the time from which the patient can give a clear and consecutive account of what was happening around him", and that it could be estimated "by careful questioning after recovery of full consciousness and normal orientation".

In short, although the post-traumatic phase is at the time marked by a mental state of *disorientation* (an inability to locate oneself with regard to time, place, and situation), it can subsequently be regarded as a state of *anterograde amnesia* (an inability to remember the continuous flow of ongoing new experiences). Russell and Nathan (1946) were explicit that the period of PTA terminated with the return of continuous memory for experienced events, as determined from the patient's own retrospective reports. Russell and Smith (1961, p. 16) in a similar manner described PTA as "the interval during which current events have not been stored". As Russell (1971, p. 12) remarked, "the retrospective assessment of the duration of the amnesic period after the injury is a remarkably good guide to the duration of loss of full consciousness".

There are therefore two important points to note about the contemporary concept of PTA:

1. As was indicated in the passage by Russell (1971, p. 1), which was quoted at the beginning of this chapter, this phase of recovery following closed head injury is dominated by two forms of mental dysfunction: (a) an anterograde memory disorder; and (b) a state of disorientation. The duration of the anterograde amnesia appears to be closely related to the duration of post-traumatic disorientation, and after the recovery of full consciousness the former is used as a retrospective estimate of the latter (Moore & Ruesch, 1944).
2. PTA terminates with the return of full consciousness as measured retrospectively by the return of continuous memory. However, contemporary practice follows Russell and his colleagues in measuring PTA from the time of the original head injury. In other words, the duration of PTA includes not only the period of anterograde amnesia but also the period of coma (Levin, Benton, & Grossman, 1982, p. 74; cf. Levin, O'Donnell, & Grossman, 1979).

## PTA and severity of closed head injury

The duration of PTA tends to vary directly with the duration of coma, though this relationship is by no means a perfect one (Evans et al., 1976; Guthkelch, 1980; Levin & Eisenberg, 1986; Moore & Ruesch, 1944; Norrman & Svahn, 1961) and it is to some extent an artefact since (as has just been pointed out) the latter is contained within the former. Nevertheless, the relationship tends to be weaker in the case of older patients, where relatively short periods of coma may be followed by disproportionately long periods of PTA (von Wowern, 1966).

Wilson et al. (1994) identified a group of eight patients who had been in coma for less than six hours but in whom the duration of PTA was longer than seven days. All but one of these patients had suffered falls, and they showed more extensive brain damage on MRI, especially in hemispheric regions, than patients with shorter periods of PTA. Wilson et al. argued that brain damage in such patients was not adequately reflected by assessing either the depth or the duration of coma alone.

The duration of PTA also tends to be directly related to the duration of RA, although the former is typically much longer than the latter (Russell, 1932; Russell & Nathan, 1946; Russell & Smith, 1961). Parkinson (1977) suggested that the total duration of PTA was about nine times that of the residual extent of RA, but other researchers have proposed more complex relationships (Crovitz, Horn, & Daniel, 1983). Symonds (1940, p. 87) suggested that a permanent period of RA longer than a few hours would always be associated "with a story of severe injury, with a long post-traumatic amnesia, and with some permanent defects of mental function other than the amnesia". Exceptions to this general pattern can arise, however, with cases of both disproportionately long RA (Hunkin et al., 1995; Symonds, 1962; cf. Kapur, 1997) and of PTA in the absence of any persistent RA (Crovitz et al., 1983; Russell & Nathan, 1946).

Moreover, PTA can also occur without the patient losing consciousness at all. On the basis of one such case, Fisher (1966) suggested that PTA and coma might result from damage to distinct neural mechanisms. Yarnell and Lynch (1973) described a further four American football players who demonstrated a marked post-traumatic memory impairment with no apparent alteration in their levels of consciousness. When tested immediately after their injuries, they had intact orientation and good memory for the episodes in question. They rejoined their games, but within a few minutes had great difficulty remembering the course of play, and they subsequently showed little or no recollection of the original examination.

PTA was described by Miller (1966, p. 257) as "the signature of significant closed head injury", and the duration of PTA is usually regarded by clinicians as an excellent indicator of the severity of a closed head injury (e.g. Smith, 1961). Brock (1960, p. 20) even maintained that "the degree of concussion is measured by the best yardstick presently available, namely, the degree and duration of the unconsciousness and/or abnormalities of consciousness, viz., confusion and dazed states related to it" (see also "The Best Yardstick", 1961).

Moore and Ruesch (1944) demonstrated that the duration of post-traumatic disorientation increased with the incidence of several clinical features, including raised intracranial pressure, skull fracture, and intracranial haemorrhage. Similarly, Russell and Smith (1961) showed that duration of PTA tended to increase systematically with a number of "organic" signs such as a skull fracture, anosmia, dysphasia, and motor disorders, although not with "nonorganic" symptoms such as headache, anxiety, depression, and dizziness. They did however note that the duration of PTA had much greater prognostic value in the case of closed head injuries than in the case of crushing injuries or missile wounds, in which the duration of both coma and PTA can often be remarkably short (see also von Wowern, 1966).

Wilson et al. (1994) compared the duration of coma and PTA in 38 patients with the findings of MRI carried out within the first week following a closed head injury. The duration of PTA was correlated with the amount of damage both to central brain structures (the corpus callosum, brainstem, and cerebellum) and with the amount of damage to hemispheric regions. As mentioned in Chapter 1, the duration of coma was only correlated with the amount of damage to central structures. Wilson et al. concluded that coma and PTA reflected disparate patterns of brain lesions and, in particular, that the assessment of PTA provided useful additional information concerning the severity of head injury.

For Symonds (1928, p. 832) the criterion for a diagnosis of "major contusion" was that "the patient should have been in a state of unconsciousness, or partial unconsciousness, for more than twenty-four hours following the injury". Similarly, it is nowadays common for either clinicians or researchers to distinguish between cases of "severe" closed head injury and "minor" closed head injury according to whether the period of PTA has exceeded 24 hours. This is roughly concordant with a dichotomy between "severe" and "minor" cases of head injury determined by whether or not the patients have spent more than six hours in coma (Jennett et al., 1975; see Chapter 1), although a lucid interval or complications such as an intracranial haematoma may lead to disproportionately long periods of disorientation. Patients in whom PTA extends beyond 24 hours are much more likely to have open fractures and intracranial haemorrhages, and they are therefore more likely to need surgical intervention. Nevertheless, this probably applies to fewer than 10% of all patients admitted to hospital with closed head injuries (Artiola i Fortuny, Briggs, Newcombe, Ratcliff, & Thomas, 1980).

Finer gradations of severity based upon both the duration of coma and the duration of PTA have been proposed. Russell and Smith (1961) themselves suggested a four-fold classification of patients with closed head injury: "slight concussion", PTA lasting less than one hour; "moderate concussion", PTA lasting between one and twenty-four hours; "severe concussion", PTA lasting between one and seven days; and "very severe concussion", PTA lasting more than seven days. Nowadays, however, these categories would be referred to simply as cases of "mild", "moderate", "severe", and "very severe" closed head injury. Greenwood (1997) suggested that other cut-off points (such as two weeks and eight weeks) might be more useful in predicting important outcomes.

There is considerable evidence that the duration of PTA is of value in determining the eventual prognosis. It is known to predict the extent of the patient's physical recovery (Evans et al., 1976), their long-term neurological, psychological, and social assessment (Bond, 1975, 1976), and their eventual occupational outcome

(Russell & Nathan, 1946; Russell & Smith, 1961; Symonds & Russell, 1943). Evidence on this matter will be discussed in Chapter 7. Nevertheless, this relationship is qualified by the effect of the patient's age. Older patients tend to have longer periods of PTA and a poorer prognosis, but they also show a more pronounced relationship between these two variables than younger patients. Thus, a more reliable assessment of the severity of a closed head injury may be obtained by taking both the patient's age and the duration of PTA into account (Russell & Smith, 1961).

## Measuring post-traumatic amnesia

In seeking to define and measure the duration of PTA, however, problems arise that are similar to those already discussed in connection with RA (see e.g. Schacter & Crovitz, 1977; Sisler & Penner, 1975). First, the period in question need not be characterised by a continuous memory loss. In other words, as Symonds (1942) emphasised, the patient's first memory after a closed head injury may not coincide with the return of continuous awareness, but may sometimes amount to an island of accessible memory that is then followed by a further period of amnesia (see also Symonds & Russell, 1943). Russell and Nathan (1946) mentioned just 13 cases who had shown such an island, which they likened to the phenomenon of the lucid interval (see Chapter 1). They implied that these islands occurred fairly early during the period of PTA and were often concerned with events of personal significance, such as the visit of a relative.

Gronwall and Wrightson (1980) carried out a detailed investigation of PTA in the case of 67 patients with minor head injuries. They found that 26 (or 39%) of their sample reported a total of 39 events as islands of memory during the period of PTA. Almost 80% of these events were apparently recalled from the first quarter of the period in question, and over 70% fell within the first 15 minutes after their accidents. The events in question were typically specific and personally significant, such as having their wounds sutured or the arrival of relatives at the hospital. In contrast, the patients who reported no islands of memory tended to give as their first recollections marking the return of continuous memory mundane or nonspecific events, such as being in a hospital bed or cubicle.

A second point, related to the first, is that some practitioners and researchers follow Russell and Nathan (1946) in identifying the end-point of PTA with the return of continuous normal memory, whereas others identify it with the earliest (or perhaps the earliest authenticated) memory after the closed head injury (e.g. Sisler & Penner, 1975). As Symonds (1942; Symonds & Russell, 1943) pointed out, the latter step does not of course exclude the isolated islands of memory just described. The inclusion of these islands may well make a significant difference to the estimated duration of PTA. Symonds and Russell concluded that careful questioning was necessary to differentiate between such isolated islands of memory and the beginning of continuous remembering (see also Gronwall & Wrightson, 1980).

A further point is that it may be difficult to estimate relatively brief periods of PTA with any degree of precision, because of uncertainty about the exact chronology both of the accident itself and of subsequent events. Even when they had exhausted all potential sources of information, including the statements of witnesses as well as ambulance and hospital records, Gronwall and Wrightson (1980) found that the most detailed classification of PTA possible was "less than 5 min", "between 5 and 30 min", and "more than 30 but less than 60 min", and they concluded that it was difficult to measure PTA duration accurately when it was less than one hour.

Gronwall and Wrightson (1980) had devoted considerable time and energy to carrying out a prospective study of PTA, involving repeated interviews every 15 minutes from the patient's admission until the return of continuous memory and full orientation. Providing such routine yet skilled observation of individual patients is clearly not practicable in most clinical settings. Because of this, Russell (1932; see also Russell, 1971, p. 12) advocated the retrospective assessment of PTA following the restoration of continuous normal memory. This was also taken to provide a means of distinguishing between the occurrence of isolated islands of memory and the return of full consciousness and continuous memory that marks the true end of PTA (Russell & Nathan, 1946; Symonds & Russell, 1943).

In Gronwall and Wrightson's (1980) study, retrospective assessments were concordant with their own prospective assessment of PTA in 75% of the total sample of 67 patients with minor closed head injury. The likelihood of any discrepancy was not affected by the timing of the retrospective interview anywhere between one week and three months after the original accidents. Moreover, when 36 of the patients received a second retrospective interview two to three months after the first, only four produced different estimates of PTA duration on the two occasions. These results tended to confirm Russell and Nathan's (1946) assertion that retrospective estimates of PTA remained relatively constant over time, and they contradict a suggestion made by Sisler and Penner (1975) that the duration of PTA varies on repeated assessment.

In principle, patients' retrospective reports may tend inadvertently to incorporate information concerning the earlier stages of their recovery which has subsequently been provided by relatives or nursing staff (Forrester, Encel, & Geffen, 1994; Levin, Benton, & Grossman, 1982, p. 75). Against this idea, however, Gronwall and Wrightson (1980) found that nearly all discrepancies in the retrospective assessment of PTA arose from patients' giving progressively *longer* estimates of PTA duration. Such discrepancies clearly could not be the result of confabulation to "fill in the gap", as Gronwall and Wrightson themselves noted, nor could they result from the incorporation of second-hand accounts. (Nor, incidentally, do they constitute "shrinkage" of the sort observed in the case of RA.) Gronwall and Wrightson did however suggest that these discrepancies might reflect the patients' increasing confusion between their own veridical memories and what they had subsequently been told by eyewitnesses, or changes in their criteria for deciding whether apparent memories were genuine experiences or merely second-hand information.

Of course, in the absence of any standardised procedure for obtaining retrospective reports, one might well question how different examiners could be expected to give consistent estimates of PTA duration (Levin, O'Donnell, & Grossman, 1979). King et al. (1997) tried to deal with this issue by proposing a standard procedure for the retrospective questioning of head-injured patients, the Rivermead post-traumatic amnesia protocol. This showed a satisfactory level of test–retest reliability (0.79) when administered to the same patients by different clinicians, but it was less satisfactory when the duration of PTA was less than 24 hours or the test–retest delay was more than six months.

However, even this procedure does not address the more fundamental problem that, unless the patients' progress has been continuously monitored, it may be difficult to establish the veracity of their retrospective reports (Greenwood, 1997). Indeed, these may in principle be far from accurate (especially in terms of their chronology), given the anxiety and disruption engendered by emergency hospitalisation (see Chapter 4) and the unfamiliar and depersonalised setting of a hospital ward. The routine nature of ward activity also means that there are few significant events that would serve to date emergence from PTA (Schwartz et al., 1998).

## PTA scales

In order to handle these problems, a number of researchers have tried to develop objective, quantifiable techniques for measuring the duration of PTA. These include a concurrent assessment of a patient's orientation (that is, basic awareness of time and place) of the sort contained in the Wechsler Memory Scale (WMS: Wechsler, 1945; see Chapter 4):

1. What year is this?
2. What month is this?
3. What day of the month is this?
4. What is the name of the place you are in?
5. In what city is it?

Groher (1977) administered the WMS to 14 patients with severe closed head injuries who had been unconscious for an average of 17 days. They were tested "after regaining consciousness or as soon as they demonstrated an ability to tolerate a one-hour testing session. … In the majority of cases, this was a one-week period" (p. 214). The Orientation subtest was scored out of a maximum of six, presumably having been supplemented by the question, "What day of the week is this?" The head-injured patients were profoundly impaired on this subtest: their average score was less than one question answered correctly. They were also impaired on all the other subtests of the WMS, implying a generalised memory dysfunction.

What is perhaps more surprising is that they continued to be impaired on the Orientation subtest through four successive retests on the WMS during the subsequent 120 days, so that they were on average still only able to answer three questions correctly nearly five months after their accidents. Groher (1977) also presented data from 14 comparable patients who showed persistent language and memory disorders more than a year after they had sustained a closed head injury; across five successive testing sessions, they consistently achieved an average of only about four items correct on the Orientation subtest. Since these patients were undoubtedly beyond the phase of PTA, these results suggest that the assessment even of a simple awareness of time and place among head-injured patients is by no means a straightforward matter (see also Kapur, 1988, pp. 19–20).

In their prospective analysis of PTA, Gronwall and Wrightson (1980) administered an orientation questionnaire every 15 minutes after the patients had arrived at the accident and emergency department. They were scored out of a maximum of 18 points on their name, address, and date of birth, the year, month, and day of the week, and where they were and why they were there. Each of a control group of 12 patients without head injuries who were also tested in the accident and emergency department achieved at least 17 points on this questionnaire, and so a score of 16 or less was taken to signify disorientation. In the case of the patients with minor head injuries, there was a significant relationship between the recovery of full orientation and the return of continuous memory, such that the proportion of disorientated cases was greater among 13 patients who were tested before the return of continuous memory than among 44 patients tested after the return of continuous memory (as confirmed at subsequent interviews). Nevertheless, eight patients were still disorientated after the return of continuous memory, whereas five patients showed persistently impaired recall of ongoing events despite normal orientation.

Gronwall and Wrightson (1980, p. 57) concluded that "the proposition that the return of full orientation signals the end of PTA (Russell, 1971) is clearly untenable". It should however be clear from the account that was given earlier that for Russell this proposition was a matter of definition rather than one of empirical fact. The empirical claim which was made by Russell was simply the one quoted earlier (1971, p. 12), namely that "the retrospective assessment of the duration of the amnesic period is a remarkably good guide to the duration of loss of full consciousness". Gronwall and Wrightson (p. 59) made the claim that there was "no consistent relationship" between the duration of anterograde amnesia and the duration of disorientation, but they presented no evidence on this point and their own data would tend to refute such an extreme position (cf. also Sisler & Penner, 1975).

On the basis of an earlier brief test of temporal orientation (Benton, Van Allen, & Fogel, 1964), Levin, O'Donnell, and Grossman (1979) developed the Galveston

Orientation and Amnesia Test (GOAT); this contains 12 questions covering simple biographical information, the circumstances of the patient's injury, and the patient's knowledge of the current time, place, and situation. The GOAT yields a global index of amnesia and disorientation out of a possible maximum score of 100, together with separate estimates of retrograde and anterograde amnesia (defined in terms of the latest memory before the head injury and the earliest memory after the injury). The GOAT is intended to be administered at least once a day, though in coma the GOAT score is zero (Levin, Papanicolaou, & Eisenberg, 1984). The duration of PTA is defined as the period in which the total score is less than or equal to 75 (the borderline level of performance according to a standardisation group of patients who had recovered following mild closed head injury).

In a series of 52 adult patients with closed head injuries, those cases in whom this period extended beyond two weeks tended to show evidence of diffuse or bilateral mass lesions on angiography or computerised tomography, and especially of compressed ventricles as the result of brain swelling. In this study, the duration of PTA according to the GOAT was found to be inversely related to eye opening, motor responses, and verbal responses on the day of admission according to the Glasgow Coma Scale (GCS), which was taken to demonstrate the broad validity of the GOAT.

However, in a subsequent study, Levin et al. (1984) found only a rather weak relationship between the duration of coma and the duration of PTA according to the GOAT among 50 consecutive admissions with severe closed head injuries; in particular, there were several cases who showed prolonged PTA in spite of relatively brief periods of coma. Levin et al. concluded that there might be other important determinants of the duration of PTA than the duration of coma. Ewing-Cobbs, Levin, Fletcher, Miner, and Eisenberg (1990) went on to adapt the GOAT for children and adolescents, yielding the Children's Orientation and Amnesia Test, and these instruments have become widely used in North American hospitals.

A similar procedure to the GOAT was developed by Artiola i Fortuny et al. (1980), but this also included a simple memory test for the examiner's face and name and for three pictured objects. Patients were tested daily, and the end of PTA was defined as the first of three consecutive days on which each patient correctly identified the three original objects out of a set that contained five distractor items. Estimates of PTA duration obtained from 80 patients participating in this study produced a very similar distribution to independent estimates obtained from the same patients by neurosurgical staff using traditional clinical methods. The correspondence between measures of PTA and orientation obtained using this technique was said to be "close", and it was claimed to offer an efficient and rapid means of detecting slight deterioration in a patient's condition that might require urgent intervention.

Subsequently, Shores, Marosszeky, Sandanam, and Batchelor (1986) extended this test to produce the Westmead PTA Scale. This contained two questions concerning biographical information, five questions to test the patient's orientation for time, date, and place, two questions on the examiner's face and name, and three questions on the retention of pictured objects. The end of PTA was defined as the first of three consecutive days on which each patient answered all 12 questions correctly. This Scale was claimed to have shown a high degree of inter-rater reliability and to have been satisfactorily used with only a minimum of training by medical staff, nurses, and occupational therapists; moreover, the duration of PTA according to the Scale was found to be a much better predictor of the neuropsychological outcome following severe closed head injury than duration of coma according to the Glasgow Coma Scale (Shores, 1989).

In common with the procedures devised by Levin, O'Donnell, and Grossman (1979) and by Artiola i Fortuny et al. (1980), the Westmead PTA Scale was developed primarily for clinical rather than experimental use, and it therefore combined the assessment of amnesia with that of orientation. This was in accordance with the view expressed by Russell (1932) that in order to be considered to have recovered full consciousness following a closed head injury the patient should be *both* fully orientated *and* reliably capable of laying down new memories (Shores, personal communication). Strictly speaking, this view entails that head-injured patients who exhibit a chronic global amnesia (e.g. Corkin et al., 1985) are in a permanent state of PTA.

Nevertheless, there are a number practical difficulties in the administration of the Westmead PTA Scale. These were noted by Forrester et al. (1994), who derived yet another instrument for the prospective assessment of PTA. This included simple memory items that were administered only when patients were fully orientated. Forrester et al. claimed that their instrument showed good interrater reliability and a strong correlation with performance on the GOAT. However, as Newcombe (1982) commented, there remains the need for a comprehensive instrument that measures different aspects of autobiographical memory, as well as orientation for person, time, and place.

Schwartz et al. (1998) explored this issue further in a prospective study where both head-injured and control patients were given the GOAT together with simple tests of free recall and recognition memory on a daily basis. The patients with head injuries typically were impaired in the free recall of groups of three words after a 24-hour delay for two to three days after their scores on the GOAT had returned to a normal level. Schwartz et al. concluded that the use of the GOAT alone would not provide a satisfactory measure of the recovery of continuous memory and that it could lead to the premature discharge of head-injured patients to their homes or to rehabilitation programmes.

## Theories of post-traumatic amnesia

Early theoretical discussions of the nature of PTA emphasised the wide variety of psychological disturbances shown by head-injured patients during the acute post-traumatic phase. Schilder (1934) presented case material to argue that PTA was characterised by a generalised cognitive dysfunction, and he argued (p. 184) that this could be attributed to "a confusion concerning the perception and synthesis of impersonal material".

Symonds (1937) agreed that this played a large part, but he considered (p. 1082) that other features were equally important:

> There is profound disorientation in space and time, with a tendency to interpret the surroundings in terms of past experience. There is defect of perception and inability to synthesize perceptual data. Memory and judgment are grossly impaired. Thought is constantly impeded by perseveration. Disturbance of the speech function is conspicuous. The mood is often elated and there is sometimes a push of talk resembling that seen in hypomanic states.

He also mentioned (p. 1084) "the inability to distinguish clearly between figure and background in the thought process".

Subsequently, Ruesch and Moore (1943) tested 120 patients within 24 hours of their closed head injuries on a variety of simple cognitive tasks. Any pronounced impairment was mainly restricted to a serial subtraction test (see also Ruesch, 1944b). Schacter and Crovitz (1977) noted that this task depended upon intact immediate memory for its adequate performance, but Ruesch and Moore had found that the immediate memory spans of their patients were essentially normal. Nevertheless, the latter investigators had excluded any patients who appeared comatose, confused, or delirious, and it was suggested by Mandleberg (1975) that they may have inadvertently confined their attention mainly to those who were fully conscious and out of PTA.

Like the theoretical discussions concerning the nature of RA, those concerning the nature of PTA have been based upon the traditional notions of consolidation and retrieval. For instance, Benson and Geschwind (1967, p. 542) argued that PTA "seems most likely to represent not a failure of retrieval but a failure to establish new memory traces". However, they did observe (p. 542) that the correlation between the duration of PTA and the residual duration of RA suggested that "the retrieval process depends on the same system that is necessary for the laying down of new memories". Similarly, Yarnell and Lynch (1973) regarded their observations concerning PTA in the absence of impaired consciousness as providing further evidence for a specific effect of closed head injury upon the consolidation of new information in a long-term memory system. On the latter point, immediate memory span may well be preserved during PTA (e.g. Ruesch, 1944b; Ruesch & Moore, 1943; Schilder, 1934; but cf. Mandleberg, 1975), whereas measures of long-term memory typically show a pronounced decrement in performance (Shores et al., 1986).

Gronwall and Wrightson (1980) attributed the fact that personally salient episodes occurring during PTA could sometimes be subsequently recalled to fluctuating levels of arousal during the post-traumatic period. An alternative interpretation of the phenomenon of islands of memory is that the anterograde amnesia associated with closed head injuries may involve a retrieval problem. This is also the implication of evidence that, like RA, this amnesic state may perhaps be alleviated to some extent by the application of barbiturates (Russell & Nathan, 1946), hormonal preparations (Oliveros et al., 1978), and hypnosis (Milos, 1975). This is not inconsistent with an explanation in terms of altered levels of arousal, since, as mentioned earlier, at least some of these procedures appear to influence memory performance by enhancing a person's general level of arousal rather than by affecting specific aspects of retention (Sahgal, 1984; Wolkowitz et al., 1985).

In general, one possible reason for a retrieval deficit is that the relevant experiences are represented in memory, but are not encoded or organised in a way that would permit efficient retrieval using the usual forms of memory search. However, Dunn and Brooks (1974) showed that head-injured patients tested during PTA used both phonemic and semantic structure in a normal fashion. This was taken to imply that PTA did not implicate a qualitatively different pattern of memory encoding, although subsequently Brooks (1984) advocated caution in attempting to generalise from these findings because they were based upon the results of just five head-injured patients.

PTA appears to be predominantly a condition that affects mainly attention and declarative memory rather than procedural memory, though there is little concrete evidence on the matter. Ewert, Levin, Watson, and Kalisky (1989) tested a group of 16 severely head-injured patients in PTA and found that they were consistently impaired on tests of declarative memory (even for memory of the previous testing session). In contrast, although they were impaired on skilled tasks (mirror reading, mazes, and pursuit rotor), they showed improvement across successive test sessions, indicating relatively preserved procedural learning. Similar results were obtained by Wilson, Baddeley, Shiel, and Patton (1992).

Nevertheless, it would be naive to characterise PTA purely as a state of confusion or disorientation. Patients who have sustained a closed head injury leading to a relatively long period of unconsciousness may demonstrate a stage of recovery marked by thrashing, combativeness, yelling, and excessive movement (Hayden & Hart, 1986). By virtue of their confusion, patients in this agitated state may have little insight into their condition. It may therefore give rise to considerable distress on the part of their relatives or carers and also constitute a major challenge to professional rehabilitation workers (Gans, 1983; Malkmus, 1983). Corrigan, Mysiw, Gribble, and Chock (1992) monitored behaviour and cognitive performance in 20 patients with severe head injuries during PTA. Cognitive impairment tended to vary with the degree of agitation, and Corrigan et al. claimed that both reflected a pathophysiology that was manifested primarily in attentional deficits.

## Disorientation and cognitive impairment

Mandleberg (1975) compared a group of severely head-injured patients tested during PTA with a matched group of severely head-injured cases out of PTA on the Wechsler Adult Intelligence Scale (WAIS: Wechsler, 1955). This contains six Verbal subtests (Information, Comprehension, Arithmetic, Similarities, Digit Span, and Vocabulary) and five Performance subtests (Digit Symbol, Picture Completion, Block Design, Picture Arrangement, and Object Assembly). The patients tested during PTA produced a generalised impairment that was more pronounced on the Performance subtests than on the Verbal subtests. There were no significant differences between the two groups of patients when they were all retested out of PTA, which showed that they were essentially equivalent in their general intellectual capacity. It was concluded that PTA was a qualitatively distinct phase of recovery from head injury characterised by a general disorder of cognitive ability.

However, this investigation suffers from the opposite problem of interpretation to that raised in connection with the study by Ruesch and Moore (1943). The patients tested within PTA undoubtedly had very severe injuries (their mean duration of PTA was 110 days), and it is conceivable that some had not recovered full awareness on assessment. In this regard, it is relevant that the impairment shown by these patients extended to the Vocabulary subtest of the WAIS, which tests a knowledge of word meanings. Tests of this sort are normally assumed to be somewhat less vulnerable to disruption by brain damage, and are often used as an index of a patient's premorbid level of attainment, provided that there is no evidence of any dysphasia (Milberg, Hebben, & Kaplan, 1986). For instance, Babcock (1930, p. 5) argued that differences in premorbid intellectual level "are shown in interests, in the data to which one spontaneously attends, and especially in the vocabulary. Words when once learned are not quickly forgotten, and remain as indications of the ability a person once had".

Nelson and McKenna (1975) found that patients with dementing diseases produced significantly poorer performance on the Vocabulary subtest of the WAIS than a group of normal control subjects. They concluded that vocabulary-type tests were affected by generalised intellectual deterioration. Nevertheless, the average age-scaled score of their dementing patients was at the normal level, which suggests that the control patients in this study (who were patients with extracerebral disorders and nonacademic employees of a university college) may have been atypical in terms of their knowledge of word meanings.

The two groups of subjects in Nelson and McKenna's (1975) study showed no difference in their scores on the Schonell Graded Word Reading Test, and the researchers concluded that reading ability was potentially a better indicator of premorbid level of functioning than vocabulary level. Nelson and O'Connell (1978) therefore devised the New Adult Reading Test, which was later renamed the National Adult Reading Test (NART: Nelson, 1982), as a measure of premorbid attainment. Crawford, Parker, and Besson (1988) confirmed that the Vocabulary subtest of the WAIS tended to give lower estimates of premorbid IQ than did the NART. Moreover, when administered to diverse groups of neurological patients, the NART yielded scores consistent with the performance of control subjects, except in the case of patients with Korsakoff's psychosis and Huntington's disease.

Subsequently, the content and the scoring procedure of the NART were revised for use in both the United Kingdom and the United States, and the resulting instruments provide highly efficient ways of assessing premorbid intelligence (Crawford, 1992).

In the study that was carried out by Shores et al. (1986), no difference was found between head-injured patients tested during PTA (roughly 7 weeks after their injuries) and head-injured patients tested out of PTA (roughly 33 weeks after their injuries) in terms of their standardised scores on the NART: both groups achieved normal scores on this test. Nevertheless, results analogous to those of Mandleberg (1975) were obtained by Bond and Brooks (1976) using alternative tests of verbal and nonverbal intelligence. Seven patients with severe head injury were assessed during PTA on both the Mill Hill Vocabulary Scale (Raven, 1962) and the Progressive Matrices Test (Raven, 1960). In comparison with published normative data, these patients were substantially impaired on both tests, although more so in the case of the latter. This tends to confirm Symonds' (1940) notion that PTA implicates a generalised impairment of intellectual function.

Benson, Gardner, and Meadows (1976) described three patients who had suffered closed head injuries and who demonstrated a persistent disorder of orientation for place, relocating their hospital at a different though personally significant geographical location, despite the fact that their memory for ongoing events had largely recovered. The converse pattern was described by Gronwall and Wrightson (1980), who found a number of patients who demonstrated persistently impaired retention of ongoing events despite normal orientation. The latter researchers had interviewed patients with mild closed head injuries on a number of occasions after their arrival in the accident and emergency department in order to determine separately the patients' level of orientation and the recall of ongoing events. Although Gronwall and Wrightson had obtained a significant relationship between the recovery of normal orientation and the return of continuous memory, their results led them to question whether post-traumatic amnesia and post-traumatic disorientation were functionally equivalent (see also Sisler & Penner, 1975).

Papanicolaou et al. (1984) demonstrated a physiological correlate of PTA in the form of the P-300 component of the human average evoked potential. This is a characteristic feature of the electrophysiological response to a distinct and infrequent stimulus interspersed within a regular series of otherwise constant, regularly occurring stimuli (such as physical tones). Its precise latency, though typically around 300msec following stimulus presentation, is thought to be an index of cognitive efficiency: It is sensitive to manipulations of processing capacity but appears to be independent both of intrinsic stimulus information and also of response selection (Pritchard, 1981). Papanicolaou et al. found that the P-300 latency was significantly delayed in eight patients who were still in PTA according to their scores on the GOAT in comparison with 10 patients who were normally orientated after recovery from PTA. Since the latter group did not differ significantly from a control group of seven hospital staff, it was concluded that the P-300 latency was not merely a function of the severity of a closed head injury, but was a specific physiological index of indicator of cognitive function in PTA. However, other researchers have found abnormal P-300 responses in patients tested many months after recovery from PTA (e.g. Campbell, Suffield, & Deacon, 1990; Ruijs, Keyser, Gabreëls, & Notermans, 1993).

Stuss et al. (1999) followed up the study by Schwartz et al. (1998) which showed different rates of recovery in the GOAT and the recall of groups of three words after a 24-hour delay. They employed a wider variety of tasks in a further prospective study, including tests of vigilance and mental control (simple counting tasks) in addition to tests of recall and recognition. They found that performance on simple automatic tasks recovered before recognition memory, which in turn preceded the recovery of performance on more attention-demanding tasks and, finally, that on effortful free recall.

Stuss et al. (1999) argued that the "amnesia" of PTA seemed to be secondary to the inability to attend during encoding (measured by tests of recognition memory) or to engage in the effortful retrieval of information (measured by tests of delayed recall). They also claimed that attentional problems were prominent, if not the most dominant disorder, in the acute phase of recovery after closed head injury, and that this phase would be better characterised as a post-traumatic confusional state, whether or not it was accompanied by an amnesic condition.

## OVERVIEW

Following the cessation of coma, patients with closed head injury show a characteristic impairment of memory function. This takes the form of: (a) a specific inability to remember events that were experienced during a short interval immediately before the injury itself (retrograde amnesia or RA); and (b) a specific inability to retain information about experienced ongoing events (post-traumatic amnesia or PTA). The duration of RA and the duration of PTA tend to vary both with each other and with the severity of the injury, as measured by the duration of coma.

RA develops within a few minutes of a closed head injury even when the patient has not lost consciousness. The duration of RA is difficult to measure with any degree of accuracy, and it is subject to "shrinkage" during the course of the patient's recovery. The transient component of RA is usually attributed to a failure of retrieval processes, and this is supported by evidence that it can be alleviated by drugs or hypnosis. The residual component that persists indefinitely after the injury is usually attributed to the disruption of memory consolidation. RA does not appear to affect the retention of information within short-term memory, and there is a suggestion that memory for general knowledge and for learned skills can also be relatively well preserved. These considerations imply that RA is a selective impairment of long-term episodic memory.

The state of PTA is marked by disorientation and anterograde amnesia; the duration of the latter according to retrospective questioning is taken to be an estimate of the duration of the former. Because of difficulties in accurately measuring the duration of PTA, a number of standard scales have been developed that assess recall of the circumstances of the injury, basic awareness of current time and place, and continuous autobiographical memory. PTA predominantly involves a specific failure to consolidate new information in long-term memory; however, it also implicates a generalised though less pronounced impairment of intellectual function and behavioural problems may be evident.

CHAPTER FOUR

# Memory function

Even after the return of normal awareness and orientation, and even after the period of profound memory loss described in the previous chapter, many patients with closed head injuries continue to complain of a wide variety of disabling symptoms. Most particularly, many head-injured patients complain of an impaired ability to remember. Tooth (1947, p. 6) gave a more detailed account of the nature of this impairment: "This complaint is usually described by the patient as absentmindedness: inability to recall names, faces, telephone numbers, and, in the Services, orders. Many patients with this complaint mentioned that they had to rely on a notebook for facts which they would formerly have retained in memory."

Russell (1934) found that 25% of all patients with closed head injuries reported "loss of memory or mental ability" during a period of at least two months after leaving hospital, although this was more common among older patients. One or two studies have suggested that the incidence of memory impairment might be only around 10% of all patients admitted to hospital with head injury in the case of both adults (Lidvall, Linderoth, & Norlin, 1974) and children (Klonoff & Paris, 1974). However, the true figure is likely to be much greater.

Oddy, Humphrey, and Uttley (1978b) administered a symptom checklist to patients with severe closed head injuries roughly six months after their accidents. "Trouble remembering things" was both the symptom that was most frequently reported by the patients themselves (38% of the sample) and also the symptom most frequently attributed to the patients by their relatives (44% of the sample). Similarly, Rimel et al. (1981) found that roughly 59% out of 424 patients with minor closed head injuries complained of impaired memory three months after their accidents, whereas interviews with their family members and close friends (p. 224) "indicated an even greater problem with the patients' memory than the patients recognized or were willing to admit".

This chapter will be concerned with whether measurable disturbances of memory function persisting beyond the period of post-traumatic amnesia (PTA) can be confirmed by objective psychometric testing. It will be useful to consider this matter separately with regard to minor and severe head injuries.

## MEMORY FUNCTION FOLLOWING MINOR CLOSED HEAD INJURY

### Empirical findings

The first systematic follow-up study of memory function in patients with minor closed head injury was carried out by Conkey (1938). Her patients were 25 cases of simple concussion, including some with no apparent loss of consciousness. When tested on up to five occasions after their accidents and compared with a control group of normal subjects of similar age and educational, economic, and social status, the head-injured patients showed a general cognitive impairment, which tended to resolve over a period of 34 weeks following the injury. Most particularly, these patients demonstrated a persistent and pronounced decrement in performance on tests of learning and remembering, and this appeared to be associated with a specific deficit in the acquisition of new memories. Conkey argued that much of the generalised impairment of cognitive functioning that had been shown by her patients could be attributed to this deficit, which following Goldstein (1936) she ascribed to "the impairment of the ability to perceive abstract relationships" (1938, p. 53) in the material to be remembered.

As Brooks et al. (1984) pointed out, the control subjects in Conkey's (1938) study were tested only once, and so they did not match the head-injured patients in terms of their overall level of practice or familiarity with the test procedures. However, in order to evaluate the effects of hospitalisation on performance, Conkey had tested a second control group that consisted of surgical patients examined once in hospital and once out of hospital, with an interval which was roughly equivalent to that between the first and second testings of the head-injured patients. There was virtually no difference between the levels of performance which these control patients achieved at the two sessions, which indicated "that the effect of hospitalization on performance is little or nothing" (p. 23). In fact, these patients tended if anything to produce poorer results at the second session; as Conkey pointed out, this suggests that any effects of their increased familiarity with the test situation were counterbalanced by the effects of novelty at the first session or of indifference at the second. Even so, this does not rule out the possibility that practice effects might be more apparent over three or more sessions, and hence the pattern of results produced by Conkey's head-injured patients may still have been contaminated by practice effects.

Levin, Grossman, and Kelly (1976b) compared nine patients who had been conscious on their admission and throughout their hospitalisation with 23 control patients suffering from peripheral neurological disorders in their short-term memory for random shapes using a forced-choice recognition procedure. Unfortunately, their results were subject to a ceiling effect: only one of the head-injured patients and only two of the control patients made any errors on this task. Subsequently, Hannay, Levin, and Grossman (1979) assessed 19 patients with mild closed head injuries who had been conscious on admission and throughout their period of hospitalisation on a continuous memory task for line drawings of familiar living things. They showed no sign of any impairment in terms of their recognition scores in comparison with a control group of 19 patients with diverse somatic complaints. Payne-Johnson (1986) used the same task as Hannay et al. to compare 20 patients with closed head injuries of varying degrees of severity with 15 other accident victims. The 11 patients with relatively mild head injuries were tested within three days of their admission to hospital. Their performance was no better than that of the more serious cases, and the head-injured patients as a group were significantly impaired in comparison with the control patients.

A number of researchers have studied the performance of head-injured patients using the selective reminding procedure (Buschke, 1973; Buschke & Fuld, 1974). This is a modified multitrial free-recall task in which only the items that have *not* been recalled on a given trial are presented again for learning on the subsequent trial: that is, the subject is "selectively reminded" of the items not recalled on the previous trial. The encoding of items into long-term storage is supposed to be shown by their correct recall on two consecutive trials (that is, without having been presented on the second of the two trials); the consistent retrieval of items from long-term storage is supposedly shown by their correct recall on subsequent trials (that is, without any further "reminding"). However, the selective reminding procedure yields a number of other indices of immediate and delayed recall and recognition. The strengths and weaknesses of this task were discussed by Loring and Papanicolaou (1987), but the evidence is consistent that patients with mild head injuries achieve normal scores on this test (Barth et al., 1983; Levin, Benton, & Grossman, 1982, pp. 109–112; McLean, Temkin, Dikmen, & Wyler, 1983).

Gentilini et al. (1985) administered a battery of cognitive tasks to 50 consecutive cases of mild head injury (defined as a loss of consciousness lasting less than 20 minutes) and 50 normal controls drawn from among their relatives and friends. The battery included immediate memory span, a word recognition test, and a free-recall test using the selective reminding procedure. The head-injured patients, who were tested roughly one month after their accidents, were not significantly impaired either in terms of their overall performance on the battery as a whole or in terms of their performance on any of these memory tests. Gentilini et al. concluded (p. 139): "if there is structural damage after mild head injury, it generally recovers from the neuropsychological standpoint within one month after the trauma".

A multicentre investigation by Levin, Mattis, et al. (1987) considered 57 patients with minor closed head injury (defined as a loss of consciousness lasting 20 minutes or less) in terms of their performance on memory span, the free recall of a list of animal names using the selective reminding procedure, and the reproduction of visual geometrical designs. When compared with a control group of 56 healthy volunteers, the head-injured patients were found to be impaired on all three tasks (and especially on the verbal-memory task) when tested a week after their accidents, but not when retested a month afterwards.

Levin, Amparo, et al. (1987) carried out a similar investigation of 20 patients with minor closed head injuries, who received computerised tomography (CT) and magnetic resonance imaging (MRI) as well as neuropsychological assessment. The baseline performance of these patients (conducted on average nine days after their injuries and within 24 hours of the MRI scan) was impaired with reference to a group of 13 normal controls on free recall using the selective reminding procedure and on a spatial analogue of that task. Those patients with MRI-defined lesions within the temporal lobes tended to show an even greater degree of impairment on both tasks at the baseline examination than those with lesions within the frontal lobes. Moreover, the magnitude of the impairment on these tasks was significantly related to the size of lesions within the right temporal lobe, though not to the size of lesions within the left temporal lobe. Those patients who were subsequently available for retest at one month and three months after their injuries showed a reduction in the size of their lesions on MRI and a concomitant improvement in their performance on the cognitive tasks, but they continued to be impaired on the verbal-memory task.

One problem is that several of these studies compared the performance of head-injured patients over repeated testing with that of a normal control group on a single administration of a free-recall test using the selective reminding procedure. This task shows a significant practice effect even when alternative materials are used at different sessions (see Hannay & Levin, 1985), and any improvement on the part of the head-injured patients can therefore be attributed merely to the effects of practice. A second problem is that the comparison groups in these studies consisted of normal, healthy individuals who had not been involved in major accidents. As I shall explain later in this chapter, any decrement on the part of the head-injured patients can be attributed as much to the anxiety-producing effects of involvement in a major accident and of rapid and unanticipated admission to hospital as to the specific effects of the injury itself upon cerebral function.

In a careful analysis of the neuropsychology of moderate head injury, McMillan and Glucksman (1987, p. 393) made the following proposal:

> Ideally a control group should differ from a head injured group only by not having sustained a brain injury. Hence a comparison group should control for the physical damage, shock, stress and disability arising from the injury. Controls should also belong to a population that has a similar likelihood of sustaining a head injury.

In order to control both the nonspecific aspects of accidents involving a head injury as well as "at risk" factors or predisposing characteristics of the victims of such accidents, McMillan and Glucksman employed control subjects who had sustained an orthopaedic injury (usually involving an arm fracture or sprain). They assessed 24 patients with moderate head injury (defined by a duration of PTA of between 1 and 24 hours) and 20 patients with orthopaedic injury within seven days of their accidents, and they found no difference between these two groups on tests of associative learning, narrative recall, and visual reproduction. The patients in this study also described their everyday memory abilities by using the Subjective Memory Questionnaire (Bennett-Levy & Powell, 1980), and the resulting ratings were found to be significantly lower in the case of the head-injured group. However, when each patient was assessed by a relative or close friend, the ratings of everyday memory that were given to the head-injured patients were not significantly different from those given to the orthopaedic controls.

Newcombe, Rabbitt, and Briggs (1994) similarly assessed 20 patients with minor head injury on a battery of tests including immediate and delayed recall of stories, continuous recognition memory for words or faces, probed recall for sequences of seven digits, a complex running-span task, which required the patients to keep track of four different categories of stimuli, and a simple prospective memory task (returning a form by post to the experimenter to report their return to work). The patients were tested within 48 hours of their injuries, and 14 were retested a month later. Their results were compared with those obtained by a control group of 20 orthopaedic and surgical patients, who were similarly tested within one week of their admission and of whom 14 were retested one month later.

There were significant differences between the two groups on just two of the tasks. First, the head-injured patients made more errors at both test sessions when deciding whether a probe item had been presented in a sequence of digits. Second, at the initial test session, the head-injured patients reported fewer items in the running-span task. There was however no difference on the latter task between the two groups of patients that were retested after a month. In this and other respects, the results obtained by Newcombe et al. (1994) confirm that the effects of minor closed head injury on the mechanisms subserving learning and memory dissipate within the first week or so after the injury.

It should nevertheless be emphasised that all the research studies on which this conclusion is based have concerned groups of patients rather than individual cases. The failure to find a *statistically* significant difference in performance between a group of head-injured patients and an appropriate control group does not rule out the possibility that some individual patients will continue to demonstrate *clinically* significant deficits in their performance on neuropsychological tests. In Chapter 2, it was pointed out that even a minor closed head injury might give rise to detectable structural damage. Many researchers nowadays consider that, in spite of the nonsignificant results obtained in group studies, a small proportion of patients who sustain minor head injuries exhibit persistent deficits that cannot be readily ascribed to emotional reactions to their accidents.

## Theoretical interpretations

Richardson (1979) investigated the role of mental imagery in the performance of 40 cases of minor closed head injury (with PTA at most seven hours) and a control group of 40 orthopaedic patients. All of these patients were tested within a few days of their injuries on the immediate free recall of five lists of concrete words and five lists of abstract words, and they then received an unexpected final recall test on all of the words presented. The results are shown in Table 4.1.

The head-injured patients were found to be impaired with respect to the control subjects in their recall of lists of concrete words, but not in their recall of lists of abstract words. Consistent with a large amount of experimental research with normal subjects, the orthopaedic controls produced better performance on the lists of concrete words than on the lists of abstract words. However, the head-injured patients failed to demonstrate a significant advantage in their recall of concrete material in comparison with their recall of abstract material. Within the head-injured sample, the magnitude of the difference between the recall of concrete words and the recall of abstract words for each patient varied inversely with the duration of PTA, but neither the site of the impact nor the incidence of concussion seemed to affect the test results. Finally, because the same pattern of results was obtained in the initial recall test and in the final, delayed recall test, it was concluded that closed head injury gave rise to a specific impairment of long-term memory rather than of short-term memory.

Richardson (1979) noted that his findings refuted the view that closed head injury resulted in an impairment of abstract thinking, because this would have predicted quite the opposite pattern of results: in other words, a more pronounced deficit in the case of abstract material than in the case of concrete material. Instead, he interpreted the results in terms of the "dual coding" theory devised by Paivio (1971), in which "images and verbal processes are viewed as alternative coding systems, or modes of symbolic representation" (p. 8). The superior performance of the control subjects in their recall of concrete items was attributed to their use of mental

TABLE 4.1

Mean per cent correct in free recall for head-injured patients and for orthopaedic control subjects on concrete and abstract material in initial and final testing

| | *Initial testing* | | *Final testing* | |
|---|---|---|---|---|
| | *Concrete* | *Abstract* | *Concrete* | *Abstract* |
| Orthopaedic controls | 46.9 | 35.3 | 17.4 | 10.8 |
| Head-injured patients | 41.6 | 36.7 | 12.2 | 10.5 |

Mental imagery, human memory, and the effects of closed head injury, by J.T.E. Richardson (1979), *British Journal of Social and Clinical Psychology, 18,* p. 322. 

imagery either as an additional memory code or as a more effective memory code in the case of concrete material. Conversely, the failure of the head-injured patients to demonstrate a significant difference in their performance between concrete and abstract items was taken as evidence that imagery was not being effectively employed by these subjects. Richardson concluded that closed head injury gave rise to a selective impairment in the use of imagery as a form of elaborative encoding in long-term memory.

Evidence that the effect of minor closed head injuries on memory was specific to the imaginal encoding of *verbal* material was found in two experiments by Richardson and Barry (1985). They eliminated the necessity for transforming verbal information into an imaginal representation by presenting the original material in a pictorial form (as unfamiliar faces or as line drawings of common objects). In neither case did head-injured patients tested within a few days of their injuries show any impairment in their retention of such material.

Richardson and Barry (1985) then asked whether head-injured patients might be induced to encode verbal information using mental imagery by means of suitable training instructions. They therefore repeated the earlier study of free recall carried out by Richardson (1979) using additional patients who were instructed to make up mental images that related to the things described by the words in each list. Experimental research with normal subjects had shown that instructions of this sort give rise to substantially enhanced performance. When given these relatively simple instructions, Richardson and Barry found that both head-injured patients and orthopaedic controls produced better performance with concrete items than with abstract items, and indeed there was no sign of any difference between the two groups in their level of retention (see Table 4.2). In other words, instructions to use imagery in learning lists of single words had increased the head-injured patients' performance to the level demonstrated by the normal control subjects, and had reinstated the effect upon recall of the concreteness of the items to be remembered.

TABLE 4.2

Mean per cent correct in free recall for head-injured patients and for orthopaedic control subjects on concrete and abstract material in initial and final testing, under standard learning instructions and imagery mnemonic instructions

| | *Initial testing* | | *Final testing* | |
|---|---|---|---|---|
| | *Concrete* | *Abstract* | *Concrete* | *Abstract* |
| Standard instructions | | | | |
| Orthopaedic controls | 51.8 | 40.9 | 18.8 | 13.3 |
| Head-injured patients | 40.8 | 39.7 | 10.3 | 11.2 |
| Imagery instructions | | | | |
| Orthopaedic controls | 56.6 | 48.8 | 22.3 | 10.2 |
| Head-injured patients | 54.3 | 47.5 | 20.5 | 9.1 |

From the effects of minor closed head injury upon human memory: further evidence on the role of mental imagery, by J.T.E. Richardson & C. Barry (1985). *Cognitive Neuropsychology, 2,* 160. 

Richardson and Barry (1985) concluded that the effects of closed head injury on human memory should be regarded as a functional deficit attributable to the patients' failure to adopt the optional strategy of constructing interactive images. One might say that the problem exhibited by these patients lies not so much in their ability to remember *per se*, nor in their ability to use mental imagery or any other mnemonic strategy, but in their efficient and spontaneous use of such strategies. In other words, the effects of minor closed head injury appear to be principally upon *metamemory*: the strategic knowledge of how, when, and where to use mental imagery and other techniques to support effective learning and remembering in everyday life (Pressley, Borkowski, & Johnson, 1987).

## MEMORY FUNCTION FOLLOWING SEVERE CLOSED HEAD INJURY

Given that even a minor closed head injury can give rise to deficits in learning and remembering that persist beyond the period of PTA, it is not surprising that more severe cases also exhibit this sort of impairment. There have been many clinical reports of such impairment since Russell's seminal paper in 1934, but in these accounts it is often not clear how memory performance or deficits in memory performance were assessed. Nevertheless, a considerable amount of formal research has been devoted to the study of learning and remembering in patients with severe closed head injuries. It is beyond doubt that such patients manifest a generalised impairment of episodic memory (that is, the retention of particular biographical events and episodes). Such an impairment has been observed in a variety of tasks, with both verbal and pictorial material, and with lists of unrelated words as well as coherent narrative.

### The Wechsler Memory Scale

This research was undoubtedly facilitated by the development of standardised tests of memory performance for use in clinical settings. Until the 1980s, the most widely used instrument in this connection was undoubtedly the Wechsler Memory Scale (WMS: Wechsler, 1945), which contains seven subtests:

1. Personal and Current Information (regarding the patient's age, date of birth, and major Government figures);
2. Orientation (with respect to date and place);
3. Mental Control (assessed in terms of simple counting and recitation tasks);
4. Logical Memory (recalling the gist of two short pieces of narrative);
5. Memory Span (recalling sequences of digits in both a forward and a backward direction);
6. Visual Reproduction (drawing simple geometric figures from memory); and
7. Associate Learning (a multitrial paired-associate task).

An age correction factor is added to the patient's total score across the seven subtests to yield a "Memory Quotient" (MQ). This index was intended to be broadly analogous to and directly comparable with the patient's Intelligence Quotient (IQ) as measured by the Wechsler–Bellevue Intelligence Scale (Wechsler, 1944), the predecessor to the Wechsler Adult Intelligence Scale (WAIS: Wechsler, 1955). Since the MQ was in fact standardised against the Wechsler–Bellevue Performance scores of 100 normal adults, it is not surprising that among normal subjects the MQ is highly correlated with the IQ. There also seems to be a high degree of communality among the various subtests of the WMS.

In contrast, when neurological or psychiatric patients are tested, there may prove to be discrepancies between the IQ and the MQ, and the structure of the WMS breaks down into two and perhaps three major factors: one is measured by the Mental Control and Memory Span subtests, a second is associated with the Logical Memory, Visual Reproduction, and Associate Learning subtests, whereas a third may be associated with the Personal and Current Information and Orientation subtests (Skilbeck & Woods, 1980). Both the absolute MQ and the discrepancy between the IQ and the MQ are affected by brain damage, but impairment on the WMS is most clearly observed in patients with lesions of the left medial temporal lobe. All these issues were discussed in detail in a review paper by Prigatano (1978).

The factorial structure of the WMS that emerged from the study of clinical patients makes good sense in terms of modern theoretical assumptions about human memory. Atkinson and Shiffrin (1968) accepted the general distinction between long-term storage and short-term storage, but they argued that the latter should be regarded not simply as a temporary store of information but as a *working memory* responsible for a variety of additional control processes such as rehearsal, encoding, decision making, and retrieval. Baddeley and Hitch (1974) found that performance in a variety of cognitive tasks was disrupted by making subjects carry them out whilst holding a sequence of digits or consonants in their heads, and they took this to support the notion of working memory as a flexible but limited-capacity processing system. This idea proved very influential in subsequent work with both normal and brain-damaged subjects (Baddeley, 1986). The subtests of the WMS that were identified with the first of the three factors mentioned earlier seem to be measures of the efficiency of working memory, and the subtests that were identified with the second of those factors seem to be measures of the efficiency of long-term or permanent memory (cf. Russell, 1975).

## IQ and MQ following severe head injury

The first systematic study of memory disorders in patients with severe closed head injury was carried out by Dailey (1956), who used the Wechsler–Bellevue Intelligence Scale and the WMS in the psychological assessment of 31 patients with post-traumatic epilepsy roughly five years after their head injuries. There was no control group in this study, nor were any summary statistics given, but the severity of the injury (measured by the duration of post-traumatic unconsciousness) was reported to show a substantial correlation with the discrepancy between IQ and MQ.

Subsequently, Black (1973) compared 50 patients with closed head injuries and 50 patients with penetrating missile wounds of the brain on the WAIS and the WMS. The latter group achieved a mean IQ of 95.5 and a mean MQ of 90.5, which Black considered to be "within normal limits". The patients with closed head injuries achieved a mean IQ of 84.5 and a mean MQ of 79.1, representing a significant deficit in both cases. As Corrigan and Hinkeldey (1987) noted, however, the discrepancy between IQ and MQ was obviously very similar in the two groups.

An unpublished study by Prigatano found a mean (IQ–MQ) discrepancy of +10.07 in 15 patients with traumatic head injury, compared with a mean (IQ–MQ) discrepancy of –2.42 in 11 psychiatric controls (see Prigatano, 1978). Gronwall and Wrightson (1981) administered the WMS to 71 head-injured patients with durations of PTA from a few seconds to several days. Those patients in whom PTA had lasted more than 24 hours achieved lower MQs than the remainder of the sample.

Corkin et al. (1985) described five cases of chronic global amnesia resulting from closed head injuries. Their average IQ on the WAIS was 98.0, and none achieved less than 90. However, their mean MQ was 75.8, representing a mean (IQ–MQ) discrepancy of +22.2, and all of them scored less than 90 on this test. Nevertheless, Solomon, Greene, Farr, and Kelly (1986) reported a mean discrepancy of only +3.14 points in 126 patients with closed head injury; they tentatively suggested that diffuse or generalised lesions were normally associated only with relatively small discrepancy scores.

Corrigan and Hinkeldey (1987) compared 38 patients with closed head injuries and 21 patients who had suffered strokes on the WAIS and the WMS. The latter patients achieved a mean IQ of 93.81 and a mean MQ of 94.67, whereas those with closed head injuries achieved a mean IQ of 89.05 and a mean MQ of 79.92. The corresponding (IQ–MQ) discrepancy scores (i.e. –0.86 and +9.13) were to be significantly different by a simple pairwise test (implying that the head-injured patients were selectively impaired in terms of memory function), but not when their age, education, and time since onset were taken into account.

In 1981, however, the Wechsler Adult Intelligence Scale—Revised (WAIS-R: Wechsler, 1981) had been published. Corrigan and Hinkeldey (1987) presented data on the WMS and the WAIS-R from a further 98 patients who had suffered traumatic head injuries and another 52 patients who had suffered strokes. The latter patients achieved a mean IQ of 87.79 and a mean MQ of 102.73, and those with closed head injuries achieved a mean IQ of 82.24 and a mean MQ of 85.31. The corresponding (IQ–MQ) discrepancy scores were still significantly different, but this was now because the patients with cerebrovascular accidents produced a mean MQ that was substantially *higher* than their mean IQ.

The pattern of results that Corrigan and Hinkeldey (1987) found with stroke patients had been obtained with other populations as well (Prifitera & Barley, 1985). They noted that their own results also showed a difference of 6–7 points between the mean IQ values produced by the WAIS and the WAIS-R. They offered no explanation for this result, however, and suggested that it could not explain the (IQ–MQ) discrepancy of –14.94 that they had obtained in stroke patients using the WAIS-R.

Nevertheless, Larrabee (1987) pointed out that the WAIS itself yields mean IQs that are roughly 4–5 points higher than those generated by the Wechsler–Bellevue Intelligence Scale, on which of course the WMS was standardised (see Wechsler, 1945). Larrabee attributed this to the general pattern for successive standardisations of intelligence tests to yield lower scores when they are administered to the same groups of subjects. In discussing this general pattern, Flynn (1984) noted yet another problem with the Wechsler–Bellevue Intelligence Scale, namely that it had been standardised on an urban sample and therefore yielded mean IQs for the general population that were probably 3–4 points too low. The upshot of all this is that an (IQ–MQ) discrepancy of anywhere between –12 and –16 is entirely to be expected if the WAIS-R and the WMS are used with normal samples of subjects. Larrabee (1987) also provided further reasons for questioning the practical utility of making direct comparisons between the IQ and the MQ.

The validity of the MQ and of the WMS itself came under scrutiny for a number of reasons, and Prigatano (1978, p. 828) listed several weaknesses of the WMS as a psychometric instrument:

> They include (1) no scaled or standard scores available for individual subtests; (2) problems of scoring the Logical Memory subtest and the need to take into consideration the tendency of the patient to guess or not to guess on the test; (3) lack of norms for a large representative sample. … (4) lack of good numerical determinations of the test-retest reliability of the MQ scores in normals; (5) lack of information as to the distribution of Full Scale IQ minus MQ scores, especially in individuals with Superior IQ scores; and (6) a need for restandardization of the MQ scores with the WAIS Full Scale IQ (or the now-being-standardized WAIS-R) as opposed to the Wechsler-Bellevue.

Prigatano concluded (p. 828) that "the WMS needs to be improved substantially if it is to continue as a viable measure of memory function".

## Further studies using the Wechsler Memory Scale

Some investigators continued to use the WMS or its constituent subtests as a research tool despite its evident limitations. In their research, the use of appropriate control groups obviated a need to rely on normative data of doubtful validity. Several different studies showed that patients with severe head injury were particularly impaired on the Logical Memory and Associate Learning subtests of the WMS, especially if they were retested after a 30-minute delay, but that they tended not to be impaired on the remaining subtests (Brooks, 1972, 1976; Corkin et al., 1985; Gronwall & Wrightson, 1981; Kear-Colwell & Heller, 1980; Levin & Goldstein, 1986; Levin & Peters, 1976).

Groher (1977) administered the WMS to 14 patients who had been unconscious for an average of 17 days after head injuries. They were tested after they had regained consciousness and at four successive intervals of 30 days thereafter. On all seven subtests, they were profoundly impaired at the first testing session but showed considerable subsequent improvement. Their performance was evaluated as being "within normal limits" on the Mental Control, Logical Memory, and Memory Span subtests by the third session and on the Personal Information subtest by the final session. Their average MQ increased from 58.3 at the first session to 74.7 at the final session, but they showed persistent deficits on the Orientation, Visual Reproduction, and Associate Learning subtests.

However, some investigators sought to amend the WMS and to submit it to more careful psychometric evaluation. Russell (1975) devised a revised version of the WMS using just the Logical Memory and Visual Reproduction subtests, but supplemented by additional retention tests after a 30-minute delay. Other researchers tried to improve the usefulness of the original WMS by adding further items and forms of assessment (Milberg et al., 1986). Nevertheless, there were many residual problems with these variants of the WMS (see Loring & Papanicolaou, 1987).

An attempt to handle these problems was made in developing the Wechsler Memory Scale—Revised (WMS-R: Wechsler, 1987). This incorporated an extended and modified battery of subtests; scoring procedures for indices of Verbal Memory, Visual Memory, Delayed Memory, and Attention-Concentration, as well as a General Memory index; and validation material involving several clinical groups. Results from a sample of head-injured patients were included in the test manual, but no information was given on either the severity of their injuries or its relationship with their objective memory performance.

Initial analyses of the WMS-R's factor structure generated rather inconsistent results, but this may have been due to the use of heterogeneous patient groups. Roth, Conboy, Reeder, and Boll (1990) carried out confirmatory factor analysis upon the scores obtained by 107 head-injured patients. They found that the best fit to the data was provided by a model based on three factors: attention-concentration, immediate memory, and delayed recall. There was no evidence for separate visual and verbal factors. However, these factors were highly correlated, which implied that they reflected a single, global memory construct.

The latter factor solution was broadly replicated in other clinical populations (Bowden et al., 1997; Woodard, 1993; see also Spreen & Strauss, 1998, pp. 397–398). It has recently been incorporated in the third edition of this test (WMS-III), which includes a broader range of tests validated on individuals from a wider age range, and which yields measures of working memory, immediate memory, and delayed memory (Wechsler, 1997b). This is likely to become the standard instrument for assessing deficits in learning and memory following closed head injury. Moreover, the fact that a third edition of the WAIS has been produced and standardised alongside the WMS-III (see Chapter 5) should mean that in future it will be possible to make sensible comparisons between IQ and MQ within the same individuals.

## Other procedures for assessing memory function

Patients with severe closed head injuries have been found to be impaired on a wide variety of other procedures for testing the recall of both verbal and pictorial material (Brooks & Aughton, 1979a, 1979b; Brooks, Hosie, Bond, Jennett, & Aughton, 1986; Gronwall & Wrightson, 1981; Levin & Peters, 1976; Lezak, 1979). This includes the selective reminding procedure described previously (Gronwall & Wrightson, 1981; Levin, Benton, & Grossman, 1982, pp. 109–114; Levin & Eisenberg, 1979a, 1979b; Levin, Eisenberg, Wigg, & Kobayashi, 1982; Levin, Meyers, et al., 1981; McLean et al., 1983; Shores et al., 1986).

In addition to tests of recall, in which the participants are required to reproduce the items that had to be remembered, researchers have used tests of recognition, in which they have to identify those items among a larger set that includes some "distractor" items that have not been previously encountered. Once again, patients with severe head injuries have been found to be impaired on these tasks (Alexandre, Nertempi, Farinello, & Rubini, 1979; Brooks, 1972, 1974b; Corkin et al., 1985; Hannay & Levin, 1988; Hannay et al., 1979; Levin, Eisenberg, et al., 1982; Levin et al., 1976b; Levin, Meyers, et al., 1981; Levin & Peters, 1976; Payne-Johnson, 1986). There is, however, a problem in separating differences in recognition memory from differences in response bias in assessing patients' performance in these tasks (Richardson, 1994).

Sunderland, Harris, and Baddeley (1983) administered a battery of memory tests to 33 patients with severe head injuries (PTA lasting between 2 and 90 days) between two and eight months after their accidents. In comparison with a group of 37 orthopaedic patients, they showed an impairment across most of the tests of episodic memory and on a test of speed of access to semantic memory, though not on a multiple-choice vocabulary test. Sunderland et al. also devised a retrospective questionnaire and a daily checklist to be completed both by each patient and independently by a close relative concerning the patient's memory failures in everyday life. The relatives of the head-injured patients reported significantly more memory failures than the relatives of the control subjects. In both groups the most commonly reported memory failures were:

> Finding that a word is "on the tip of your tongue". You know what it is but can't quite find it.

Forgetting something you were told a few minutes ago. Perhaps something your wife or a friend has just said.
Forgetting something you were told yesterday or a few days ago.
Forgetting where you have put something. Losing things around the house.

Nevertheless, the head-injured patients themselves did not report significantly more memory failures than the orthopaedic control patients, and there was essentially no relationship between the performance of individual subjects in either group on the formal memory tests and the total number of memory failures reported either by the patients or by their relatives.

Sunderland et al. (1983) suggested that any residual memory problems might have been obscured by a tendency for both the head-injured patients and their relatives to compare the patients' condition at the time of assessment with the major cognitive dysfunction suffered during the comparatively recent period of PTA and the very early stages of recovery. However, they also suggested (p. 353) that the absence of correlations between "objective" performance and "subjective" reports was also due to differential exposure to cognitive demands:

> Having only just returned home, the most severely injured recent patients were less often back at work and may have been sheltered by relatives from cognitively demanding situations. Few memory errors will be made in an environment that makes few demands on memory, despite the poor performance of these patients on objective tests. The less seriously injured recent patients were more often back at work or were at least likely to be taking on domestic duties and to be venturing out, thus exposing themselves to problems and thereby making errors. Such a difference in exposure would tend to cancel out any subjective-objective correlations that might otherwise have occurred.

Most of the formal procedures described so far stem from laboratory research on human learning and memory and may not provide an accurate assessment of head-injured patients' abilities in daily life. The Rivermead Behavioural Memory Test was developed by Wilson (1987, chap. 5) to diagnose impairment in everyday memory functioning and to monitor change resulting from treatment for memory difficulties. It contains 11 subtests designed to provide analogues of a range of everyday memory tasks that appeared to be troublesome for brain-damaged patients, and selected on the basis of the types of memory failure reported by the patients in the study by Sunderland et al. (1983) and on the basis of behavioural observations of patients in a rehabilitation setting:

1 Remembering a name
2 Remembering a hidden belonging
3 Remembering an appointment
4 Picture recognition
5 Prose recall
6 Remembering a short route

7 Remembering an errand
8 Orientation (based on the Orientation subtest and the Personal and Current Information subtest of the WMS)
9 Date
10 Face recognition
11 Learning a new skill

Each of these items was shown to discriminate effectively between a group of 25 patients assessed as having everyday memory problems and a separate group of 16 patients assessed as not having such problems by occupational therapists. (All 41 patients had brain damage, in 24 cases as the result of head injury.) The number of items performed correctly by each subject showed a highly significant difference between the two groups of patients, demonstrated good interrater reliability, test–retest reliability, and parallel-form reliability, and was highly correlated both with therapists' observations of memory failures and with performance on standard tests of memory performance (including the Logical Memory test from the WMS), but not with measures of IQ according to the WAIS.

In short, patients with severe head injuries tend to show deficits across a wide range of tasks requiring explicit memory for the occurrence of specific episodes. Nowadays, clinicians are making use of an increasing variety of psychological tests in assessment of learning and memory (see e.g. Mayes, 1995). At the time of writing, these have not figured in any research publications concerned with the effects of closed head injury, but it would be very surprising if they led to any substantial change in the picture that has been painted earlier.

A major exception is tests of "implicit" memory (Schacter, 1987; see Chapter 3). Vakil, Biederman, Liran, Groswasser, and Aberbuch (1994) asked 14 head-injured patients and 15 healthy volunteers to learn a list of words. Unbeknownst to any of the participants, twelve of the items were presented once, three items were presented three times, and three items were presented six times. The participants were then given a word-stem completion task, in which they were given the first two letters of a word and had to supply the first word that came to mind. Scoring the number of list items supplied in this task is generally agreed to be a measure of priming in implicit memory that is typically intact in amnesic patients (see Graf, Squire, & Mandler, 1984; Shimamura, 1986). Vakil et al. found no sign of any impairment on this task in their head-injured patients. In contrast, the head-injured patients produced fewer words than the controls in a conventional test of free recall, and they were less accurate at saying how often each word had originally been presented.

Several investigators have shown that the degree of memory impairment after severe head injury is directly related to the duration of PTA (Brooks, 1974a, 1976; Brooks & Aughton, 1979b; Brooks, Aughton, Bond, Jones, & Rizvi, 1980; Dailey, 1956; Levin et al., 1976b; Parker & Serrats, 1976). This relationship may be more pronounced in older patients (Brooks, 1972, 1974b). However, Ewing-Cobbs et al. (1990) found that in children and adolescents the duration of PTA assessed using the Children's Orientation and Amnesia Test was a better predictor of their memory performance at six and twelve months after injury than their GCS scores on admission.

The degree of impairment may also be associated with the level of consciousness on admission according to the Glasgow Coma Scale (Hanny & Levin, 1988; Levin & Eisenberg, 1979a, 1979b), the duration of post-traumatic unconsciousness (Dailey, 1956; Groher, 1977; Hannay & Levin, 1988; Hannay et al., 1979; Kløve & Cleeland, 1972; Levin & Eisenberg, 1979a, 1979b; Levin, Eisenberg, et al., 1982; but cf. Brooks et al., 1980), and with the incidence of neurological signs of brain-stem damage (Levin et al., 1976b). On the basis of the discussion in Chapter 2, therefore, one might conclude that postconcussional disorders of learning and remembering are produced by rotational movement of the brain at the time of head impact.

Conversely, measures of focal brain damage do not show a consistent relationship with the degree of residual impairment (Brooks, 1975, 1976; Brooks et al., 1980; Levin et al., 1976b; Levin & Eisenberg, 1979a; Levin, Eisenberg, et al., 1982). In particular, the extent of memory impairment does not appear to be affected by the presence of a skull fracture (Brooks et al., 1980; Kløve & Cleeland, 1972; Levin et al., 1976b; but cf. Brooks, 1975; Smith-Seemiller, Lovell, Smith, Markosian, & Townsend, 1997). It is, however, not clear whether dysphasia should be regarded as a focal neurological sign that affects the extent of memory impairment (Brooks, 1974b; Levin et al., 1976a, 1976b; Thomsen, 1977; see Chapter 5).

Moreover, the prognostic significance of intracranial haematomas is also unclear (see Alexandre et al., 1979; Cullum & Bigler, 1985; Timming, Orrison, & Mikula, 1982). Indeed, in the study by Brooks et al. (1980), patients who had undergone surgical removal of a haematoma were found to perform significantly better on story recall than nonoperated patients, which was taken to reflect a bias in the selection of patients for neurosurgical treatment. This study found that the side of haematoma was irrelevant as a predictor of memory performance. Levin, Benton, and Grossman (1982, pp. 109–114) described unpublished results suggesting focal damage to the left temporal lobe might be important. Such effects could be ascribed to uncontrolled variation in the severity of damage (Hannay & Levin, 1988). However, Bigler et al. (1996) showed that memory impairment in head-injured patients varied with the degree of hippocampal atrophy according to MRI. This link was apparent only in patients tested more than 90 days postinjury, and was more evident in the left hippocampus than the right.

## Theoretical interpretations

One theoretical interpretation of the effects of severe closed head injury on memory function has been in terms of the theory of short-term and long-term storage that was proposed by Atkinson and Shiffrin (1968). Brooks (1975) compared patients with closed head injuries and other accident victims who were undergoing the treatment of limb injuries. He found that the patients with head injuries were impaired in the free recall of common words but not in their immediate memory span for digits. The head-injured patients were also more impaired in the former task when they were tested after a delay of 20 seconds during which they were required to engage in an irrelevant counting task.

These results might suggest that severe closed head injury disrupts long-term storage but not short-term storage. However, other investigators have not found such a clear dissociation between memory span and tests of long-term retention (Becker, 1975; Levin & Goldstein, 1986; Lezak, 1979; Thomsen, 1977). Indeed, when Brooks (1975) examined the influence of the time between injury and testing, the patients who had been tested within six months of their accidents produced poorer performance in memory span than those who had been tested more than six months afterwards; no such difference was obtained in the measures of long-term retention. This suggests that short-term memory is impaired by severe head injury but rapidly improves to a normal level, whereas long-term memory recovers much more slowly and exhibits a persistent residual impairment.

The discussion thus far has implied that the rotational acceleration of the brain that is induced by a severe closed head injury leads to a specific impairment of the encoding of material into long-term storage. However, it is important to remember that qualitatively different forms of impairment can arise from the focal lesions that result from skull fractures or intracranial haematomas. An interesting example of this was a patient reported by Warrington and Shallice (1970), who had suffered a left parieto-occipital fracture in a road accident and subsequently had to undergo surgery for the evacuation of a left parietal subdural haematoma. When assessed 11 years later, his performance in tests of long-term memory (including the Associate Learning subtest of the WAIS and a multitrial free-recall task) was essentially normal. However, his digit span was just two, and he proved to have a general impairment in the repetition of auditory verbal stimuli. Shallice and Warrington (1970) presented further evidence to show that this patient had a selective reduction in the capacity of short-term memory.

Because of epileptic seizures, the patient then underwent exploratory craniotomy, enabling the extent of the damage to be macroscopically visualised. Warrington, Logue, and Pratt (1971, p. 378) reported that "the lesion was both to cortex and white matter, but mainly to the former, which in places was totally lacking, the white matter being exposed". Warrington et al. presented the findings of their postoperative assessment, in which the patient performed at or above the normal level on the Performance subtests of the WAIS and roughly within the normal range on the Logical Memory and Associate Learning subtests of the WMS. However, his performance was more variable on the Verbal subtests of the WAIS, where he was impaired on the Arithmetic subtest and especially on the Digit Span subtest.

At that time, it was the conventional wisdom that verbal information could only be encoded in long-term memory by being held and rehearsed within short-term memory: in other words, short-term memory served as some kind of gateway between sensory input and long-term storage. As Shallice and Warrington (1970) pointed out, the fact that their patient's long-term retention was largely intact in the face of a gross impairment of short-term retention created difficulties for this view. As an alternative, they argued short-term memory and long-term memory constituted functionally independent forms of storage. Largely thanks to their research findings but also to evidence from other individual patients with similar patterns of memory dysfunction, this is now very much the prevailing conception of the functional architecture of human memory (Richardson, 1996).

Earlier in this chapter, I suggested that a minor closed head injury impaired memory function by disrupting the use of mental imagery as a form of coding within long-term memory. A study by Thomsen (1977) compared 41 patients with severe closed head injuries and 21 control subjects on the multitrial free recall of a single list of 10 concrete nouns and a single list of 10 abstract nouns. The head-injured patients proved to be significantly impaired on the abstract list as well as on the concrete list. This result might suggest that the persistent and pronounced impairment of memory function that follows the occurrence of a severe closed head injury is not to be ascribed merely to an impairment in the use of mental imagery.

Nevertheless, Thomsen's (1977) control subjects were students from a college of further education, and it is quite possible that they were not really an appropriate comparison group. College students are very atypical of the general population in terms of a range of characteristics, most obviously their age, intelligence, educational level, and social class (Richardson, 1987). The control subjects used in Thomsen's study were in fact of a similar age range and occupational status to her head-injured patients, and they "had not had any known damage to the brain" (p. 73). There was, however, no suggestion that any of this particular comparison group had ever been involved in serious accidents. This is an important point, and one that is worth considering in some detail.

## Choice of control subjects

In the assessment of individual patients in clinical practice, it may be important to establish whether they are functioning at a lower level than their educational or occupational history would suggest, regardless of whether this is caused by the organic effects of head injury or to the broader social and psychological factors that are of necessity attendant upon an individual's involvement in a major accident. In these circumstances it will often be appropriate to use standard normative data in arriving at a formal evaluation. It may even be possible to arrive at an estimate of a patient's premorbid performance on the basis of demographic characteristics such as age, education, and occupation (Barona, Reynolds, & Chastain, 1984; Crawford & Allan, 1997; Reynolds & Gutkin, 1979).

In some instances, test results may be available from before the person's injury. These might be obtained as a formal consequence of a research design, as in some investigations of closed head injuries in contact sports where players have been systematically assessed during the preseason (Barth et al., 1989; Hinton-Bayre, Geffen, & McFarland, 1997). Alternatively, premorbid test results might be available by virtue of the choice of the population to be studied. This would be the case in studies of closed head injuries among the members of the armed services, who will have undergone routine psychological assessment during their induction (Becker, 1975; Dresser et al., 1973; Russell, 1981). It would also be likely in the case of research involving head-injured schoolchildren, who might well have received tests of mental or scholastic ability (e.g. Levin & Eisenberg, 1979a). Even so, premorbid data of this sort need to be considered with care and even scepticism (see Teuber, 1969). Once the psychologist wishes to go beyond the circumstances of the individual patient, however, and to make general statements concerning the effects of head injuries on mental function, whether for the purposes of assessment, rehabilitation, or research, then the need arises to establish a suitable group with which to compare the head-injured sample.

In experimental research, a control group is a group of subjects who are treated in an identical manner to those in the experimental group with the exception that they are not exposed to the manipulation that is under investigation. In other words, the two groups differ only with respect to the critical independent variable whose effect is being studied. This can normally be achieved by assigning individual subjects at random to one of the two groups, so that the experimental manipulation is systematically either imposed upon or withheld from subjects who are otherwise drawn from the same underlying population.

In research in clinical neuropsychology, however, it is neither ethically permissible nor practically possible to allocate participants at random to control and experimental groups by systematically exposing them to or protecting them from disease or trauma. Membership of the two groups is thus a "classification" variable that is determined in advance of the study in question rather than a "treatment" variable resulting from the manipulations of the investigator, and it follows that research of this sort is intrinsically correlational rather than experimental in nature (see Ferguson & Takane, 1989, pp. 246–247). Under these circumstances the selection of a suitable control group will be of considerable importance, since the researcher will otherwise be seeking to attribute differences in performance between a clinical sample and a control group to some neurological indicator in the full knowledge that the two groups may well differ on many other relevant characteristics (Richardson, 1982).

In the case of research into the effects of closed head injury, it is normally considered necessary to select control subjects who are similar to the head-injured sample in every relevant respect, save that of having received a blow to the head (see McKinlay & Brooks, 1984; McMillan & Glucksman, 1987; Rutter et al., 1980). In particular, it is common for control subjects to be chosen from accident victims who have been admitted to hospital for orthopaedic treatment of major fractures, because these patients will also have suffered traumatic injury leading to rapid, unexpected hospitalisation (Brooks, 1976; cf. Brooks et al., 1984). This also allows for the fact that accident victims are not a representative or random subgroup of the general population, but appear to differ from the rest of the population in important respects (Aitken et al., 1982; Mandleberg & Brooks, 1975). In particular, as McKinlay and Brooks (1984, p. 96) pointed out, the use of orthopaedic cases as control patients means that they are "drawn from a similar 'at risk' population with the over-representation of the young, of males, and of the lower socioeconomic classes", unlike other comparison groups such as cardiac patients or those with severe burns (see also Chapter 1).

Of course, the use of orthopaedic patients as a control population also assumes that head-injured patients are broadly similar to other accident victims. One might seek to justify this on the grounds that whether or not an accident leads to a head injury (as opposed to an injury to some other part of the body) is often a matter of chance. Of particular relevance to the assessment of post-traumatic cognitive function is the relatively poor premorbid academic attainment of patients with closed head injuries (Haas et al., 1987; Rutter et al., 1980), and this seems equally to be a characteristic of other accident victims (Hall et al., 1987; Wilmot et al., 1985). Nevertheless, Brown, Chadwick, Shaffer, Rutter, and Traub (1981) found that children with mild head injuries (unlike those with severe head injuries) showed a rate of premorbid behavioural disturbance that was markedly higher than that of children who had suffered orthopaedic injuries not involving the head.

In research on the effects of severe head injury, McKinlay and Brooks (1984) argued that the control subjects should have sustained a traumatic injury that was life-threatening in at least a proportion of cases and involved a significant degree of disability, leading to an associated re-evaluation of life plans and the possibility of adverse psychological reactions. They suggested (p. 97) that orthopaedic patients "are less severely injured and can be expected to make a more or less full recovery over a few months; adverse psychological reaction to disability would therefore be expected to be less marked and less prolonged". Instead, they argued that cases of traumatic paraplegia come closer to meeting the requirements for appropriate control subjects (cf. Rosenbaum & Najenson, 1976). However, McKinlay and Brooks acknowledged that the disabilities of paraplegic patients were permanent and severe, which might make any psychological reactions particularly acute, and yet at the same time visible and public, which might mean that they were easier to accommodate and less subject to stigma than mental disabilities.

## Brain function in orthopaedic patients

The choice of orthopaedic patients as control subjects appears to be more appropriate in the case of research into the effects of minor closed head injury. Nevertheless, there are at least four different reasons why this might be expected in principle to give only a rather conservative assessment of the effects of traumatic brain damage upon psychological function.

First, an accident victim might have received a head injury that was not sufficiently conspicuous to be noted on medical examination. For example, it would seem that as many as 50% of patients admitted to hospital with spinal-cord injuries also have closed head injuries (Silver, Morris, & Otfinowski, 1980). Whether these are detected will depend upon the vigilance of the receiving medical staff (Kopaniky & Wagner, 1987) and the level of expertise in the unit to which they are admitted (Silver et al., 1980). For instance, Davidoff, Morris, Roth, and Bleiberg (1985) found that only 25% of patients with traumatic spinal-cord injuries were assessed for PTA. They concluded that a closed head injury was a frequent concomitant of traumatic spinal-cord injury but that "many of these closed head injuries remain undetected and their sequelae unevaluated" (p. 42). Kopaniky and Wagner (1987) also argued that evidence of a possible head injury may be inadvertently dropped from the patient's medical record as the spinal-cord injury becomes the major focus for medical attention. Equally, however, as Cope (1987, p. 100) pointed out, it may well be very difficult to assess mental function in patients with spinal-cord injuries since they "are not only paralyzed but their initial course is also characterized by passivity and dependency".

A prospective study by Enderson et al. (1990) attempted to measure the incidence of missed injuries among patients who had been admitted to a medical centre where best practice was being followed when identifying injuries in trauma patients. Injuries that had been missed on original assessment were identified in 9% of all patients. However, nearly all of these were thoracic, abdominal, or musculoskeletal injuries, and they had often been missed in patients whose consciousness was impaired by alcohol, drugs, or head injury. The results of this study indicate that nowadays the incidence of missed head injuries in patients with other kinds of injury may actually be very low.

Second, an accident victim whose orthopaedic injuries were sufficiently serious to warrant emergency hospitalisation might have received a bodily impact which transmitted an inertial loading to the brain even without a direct impact to the head (see Chapter 2). This may of course be evidenced by a loss of consciousness at the time of the accident and by a subsequent period of PTA. Hall et al. (1987) assessed a consecutive series of 130 patients with spinal-cord injury and found that 56% were quadriplegic as the result of a high-energy deceleration accident, 36% had lost consciousness at the time of their injuries, and 15% had neurological indicators of significant brainstem or cortical damage.

Third, even without causing mechanical damage to the brain, orthopaedic injuries can give rise to brain injury. The latter is often an "occult" injury in the sense that its onset may be delayed and so the symptoms and signs of cerebral involvement may not be present at the time of admission. There are at least two major mechanisms by which this can happen. On the one hand, a blunt injury to the neck can lead to the intimal dissection of a major cerebral artery resulting in the occlusion of blood flow or focal cerebral infarction (see Kopaniky & Wagner, 1987). Lampert and Hardman (1984) noted that this was an indirect source of brain damage in boxing. On the other hand, an injury to the spinal cord often gives rise to respiratory insufficiency with the consequent risk of hypoxic damage to the brain (Cope, 1987). By a similar means, hypoxia can also result from traumatic chest injury as well as other disorders such as pulmonary oedema (Teasdale & Mendelow, 1984).

Finally, even relatively minor orthopaedic cases might be undergoing uncomfortable or distressing treatment, and this might affect their performance in psychometric testing. In this context, it is interesting that Rutter et al. (1980) found that some form of surgical intervention had been necessary in 21% of children with moderate head injuries, in 25% of children with severe head injuries, but in 57% of children with orthopaedic injuries. Wilmot et al. (1985) assessed 67 victims of traumatic spinal-cord injuries on a neuropsychological test battery, and found that 43 of them were impaired, 7 of them profoundly so. Despite the fact that their physicians were aware of this study, only 10 patients had been diagnosed as having a head injury or a cognitive problem (see also Hall et al., 1987). Very similar results were obtained in a prospective study by Davidoff, Roth, Morris, and Bleiberg (1987).

When some of the patients studied by Hall et al. (1987) received a follow-up assessment an average of 16 months after their injuries, precisely half of them were found still to be impaired. More recently, Dowler et al. (1997) assessed 91 patients on average 17 years after they had sustained traumatic spinal-cord injury. Patients were included if they had incurred their injuries in either vehicular accidents or falls (where a concomitant head injury was thought to be probable). By means of cluster analysis on their patients' scores across a battery of tests, Dowler et al. inferred that 60% exhibited clinically significant deficits in one or more cognitive domains, and they attributed these to a concomitant undiagnosed head injury.

From a practical point of view, then, the possibility of concurrent cerebral injury has to be taken seriously in the management of traumatic orthopaedic cases. Moreover, any residual cognitive impairment will have important implications for the treatment and rehabilitation of such patients. In particular, such deficits may well impede the learning of new skills and information (Davidoff et al., 1987), and, as Cope (1987) pointed out, they may explain some of the psychological problems of patients recovering from spinal-cord injuries that have been thought in the past to be purely characterological or psychodynamic in nature. For present purposes, however, the main point is that the use of hospitalised orthopaedic control subjects might tend in principle to underestimate the effects of closed head injuries upon cognitive function.

## Physical trauma and psychological function

Some researchers have used normal, healthy volunteers as control subjects in evaluating the effects of closed head injury. Brooks et al. (1984) noted that this provided an estimate of the asymptotic level of performance which might in principle be approached during the course of recovery by head-injured patients, and that the healthy working population might well provide an important frame of reference, especially for medico-legal purposes. Other researchers have obtained control subjects from among nonemergency hospital admissions.

As mentioned earlier in this chapter, Conkey (1938) tested a group of surgical patients both in and out of hospital, and found no difference between the two testing sessions. Moreover, these control patients showed a similar pattern of performance to the normal subjects which she used as the comparison group in evaluating the effects of closed head injury. This tends to confirm that hospitalisation itself has little or no effect on performance in psychological tests. Nevertheless, as Conkey herself acknowledged (p. 18), "none of these patients was suffering from physical trauma of any type", and so her results do not distinguish between the effects of trauma in general and the specific consequences of traumatic brain injury.

As McKinlay and Brooks (1984, p. 98) observed, the empirical phenomena that are observed and reported in patients with closed head injury "will be a mixture of specific effects of brain injury and general effects due to reactions to injury, hospitalisation, threat to life and so on". However, little is known about the generalised effects of serious trauma and consequent emergency admission to hospital on psychological functioning. Richardson and Snape (1984) pointed out (as indeed is immediately apparent to anyone involved in the treatment and care of accident victims) that these events constitute a major source of stress that is predominantly expressed as a profound anxiety about oneself, one's family, one's job, and so on. The nature, complications, and clinical management of this acute response to trauma were discussed by Peterson (1986).

In experimental research, it is generally agreed that effects of situational stress upon cognitive performance are likely to be mediated by the amount of experienced anxiety or "state anxiety" that is engendered by the situation in question (Eysenck, 1982, p. 96). The latter was defined by Spielberger (1972, p. 39) as a condition "characterized by subjective, consciously perceived feelings of tension and apprehension, and activation of the autonomic nervous system" (see also Spielberger, 1966). It was claimed by Liebert and Morris (1967; see also Morris & Liebert, 1970) that state anxiety had both cognitive components ("worry") and autonomic components ("emotionality"), and that it was the former that were responsible for cognitive dysfunction. The evidence for this distinction is not entirely unequivocal (Richardson, O'Neil, Whitmore, & Judd, 1977), but it is generally accepted that anxiety (and other affective states) may interfere with human cognition (see Eysenck, 1982, chap. 6; Messick, 1965).

Eysenck (1982, p. 99) made a specific theoretical assertion about the likely effects of state anxiety upon cognitive functioning:

> Worry and other task-irrelevant cognitive activities associated with anxiety always impair the quality of performance because the task-irrelevant information involved in worry and cognitive self-concern competes with task-relevant information for space in the processing system.

In particular, he proposed that the principal manifestation of the concurrent processing of task-irrelevant information should be a reduction in the available capacity of working memory. This idea is supported by the fact that state anxiety has a pronounced effect upon performance in tests of memory span (see Eysenck, 1979; Hodges & Spielberger, 1969).

Richardson and Snape (1984) suggested that the worries that are shown by accident victims were precisely the sort of task-irrelevant information that might be expected to pre-empt the limited processing space available within working memory. They compared two samples of 30 orthopaedic patients: one group was tested as inpatients within a few days of their accidents, whereas the other group was tested as outpatients several weeks later. The former group was found to be severely impaired in comparison with the latter group on the task that had been used by Richardson (1979) to measure the free recall of lists of concrete and abstract words (see the first two rows of Table 4.3). This was true, however, only on the initial, immediate test, not on the final, cumulative test. This pattern of impairment was clearly to be attributed to a specific problem in the use of a short-term store or working memory, rather than to any disruption of long-term or permanent memory. In short, this was precisely the outcome that was to be expected on the basis of current understanding of the effects of stress and anxiety upon learning and memory, but one that also has important implications for the choice of an appropriate control group in research into closed head injury.

As explained earlier in this chapter, working memory is construed as a flexible, limited-capacity processing system that is involved in a wide variety of cognitive functions. Nevertheless, the experimental findings that led Baddeley and Hitch (1974) to develop this notion indicated that it was not a unitary device, but should be conceptualised as a complex system consisting of a central executive processor together with a number of "slave" subsystems. Considerable support was obtained for this sort of account in subsequent research (see Baddeley, 1986). Two hypothetical subsystems of working memory have received particular attention. One is a "visuo-spatial sketchpad" that is assumed to be mainly responsible for the construction and manipulation of spatial and pictorial representations and hence

TABLE 4.3

Mean per cent correct in free recall for outpatient controls, inpatient controls, and patients with minor and severe closed head injuries on concrete and abstract material in initial and final testing

| | *Initial testing* | | *Final testing* | |
|---|---|---|---|---|
| | *Concrete* | *Abstract* | *Concrete* | *Abstract* |
| Outpatient controls | 56.3 | 46.9 | 19.1 | 12.9 |
| Inpatient controls | 47.0 | 36.1 | 17.0 | 10.6 |
| Minor head injuries | 44.9 | 37.8 | 9.9 | 9.5 |
| Severe head injuries | 37.3 | 35.0 | 6.0 | 6.5 |

Adapted from Richardson and Snape (1984), p.255. Copyright 1984 by Lawrence Erlbaum Associates Ltd. Adapted by permission of Psychology Press, UK.

to be an important component in the utilisation of mental imagery (see Logie, 1995). The other subsystem is a short-term phonological store or response buffer that is assumed to be involved in the immediate serial recall of verbal items (see Longoni, Richardson, & Aiello, 1993).

Imposing a concurrent memory load upon subjects engaged in a short-term verbal memory task preempts some of the limited capacity of this store and therefore reduces its contribution to the overall level of performance (Richardson, 1984). However, the worries and cognitive self-concern that are associated with involvement in a major accident requiring emergency hospitalisation would presumably be effectively registered within long-term or permanent memory, and would not need to be maintained or rehearsed within the phonological buffer store. Rather, the cognitive disruption that is engendered by anxiety amongst accident victims should result from competition with task-relevant information for space within the central executive processor itself, and should therefore be manifested across a wide range of intellectual activities.

This last conclusion is interesting from a theoretical point of view, but the converse is more significant in the practical context of clinical assessment. The observation of cognitive impairment in head-injured patients need not be taken as evidence for brain damage but may simply reflect the generic effects of post-traumatic stress and anxiety. This alternative explanation needs to be considered especially when the patient is assessed soon after their accident and when there is little or no neurological or radiological evidence to corroborate the presumption of physical damage to the brain.

## Imagery and memory following severe head injury

Nevertheless, the results obtained by Richardson and Snape (1984) suggest that the effects of the stress caused by involvement in a major accident tend to dissipate within a few weeks. It would appear that any long-term residual impact of emergency hospitalisation is likely to be minimal in the case of patients who have sustained severe closed head injuries. Effects of this sort are unlikely to have influenced the performance of the head-injured patients described by Thomsen (1977), since they were assessed at least one year after their accidents. It remains true, however, that these patients were not comparable in certain important respects with the sample of college students that Thomsen selected as control subjects.

To respond to Thomsen's findings, therefore, Richardson and Snape (1984) used their recently hospitalised orthopaedic patients as controls in a replication of Richardson's (1979) original study using a sample that included eight cases of severe closed head injury (defined as a PTA lasting longer than 24 hours) and twenty-two cases of minor closed head injury. Their results are contained in the last two rows of Table 4.3. The severely injured patients showed an even more pronounced impairment on the concrete items, but they were not impaired on the abstract items. Whereas the patients with minor head injury still showed a modest difference in the recall of concrete and abstract items, those with severe head injury showed no difference at all.

Thus, the conclusions of Richardson (1979) seem to apply even to patients who have suffered severe closed head injuries. Provided that these patients are tested beyond the period of PTA and provided that they are not suffering from peripheral defects, their ability to recall lists of abstract words appears to be essentially normal. Richardson and Snape concluded (1984, p. 228): "there is at present no reason to think that Richardson's imagery account is not entirely adequate as an explanation of the persistent disturbance of memory function which results from closed head injury". It is, in fact, intriguing that Thomsen (1977) herself suggested that some of her patients had not realised the difference between the concrete and abstract words and had therefore been unable to visualise the former in attempting to learn them.

It is also interesting to note that the pattern of results obtained by Richardson (1979) and replicated by Richardson and Snape (1984) is not peculiar to patients with closed head injuries. Many groups of patients with localised or generalised cerebral dysfunction show a normal superiority in their recall of concrete words relative to that of abstract words (Richardson, 1991). However, Weingartner, Caine, and Ebert (1979a, 1979b; see also Caine, Ebert, and Weingartner, 1977) found that patients with Huntington's disease showed no difference in their recall of the two types of word. Some of these patients were asked to provide imageability ratings of the individual words, and their judgements broadly reproduced the mean ratings generated by large normative samples. Weingartner et al. (1979a, 1979b) concluded that Huntington's patients were sensitive to the varying imageability of words but failed to use this attribute when encoding material for later recall.

Weingartner et al. (1979a) also found no difference in the recall of concrete and abstract words on the part of normal volunteers given intramuscular injections of scopolamine, which is an acetylcholine receptor blocker that is well known to disrupt memory function. Because of the similarity between these data and those obtained with Huntington's patients, Weingartner et al. raised the question whether the memory impairment in Huntington's disease was caused by some disorder of acetylcholine-mediated neurotransmission. However, Sitaram, Weingartner, Caine, and Gillin (1978) also found no difference between the recall of concrete and abstract words in normal volunteers who had been given a single oral dose of choline (which gave rise to an *increase* in the overall level of recall performance). It is important, too, to note that all of these studies employed the selective reminding procedure, and that none of these findings is replicable if more conventional testing procedures are employed (Richardson, 1991).

It is equally pertinent to enquire whether the memory deficits shown by head-injured patients are really confined to the use of mental imagery in memory tasks. Earlier in this chapter it was noted that instructions to use mental imagery can alleviate the memory impairment seen in patients with minor closed head injury (see Richardson & Barry, 1985), and hence that the underlying problem is one of metamemory rather than of memory itself. In this case, there is no reason to assume that effects of head injury are confined to the strategy of employing interactive imagery. Indeed, Marschark, Richman, Yuille, and Hunt (1987) argued that concrete and abstract words differ not just in their imageability but in the relative ease with which they can be subjected to relational processing.

Although this proposal was originally intended to explain apparently problematic findings concerning the retention of narrative, it yields a very coherent analysis of the effects of concreteness and imageability in both paired-associate learning (Marschark & Hunt, 1989) and free recall (Marschark & Surian, 1989). This prompts a quite different sort of account of the effects of a closed head injury upon learning and memory (Marschark, personal communication), namely that head-injured patients fail to engage in relational processing during the presentation of word lists unless they receive instructions that specifically encourage them to do so (for instance, by constructing interactive images).

A study carried out by Levin and Goldstein (1986) is of direct relevance to this account. These researchers compared 12 patients with severe closed head injury and 10 normal controls on the multitrial free recall of word lists designed to measure the use of semantic organisation in learning and remembering. The head-injured patients were found to be impaired not just in terms of the amount that was recalled but also on measures of categorical clustering and subjective organisation. Indeed, an index of the consistency of order of recall between successive trials was below chance in the head-injured patients (see also van Zomeren, 1981, p. 111). Analogous results were obtained by Crosson, Novack, Trenerry, and Craig (1988) and by Stallings, Boake, and Sherer (1995).

A subsequent study by Twum and Parenté (1994) investigated the effects of learning instructions in 60 patients with severe head injuries on the visual and verbal paired associates tasks in the WMS-R. The former task assesses memory for abstract line drawings paired with different colours, whereas the latter task assesses memory for pairs of common words. Half of the patients were instructed to use verbal labelling on the visual task, but the remainder received no specific instructions for this task. Independently of this manipulation, half of the patients were instructed to use associative imagery on the verbal task, whereas the remainder received no specific instructions for this task. In each case, the learning instructions led to better immediate recall, faster learning (i.e. fewer trials to criterion), and better recall after a 30-minute delay on the relevant materials. These results cannot be handled by an account based solely upon the impaired use of mental imagery, but they are consistent with an analysis in terms of impaired relational organisation.

## OVERVIEW

An impairment of learning and remembering is the most frequent subjective complaint and the most prominent residual deficit in patients who have sustained a closed head injury. Provided that it is sufficiently serious to warrant hospitalisation, even a minor closed head injury can produce a measurable decrement on tests of memory function that persists beyond the period of post-traumatic amnesia. Nevertheless, in the latter case, the magnitude of any impairment is relatively slight, it tends to resolve within the first week or so following the head injury, and it is very doubtful whether it gives rise to any major handicap in everyday activities. This transient disruption of learning and remembering can be attributed to a selective impairment in the use of mental imagery as a form of elaborative encoding in long-term episodic memory, which can itself be abolished by the administration of imagery mnemonic instructions.

Severe closed head injury gives rise to a more pronounced and more persistent memory dysfunction that is manifested across a wide variety of tasks. It can be readily demonstrated on the Wechsler Memory Scale and its constituent subtests, especially when patients are retested on the Logical Memory and Associate Learning tasks after a 30-minute delay. The magnitude of this impairment varies directly with the severity of the injury but is not consistently related to measures of focal cerebral damage, and it is also largely independent of the incidence of memory failures in daily life. Memory dysfunction following severe head injury can also be ascribed to a selective impairment in the use of mental imagery as an elaborative memory code, although there is evidence that it involves a more widespread disruption of relational processing in long-term storage. It should, of course, be acknowledged that memory impairment need not take one single form. There is evidence for several types of head-injured patients who differ in their patterns of test scores (Deshpande, Millis, Reeder, Fuerst, & Ricker, 1996).

Attempts to evaluate different theoretical accounts of the effects of closed head injury upon memory function have been bedevilled by problems over the choice of an appropriate control group. Involvement in a major accident followed by rapid and unexpected admission to hospital engenders anxiety, and the resulting cognitive self-concern leads to a reduction in the available capacity of a short-term store or working memory. This can be manifested across a wide range of cognitive tasks but is conceptually distinct from the specific effects of brain injury. These considerations tend to motivate the choice of orthopaedic patients as a suitable control population, although for a number of different reasons this might provide only a conservative assessment of the effects of closed head injury upon psychological function.

CHAPTER FIVE

# Cognition and language

Apart from memory, the cognitive abilities of human beings include perception, attention, communication, comprehension, thinking, and reasoning. Given that even mild cases of closed head injury can demonstrate a measurable reduction in the ability to learn and remember that endures (at least for a limited time) beyond the period of post-traumatic amnesia (PTA), it is important to determine the incidence and the severity of persistent disorders in other aspects of cognition. In fact, head-injured patients do tend to show impaired performance across a wide range of intellectual functions.

In this chapter, I shall discuss the general nature of the cognitive impairment shown by head-injured patients and its relationship to various possible prognostic indicators. I shall then go on to consider the relative vulnerability of verbal and nonverbal cognitive functioning, as measured by formal psychometric instruments. Finally, I shall review what is known about the disorders of language and communication that tend to result from closed head injury. This is not, of course, to assume that memory and language are distinct from cognition: indeed, I shall emphasise parallels between the impact of head injury on memory and its impact on other aspects of cognition, and I shall also stress the close relationship between language disturbances and a more general disruption of cognitive skills.

## COGNITIVE FUNCTION

### Early studies

The first systematic study of intellectual abilities following closed head injury was that reported by Conkey (1938), who administered an extensive battery of psychological tests to 25 patients with simple concussion. The results of the tests that were specifically concerned with memory function were described in the previous chapter. Conkey classified the remainder into three levels of difficulty or "levels of mental functioning". Both the magnitude of the patients' impairment at the initial examination two to three weeks after their injuries and their rate of recovery were a direct function of task difficulty.

However, Conkey (1938) suggested that the three groups of tests differed from each other in the nature of the impairment in question. Simple tests of orientation, personal information, and recitation produced impaired performance largely because the head-injured patients took an appreciably longer time to carry out the tasks than normal controls. More complicated tests tended to produce poorer performance because they often depended upon the use of "old knowledge and associations" (or what would nowadays be characterised as the retrieval of information from "semantic memory": Tulving, 1972; see also Chapter 3). The most complex tests emphasised high-level reasoning and problem solving, and Conkey suggested (p. 39) that her head-injured patients had failed on these latter tasks because they were deficient in "the use of symbolism, the perception of logical relations and the ability to abstract".

In each category of test, however, the performance of the head-injured patients approached that of normal controls over a period of 34 weeks, although there was a suggestion of a slight residual impairment on the tests of intermediate difficulty. Unfortunately, the interpretation of Conkey's findings is made complicated by the very high attrition rate across the test sessions among her head-injured patients. She ascribed this (p. 20) to the fact that a large number of her subjects "belong to the 'unfortunates' of society and are unreliable and shiftless", and she characterised it (p. 20) as a "weeding out process … in which the more reliable and more desirable individuals were obtained for study".

It could however equally be argued that it is the patients who have made a good recovery and returned to their previous employment who are unwilling to take time away from their work or other responsibilities to participate in repeated testing sessions purely for the sake of clinical research. This seems to have been the case in a more recent study in which only 37% of the original sample returned for follow-up evaluation (Levin, Mattis, et al., 1987). Nowadays, patient drop-out for whatever reason is recognised as a serious methodological problem in longitudinal research (see Brooks et al., 1984).

Ruesch and Moore (1943; Ruesch, 1944b) developed batteries of tests which they administered repeatedly to patients during the days or weeks following their head injuries. As I mentioned in Chapter 3, any pronounced deficit was chiefly restricted to a task that required the subjects to count backwards by sevens from 100. On repeated testing, there were slight improvements, most often on this subtraction test and a psychomotor search test. Ruesch (1944b, p. 494) inferred that as a result of head injury "mental speed is retarded, the ability to keep up a sustained effort is reduced, and judgment in general is defective".

Gronwall and Sampson (1974, p. 22) argued that the methods used by Ruesch confounded improvements due to the recovery of function with improvements due to practice. However, Ruesch et al. (1945) obtained similar results in comparing groups of patients tested at different times after head injury. Chadwick, Rutter, Brown, Shaffer, and Traub (1981) also argued that impairment could be inferred from subsequent improvement, but they had compared head-injured and orthopaedic patients who followed the same schedule of testing, thus enabling effects of recovery to be differentiated from effects of practice.

Ruesch (1944b) experimented with other tasks designed to assess mental speed (naming colours and reading the names of colours), spatial thinking ability, flicker-fusion threshold, and tachistoscopic recognition. He found no significant differences in performance on these tasks between 33 patients with simple concussion and 15 patients with more severe injuries. As Denny-Brown (1945b, p. 469) observed, these findings indicated "that the type of disorder early in the course of a mild head injury was not distinguishable from the type of disorder in a comparable stage of recovery from a severe injury with prolonged unconsciousness".

In subsequent work, Ruesch (1944a) evaluated simple visual reaction time and the tachistoscopic recognition of three-digit numbers among 25 patients with recent head injuries, 32 chronic cases with persistent post-traumatic symptoms, and 25 hospital employees as control subjects. The recently injured patients were found to be significantly impaired on both tasks, whereas the chronic cases were impaired in the case of simple visual reaction time but not in the case of tachiscopic recognition. A more recent study by Hannay, Levin, and Kay (1982) found that tachistocopic recognition tended to be related to the severity of closed head injury, as indexed by the duration of coma.

## An information-processing framework

Based on his experience with patients who had suffered brain damage as the result of gunshot wounds sustained during wartime (see Goldstein, 1942, chap. 5), Goldstein (1943) described a battery of psychological tasks based upon laboratory research that would be useful in evaluating cognitive disturbances after concussion. This comprised: a self-paced, continuous addition task in which subjects had to add together pairs of digits that were printed on a sheet of paper; tests of simple and choice reaction time; a block-design test of abstract thinking; and recognition of tachistoscopically presented words and objects.

The continuous addition task was intended to provide an index of the subject's "general performance capacity" (p. 331). For the reaction-time tasks, Goldstein, (1943, p. 232) provided the following rationale: "if the subject shows normal behavior in the single [i.e. simple] reaction test but definite deviation in the choice reaction test, both as to protracted reaction time and fluctuation with more or less errors, it is an indication of impairment of the higher mental capacities". Norrman and Svahn (1961) found that patients with severe closed head injuries were impaired on a three-choice reaction-time task, but not on a test of simple reaction time.

Choice reaction-time tasks came to be used frequently by experimental psychologists during the 1950s and 1960s. This was prompted by the analogy of the individual subject responding to external stimuli as akin to a communication channel that had a limited capacity for processing and transmitting information during a particular period of time (e.g. Broadbent, 1958). The classic demonstration of humans' limited information-processing capacity was Hick's law: the finding that response latencies in a choice-reaction-time experiment increased with the number of stimuli and more specifically that they varied as a logarithmic function of the number of alternatives (Hick, 1952).

Miller (1970) evaluated performance in this procedure in five patients with severe closed head injuries in whom PTA had lasted for more than a week; they were tested between three and twelve months after their injuries, when they had no residual motor deficits. These patients produced slower response latencies than a group of five normal control subjects, and the magnitude of their impairment varied directly with the number of possible alternative stimuli. Miller argued that the effect of a closed head injury was to slow down the individual's decision-making and information-processing abilities, and that this could not be attributed to any disruption of sensory or motor processes. This is clearly in accord with Ruesch's (1944b, p. 494) suggestion that "mental speed is retarded" in head-injured patients.

## Gronwall and Sampson's experiments

Gronwall and Sampson (1974) carried out a series of experiments to apply an information-processing analysis to performance in head-injured patients. Their first experiment employed a paced auditory serial addition task (PASAT: Sampson, 1956), in which subjects were presented with a random series of digits and were required to report the sum of each number and the number that had immediately preceded it. As Gronwall and Sampson noted (p. 26), "PASAT thus yields an estimate of the subject's ability to register sensory input, respond verbally, and retain and use a complex set of instructions. He must also hold each item after processing, retrieve the held item for addition to the next digit, and perform at an externally determined pace".

The task was administered to 10 cases of "mild concussion" in whom PTA had lasted for less than one hour and to 10 cases of "severe concussion" in whom PTA had lasted for between one hour and seven days. They were all tested within 48 hours of admission, as soon as they were capable of responding to simple questions, and testing was repeated every 24 hours until their discharge from hospital, with a final retest about five weeks later. Their performance was compared with that of

10 accident victims and 10 normal controls. All of the subjects were able to perform an unpaced version of the task without error, which suggested that the demands being made upon memory and general intellectual skills were within the capabilities of head-injured subjects.

However, the patients with severe concussion proved to be very impaired on the PASAT itself relative to the other three groups. The deficit was more pronounced at the first test, when half of these patients were still apparently in PTA (Gronwall & Sampson, 1974, pp. 33–34), but was still evident at the final retest. The patients with mild concussion were significantly impaired relative to the accident victims at the first test but not at the final retest. Unfortunately, as Miller (1979) noted, interpretation of these results is problematic, because performance on the PASAT shows large effects of practice (Barth et al., 1989; Newcombe et al., 1994; Sampson, 1961).

Comparable data from a much larger sample of 80 patients with minor closed head injuries were subsequently presented by Gronwall and Wrightson (1974). Seventy-five of these patients achieved PASAT scores within the normal range at a retest 30–35 days after their accidents, and the remaining five patients received an unspecified number of weekly retests until their scores, too, were within the normal range. This progressive improvement in performance was interpreted as a manifestation of the spontaneous process of recovery, but the possibility of practice effects was clearly as great as in the previous study. Gronwall and Sampson (1974) concluded from their results that concussion affected the rate of human information transmission.

Gronwall and Wrightson (1975) used the PASAT to evaluate the effects of multiple concussion upon information processing. They tested 20 head-injured patients with a history of previous head injury requiring hospital admission. Ten of these patients had suffered relatively mild injuries, with PTA lasting less than an hour, whereas the remaining patients had suffered more severe injuries, with PTA lasting for one to twenty-four hours. They were individually matched with 20 patients who had been admitted to hospital for the first time with injuries of similar severity. Unsurprisingly, when initially tested within 48 hours of their accidents, the head-injured patients were very impaired on the PASAT in comparison with a group of 60 normal control subjects.

In addition, the patients who had a history of a previous head injury were significantly impaired relative to those with no such history, both in terms of their initial performance on the PASAT and in terms of the time that elapsed before their performance approached normal levels. These results confirmed the earlier observation that even a minor closed head injury impairs human information-processing capacity, but they also imply that this impairment is both greater and longer-lasting among patients who have suffered a previous concussional head injury (although cf. Bijur, Haslum, & Golding, 1995).

Gronwall and Sampson (1974) argued that the reduced information-processing capacity of patients with mild concussion meant that they were unable to analyse incoming stimuli and simultaneously to amend their responses to previous stimuli. This implied that the effects of concussion might be simulated by making normal individuals engage in a concurrent secondary task that imposed demands upon their central processing capacity. Normal subjects were asked to carry out the PASAT while performing a two-choice reaction-time task. The pattern of results produced by subjects carrying out the PASAT with and without the secondary task was qualitatively similar to the results produced by patients with concussion tested on admission to hospital and at follow-up.

## Further research on choice reaction time

Van Zomeren and Deelman (1976) carried out further experiments on simple and choice reaction time. Head-injured patients were found to produce slower responses than normal controls, but the magnitude of this impairment varied with the complexity of the task and the duration of coma. Van Zomeren and Deelman (1978) obtained similar results in a two-year follow-up study, and they concluded that head injury influenced the rate of information transmission in the central nervous system (see also Zwaagstra, Schmidt, & Vanier, 1996).

Miller and Cruzat (1981) carried out a further study of the effects of irrelevant information on cognitive performance in patients with severe or minor closed head injury and normal controls. The subjects were required to sort packs of cards into two piles according to whether there was a letter A or a letter B on their faces. The cards in different packs contained zero, one, four, or eight irrelevant letters distributed at random across their faces. The time taken to sort a pack of cards increased with the amount of irrelevant information for all three groups of subjects. The patients with minor closed head injuries were not at all impaired on this task, whereas those with severe closed head injuries showed a substantial deficit. However, there was no sign of an interaction between the effects of head injury and of irrelevant information, and this was taken to mean that the relatively poor performance of the patients with severe head injuries was caused not by poor selective attention but rather by a central processing deficit.

Van Zomeren, Brouwer, and Deelman (1984) discussed the effects of closed head injury with reference to a theoretical distinction proposed by Shiffrin and Schneider (1977) between *automatic* and *controlled* information processing. Van Zomeren et al. argued that a reduced capacity for information processing might explain certain aspects of the deficits in learning and remembering shown by head-injured patients, although they acknowledged that residual memory deficits were occasionally seen in patients whose information-processing capacity (as determined from reaction-time tasks) was essentially normal. They also concluded that head-injured patients might be said to suffer from "attentional" deficits in the specific sense that they showed a slower rate of controlled processing, but that they showed no evidence of any deficits of focused or selective attention nor (apart from patients with very severe injuries) any deficits in tonic alertness in tasks demanding sustained attention. For ways of assessing these different aspects of attention, see van Zomeren and Brouwer (1992).

However, subsequent evidence relevant to the second half of this conclusion has proved equivocal (see Manly & Robertson, 1997; Ponsford & Kinsella, 1992). Robertson, Manly, Andrade, Baddeley, and Yiend (1997) devised a test in which subjects were required to respond to regularly presented digits, but to withhold their responses to specific, rarely presented targets (such as the digit 3). The number of errors (false presses) was greater in head-injured patients than in normal controls, but their responses were not significantly slower. The patients' scores varied with their tendency to show cognitive failures in daily life, as reported by their friends or relatives (although not with everyday cognitive failures reported by the patients themselves). Nevertheless, van Zomeren (1997) argued that this task demanded not just sustained attention but also strategic control in the inhibition of potentially automated reactions.

To try to clarify matters, Spikman, van Zomeren, and Deelman (1996) compared 60 severely head-injured patients and 60 healthy controls on a range of tasks designed to measure focused, divided, and sustained attention. In each case, the severely head-injured patients produced slower responses than the controls, but the difference was no longer significant when the researchers used analysis of covariance to control for the performance in a baseline condition supposedly measuring speed of information processing alone. Spikman et al. concluded that apparent deficits in focused, divided, and sustained attention were just a result of mental slowness.

Veltman, Brouwer, van Zomeren, and van Wolffelaar (1996) investigated the effect of irrelevant stimuli on reaction time. The presence of distracting stimuli increased the mean response latencies of both head-injured patients and healthy controls by roughly 30%, which suggested that there was no selective effect of distraction in the head-injured patients. Similar patterns of results were obtained by Spikman et al. (1996) and by Whyte, Fleming, Polansky, Cavallucci, and Coslett (1998).

Schmitter-Edgecombe and Kibby (1998) compared 20 patients who had sustained severe closed head injury at least one year and in the majority of cases at least five years before with 20 intact college students in their performance on a visual reaction-time task. The head-injured patients responded more slowly than the control subjects under all conditions, and their responses were disproportionately affected by the presence of irrelevant items when the location of the target was unknown or the targets were visually similar to the distractors. However, the patients did not produce significantly slower responses when the location of the target was known in advance and the targets were different from the distractors. Thus, severely head-injured patients may show impairment of focused attention in situations that demand visual search or where the discriminability of targets is low.

## Other studies of information processing

Gronwall and Wrightson (1981) carried out a factor analysis on the data obtained from 71 patients with closed head injury on the PASAT and the constituent subtests of the Wechsler Memory Scale (WMS; see Chapter 4). Of the three factors extracted, one showed significant loadings on the PASAT as well as on Personal Information and Orientation, but not on the other WMS subtests. The other factors were identified with (a) learning and memory and (b) general knowledge and verbal competence. Gronwall and Wrightson then administered the PASAT in a battery of tests to another 20 head-injured patients. Their PASAT scores were very highly correlated with those on the Visual Sequential Memory subtest from the Illinois Test of Psycholinguistic Abilities, but they were not significantly related to different measures of performance derived from a recall test using the selective reminding procedure. Gronwall and Wrightson concluded (p. 894) that the deficit in information processing "is related to performance in memory tasks only when the tasks require complex processing, or where time constraints are imposed".

Sunderland et al. (1983) gave a four-choice reaction-time test to 33 patients with severe head injuries between two and eight months after their accidents. To measure the motor component of this task, they also asked the subjects to press the response keys in rapid succession for 1min without reference to the stimuli. In comparison with the control group of 37 orthopaedic patients, the head-injured patients produced significantly longer latencies on both tasks. Nevertheless, the mean increase in choice reaction time was 113msec, whereas the increase in finger-tapping time was only 31msec. This suggests that most of the increase in the patients' choice reaction time was attributable to central (that is, cortical) factors rather than to peripheral (that is, motor) ones.

Gentilini et al. (1985) compared 50 patients with mild head injury (defined as a loss of consciousness lasting less than 20 minutes) tested one month after their accidents and 50 normal controls recruited from amongst their friends and relatives. The head-injured group was found to be significantly impaired on a visual search task in which they were required to cancel instances of one, two, or three digits from a 13 x 10 array. These patients were not however impaired on any of five other tests of memory and cognition, including a card-sorting task that made similar processing demands to the PASAT.

Subsequently, Gentilini, Nichelli, and Schoenhuber (1989) compared another group of 48 patients with mild head injury and 48 normal controls on their visual search task. When tested one month after their accidents, the groups differed significantly in their response times but not in their accuracy. In a further experiment, Gentilini et al. found that patients with mild head injury were significantly slowed in their choice reaction time for stimuli presented either to the left or to the right of a central fixation point. Although these researchers interpreted these findings in terms of "a specific impairment of attention"

(p. 174), they are actually much more consistent with the idea that head-injured patients suffer mainly from a reduced central information-processing capacity.

The study by Levin, Mattis, et al. (1987) considered 57 patients with minor closed head injuries and 56 normal controls in their performance on the PASAT. The head-injured patients were found to be impaired when tested a week after their accidents but not when retested one month or three months later. However, the increased performance of the head-injured patients on retesting may only have reflected the effects of practice on the PASAT, since the control subjects were tested on just one occasion. At the same time, because the control subjects were normal individuals who had not been involved in accidents, even the initial, transient deficit shown by the patients with closed head injuries can be ascribed to the generalised anxiety-producing effects of their involvement in a major accident that had necessitated rapid and unexpected hospitalisation (see also Waddell & Gronwall, 1984).

As I mentioned in the previous chapter, the matter of the appropriate comparison group was directly addressed by McMillan and Glucksman (1987). Their own study involved 24 patients with moderate head injuries (in whom PTA had lasted between one and twenty-four hours) and 20 patients with orthopaedic injuries, all tested within seven days of their accidents. The head-injured patients were found to be impaired on the PASAT when the digits were presented at a relatively fast rate (one every 2sec), but not when they were presented at a relatively slow rate (one every 4sec). This was taken to support the position that head-injured patients exhibited a reduced rate of information processing.

However, most of the head-injured patients in this study had been involved in road accidents or assaults, whereas most of the control patients had merely suffered falls (and all of them had sustained simple arm fractures or sprains). McMillan and Glucksman (1987) acknowledged that the impairment shown by their head-injured patients on the PASAT might have resulted from higher levels of anxiety associated with their involvement in more serious accidents. Consistent with this idea, 55% of the head-injured patients but only 32% of the orthopaedic patients were prescribed analgesic drugs during their hospitalisation.

Shum, McFarland, Bain, and Humphreys (1990) compared adult patients who had suffered severe or mild head injuries in their performance on a visual-spatial choice reaction-time task. This task was presumed to involve four information-processing stages (feature extraction, stimulus identification, response choice, and motor adjustment), and task variables were manipulated that were intended to have specific effects on each of these stages. The patients with mild head injuries were not impaired on this task. Patients tested within two years of suffering a severe head injury were significantly impaired in terms of identification, response selection, and motor execution, but those tested more than two years after a severe head injury were impaired only in terms of response selection and motor execution. Murray, Shum, and McFarland (1992) obtained similar findings in head-injured children, and Shum, McFarland, and Bain (1994) replicated their original results using a name-matching task.

Another study mentioned in the previous chapter was that of Newcombe et al. (1994), who tested 20 patients with minor head injuries and a control group consisting of 20 orthopaedic and surgical patients. They received a battery of tests within a few days of their admission, and 14 patients in both groups were retested a month later. The tests included a card-sorting task, a paced mental addition test, and the PASAT at two rates of presentation. There were no significant differences between the two groups on any of these tasks at either testing session.

## The Halstead–Reitan battery

The higher executive functions discussed so far in this chapter have often been linked by neuropsychologists to the anatomical structures of the frontal lobes, and a variety of psychological tests have been developed for measuring brain damage in these regions, usually with mixed success (see e.g. Lezak, 1982; Stuss & Benson, 1984; Walsh, 1978, chap. 4). For instance, the battery of tests developed by Halstead (1947) and revised by Reitan (1966) contains a number of subtests that are supposedly sensitive to frontal damage, including a complex sorting task, the Halstead Category Test (see Reitan, 1986, for a discussion of the battery's theoretical and methodological foundations). The proportion of tests in the battery on which a patient produces performance below a certain standard can also be used as a global index of impairment (Reitan & Davison, 1974).

Dikmen and Reitan (1976) administered the Halstead–Reitan battery to 34 patients with "significant head injuries" soon after their accidents and again 12 and 18 months later (see also Dikmen, Reitan, & Temkin, 1983). Most of the psychometric measures derived from the battery showed an initial impairment followed by highly significant improvements across the three testing sessions, especially during the first 12 months. To control for practice effects, a subgroup of 23 patients was compared with normal control subjects matched for educational level who received a similar schedule of testing. The degree of improvement shown by the head-injured patients was generally greater than the effects of practice shown by the control subjects, significantly so in seven of the fourteen measures studied.

Dye, Milby, and Saxon (1979) compared 48 head-injured patients in whom the duration of coma had been on average two days with 16 other accident victims who had not sustained head injuries. The two groups were significantly different on most of the subtests and on the overall impairment index of the Halstead–Reitan battery, and the degree of impairment on the part of the head-injured patients was a direct function of their initial neurological status. Long and Webb (1983) also described impaired performance on the Halstead–Reitan battery in patients with closed head injuries. They concluded (p. 56) that the battery "appears to be highly sensitive to the type of impairment experienced by head trauma patients and to subtle effects present during the chronic phase of recovery that are not directly observable".

Rimel et al. (1981) presented preliminary findings from an assessment of 69 patients roughly three months after they had sustained minor closed head injuries associated with a period of coma not exceeding 20 minutes, a Glasgow Coma Scale score on admission of 13 or more, and a period of hospitalisation of 48 hours or less. They concluded (p. 226) that "mild neuropsychological impairment was evident on the vast majority of the Halstead–Reitan Neuropsychological Test Procedures, including the tests of higher level cognitive functioning, new problem-solving skills, and attention and concentration".

Stewart, Kaylor, and Koutanis (1996) used the Halstead–Reitan battery to assess 36 patients just one week after they had sustained minor head injury. All the patients had had Glasgow Coma Scale scores of 15 at initial presentation, and none had abnormal radiological findings or a history of prior admission to hospital. Even so, 15 (or 42%) of these patients were judged to have either mild or moderate cognitive deficits according to their overall impairment index. The only clinical sign at presentation significantly associated with cognitive impairment was defective performance on the "finger–nose" test, which is normally regarded as a sign of cerebellar dysfunction. Stewart et al. speculated that both deficits might result from diffuse axonal injury involving the cerebral hemispheres and the posterior fossa (i.e. the cerebellum and the brainstem).

## Further research on higher executive functions

Other tasks designed to evaluate the functioning of the frontal lobes include Nelson's (1976) modified card-sorting test, Benton's (1968) test of verbal fluency, in which subjects are required to produce as many words as possible beginning with a specified letter within 1min, and an analogous test of design fluency (Jones-Gotman & Milner, 1977), in which subjects are required to invent novel designs.

Levin, Amparo, et al. (1987) used these three tasks to compare 20 patients with minor closed head injuries and 13 normal control subjects. The performance of the head-injured patients at their initial assessment (on average nine days after their injuries) proved to be significantly impaired on all three tasks. The amount of damage to the frontal lobes, as estimated by means of magnetic resonance imaging (MRI), showed a significant negative correlation with performance on the design fluency test, but not with performance on the other two tasks. Nevertheless, performance on all three of the tests showed a significant relationship with the amount of damage to the *temporal* lobes.

Impaired performance on the modified card-sorting test in patients tested some years after severe closed head injury was found by Levin and Goldstein (1986), and a similar impairment during the subacute phase of recovery (in practice, between 15 and 55 days after injury) was found by Spikman et al. (1996). Chadwick et al. (Chadwick, Rutter, Brown, Shaffer, & Traub, 1981; Chadwick, Rutter, Shaffer, & Shrout, 1981) found no sign of any impairment in verbal fluency among severely injured children tested a year after their accidents. However, Levin et al. (1993)

found that younger children (six to ten years) tested one to two years after severe head injuries were impaired on card sorting, verbal fluency, and design fluency.

Anderson, Bigler, and Blatter (1995) also found that patients with head injuries of varying degrees of severity were impaired on the Halstead Category Test and a card-sorting test. Nevertheless, there were no significant differences between the patients who had lesions of the frontal lobes according to MRI and the patients with no such lesions. Anderson et al. argued that impaired performance on these tests reflected diffuse pathology in head-injured patients and was not diagnostic of frontal damage. However, Levin, Song, et al. (1997) confirmed that severely injured children were impaired in card sorting when tested after an average of five years, and they found that this was more pronounced in those with damage to the frontal lobes.

One further task that has been used to measure processing speed and response selection is the colour–word test devised by Stroop (1935). This requires subjects to read aloud the names of colours and to name the colour of ink in which stimuli are printed. Their response latencies are found to be slower (more so in the second condition) when the stimuli are the names of colours printed in a different colour of ink, and this effect is usually attributed to competition or interference between the two alternative responses that are evoked by the stimuli.

Van Zomeren (1981, pp. 83, 86) mentioned two unpublished studies (one with adults, the other with children) showing that head-injured patients were impaired to roughly the same extent across the various conditions of the Stroop test. This implies that closed head injuries give rise to a reduced capacity for information processing but do not have any specific effect on attentional selectivity (see Spikman et al., 1996). However, Chadwick, Rutter, Brown, Shaffer, and Traub (1981) and Chadwick, Rutter, Thompson, and Shaffer (1981) found that neither severely nor mildly injured children were significantly impaired on this task at a follow-up session one year after their accidents.

In short, in patients with minor closed head injury, it is possible to demonstrate a persistent disturbance of cognitive function that affects their performance in a wide variety of intellectual tasks and which can be attributed to a reduction in their central processing capacity. The tasks in question include several psychometric tests intended to be sensitive to lesions of the frontal lobes, and this is entirely consistent with what is known about the probable sites of cortical damage following head injury (Mattson & Levin, 1990; see Chapter 2). Although the deficits may be relatively subtle, it will be noted in the next section that they may have an impact upon patients' cognitive performance in daily life. In particular, the effort involved in endeavouring to maintain the previous level of work performance in the face of a reduced processing capacity may in turn lead to increased fatigue or avoidance of social activity.

Among patients with severe closed head injury there tends to be an even more pronounced and widespread impairment of their cognitive abilities (e.g. Vigouroux et al., 1971). This impairment may extend even to simple mental abilities, such as counting backwards and giving items of general information (Brooks, 1976; Conkey, 1938), and in very severe cases can constitute a persistent condition of post-traumatic dementia (Denny-Brown, 1945b; Symonds, 1937). The latter was well documented as a progressive and relatively stereotyped disorder among ex-professional boxers before the introduction of stricter medical controls in boxing (Roberts, 1969).

When considered across all head-injured patients, the magnitude and extent of intellectual impairment are related to several prognostic indicators. First, the degree of cognitive deficit tends to be correlated with the duration of coma (see Brink, Garrett, Hale, Woo-Sam, & Nickel, 1970; Levin & Eisenberg, 1979a, 1979b; Levin, Grossman, & Kelly, 1977b; Ruesch, 1944b; van Zomeren & Deelman, 1976, 1978; Winogron et al., 1984). However, Kløve and Cleeland (1972) found that this relationship applied only within the first three months following the head injury, and that it was no longer significant when the effects of other clinical variables were taken into account. Zwaagstra et al. (1996) found that patients with longer coma durations were more impaired but showed faster recovery than less severely injured patients.

Second, the degree of cognitive impairment after closed head injury may be related to the depth of coma on admission to hospital according to the Glasgow Coma Scale (Anderson et al., 1995; Levin & Eisenberg, 1979a, 1979b; Winogron et al., 1984; cf. Zwaagstra et al., 1996). Third, the degree of deficit is related to the duration of PTA (Chadwick, Rutter, Brown, Shafer, & Traub, 1981; Gronwall & Sampson, 1974, Exp. I; Gronwall & Wrightson, 1981; Klonoff & Paris, 1974; Ruesch, 1944b; van Zomeren & Deelman, 1978). Finally, the degree of cognitive deficit is related to the incidence of intracranial haematomas, positive neurological signs, electroencephalographic abnormalities or abnormalities revealed by computerised tomography (CT), but not to the incidence of skull fractures or measures of acute intracranial pressure (Dye et al., 1979; Kløve & Cleeland, 1972; Levin et al., 1977b; Ruesch, 1944b; Ruesch & Moore, 1943; Smith-Seemiller et al., 1997; van Zomeren & Deelman, 1978; Winogron et al., 1984).

## Executive control in head-injured patients

In Chapter 4, I mentioned that Baddeley and Hitch (1974) had postulated that working memory consisted of a central executive processor together with two "slave" systems responsible for the temporary storage of verbal and visuospatial information. In developing the notion of a central executive, Baddeley (1986, chap. 10) adopted an existing account of the control of action that had been devised by Norman and Shallice (1982/1986; Shallice, 1982). This account incorporated a limited-capacity supervisory attentional system, which served as the locus of conscious control in tasks involving planning or decision making or in problematic situations. Consequently, the processing capacity of this system could be occupied by an irrelevant task that demanded the organised planning of ongoing behaviour.

The main example of such a task given by Baddeley was that of the random generation of sequences of digits or letters of the alphabet.

Shallice (1982) had originally proposed that impairment of this system would generate the pattern of behavioural deficits usually associated with damage to the frontal lobes, a pattern that Baddeley (1986, p. 238) characterised as the "dysexecutive syndrome". However, it was subsequently acknowledged that poor performance on so-called "frontal" tests was not unequivocally linked either to frontal lesions or to behavioural disturbances in patients who did have frontal damage (Baddeley, Della Sala, Papagno, & Spinnler, 1997; Shallice & Burgess, 1991). Nowadays, "executive function" is typically used to refer to the forms of controlled processing that are tapped by frontal tests without assuming that performance in these tasks depends critically and solely on neural structures in the frontal lobes (see Baddeley & Della Sala, 1996; Tranel, Anderson, & Benton, 1994).

A task that was devised specifically to measure executive function is the Tower of London, in which the participants are required to rearrange a number of disks placed on various rods in order to achieve a specified goal pattern (Shallice, 1982). Veltman et al. (1996) found that severely head-injured patients were unimpaired on this task, whereas Ponsford and Kinsella (1992) found deficits in solution time rather than errors, which they interpreted as a general effect upon processing speed rather a specific impairment of executive function. Nevertheless, Levin et al. (1993, 1994; Levin, Song, et al., 1997) found that children with severe head injury were less accurate than children with mild head injury or controls; this impairment was more pronounced among younger children and tended to vary with the amount of damage to the frontal lobes according to MRI. Moreover, the patients tested by Veltman et al. (1996) were impaired on a driving simulator test that involved continuously changing task demands.

A different strategy is to examine the role of the central executive in coordinating different activities by requiring the participants to carry out two tasks simultaneously. The use of dual-task methodologies appears to be important from a clinical point of view, because impaired performance is associated with gross disturbances of executive function in everyday activities (Baddeley et al., 1997). Spikman et al. (1996) combined visual and auditory reaction-time tasks, and found that the response latencies of severely injured patients could be predicted from their response latencies on the separate tasks. Veltman et al. (1996) obtained similar results when they combined the driving simulator task with a visual reaction-time task. They ascribed these results to a generalised mental slowing.

Azouvi, Jokic, Van Der Linden, Marlier, and Bussel (1996) carried out two experiments in which patients with severe head injuries and normal controls were asked to carry out cognitive tasks with and without concurrent random number generation. In the first experiment, the task in question was the Stroop task. When tested on each task in isolation, the patients were slower than the normal controls. Under dual-task conditions, there was a comparable slowing of responses in both groups on both tasks. In the second experiment, the additional task was card sorting, and the Trail Making Test was used to obtain a separate measure of processing speed. Under dual-task conditions, there was no overall difference between the two groups in random generation when their processing speed was statistically controlled, but the patients were still slower at card sorting than the normal controls, and the difference between the groups increased with the complexity of the sorting task. Clearly, all these results can be handled by the parsimonious hypothesis that head-injured patients have a reduced information-processing capacity.

## VERBAL AND NONVERBAL INTELLIGENCE

### The Wechsler Adult Intelligence Scale

In neuropsychological assessment, the obvious way to evaluate acquired disorders of cognitive function is by means of formal psychometric testing on standardised intelligence scales. The most widely used test is the Wechsler Adult Intelligence Scale (WAIS: Wechsler, 1955). As I mentioned in Chapter 3, this test consists of 11 subtests:

| *Verbal subtests* | *Performance subtests* |
|---|---|
| Information | Digit Symbol |
| Comprehension | Picture Completion |
| Arithmetic | Block Design |
| Similarities | Picture Arrangement |
| Digit Span | Object Assembly |
| Vocabulary | |

The raw scores on the individual subtests are transformed into a common scale between 0 and 19, and the total of the scaled scores is converted to an Intelligence Quotient (IQ) by comparison with the total scores achieved by a standardisation sample of the appropriate age-range. Separate Verbal and Performance IQs may be obtained by summing the scaled scores on the relevant subtests, or else a Full Scale IQ may be derived from the scaled scores on all 11 subtests. In 1981, the Wechsler Adult Intelligence Scale—Revised (WAIS-R; Wechsler, 1981) was published; some of the original test items were replaced, the order of the constituent subtests was changed, and a new set of population norms was produced.

In the earliest study of this sort, Ruesch (1944b) gave four tests from the Wechsler–Bellevue Intelligence Scale (the predecessor to the WAIS: Wechsler, 1944) to 70 patients between one and three months after closed head injuries. The mean IQ prorated from the scaled scores on these four tests was 94.5, which was essentially what was expected on the basis of the patients' educational background. Cole (1945) reported preliminary findings from 119 patients in the same series when they were similarly tested on portions of the Wechsler–Bellevue Intelligence Scale roughly six months after their discharge from hospital. Only four cases achieved poorer performance than had been expected on the basis of their educational background, and in each case the patient's psychiatric history cast some doubt on the validity of the latter estimate.

Ruesch et al. (1945) employed a slightly different set of four subtests from the Wechsler–Bellevue to assess 128 patients with head injuries. The mean prorated IQ was 96 in the case of 49 patients tested within four weeks of their accidents and 107 in the case of 79 patients tested more than four weeks (in most cases more than one year) after their accidents. The difference between these means was statistically significant, but both are within the normal range.

Dailey (1956) administered the entire Wechsler–Bellevue Intelligence Scale to 31 patients with post-traumatic epilepsy about five years after their head injuries. No results were presented concerning their Full Scale IQs, but their Verbal IQs were found to be negatively related to the duration of post-traumatic unconsciousness, even when variations in their premorbid intellectual status were taken into account by controlling for the number of years of education. Black (1973) administered the WAIS to 50 patients with closed head injuries and obtained an average Full Scale IQ of 84.5; as I mentioned in Chapter 4, this was significantly poorer than the mean IQ achieved by 50 cases with penetrating brain injuries and significantly poorer than the population mean of 100.

Bond (1975, 1976) reported findings on the WAIS from 40 patients with severe head injury at intervals between three and more than twenty-four months after their accidents. Those who were tested within the first six months showed a pronounced decrement in Full Scale IQ that varied with the duration of PTA. Subsequently, those patients in whom PTA had lasted for less than 12 weeks achieved mean IQs that were within the normal range; however, those in whom PTA had lasted for more than 12 weeks continued to demonstrate impaired performance with little sign of any restitution of function.

Dye et al. (1979) found a mean Full Scale IQ of 88.0 on the WAIS among 48 head-injured patients, but a mean IQ of 101.3 among 16 control patients drawn from other accident victims who had not sustained head injuries. Levin, Grossman, Sarwar, and Meyers (1981) assessed 21 patients with severe head injury who had been aphasic during their initial hospitalisation. Those who showed a persistent generalised disruption of language function at least six months later were substantially impaired in terms of both their Verbal IQ and their Performance IQ, whereas those whose language function had returned to normal showed no sign of any deficit on the WAIS. Rimel et al. (1981) administered the WAIS to 69 patients with minor closed head injuries roughly three months after their accidents; no quantitative data were presented, but they apparently found "no significant differences from established norms" (p. 226).

In contrast, Timming et al. (1982) assessed 30 patients with severe head injuries before their discharge roughly 13 weeks following their accidents and found an average Full Scale IQ among the 19 patients who completed the WAIS of only 76.3. When considering five cases of chronic global amnesia resulting from closed head injuries, Corkin et al. (1985) found an average Full Scale IQ on the WAIS or the WAIS-R of 98.0, which was taken to be within the normal range. Finally, Solomon et al. (1986) reported a mean Full Scale IQ of 93.85 in 126 patients with closed head injury; this reflects a significant impairment for the sample as a whole, even though such a score would be within normal limits for an individual patient.

Some researchers have focused upon particular subtests of the WAIS. This has been motivated partly by the practical need to reduce the amount of time that would otherwise need to be devoted to administering the test in its entirety. With this aim in mind, various proposals have been made for abbreviating both the WAIS (e.g. Levy, 1968; Maxwell, 1957) and the WAIS-R (e.g. Cyr & Brooker, 1984; Roth, Hughes, Monkowski, & Crosson, 1984; Silverstein, 1982). As I mentioned earlier, Ruesch (1944b) gave four subtests from the Wechsler–Bellevue Intelligence Scale (Similarities, Comprehension, Block Design, and Digit Symbol) to 70 patients between one and three months after closed head injuries.

In a similar manner, Reynell (1944) selected six subtests from those described by Wechsler (1941): three of these tests (Vocabulary, General Information, and General Comprehension) were chosen because they were expected to be relatively insensitive to brain damage, whereas the other three (Arithmetic Reasoning, Digit Retention, and Similarities) were chosen because they were expected to be particularly sensitive to brain damage. These tests were administered to 520 military personnel with head injuries (of whom 95% were cases of closed head injury), and Full Scale IQs were prorated from performance on each set of tests. In 117 patients, most of whom were cases of moderate or severe head injury (in the sense that they had suffered a period of PTA lasting at least a few hours), the two estimates of IQ differed by 10 points or more. The most obvious deterioration was in the ability to repeat sequences of digits backwards (cf. Lezak, 1979). Similar results were obtained by Tooth (1947).

Somewhat different findings were obtained in a more recent study by Levin and Goldstein (1986), who compared 12 patients with severe closed head injury and 10 normal controls. These head-injured patients were found to be significantly impaired in terms of their age-corrected scores on the Comprehension, Information, and Digit Span subtests of the WAIS-R, though not on the Similarities subtest. Not surprisingly, they were also significantly impaired in terms of their Verbal IQs, prorated from their performance on these four subtests. Indeed, their average Verbal IQ of 86.7 was found to be 16.7 points below their average premorbid Verbal IQ, estimated from their age, race, sex, education, and occupation, and across individual cases the degree of estimated intellectual deterioration tended to increase with the duration of impaired consciousness.

Levin, Mattis, et al. (1987) similarly compared 57 cases of minor closed head injury (defined as a loss of consciousness lasting 20 minutes or less) with 56 normal controls on the Digit Span and Digit Symbol subtests of the WAIS. The head-injured patients were found to be significantly impaired on both tasks when tested within a week of their accidents, but not when retested one month or three months later.

However, as I mentioned earlier in this chapter, the initial impairment shown by the head-injured patients in this study can be ascribed to the generalised anxiety-producing effects of their involvement in a major accident, and their subsequent improvement might merely reflect the results of practice. McMillan and Glucksman (1987) found no sign of any difference in performance on an abbreviated version of the WAIS-R administered within seven days of the accident between 24 patients who had sustained a moderate head injury and 20 patients who had sustained an orthopaedic injury.

## Verbal IQ and Performance IQ

Wechsler's distinction between Verbal IQ and Performance IQ was based upon an a priori classification of the relevant subtests, and was not necessarily intended to correspond to qualitatively distinct forms of cognitive function. Nevertheless, it received empirical confirmation from results of factor analyses carried out upon the subtest scores obtained by samples of participants on the WAIS (Maxwell, 1960) and the WAIS-R (Atkinson, Cyr, Doxey, & Vigna, 1989; Canavan, Dunn, & McMillan, 1986), as well as the responses to individual items (Beck et al., 1989). Vigouroux et al. (1971) found that patients with severe closed head injury were impaired on both Verbal IQ and Performance IQ, and they concluded (p. 337) that "the disturbance led to a generalized modification of mental functions". However, subsequent research has suggested that Performance IQs are more vulnerable to disruption following closed head injury than are Verbal IQs.

Becker (1975) carried out a particularly well-designed study in which 10 head-injured patients were compared with a control group that consisted of hospital staff and orthopaedic patients. Since the head-injured patients had been enlisted in the US Navy, their premorbid IQs could be estimated from the General Classification Test scores that they had obtained on induction into service. It was therefore possible to show that the control group was well matched on this variable as well as other pertinent characteristics. The WAIS was administered to each head-injured patient within 2 weeks of their accidents and again about 10–11 weeks later. The control subjects were also tested on two occasions with the same intervening interval. The results are shown in Table 5.1.

The first point to note about these results is that the head-injured patients were impaired relative to the control subjects in terms of their Full Scale IQs and in terms of most of the constituent subtests, but that this impairment was rather more pronounced in the case of the Performance subtests than in the case of the Verbal subtests. This pattern of results has been obtained in other studies, which have also shown that Performance IQs show a clearer correlation with independent neurological measures of the severity of a closed head injury than Verbal IQs (Bond, 1975, 1976; Corkin et al., 1985; Dye et al., 1979; Kløve & Cleeland, 1972; Kunishio et al., 1993; Levin, Eisenberg, et al., 1982; Mandleberg, 1975, 1976; Mandleberg & Brooks, 1975; Prigatano et al., 1984; Timming et al., 1982; cf. McMillan &

TABLE 5.1

Mean IQ and subtest scores for head-injured patients and controls on two successive administrations of the Wechsler Adult Intelligence Scale

| | *Head-injured* | | *Control* | |
|---|---|---|---|---|
| | *Original* | *Retest* | *Original* | *Retest* |
| Information | 9.1 | 9.5 | 10.8 | 11.2 |
| Comprehension | 8.6 | 10.5 | 11.5 | 12.6 |
| Arithmetic | 8.2 | 9.5 | 9.7 | 10.6 |
| Similarities | 8.7 | 10.1 | 11.9 | 12.5 |
| Digit span | 8.2 | 9.9 | 11.0 | 11.1 |
| Vocabulary | 9.6 | 10.3 | 11.1 | 11.3 |
| Verbal IQ | 93.7 | 100.7 | 106.0 | 109.2 |
| Digit symbol | 6.4 | 8.0 | 11.4 | 12.7 |
| Picture completion | 8.5 | 10.9 | 11.3 | 11.9 |
| Block design | 6.6 | 9.9 | 11.6 | 11.8 |
| Picture arrangement | 7.3 | 8.9 | 9.7 | 11.1 |
| Object assembly | 6.1 | 8.9 | 11.8 | 13.3 |
| Performance IQ | 80.3 | 95.7 | 107.1 | 113.5 |
| Full scale IQ | 87.1 | 98.4 | 106.9 | 111.9 |

From "Intellectual changes after closed head injury," by B. Becker (1975), *Journal of Clinical Psychology, 31*, p. 308. Copyright 1975 by Clinical Psychology Publishing Co., Inc. Reprinted by permission of John Wiley & Sons, Inc.

Glucksman, 1987; Solomon et al., 1986). Similar results have been obtained in studies of intellectual deficits in head-injured children (Chadwick, Rutter, Brown, Shaffer, & Traub, 1981; Chadwick, Rutter, Shaffer, & Shrout, 1981; Chadwick, Rutter, Thompson, & Shaffer, 1981; Winogron et al., 1984; cf. Woo-Sam, Zimmerman, Brink, Uyehara, & Miller, 1970) that have used the Wechsler Intelligence Scale for Children (WISC: Wechsler, 1949).

Other researchers have used the Mill Hill Vocabulary Scale (Raven, 1962) together with Raven's (1960) Progressive Matrices Test. This is a nonverbal test of problem solving and reasoning that requires the ability to conceptualise spatial or numerical relationships of an abstract nature. Head-injured patients show a pronounced impairment on the Progressive Matrices Test that increases with the severity of their injury according to the duration of PTA, whereas they show much less impairment on the Mill Hill Vocabulary Scale in comparison with orthopaedic control patients (Brooks & Aughton, 1979a, 1979b; Sunderland et al., 1983) or with published normative data (Brooks et al., 1980; cf. Bond & Brooks, 1976). Nevertheless, Gentilini et al. (1985) found no impairment in the performance of 50 patients tested one month after sustaining minor head injuries on the Progressive Matrices test in comparison with a control group drawn from their friends and relatives.

The second point is that both of the groups of subjects in Becker's (1975) study showed a significant improvement on all three IQ measures but that the improvement demonstrated by the head-injured patients was not significantly greater than that shown by the control subjects. As Becker himself commented

(p. 307), "This suggests, of course, that much of the 'improvement' shown on retesting with the WAIS over relatively short time intervals must be attributed to practice and the experience of having taken the test". Indeed, the improvement shown by the head-injured patients was significantly greater than that shown by the control subjects on only two of the 11 subtests (Digit Span and Block Design). This outcome could be ascribed not to any particularly conspicuous improvement in the case of Becker's head-injured sample, but to the fact that his control sample showed no improvement on these subtests at all.

However, some factor analyses carried out on the subtest scores obtained by samples of participants on the WAIS-R found clear evidence for a third factor (variously termed "attention/concentration" and "freedom from distractibility"), with loadings on the Digit Span, Arithmetic, and Digit Symbol subtests (Atkinson et al., 1989; Crawford, 1992; Crawford, Allan, Stephen, Parker, & Besson, 1989; cf. Spreen & Strauss, 1998, p. 98). Crawford, Johnson, Mychalkiw, and Moore (1997) observed that the most pronounced deficits shown by patients with closed head injury on the WAIS-R seemed to occur precisely on the subtests defining the attention/concentration factor.

To test this idea, Crawford et al. (1989) compared 233 patients hospitalised following head injury and a control group of 117 normal individuals matched for age, sex, and education in their estimated scores on the three hypothesised factors underlying the WAIS-R. The difference between the means of the two groups was nonsignificant on the verbal factor, but significant on the performance factor and highly significant on the factor that was concerned with attention/concentration. This indicates that the deficits shown by head-injured patients on the WAIS-R vary with the information-processing demands of different subtests, and there is some independent support for this idea. Deary, Langan, Hepburn, and Frier (1991) found in people with Type 1 (insulin-dependent) diabetes mellitus that scores on the PASAT loaded highly on the attention/concentration factor, but not on the verbal or performance factors. Crawford, Obansawin, and Allan (1998) obtained similar results in normal individuals.

In other clinical populations, there is some evidence of yet a fourth factor, which has been termed "processing speed" (Spreen & Strauss, 1998, p. 99). The multifactorial structure of this instrument has recently been acknowledged in a third edition, the WAIS-III. This incorporates three new subtests and provides separate measures of verbal comprehension, perceptual organisation, working memory, and processing speed, as well as measures of Verbal and Performance IQ (Wechsler, 1997a). As was mentioned in the previous chapter, the WAIS-III was developed and standardised alongside the third edition of the WMS.

## The left hemisphere and the right hemisphere

The distinction between the Verbal and Performance subtests of the WAIS is of theoretical interest, because it is commonly thought to map onto the functional asymmetry of the cerebral cortex. In particular, achievement in the Verbal subtests is assumed to depend upon the neural structures located within the cerebral hemisphere that is "dominant" or specialised for language function (normally the left hemisphere), whereas achievement in the Performance subtests is assumed to depend more upon neural structures within the nondominant cerebral hemisphere (normally the right hemisphere).

Consequently, differential performance on the two groups of subtests by patients with neurological deficits should be very informative as to the anatomical lateralisation of the underlying lesions. However, until the advent of sophisticated medical imaging technology, the empirical evidence for this interpretation of the Verbal–Performance distinction was quite unconvincing (see Walsh, 1978, pp. 291–292), and it was really little more than a convenient myth within psychometric testing. Early investigations relating scores on intelligence tests with the results of computerised tomography (CT) were not reassuring (e.g. Warrington, James, & Maciejewski, 1986; Wood, 1979).

Uzzell, Zimmerman, Dolinskas, and Obrist (1979) compared CT findings and WAIS results in 26 patients with head injuries of varying degrees of severity. The mean Verbal IQ and Performance IQ for the eight patients with CT evidence of a left-hemisphere lesion were 72.1 and 80.8, respectively, whereas the mean Verbal and Performance IQs for the 13 patients with CT evidence of a right-hemisphere lesion were 96.4 and 78.9, respectively. The two groups differed significantly in terms of their Verbal IQs but not in terms of their Performance IQs. A detailed analysis of the patients' age-corrected scaled scores on the individual subtests confirmed that the Verbal subtests differentiated the patients with left-sided and right-sided lesions, whereas the Performance subtests did not.

Nevertheless, similar results were not found in a study of head-injured children reported by Chadwick, Rutter, Thompson, and Shaffer (1981). Each of these patients had sustained a unilateral compound depressed skull fracture, which resulted in a torn dura and surgically verified damage to the underlying cerebral hemisphere (to the left hemisphere in 44 cases and to the right hemisphere in 53 cases). They were assessed on a test battery that contained four Verbal subtests and four Performance subtests from the WISC, and the results were prorated to generate estimates of Verbal and Performance IQ. There was no significant difference between the cases with left-hemisphere damage and those with right-hemisphere damage with regard to Verbal IQ, Performance IQ, or any of the constituent subtests. Few of the remaining measures in the test battery produced a significant difference between children with damage to the left and right hemispheres.

Levin, Eisenberg, et al. (1982) obtained similar results in comparing severely injured children and adolescents in whom mass lesions had been visualised by CT within the left or right hemispheres. Moreover, in a sample of head-injured patients between 5 and 75 years of age, Kunishio et al. (1993) found no difference at all in either Verbal IQ or Performance IQ between those with left-sided damage and those with right-sided damage according to CT. Patients with bilateral lesions were more impaired than those with unilateral lesions.

## DISORDERS OF LANGUAGE

### Aphasic disturbances

The classification of aphasia is a complicated topic to which it is impossible to do justice in this book. My approach will focus on the Boston classification, because this has been most influential in research on the effects of closed head injuries.

A detailed prospective study of aphasic disorders beyond the phase of PTA was reported by Heilman et al. (1971). All patients who were admitted to a major city hospital during a 10-month period with a diagnosis of closed head trauma received an aphasia screening examination once they were alert and cooperative. Those who showed any deficit underwent further study and were assigned to a number of diagnostic categories (p. 266, italics added):

> *Anomic aphasia* was defined as a fluent aphasia in which the patient demonstrates verbal paraphasias and circumlocutions, has normal comprehension and repetition, and has abnormal naming for all kinds of material especially to confrontation. *Wernicke's aphasia* was defined as a fluent aphasia with paraphasia, poor comprehension for spoken and written language, and poor repetition. *Broca's aphasia* was defined as non-fluent aphasia with good comprehension, which may improve slightly in repetition, series speech, and singing. *Global aphasia* was defined as a non-fluent aphasia with poor comprehension, poor repetition, and poor naming. *Conduction aphasia* was defined as a fluent aphasia with literal paraphasia, good comprehension, but very poor repetition and impaired naming. We defined *the syndrome of the isolated speech area* as a fluent aphasia with poor comprehension, but with excellent repetition and echolalia.

Out of the consecutive series of 750 head-injured patients, just 15 cases of aphasia were identified. One of these was excluded from further study because he met the diagnostic criteria only when lethargic, not when alert. A second patient was excluded because surgical treatment had been carried out before the aphasiological examination. Of the other thirteen patients, nine had an anomic aphasia, while four had a Wernicke's aphasia, and no other type of aphasia was seen.

As implied in the definition quoted previously from Heilman et al. (1971), anomic aphasia (also described as *amnesic*, *amnestic*, or *nominal aphasia*) is a relatively specific disorder of language function that is marked by an inability to identify objects or people by their names. This can typically be demonstrated in formal tests of object naming ("naming to confrontation"), but may also be reflected in a patient's spontaneous conversational speech. In both cases, various kinds of anomic errors may be produced (see Levin, 1981, for examples).

In contrast to this pronounced difficulty in word finding, the patient's ability both to comprehend and to repeat aloud spoken utterances may be essentially normal, as is illustrated by the individual cases described by Heilman et al. (1971). Moreover, through either the nature of the errors or the accompanying gestures and actions, it may well be apparent that the patient understands perfectly well the use or function of the objects in question. On the other hand, Benson and Geschwind (1967) stressed that anomic aphasia after closed head injury was a generalised naming deficit that was not restricted to specific classes of objects or stimuli. They also argued that it was a direct consequence of focal brain damage and not simply one manifestation of memory disturbances, on the grounds that most patients with severe post-traumatic memory dysfunction do not suffer from anomic disorders. As an extreme example, Corkin et al. (1985) found no pronounced deficits of speech comprehension or production among patients with chronic global amnesia resulting from closed head injury.

Wernicke's aphasia (also described as *receptive* or *sensory aphasia*) is marked by an inability to comprehend both spoken language and written language (dyslexia). Among patients with severe closed head injuries it may be characterised by an impaired ability to repeat spoken utterances and by relatively fluent (indeed, unusually voluble) spontaneous speech in which incorrect words or phrases or even frank neologisms have been substituted (paraphasia). Newcombe (1982) has however noted the difficulty of giving an accurate assessment of a head-injured patient's problems in the area of speech comprehension.

Subsequent research has confirmed that anomic aphasia and Wernicke's aphasia are the most common disorders of language in head-injured patients, whereas other forms of disorder are very uncommon. In particular, although it has been suggested that Broca's aphasia may result from closed head injury (Bakay & Glasauer, 1980, p. 108), this condition has been observed rarely if at all in the detailed clinical examination of consecutive series of patients (Levin et al., 1976a; Thomsen, 1975, 1976). One case of post-traumatic conduction aphasia (which as mentioned earlier is marked by a disproportionate impairment in repetition tasks) was reported by Warrington and Shallice (1970; Warrington et al., 1971; see Chapter 4). Nevertheless, performance in tests of sentence repetition is normally preserved in cases of head injury (Levin et al., 1976; Levin & Eisenberg, 1979a; Levin, Grossman, et al., 1981).

The results obtained by Heilman et al. (1971) indicate that clinical aphasia is relatively rare following closed head injury, occurring in about 2% of all hospital admissions. A previous study by Arseni, Constantinovici, Iliescu, Dobrotá, and Gagea (1970) had similarly found just 34 cases of aphasia in a consecutive series of 1544 head-injured patients. These tended to be the consequence of assaults or accidental injury with a variety of objects rather than of traffic accidents or other causes (cf. Thomsen, 1974). The focal nature of the resulting brain damage was also shown by the high proportion (71%) of these cases who had required surgical intervention for intracranial haematoma. Arseni et al. suggested in particular that post-traumatic aphasia was generally associated with lesions of the parietal lobe of the dominant hemisphere.

Heilman et al. (1971) reported that seven of their thirteen aphasic patients had received a blow to the right orbito-frontal region of the cranium, whereas four had received blows to the left temporo-parietal region, and two had no external evidence of trauma, though there seemed to be no relation between the site of impact and the nature of the aphasic disorder that ensued. Heilman et al. speculated (p. 269) from post-mortem evidence in other patients that "contusion of the dorsolateral surface of the temporal lobe and temporoparietal junction is the most likely aetiology for these aphasias" (cf. Geschwind, 1971). The evidence that was reviewed in Chapter 2 indicates that contusions in these areas are extremely rare, which would account for the remarkably low incidence of aphasic disorders following closed head injury. The incidence of such disorders is not related to conventional measures of the severity of head injury (see de Morsier, 1973; Levin & Eisenberg, 1979a, 1979b; Sarno, 1980; cf. Heilman et al., 1971). More specifically, as Levin (1981, p. 455) noted, "prolonged coma is neither a necessary nor sufficient condition for residual aphasia" (see also Levin et al., 1976a, p. 1069).

## Subclinical disturbances of language

Subclinical disturbances in the comprehension and production of speech are much more common, especially in patients with severe closed head injuries, although these have been characterised as essentially "nonaphasic" disorders of language (Holland, 1982; Prigatano et al., 1986, p. 19).

For example, Thomsen (1975) studied 26 patients who had been in coma for at least 24 hours, and found language disorders in 12 of these cases when assessed on average four months after their accidents. Naming errors and paraphasia were the most common deficits, although comprehension and writing problems were also observed, but symptoms characteristic of expressive disorders were rarely seen. Subsequently, Thomsen (1976) described a further 16 patients with severe closed head injuries in whom focal lesions due to intracranial haematoma or severe anoxia had been surgically verified. When examined on average 15 weeks after their accidents, 11 of these patients showed a wide variety of linguistic deficits, leading Thomsen to emphasise the "multisymptomatic" nature of post-traumatic language disorders. In particular, nearly all of these patients demonstrated "impaired analysis of speech, impaired analysis of reading, amnestic aphasia, verbal paraphasia, agraphia, and perseveration" (p. 363).

Levin et al. (1976a) evaluated 50 head-injured patients on six subtests of the Multilingual Aphasia Examination (MAE: Benton, 1967, 1969). They were tested "after periodic monitoring of orientation to surroundings and time ... had disclosed an absence or at least marked reduction of confusion" (1976a, p. 1063), although 38% were still impaired on a test of temporal orientation (Benton et al., 1964) when the MAE was administered. In comparison with 30 control patients with diverse somatic disease, they were impaired on tests of visual object naming and verbal fluency and also on the Token Test (De Renzi & Vignolo, 1962), though they were not significantly impaired on tests of sentence repetition, auditory comprehension, or reading comprehension. Duration of coma and signs of brainstem involvement were negatively correlated with their performance on all six subtests, significantly so in the case of object naming, verbal fluency, auditory comprehension and reading comprehension, but their test performance was not related to the presence or absence of skull fracture, intracranial haematoma, or neurological findings of damage predominantly involving one or other cerebral hemisphere.

In the study by Groher (1977) mentioned in Chapters 3 and 4, 14 patients with severe head injuries were assessed on the Porch Index of Communicative Ability (PICA) after they had regained consciousness and were reassessed at four successive intervals of 30 days thereafter. The initial assessment revealed serious deficits, but there was subsequently considerable improvement. In particular, although all of the patients had initially shown marked anomia, their naming to confrontation was normal by the final session. Even so, their scores still showed a significant impairment in both receptive and expressive language capacities even at nearly five months after their accidents.

Najenson, Sazbon, Fiselzon, Becker, and Schechter (1978) monitored the recovery of 15 patients with prolonged coma after closed head injury. Six patients remained in a persistent vegetative state with no expressive function and minimal evidence of any comprehension. Six patients showed relatively complete recovery of both receptive and expressive functions over the nine months following their accidents. The comprehension of visual gestures and oral commands returned first of all, followed by reading and writing skills and oral expression. Najenson et al. emphasised the good potential for recovery of communicative function even following prolonged coma and the close association between the recovery of communication functions and the recovery of locomotor function. However, the three remaining cases showed persistent communication disorders, and eight of the nine patients who showed at least partial recovery were persistently impaired in terms of the motor aspects of speech and especially in the coordination of respiration, articulation, and phonation.

Levin, Grossman, et al. (1979) evaluated language function in 27 patients with severe closed head injury, defined in terms of a score on the Glasgow Coma Scale on admission to hospital of 8 or less. The MAE and three subtests from the Neurosensory Center Comprehensive Examination for Aphasia (NCCEA: Spreen & Benton, 1969) were administered on average one year after injury. By this time, all but the most severely disabled patients exhibited normal conversational speech and comprehension of commands, but many continued to show hesitancy in finding words and especially in naming objects presented either visually or tactually.

Levin and Eisenberg (1979a) used the NCCEA to carry out an assessment of persistent language deficits in 64 children and adolescents with head injuries of varying degrees of severity. Nearly a third of the sample showed some impairment of language function during the first six months following injury, especially in object naming. This study found no relationship between the children's scores on the individual subscales of the Glasgow Coma Scale and the subsequent incidence of language deficits.

Nevertheless, Johnston and Mellits (1980) found a negative relationship between the duration of coma in head-injured children and their expressive language ability when tested within the first year following injury. In addition, a study by Winogron et al. (1984) involving 51 head-injured children showed significant correlations between their total scores on the Glasgow Coma Scale and the magnitude of their subsequent impairment on both an aphasia screening battery and a test of verbal fluency. Jordan, Ozanne, and Murdoch (1988, 1990) confirmed that children show persistent language deficits after closed head injury, especially in terms of naming.

Sarno (1980) described the results of 56 patients referred to a rehabilitation centre following severe closed head injury on four subtests of the NCCEA covering object naming, verbal fluency, sentence repetition, and the Token Test. Eighteen of the patients were diagnosed as aphasic on the basis of clinical evaluation of spontaneous speech production and comprehension, and these individuals were found to be profoundly impaired on all four quantitative tests. The remaining 38 patients were not diagnosed as clinically aphasic, but they too were found to have measurable speech and language deficits on formal testing. Sarno described (p. 687) these deficits as instances of "subclinical aphasia disorder": that is, "linguistic processing deficits on testing in the absence of clinical manifestations of linguistic impairment". She concluded (p. 689) that "all traumatically brain-injured patients who have experienced coma will suffer a significant degree of verbal impairment", but she acknowledged that her sample probably consisted of patients whose injuries were particularly severe.

Levin, Grossman, et al. (1981) studied the progress of 21 patients with severe head injuries who were aphasic on the recovery of consciousness. Their residual language deficits at least six months after their accidents were assessed by means of six subtests of the MAE together with three subtests of the NCCEA. On most of the tests roughly 25% of the sample as a whole produced impaired performance and 40% showed impaired naming of visual or haptic stimuli. Altogether 12 patients proved to have persistent language deficits on formal testing: half of them showed a generalised impairment of both receptive and expressive abilities, whereas the other half showed a language deficit confined to a single function, usually that of object naming. The former patients also showed a persistent deficit in terms of both Verbal IQ and Performance IQ according to the WAIS, whereas the latter patients and the nine patients who had fully recovered from their acute aphasia and who produced normal scores on the tests of linguistic competence also produced normal levels of performance on the WAIS. A persistent generalised language impairment was consistently associated with longer periods of coma and with CT evidence of enlarged ventricles at follow-up. Moreover, across the sample as a whole the duration of coma was found to be significantly correlated with performance on visual naming, word fluency, speech comprehension, and reading comprehension. The naming of haptic stimuli was disproportionately impaired in the case of those presented to the left hand, which Levin et al. attributed to the disruption of interhemispheric connections as the result of damage to the corpus callosum.

These and other results led Levin (1981, p. 441) to sum up the research findings at the time in the following manner:

> The studies of long-term recovery of language after CHI [closed head injury] show an overall trend of improvement that may eventuate in restoration of language or specific deficits ("subclinical" language disorder) in naming or word finding in about two-thirds of the patients who are acutely aphasic. Generalized language deficit, which is associated with global cognitive impairment, persists in patients who sustain severe CHI.

As mentioned earlier in this chapter, Sunderland et al. (1983) tested 33 patients with severe closed head injuries between two and eight months after their accidents. They showed no sign of any impairment on the Mill Hill Vocabulary test in comparison with 37 orthopaedic control patients. They were also given a simple test of semantic processing (subsequently called the "Silly Sentences" test). The head-injured patients were found to be significantly slower than the control patients, producing barely 70% as many correct responses within the allotted time interval, but they were not significantly impaired in terms of the proportion of errors that they made. The two groups still proved to be significantly different from one another when their speed in a finger-tapping task was used to control for the motor component of the semantic-processing task. These results are consistent with the idea that even patients with severe head injuries are largely intact in terms of their comprehension ability, but have a general impairment in terms of their speed of cognitive processing. Similar results were obtained by Hinton-Bayre et al. (1997) when the performance of rugby football players with mild head injuries on the Silly Sentences test was compared with their baseline performance at the start of the relevant season.

Nevertheless, head-injured patients also appear to have specific word-finding difficulties, and these are demonstrated in tests of object naming and of verbal fluency. In principle, impairment on the latter kind of test could also be attributed to slower mental processing, in that (as was mentioned earlier) tests of verbal fluency are often regarded as measures of the efficiency of the frontal lobes. However, impairment in naming following closed head injury can typically be associated with specific linguistic deficits in both semantic and phonological processing (see Kerr, 1995).

## Language and communication

Although it is clear that patients with closed head injury may show language-processing deficits on formal testing in the absence of clinical manifestations of classical aphasia (Sarno, 1980), the results obtained by Sunderland et al. (1983)

raise the possibility that such deficits simply reflect a broadly based limitation upon the patients' capacity for complex information processing. Indeed, Halpern, Darley, and Brown (1973) found that the language disorders caused by head injury were unlikely to represent a specific impairment of the capacity to interpret and formulate linguistic utterances that was disproportionate to any impairment of other intellectual functions. Rather, they were much more likely to be particular aspects of a condition of "confused language" in which there was "reduced recognition and understanding of and responsiveness to the environment, faulty short-term memory, mistaken reasoning, disorientation in time and space, and behavior which is less adaptive and appropriate than normal" (p. 163).

Levin et al. (1976a) also entertained the notion that post-traumatic linguistic defects might be viewed as instances of general mental impairment, but rejected it on the somewhat tenuous grounds that head-injured patients were typically unimpaired in the repetition of even quite lengthy sentences. Although not wholly explicit, their own view seems to have been that post-traumatic linguistic defects were subclinical forms of specific aphasic disorders. This was certainly the position adopted by Sarno (1980) and by Levin (1981) in the passages quoted previously. In contrast, Holland (1982) argued that post-traumatic language disorders were secondary to deficits of memory and cognition and should not be regarded as "subclinical aphasia". Hagen (1984) also suggested that cognitive impairment following closed head injury disrupted language processes.

In order to contrast these two viewpoints, Payne-Johnson (1986) tested 20 patients who had sustained head injuries of varying degrees of severity on a broad "communication competence" test battery designed to assess intelligence, expressive and receptive language, articulation, both auditory and visual short-term memory, oral agility, automatic speech, writing, reading, and simple mathematics. The scores of the head-injured patients were very similar to those of 15 other accident victims on a standard audiological evaluation, on a test of articulation, and on five subtests concerned with reading, writing, and arithmetic skills. However, they were significantly impaired on the remaining 15 subtests concerned with "verbal recognition, intelligence, speech, language, and memory" (p. 245). The most pronounced deficit was demonstrated on an Oral Agility subtest, which "taps subjects' ability to manipulate the articulators for speech upon command and through imitation" (p. 245), and which Payne-Johnson claimed to be mediated by motor centres in the frontal lobe.

This, too, is consistent with the effects of brain damage on the frontal lobes. As Mattson and Levin (1990) pointed out, formal language is typically preserved following frontal lobe damage, but the structure and coherence of speech may well be disrupted. Subsequent analyses examined the impact of severe closed head injury on communicative abilities in more detail. For instance, Hartley and Jensen (1991) found that head-injured patients were significantly impaired in the productivity, the content, and the cohesion of both their narrative discourse (telling and retelling stories) and their procedural discourse (explaining how to do things). Chapman et al. (1992) similarly found that the narrative discourse of head-injured children and adolescents was impaired in its information structure, and that this was true particularly of children in whom lesions of the frontal lobe had been identified by magnetic resonance imaging.

Coelho (1995) reviewed these and other investigations and concluded that head-injured patients demonstrated impairments in the cohesion, coherence, and structure of their discourse, as well as in initiating and sustaining topics in conversation. Indeed, nowadays there is an emerging consensus that patients with closed head injury demonstrate a "cognitive-communicative" disorder, in which discourse is disrupted primarily because of impaired executive processing following damage to the frontal lobes (see e.g. Coelho, Liles, & Duffy, 1995; Hartley, 1995). Ponsford, Sloan, and Snow (1995, chap. 5) argued more generally that head-injured patients were impaired in their "pragmatic" competence, which subsumed conversational and social skills.

## Other disorders of language

Disorders of reading (dyslexia) and writing (dysgraphia) are often observed in conjunction with post-traumatic aphasia, and occasionally they may be manifested in a selective and perhaps even persistent form (see e.g. de Morsier, 1973; Newcombe, 1982). There are also a number of speech disorders that can arise following closed head injury without aphasia. These include: *mutism*, the total abolition of speech following the period of coma, which has already been mentioned; *palilalia*, the automatic repetition of one's own words; and *echolalia*, the automatic repetition of words spoken by others. These are all relatively rare conditions in cases of closed head injury, and normally do not occur as isolated disorders of language processing (Thomsen & Skinhøj, 1976).

Thomsen (1976) suggested that post-traumatic mutism in the absence of any receptive impairment was most likely to be an extreme form of *dysarthria*, an impairment of speech function resulting from a disorder of the neuromuscular mechanism responsible for articulation. This has frequently been reported in research studies of language and speech following closed head injury (de Morsier, 1973; Gilchrist & Wilkinson, 1979; Groher, 1977; Sarno, 1980; Thomsen, 1975, 1976), and it may persist following the restoration of language function (Brooks, Campsie, Symington, Beattie, & McKinlay, 1986; Najenson et al., 1978; Thomsen, 1974, 1975, 1984). In particular, it was mentioned by Roberts (1969, p. 109) as being one feature of the "relatively stereotyped clinical pattern" of traumatic encephalopathy observed in professional boxers.

Sarno (1980) identified 21 cases of dysarthria among 50 patients referred to a rehabilitation centre following severe closed head injury, and they were found to be significantly impaired across a broad range of tests concerned with speech production and comprehension. Levin (1981) recommended that the Oral Agility subtest of the Boston Diagnostic Aphasia Examination (Goodglass & Kaplan, 1972) would be useful in evaluating dysarthria, and it was precisely this subtest which showed the best discrimination between the head-injured and control patients in the study by Payne-Johnson (1986). Cases of acquired dysarthria are of some interest to cognitive psychologists who are concerned with language and memory because they appear to be capable of phonological coding and subvocal rehearsal despite the absence of feedback from the peripheral speech musculature (Baddeley & Wilson, 1985).

Little is known concerning the exact nature and aetiology of post-traumatic dysarthria, although it probably results from lesions to the brainstem. Murdoch and Theodoros (1999) recently summarised the main findings of research on this condition, but their review mainly emphasised the considerable interindividual variability that is apparent in its severity and manifestation. Murdoch and Theodoros noted the relatively persistent nature of this disorder and suggested that the prognosis for its complete resolution in patients with severe closed head injury was poor. Nevertheless, they also noted that there was apparent scope for bringing about significant improvement in articulatory function over several years as a result of individualised interventions.

## Verbal skills and verbal memory

Given the prevalence of language disorders and dysarthria after closed head injury, it is important to consider whether they are likely to have a role in determining performance in other cognitive tasks. There at least seems to be an assocation between the two at a descriptive level; as Levin (1981, p.460) noted, "Patients with closed head injury who become aphasic frequently exhibit concomitant neuropsychological deficits". One possibility, of course, is that the residual memory impairment and persistent disturbances of language function that result from closed head injury are expressions of a common underlying deficit, perhaps resulting from disproportionate injury to the temporal lobes (cf. Levin, Benton, & Grossman, 1982, p. 145). Nevertheless, given that most tests of retention and cognition place a primary emphasis upon verbal encoding, processing, and performance, it is equally conceivable that observable deficits in these latter areas resulting from closed head injury are the result, at least in part, of impaired language function.

Confounding of this sort is obviously more likely when the materials presented to the subjects and the responses that are demanded of them are verbal in nature. This would explain why language deficits in head-injured patients have little or no effect upon recognition memory for simple geometrical figures, upon the simultaneous matching of different views of unfamiliar faces, nor upon the the performance of sensory or motor tasks (Brooks, 1974b; Levin et al., 1976a, 1977b; cf. Levin et al., 1976b). In contrast to these results, Thomsen (1977) found that the generalised impairment of verbal learning that resulted from severe closed head injury was much more pronounced in aphasic patients. A dissociation between these two forms of memory impairment had been reported earlier by Akbarova (1972). Of 18 head-injured patients with lesions predominantly confined to the left hemisphere, 13 had relatively selective deficits of verbal memory, and this group tended to demonstrate concomitant disturbances of language function; the cognitive impairment of the remaining 5 cases was relatively specific to visuospatial memory.

Groher (1977) administered both the Wechsler Memory Scale (WMS) and the Porch Index of Communicative Ability (PICA) to 14 patients on average nearly five months after they had sustained severe closed head injuries. As mentioned in Chapter 4 and earlier in the present chapter, deficits were apparent on both instruments. Analysis of the results from individual subjects in Groher's paper reveals significant relationships between the subjects' Memory Quotients on the WMS and their performance in the PICA. Of course, these are purely correlational findings, and one cannot be entirely confident in inferring causal relationships. Nevertheless, it is probably fair to say that the contribution of memory factors to performance on the PICA is minimal. It is therefore reasonable to conclude from Groher's results that language deficits, as evaluated by the PICA, are an important determinant of the scores achieved by head-injured patients on memory tasks such as the WMS.

Further evidence has been obtained from the use of intelligence tests such as the WAIS. In assessing patients on average 30 months after they had sustained severe closed head injuries, Thomsen (1974) failed to find any difference in terms of Full Scale IQ between 21 patients who showed aphasic symptoms and 29 patients who did not. Nevertheless, Levin, Grossman, et al. (1981) found that head-injured patients who showed a persistent generalised disturbance of language function were profoundly impaired in terms of both Verbal IQ and Performance IQ on the WAIS, whereas those patients whose language functions had returned to normal showed no sign of any intellectual deficit. Subsequently, Levin and Goldstein (1986) found that Verbal IQ was correlated with performance in free recall, and they concluded (p. 652) that "verbal intellectual functioning is closely linked with performance on this memory task".

## OVERVIEW

Patients who have suffered closed head injury manifest a disturbance of cognitive function beyond the period of post-traumatic amnesia across a wide variety of tasks. This impairment is to be attributed to a reduction in their central information-processing capacity rather than to a deficit of selective attention or tonic alertness. Whereas the residual cognitive dysfunction that is exhibited in patients with minor closed head injury tends to resolve within the first few weeks after the accident, severely injured patients may show persistent deficits many months later (see also Livingston & Livingston, 1985). These deficits are even more pronounced and widespread, and extend even to simple mental activities such as counting backwards and giving items of general information.

Similar deficits are shown by head-injured patients in terms of their Intelligence Quotients according to standardised psychometric instruments such as the Wechsler Adult Intelligence Scale. Performance IQ and scores on nonverbal tests are typically more vulnerable than Verbal IQ and scores on verbal tests. These two aspects of intellectual function appear to be differentially sensitive to damage within the left and right hemispheres. Both tend to improve to within normal limits over the course of two to three years after a closed head injury, although in some studies such improvements are confounded with practice effects.

Pronounced and specific disorders of language function are relatively rare after closed head injury and usually take the form of either nominal aphasia or Wernicke's aphasia. However, subclinical disturbances in word finding, discourse, and speech production are much more common, especially in severely injured patients. These seem to be manifestations of a more general disruption of cognitive and communicative skills, but it is nevertheless true that some decrements in performance in cognitive tasks following closed head injury appear to be the result of selective impairments of language function.

CHAPTER SIX

# Subjective complaints and personality disorders

Head-injured patients exhibit a wide variety of symptoms, and if these persist they may well prove to be debilitating in terms of patients' family relationships or future employment. In this chapter, I shall consider the broad pattern of postconcussional symptoms as well as the particular clinical condition of a persistent postconcussional syndrome. I shall go on to consider in more detail the affective, behavioural, and psychiatric disturbances that may result from a closed head injury, and the impact which these have upon the patient's immediate relatives and friends.

## POSTCONCUSSIONAL SYMPTOMS

Even though a patient may make a good recovery from a clinical point of view, the immediate period following a closed head injury is often marked by a particular set of subjective complaints on the part of the patient. As long ago as 1904 Meyer described the overall symptom picture as "that of a mental weakness shown by *easy fatigue, slowness of thought, inability to keep impressions, irritability, and a great number of unpleasant sensations, above all headaches and dizziness*" (p. 403, italics in original).

In a detailed study of 200 patients admitted to hospital with closed head injury, Denny-Brown (1945a, pp. 430–431) classified these symptoms into:

> complaints derived directly from observed structural injury (symptoms of direct physical disorder), psychiatric complaints (symptoms of the order of fatigue, nervousness, anxiety, depression), symptoms of change in personality (separately coded only when there was evident aggressiveness or irritability or prolonged elation, without other mental symptoms) and complaints of uncertain or variable derivation (headache, dizziness, vertigo).

In this series, 69% of the patients complained of headache at some time after their injury (see Brenner, Friedman, Merritt, & Denny-Brown, 1944), and 50% complained of dizziness at some time after their injury (see Friedman, Brenner, & Denny-Brown, 1945). In both cases the most common precipitating factors were sudden changes in posture, fatigue, or effort, and emotional stress. Only 6% complained of true vertigo (the sense that either oneself or one's surroundings are in constant movement).

In addition, 55% of the patients complained of one or more symptoms after discharge from hospital, the most frequent combination being that of headache, dizziness, and anxiety (Denny-Brown, 1945a). Accurate epidemiological information on the incidence of these symptoms does not exist, but subsequent research has tended to confirm that 50–80% of patients who are admitted to hospital following closed head injury will subsequently complain of one or more of these symptoms (Barth et al., 1989; Cook, 1969, 1972; Hjern & Nylander, 1964; Levin, Gary, et al., 1987; Lidvall et al., 1974; MacFlynn et al., 1984; McLean et al., 1983; Rutherford, Merrett, & McDonald, 1977).

Although the symptoms in question are often referred to as "postconcussional" symptoms, they are not peculiar to patients who have sustained concussional head injuries: they are in particular common among patients who have sustained mild head injuries that did not give rise to any loss of consciousness and even among patients who have sustained neck injuries without a blow to the head (Jacobson, 1969). In a study by McMillan and Glucksman (1987), a checklist of six symptoms was given to 24 patients within seven days of sustaining a closed head injury that gave rise to a period of post-traumatic amnesia (PTA) lasting between one and twenty-four hours. For comparison the same checklist was given to another 20 patients who had sustained an orthopaedic injury (usually an upper limb fracture or sprain). The results are shown in Table 6.1: the proportion of cases who reported each symptom was significantly different between the two groups (see also Oddy et al., 1978b).

McMillan and Glucksman (1987) asked a relative or close friend to describe each patient's symptoms on a more elaborate checklist. The head-injured patients

TABLE 6.1

Percentage of patients reporting six post-concussional symptoms within the first seven days of sustaining a moderate head injury or an orthopaedic injury

| *Symptom* | *Head injury* | *Orthopaedic injury* |
|---|---|---|
| Headache | 71 | 10 |
| Dizziness | 46 | 5 |
| Irritability | 64 | 16 |
| Fatigue | 75 | 25 |
| Intolerance to noise | 38 | 0 |
| Intolerance to bright lights | 33 | 0 |

From McMillan and Glucksman (1987). *Journal of Neurology, Neurosurgery, and Psychiatry, 50,* p. 395. Copyright 1987 by the British Medical Association. Reproduced by permission of BMJ Publishing Group.

were more likely than the orthopaedic controls to be described as quieter and more tense since their accidents. Nevertheless, in contrast to their own reports the two groups of patients did not differ in the extent to which they were described by their friends and relatives as being irritable, worried, impatient, angry, violent, childlike, forgetful, depressed, happy, calm, peaceful, relaxed, or "at ease". As mentioned in Chapter 4, a similar discrepancy was noted between patients and relatives concerning whether the head-injured cases were impaired relative to the orthopaedic cases in their everyday memory ability (see also McLean et al., 1983). McMillan and Glucksman suggested that these disparities between the perceptions of head-injured patients and their relatives might subsequently lead to the development of marital difficulties and other psychosocial problems.

## The postconcussional syndrome

In many head-injured patients, these characteristic symptoms of the initial postconcussional phase subside within a matter of days or within at most a few weeks. In such cases, these symptoms are usually regarded as a normal part of the process of recovery from closed head injury, not themselves warranting any clinical attention or treatment. However, a substantial proportion of head-injured patients continue to complain of postconcussional symptoms beyond the initial post-traumatic period, in which case these symptoms may interfere with their ability to return to their previous employment (Denny-Brown, 1945a; Russell & Smith, 1961). This condition of persistent postconcussional symptoms is described as the "postconcussional syndrome" (or occasionally as the "post-traumatic syndrome").

Once again, accurate statistics are difficult to obtain on the likely incidence of this condition (see Rutherford, 1989). The earliest evidence was obtained by Russell (1932), who described the results of a six-month follow-up of 141 head-injured patients; 61% of the sample reported one or more persistent postconcussional symptoms. These patients were included in an 18-month follow-up of an extended sample of 200 patients (Russell, 1934), of whom 60% described such symptoms. The most common symptoms in both studies were: headache, dizziness, loss of memory or mental ability, and nervousness. A similar picture emerged in the case of the 200 head-injured patients described by Denny-Brown (1945a): 32% complained of headaches and 23% complained of dizziness more than two months after their accidents (see also Brenner et al., 1944; Friedman et al., 1945). Moreover, Adler (1945) found that 35% of the 200 patients reported persistent psychiatric symptoms, and of these by far the largest group (48 cases) consisted of patients showing fears and anxiety states (see also Kozol, 1945).

Subsequent studies tended to suggest that 10–25% of adult patients experience persistent postconcussional symptoms (see e.g. Lidvall et al., 1974; MacFlynn et al., 1984; Rutherford, Merrett, & McDonald, 1979; Steadman & Graham, 1970;

Wrightson & Gronwall, 1981). However, a much higher incidence was found by Klonoff and Paris (1974), who interviewed the parents of 196 children one year after they had been admitted to hospital with a head injury and the parents of 163 of them again one year later. Postconcussional symptoms were reported in 56% of cases at the first interview and in 44% at the second interview. The most common complaints from the parents were of personality changes, headaches, learning difficulties, fatigue, and irritability.

A fundamental problem in evaluating these findings is that the proportion of normal individuals who report these symptoms is typically unknown. Kozol (1946) carried out an intensive diagnostic interview with 101 head-injured patients, on the basis of which he rated 60 "personality traits, tendencies or characteristics" (p. 248) on a 4-point scale with regard to their magnitude or severity prior to the accident and at various occasions after their discharge from hospital. In comparison with their estimated premorbid ratings, more than 25% of Kozol's sample showed an increase in periodic headaches, fatigability, dizziness, anxiety regarding their heads, emotional instability, tension, insomnia, irritability, timorousness, and abulia (loss of will power). These traits had in most cases simply not been present in any appreciable degree before the head injury: they tended to develop soon after a patient's discharge from hospital, reached a peak about six weeks after the accident, and were often substantially receding at about three months. However, in roughly 50% of these patients such symptoms persisted for at least six months, and in roughly 15% of cases they persisted for one year or more. In a similar manner, Lidvall et al. (1974) asked their patients about the symptoms they had experienced before their accidents, and they specifically excluded from consideration "postconcussional" symptoms that had been present before the injury. Such symptoms were reported by 35% of their total sample: anxiety and fatigue were by far the most common premorbid symptoms, but headache was relatively uncommon.

Whereas the postconcussional symptoms that immediately follow the head-injured patient's recovery of consciousness may well have an organic cause, it has typically been assumed that the continued manifestation of these symptoms is psychogenic in nature. Long and Novack (1986) pointed out two basic reasons for such an assumption. First, the development and exacerbation of such symptoms several weeks or months after the occurrence of a mild or moderate head injury is difficult to explain on an organic basis. Second, some of the symptoms that develop and persist following closed head injury, such as anxiety and depression, are by their nature not easily attributed to actual brain damage. Conversely, as Rutherford (1989) pointed out, some of the more obvious somatic complaints (such as vomiting, nausea, drowsiness, and blurred vision) are usually short-lived. There are, however, further arguments that need to be considered relating to the severity of the injury, the role of litigation for compensation, objective performance, the possibility of simulation, and the patient's personality.

## Severity of injury and postconcussional symptoms

It is presumably the case that the incidence of a clinical syndrome that was engendered by organic brain damage would tend to be increased in those patients who had sustained more severe damage. Traditionally, indeed, it was often assumed that the postconcussional syndrome would be associated with more severe damage of the brain (e.g. Meyer, 1904).

However, there is in fact little evidence that persistent postconcussional symptoms are more likely following more severe head injuries (see e.g. Brenner et al., 1944; Cook, 1969, 1972; Elia, 1974; Friedman et al., 1945; Jacobson, 1969; Kay, Kerr, & Lassman, 1971; Kozol, 1946; Lishman, 1968; McLean et al., 1983; Norrman & Svahn, 1961; Russell & Smith, 1961; Rutherford et al., 1977, 1979; Symonds, 1940; Wrightson & Gronwall, 1981; cf. Livingston & Livingston, 1985). Indeed, Miller (1961a) presented results that showed an inverse relationship between the incidence of postconcussional symptoms and the severity of the original head injury, whether measured by the occurrence of skull fracture, the duration of unconsciousness, or the duration of PTA. In particular, out of 48 patients in whom PTA had lasted longer than 72 hours, just 3 cases were said to show "residual psychoneurosis."

On the basis of such results, Miller and Stern (1965, p. 225) asserted that postconcussional symptoms were "conspicuously infrequent" in patients with severe head injury. In a series of 100 patients in whom the duration of PTA was longer than 24 hours, they identified 10 patients with "psychoneurotic symptoms" at an initial examination (on average 3 years after their accidents) and only 4 patients with such symptoms at follow-up (on average 11 years after their accidents). Such findings contrast directly with the much earlier assertion made by Symonds (1940, p. 97) that the same pattern of symptoms was "commonly observed in the course of recovery from moderate or severe brain injury". In this regard, the literature tends to favour Symonds' position rather than Miller's.

Russell (1932) analysed the incidence of postconcussional symptoms in 61 patients with PTA lasting for less than one hour, 45 patients with PTA lasting for between one and twenty-four hours, and 35 patients with PTA lasting for more than twenty-four hours. The proportion of patients in each group who reported persistent postconcussional symptoms was 49%, 69%, and 71%, respectively, indicating that the frequency of these symptoms varied directly with the severity of injury. Russell then presented a detailed analysis, which indicated that the association between severity of head injury and the incidence of different symptoms might be positive (memory loss), negative (headache), or nonexistent (dizziness and nervousness).

A subsequent study by Lewis (1942) described 64 patients who had been admitted to a psychiatric centre for treatment following head injury. Lewis acknowledged that they had been referred to that centre rather than to a rehabilitation unit because they were considered to have made a full recovery from all the physical effects of the injury. He then added (p. 610): "They were, however, very good examples of the [postconcussional] syndrome, clinically, and many of them had had very severe head injuries."

Indeed, there are a great many studies in the literature reporting persistent postconcussional symptoms in a significant proportion of patients with severe head injuries (Adler, 1945; Brenner et al., 1944; Bruckner & Randle, 1972; Denny-Brown, 1945a; Edna & Cappelen, 1987; Friedman et al., 1945; Horowitz et al., 1983; Kelly, 1975; Landy, 1968; McKinlay, Brooks, & Bond, 1983; McKinlay, Brooks, Bond, Martinage, & Marshall, 1981; Minderhoud, Boelens, Huizenga, & Saan, 1980; Oddy et al., 1978b; van Zomeren & van den Burg, 1985). The safest conclusion to be reached on the basis of the evidence that is available is probably that the relationship between severity of closed head injury and the incidence of postconcussional symptoms is inconsistent both across symptoms and across patient samples.

## Compensation factors

Persistent postconcussional symptoms appear to be quite rare among those patients who have sustained head injuries in the context of domestic or recreational accidents, but relatively common among those who are involved in industrial or traffic accidents (e.g. Adler, 1945; Brenner et al., 1944; Cook, 1969; but cf. Kelly, 1975). In principle, the mechanism and severity of the injury could be different in these various situations, as was noted in Chapter 2. However, the crucial factor in both industrial and traffic accidents seems to be that they are much more likely to involve litigation and claims for compensation. This could affect patients' emotional reactions but also their motivation for claiming to suffer from persistent deficits.

During the 1960s, predominantly on the basis of his experience as an expert witness representing insurance companies and other defendants in litigation of this sort, Miller (1961a) had considerable influence among the medical community in maintaining that postconcussional symptoms tended to arise specifically in compensation cases and to subside once any legal claims had been settled. Of course, as McKinlay et al. (1983) noted, insofar as Miller's clinical material consisted wholly of medico-legal referrals, his claims were based upon patient samples that were grossly atypical of the broader population of patients with closed head injuries. Initially, at least, Miller was disposed to regard the postconcussional syndrome merely as a form of "accident neurosis", an emotional reaction to an accident for which blame could be attached to another person or organisation against whom or which a legal claim for financial compensation could be made (see Miller, 1961b). Subsequently, however, he came to regard the persistence of postconcussional symptoms as being essentially the product of simulation (Miller, 1966; see also Miller & Cartlidge, 1972; Miller & Stern, 1965).

Although these views met with a favourable reaction among the general medical community, the response of many researchers was to suggest that Miller had overemphasised the conscious desire for monetary gain as a causal factor in the development of the postconcussional syndrome (e.g. Cronholm, 1972). In particular, Lishman (1973) suggested that the psychological processes associated with compensation and litigation operated at many different levels of consciousness, and that the desire for compensation was merely one possible manifestation of the neurotic conflict that was elicited by the personal crisis of the original injury. In particular, he argued that this sort of emotional impact of a closed head injury would be especially likely in mild cases where there was no post-traumatic amnesia of the accident and its immediate aftermath.

This line of thinking would probably tend to identify the postconcussional syndrome as a form of "compensation neurosis" which happened to follow injuries to the head (cf. Weighill, 1983). In this connection, it is interesting that the fourth edition of the American Psychiatric Association's (1994) *Diagnostic and Statistical Manual of Mental Disorders* (DSM-IV) distinguishes between malingering and factitious disorders: in malingering, the motivation for the production of symptoms is an external incentive, whereas factitious disorders are driven by an intrapsychic need to maintain the sick role (p. 683).

Nevertheless, other researchers were led to question whether Miller's premise that the postconcussional syndrome was associated with claims for compensation was even true. Much earlier, indeed, Strauss and Savitsky (1934, p. 933) had inveighed against "the implicit confidence and the rigid finality of some observers who assert that most of the persistent complaints of the postconcussion state are psychogenic and result from the subtle suggestions of environment and from unconscious wishes for security". They argued (p. 933) that "the same complaints (headache, dizziness, fatigability, etc.) are encountered in those unconcerned with the alluring fruits of a favorable decision by a group of experts". Similarly, Symonds (1940, p. 97) argued that the development of the syndrome after a latent interval of a few days "has often been attributed unjustly to the effects of a compensation neurosis, but is in fact observed quite commonly in cases where no such possibility exists".

The research evidence again supports Symonds' position rather than Miller's. For instance, in the study by Russell (1932) that I mentioned earlier, 51% out of the total of 141 patients reported postconcussional symptoms in the absence of any outstanding litigation. Russell (1934) did not provide detailed information from his 18-month follow-up study of 200 patients. However, he remarked (p. 134): "In assessing the significance of the compensation factor, however, it must be noted that many of the non-compensation cases returned to work while still suffering from severe post-concussional symptoms."

In the 200 patients described by Denny-Brown (1945a) and his colleagues, the incidence of persistent postconcussional symptoms was increased in those with pending litigation but also in those with domestic or occupational difficulties that were uncomplicated by the possibility of compensation (Adler, 1945; Brenner et al., 1944; Friedman et al., 1945). This was taken to mean that litigation was merely one of several factors that might increase emotional strain in head-injured patients. Subsequent studies confirmed that the relevant symptoms can be seen where there is no question of litigation because claims for compensation have not been made or have been settled (e.g. Kelly, 1975; Merskey & Woodforde, 1972; Rimel et al., 1981; Taylor & Bell, 1966; Tooth, 1947).

Wrightson and Gronwall (1981) found that postconcussional symptoms persisted for more than 90 days in 13 out of a total of 66 patients admitted to two hospitals in New Zealand with minor head injuries. An important feature of this series was that none of the patients had made any formal legal complaint about their symptoms, and none had outstanding claims for compensation, perhaps because of the existence of a no-fault system of compensation for occupational injuries. Despite this, the incidence of persistent symptoms was similar to that found in earlier studies conducted in the UK, where there is no such system and where a significant proportion of the patients concerned are likely to have sought compensation (e.g. Cook, 1972; Rutherford et al., 1977, 1979).

McKinlay et al. (1981) selected two samples of 21 patients consisting of patients who had consistently maintained either that they had grounds to pursue a claim for compensation or that they had no such grounds. There was a tendency for the former patients to have been more severely injured in terms of the duration of PTA, but there were no significant differences between the two groups in the incidence of psychosocial changes reported by their relatives. McKinlay et al. (1983) found that the former group were slightly more likely to report poor concentration, dizziness, or irritability, but that there was little sign of any difference between the two groups in terms of their performance on objective cognitive tests. Once again, these results show that compensation factors have little role in the development or persistence of postconcussional symptoms.

A similar conclusion was reached by Mayou (1995), based on a prospective study of patients who had been injured in traffic accidents but who had not sustained head injuries. As he noted (p. 795), “Overall, there was no evidence that there were significant differences in any aspect of outcome between those who sought compensation and those who did not”. He acknowledged that, in principle, one or two patients in the series may have had financial incentives to make the most of their limitations, but, equally, he suggested that many people avoided litigation or settled quickly to avoid protracted legal proceedings.

## Subjective complaints and objective performance

Some researchers have addressed the question of the nature and aetiology of the postconcussional syndrome by measuring patients’ performance on objective psychological tests. For instance, Tooth (1947) evaluated head-injured naval personnel on an abbreviated form of Wechsler’s (1941) verbal intelligence test. (The sample contained an unspecified number of cases of gunshot wounds, but Tooth argued that they were nevertheless representative of concussional injuries.) Poorer levels of performance on the Similarities subtest were achieved by those who complained of memory disturbance or irritability. There were however no such differences in the case of complaints of headache and dizziness, nor in the case of the other subtests used in this investigation.

Gronwall and Wrightson (1974) administered their paced auditory serial addition task (PASAT) to 10 patients who had returned to work following a closed head injury but who had been unable to continue because of poor concentration, fatigue, irritability, and headache. When compared with a control group of 10 head-injured patients who did not report such symptoms, they were significantly impaired on an initial assessment on the PASAT and took significantly longer to achieve normal performance on repeated testing. Gronwall and Wrightson suggested that the postconcussional syndrome was caused by a reduced rate of information transmission, which manifested itself in subjective complaints of poor concentration in tasks that involved a high information load. Gronwall (1976) confirmed that the reduction in information-processing rate on the PASAT was correlated significantly with subjective reports of postconcussional symptoms, and that scores on the repeated administration of the PASAT improved in a manner that was roughly commensurate with the resolution of those symptoms.

Waddell and Gronwall (1984) measured the tolerance to light and sound of nine patients with minor head injury who were not admitted to hospital but were referred to their general practitioners. When tested between seven and nineteen days after their accidents and compared with a group of matched control subjects drawn from hospital staff and the local community, they were found to be impaired in their objective tolerance to light and sound. However, there was no relationship between the patients' subjective ratings of hypersensitivity to light and sound and their objective tolerance. The head-injured patients in this study were also given the PASAT, but their scores on this task were not significantly correlated with either their self-ratings or their objective assessment of hypersensitivity.

Dikmen and Reitan (1977) assessed 27 head-injured patients on the Minnesota Multiphasic Personality Inventory (MMPI: Dahlstrom, Welsh, & Dahlstrom, 1972) soon after their accidents and again 12 and 18 months later. They were divided into two groups based on whether or not they had initially been found to have at least moderate deficits on the Halstead–Reitan battery. Over the three test sessions, significant reductions were found on the Hypochondriasis, Depression, Hysteria, Psychasthenia, and Schizophrenia scales of the MMPI; this pattern was taken to suggest that "head-injured patients in general complain of more depression, anxiety, somatic problems, and strange experiences soon after the injury" (p. 493). Moreover, at both the 12-month and the 18-month sessions, the patients with initial cognitive deficits showed significantly greater emotional difficulties on the Hypochondriasis, Depression, and Mania scales of the MMPI. Dikmen and Reitan argued that impairment of neuropsychological functions could be used as an index of the severity of a head injury, and they implied that their data were inconsistent with psychogenic accounts of the consequences of closed head injury.

Bohnen, Jolles, and Twijnstra (1992) studied nine patients who continued to complain of postconcussional symptoms six months after they had suffered a minor head injury. They compared them with nine healthy volunteers and with nine patients who did not complain of any symptoms six months after similar head injuries. The nine patients with postconcussional symptoms were impaired in comparison with both of the other two groups (a) in terms of their response latencies (but not their response accuracy) in a computerised test of divided attention and (b) in terms of the magnitude of the colour–word interference effect in the Stroop test (see Chapter 5). These findings indicated that the former patients had reduced information-processing capacity. However, Bohnen, Jolles, Twijnstra, Mellink, and Wijnen (1995) failed to replicate these results in patients tested after 12–34 months.

Gass and Apple (1997) assessed 63 patients with closed head injury on a self-report instrument, the Cognitive Difficulties Scale, and a battery of neuropsychological tests. Their subjective complaints on the self-report instrument were associated with measures of depression and anxiety on the MMPI. They were also significantly (and negatively) correlated with their scores on the Logical Memory subtest of the WMS-R, but were not significantly correlated with scores on the Digit Span or Visual Reproduction subtests. Gass and Apple concluded that their self-report instrument was a valid measure of cognitive deficits in head-injured patients.

The broad research strategy in all these investigations was to seek to demonstrate that the subjective complaints characteristic of the postconcussional syndrome could be correlated with some objective, measurable deficit. However, a criticism of these studies is that such findings would not rule out the possibility that both the subjective complaints and the objective impairment resulted from simulation and malingering. Performance in many psychological tasks is under the control of conscious processing strategies, and it is open to patients to adopt suboptimal strategies if it serves their purposes to do so. A number of investigators have addressed this issue.

First, in the case of the PASAT, Gronwall (1977) suggested that there were certain patterns of test results that indicated either poor motivation or a deliberate attempt at faking low scores, but she acknowledged that not all cases of malingering were clear-cut. Second, Hannay and James (1981) found that students could successfully simulate the pattern of performance on a test of continuous recognition memory which had been produced by head-injured patients in an earlier study (Hannay et al., 1979). There was considerable overlap in the respective distributions of test scores, although extreme false-alarm rates tended to be characteristic of the simulators rather than of the patients.

Third, as was mentioned in the previous section, McKinlay et al. (1983) found little evidence for any difference in psychometric test performance between head-injured patients who were entertaining claims for financial compensation and those who were not. They concluded (p. 1089) that "claimants did not attempt to fake low scores in order to present as more disabled than they were". On the basis of their own clinical experience, they considered that faking low scores was rare, and that "serial testing would uncover it easily in the very few cases where it occurs" (p. 1089). However, there is now a substantial body of evidence to show that patients with financial incentives may produce poorer performance on neuropsychological testing than other head-injured patients despite the fact that they tend to have less severe injuries (see Binder & Rohling, 1996).

Moreover, clinicians and researchers have developed more sensitive procedures for detecting malingering (Binder, 1997; Spreen & Strauss, 1998, pp. 666–685). For example, Trueblood (1994) identified 12 patients with mild head injuries as malingerers, as evidenced by below-chance responding in a forced-choice test. When compared with other head-injured patients matched for age, sex, and education, the malingerers obtained lower scores on both the WAIS-R and the California Verbal Learning Test. It was, however, difficult to identify any qualitative aspects of the malingerers' performance that discriminated them from the other head-injured patients.

Suhr, Tranel, Wefel, and Barrash (1997) obtained similar findings, but they argued that there was no clear evidence to relate patients' involvement in litigation to their performance in neuropsychological assessment. They found that patients with mild head injury who were currently involved in litigation or who were otherwise seeking compensation for their head injury did not perform differently from other head-injured patients who were not seeking compensation for their injuries. Suhr et al. concluded that patients' involvement in litigation was not itself indicative of malingering or exaggeration of deficits.

Iverson and Franzen (1994) conducted an experimental study using a recognition memory test, the Digit Span subtest of the WAIS, and a nonverbal analogue of the digit-span procedure. They tested groups of students and of inmates at a US federal correction institute under either neutral instructions or instructions to simulate a memory deficit. The instructions to malinger led to much poorer performance on all three tasks in both students and inmates. A group of patients with impaired memory function following head injuries who were not involved in any litigation produced poorer performance on the Digit Span subtest than the neutrally instructed students and inmates but were largely unimpaired on the other two tasks. A discriminant function analysis classified all the patients as nonmalingerers according to their scores on the three tests.

Iverson and Franzen (1994) inferred that the tests they had employed were vulnerable to malingering and hence could be used to detect malingering in clinical patients. Unfortunately, this study serves to demonstrate a fundamental problem with attempts to detect malingering: it can never be ruled out that patterns of performance supposedly characteristic of malingering are not also dissociations that can be produced either by pre-existing conditions or by actual brain damage (see Nies & Sweet, 1994). For instance, a selective impairment on the Digit Span subtest and analogous tasks is expected in patients with developmental dyslexia, who often have problems when dealing with sequences. Moreover, in Chapter 4, I mentioned a head-injured patient who demonstrated a selective impairment of short-term memory that was unequivocally the result of brain damage, not malingering (Warrington & Shallice, 1970).

## Psychogenic aspects of postconcussional symptoms

The possibility that persistent postconcussional symptoms constitute a psychogenic reaction to closed head injury and its immediate consequences has led to an interest in factors that might be involved in the aetiology of the syndrome other than the physiological aspects of the head injury itself: both endogenous, constitutional factors properties of the patient prior to the injury and exogenous, circumstantial properties of the injury and its clinical management (Lishman, 1973).

The role of endogenous factors in the aetiology of postconcussional symptoms was first emphasised by Symonds (1928, p. 831), who recommended that "it should be a rule in such cases to inquire for a family history of mental instability and to ascertain the patient's previous biological record, with especial reference to nervous breakdowns". Russell (1934, p. 139) argued that "identical injuries to the head in two individuals may produce quite different after-effects". Subsequently, Symonds (1937, p. 1092) reiterated his earlier recommendation in an often-quoted passage:

> The later effects of head injury can only be properly understood in the light of a full psychiatric study of the individual patient, and in particular, his constitution. In other words, it is not only the kind of injury that matters, but the kind of head.

Symonds and Russell (1943, p. 8) presented initial data to support the notion that "the mental constitution before injury plays an important part in the prognosis of head injuries".

The fact that there is no clear relationship between the severity of the original head injury and the persistence of postconcussional symptoms is usually taken to imply that this condition affects only those patients with some constitutional vulnerability or susceptibility. In particular, it would be expected that the incidence of postconcussional syndrome would be higher in patients with a premorbid anxiety or neurotic instability (Behrman, 1977; Cronholm, 1972; Lishman, 1973).

The early study by Lewis (1942) compared 64 head-injured patients with postconcussional symptoms who had been admitted to a psychiatric unit for assessment and 64 neurotic patients from the same hospital. The former group was more likely to include individuals who had been of a stable, well-organised premorbid personality, and more likely to complain of severe headache, fainting, and irritability. However, in most other respects the two groups were similar in family and personal history, intelligence, symptoms, response to treatment, and outcome. Lewis concluded (p. 610) that "the long-standing, relatively intractable post-contusional syndrome is apt to occur in much the same person as develops a psychiatric syndrome in other circumstances without any brain injury at all".

In a study of 128 cases of closed head injury, Ruesch et al. (1945) found that post-traumatic personality changes were typified by complaints of increased fatigability, lowered tolerance to alcohol, unstable work history, decrease of interests, and occasional impotency. In addition, these patients produced higher scores than average on the neuroticism scales of the MMPI, and the latter showed a strong correlation with the number of post-traumatic complaints. Ruesch et al. concluded that pre-existing neurotic tendencies appeared to prolong the duration of post-traumatic symptoms. Nevertheless, the causal link might conceivably run in the reverse direction: apparent differences on items used in conventional personality inventories such as the MMPI may simply reflect genuine changes in the daily activities of head-injured patients in response to the diverse forms of post-traumatic cognitive impairment.

Kozol (1945) found that 32% of 200 head-injured patients had developed postconcussional symptoms. However, for those with previously normal personality, with premorbid neurotic personality, with premorbid psychopathic personality, and with other premorbid personality variants the corresponding figures were 30%, 26%, 35%, and 30%, respectively. Kozol concluded (p. 361) that "the pretraumatic personality is not a dominant factor in the production of post-traumatic symptoms". However, on the basis of her own work with the same patients, Adler (1945) noted that the incidence of such symptoms rose to 57% in those who had a history of pre-existing anxiety, hypochondriasis, or depression. She also found that the symptom that predominated in patients with normal premorbid personalities was almost always anxiety, whereas the symptoms that developed in those patients with pre-existing psychiatric abnormalities tended to reflect their previous clinical condition.

Kozol (1946) presented a much more detailed account of the relationship between previous personality and postconcussional symptoms in 101 of the patients from his original sample. As I noted earlier, he developed a detailed schedule of 60 individual characteristics that were assessed in diagnostic interviews in terms of their magnitude or severity prior to the accident and at various occasions after a patient's discharge from hospital. He noted that a substantial number of patients showed certain characteristics after their injury that had not been apparent previously, and that this was true in particular of specific psychoneurotic traits such as anxiety and fatigability. One might, of course, suggest that these were reasonable reactions to the experience of persistent postconcussional symptoms.

Kozol (1946, p. 256) pointed out that this "refutes the oft expressed view that post-traumatic psychiatric symptoms represent a pretraumatic psychiatric liability to such symptoms". Although patients with a premorbid neurotic personality tended to show little change on characteristics that were associated with that personality type, this was because their pretraumatic ratings on those traits were often at or approaching a ceiling. However, these patients tended to show a greater post-traumatic change on other characteristics than those patients with normal premorbid personality or with other abnormalities. As a result, the occurrence of sequelae of any kind and the occurrence of the most severe sequelae was more likely in the patients with neurotic personalities than in other patient groups.

Other evidence on the role of premorbid personality has come from the comparison of pairs of twins in whom one member has suffered closed head injury. Dencker (1958, 1960) assessed 117 such pairs, consisting of 36 monozygotic or identical twins and 81 same-sexed dizygotic or fraternal twins. At a follow-up examination conducted on average 10 years afterwards, there was no significant difference between the head-injured monozygotic twins and their co-twins in terms of the incidence of headache, vertigo or dizziness, impaired memory, increased sensitivity to noise and light, and decreased tolerance of alcohol. Moreover, the monozygotic pairs were found to be more alike or concordant than the dizygotic pairs in this respect. Those patients who did show these symptoms more than their co-twins appeared to be more accident-prone and in particular were more likely to have suffered additional head injuries. Dencker concluded that these late "postconcussional" symptoms were largely of constitutional origin rather than the result of the head injury itself.

To some extent, the study of Merskey and Woodforde (1972) supported this view, in that some of their patients who had been referred for assessment with persistent postconcussional symptoms had evidence of neurotic problems that predated their accidents. However, these researchers also remarked (p. 523) that several patients "showed quite convincing past evidence of stable personalities and successful adjustment at home and at work". In other words, in a substantial proportion of cases, the relevant symptomatology could not be related to a poor premorbid psychiatric history (Newcombe, 1982).

Greiffenstein, Baker, and Gola (1996) investigated whether patients with persistent postconcussional symptoms could be differentiated on the basis of a particular pattern of motor dysfunction. They compared 131 such cases with 54 patients with motor abnormalities following moderate or severe head injury. The latter patients were severely impaired on a pegboard task, less impaired on a finger tapping task, and least impaired on a grip strength task. This pattern was felt to be consistent with damage to central motor pathways. The patients with persistent postconcussional symptoms showed the opposite pattern, normally characteristic of peripheral disease such as flaccid paralysis. Unlike the patients with moderate or severe injuries, most of the patients with postconcussional symptoms were women, and all were engaged in litigation in connection with their injuries. Greiffenstein et al. inferred that the motor skill deficiencies of the latter group were probably psychogenic in nature.

If persistent postconcussional symptoms do constitute a variety of neurotic conflict that arises out of a closed head injury, they would be expected to depend to some extent on the circumstances of the accident itself. The putative relationship between the postconcussional syndrome and litigation implies that the possibility of ascribing blame for the accident to a separate individual or organisation may be an important factor in this regard. Indeed, Rutherford et al. (1977) confirmed that the persistence of postconcussional symptoms in patients with minor closed head injury was greater in those who blamed their employers or a large impersonal organisation for the accident.

Even if the persistence of postconcussional symptoms were determined to a large extent by the patient's premorbid personality, this would not mean that the condition was beyond clinical treatment. Indeed, Gronwall and Wrightson (1974) suggested that the postconcussional syndrome would require continued monitoring and management, and the precise form which that management takes is likely to determine whether those symptoms are satisfactorily resolved. A more extreme point of view was expressed by Gruneberg (1970) and by Kelly (1975), who argued that the condition was often the result of an unsupportive attitude on the part of the patient's doctor. Conversely, Englander, Hall, Stimpson, and Chaffin (1992) argued that education about postconcussional symptoms from the outset in the form of a brief interview and a standard leaflet may provide sufficient reassurance to most patients that they would regard further use of medical services as unnecessary.

Evans (1987) noted that the patient's involvement in litigation may exert a similar influence on the persistence of postconcussional symptoms through the attitudes adopted by the representatives of insurance companies. He cited a remark made more than 50 years before by Strauss and Savitsky (1934, p. 949):

> The harshness, injustice and brutal disregard of complaints shown by the physicians and representatives of insurance companies and their ready assumption for intent to swindle do not foster wholesome patterns of reaction in injured persons. The frequent expression of unjustifiable skepticism on the part of examiners engenders resentment, discouragement and hopelessness and too often forces these people to resort to more primitive modes of response (hysterical). The repeated psychic traumas bring out the worst that there is in them and makes manifest all their frailties and constitutional insufficiencies.

One basic piece of evidence against the idea that these symptoms are psychogenic in nature is that they can occur in people who apparently do not link them with the occurrence of closed head injury. As mentioned in Chapter 1, Gordon et al. (1998) referred to these as cases of "hidden" traumatic brain injury. These people exhibited high levels of emotional stress on standard self-report instruments, although, as was pointed out earlier in the case of the MMPI, the relevant items might just reflect changes in patients' daily activities in response to post-traumatic cognitive impairment. A fundamental problem with this study, however, is that, apart from self-reports, there was no information about the head injury in question and indeed no independent confirmation that it had ever occurred.

## Organic aspects of postconcussional symptoms

The contrary view was put more than 70 years ago by Symonds (1928, p. 831): "My impression is that the frequency of traumatic neuroses following head injury is a good deal exaggerated and that the minor mental symptoms so often encountered are mainly due to organic damage." Indeed, most modern accounts have suggested that Miller (1961a) overemphasised the importance of psychoneurotic influences upon postconcussional symptoms, and that physiological mechanisms may be responsible.

The earliest findings were obtained from arteriographic investigations, which tended to show persistent disturbances of cerebral circulation even following minor closed head injuries. For instance, Taylor and Bell (1966) found a reduction in cerebral blood flow in patients with postconcussional symptoms, and they argued that this was a result of increased arteriolar vasomotor tone. When individual patients were tested repeatedly during the course of their recovery, postconcussional symptoms and increased cerebral circulation time tended to come and go together. Normal circulation time at two to three weeks after concussion was said (p. 180) to "carry a good prognosis for the non-occurrence or early disappearance of post-concussional symptoms".

Rutherford et al. (1977) compared the persistence of postconcussional symptoms in 145 patients who had sustained minor head injuries with the incidence of various signs at neurological examination roughly 24 hours after their original accidents. The signs in question were headache, diplopia (double vision), anosmia (loss of the sense of smell), and the presence of other abnormalities of the central nervous system. In each case there proved to be a positive correlation with the incidence of postconcussional symptoms at follow-up examination six weeks later, which Rutherford et al. regarded as evidence to support the involvement of organic factors in the aetiology of such symptoms. When 131 of these patients were followed up one year after their accidents, these neurological signs were no longer associated with a higher symptom rate, but other signs did show such an association (Rutherford et al., 1979).

One might have anticipated that direct evidence on the involvement of organic factors in such symptoms would come from the use of brain imaging techniques. Computerised tomography (CT) scans typically prove to be normal in patients with persistent postconcussional symptoms (Weisberg, 1979). However, the relative insensitivity of CT scans in detecting parenchymal lesions was noted in Chapter 2. It is certainly recognised that during the early stages of recovery patients with closed head injury may show normal CT scans in the face of clinical evidence of brain damage (Stevens, 1982).

Electroencephalographic (EEG) recordings too are often normal after closed head injury, even when there is clinical evidence of cerebral dysfunction. However, even a relatively mild head injury can on occasion result in abnormal findings (see Chapter 2). MacFlynn et al. (1984) recorded both EEG and brainstem-evoked potentials in 24 cases of minor closed head injury within 48 hours of their accidents and again six weeks later. When these patients were compared with normal-hearing controls, 33% had EEG abnormalities, and nearly half showed evidence of delayed brainstem conduction time.

Single-photon emission computer tomography (SPECT) is a technique for monitoring regional cerebral blood flow. Kant, Smith-Seemiller, Isaac, and Duffy (1997) used SPECT to locate lesions in patients with persistent postconcussional symptoms following minor closed head injury. A total of 37 lesions were identified in 23 (or 53%) out of 43 such patients. As expected, most sites were in the frontal or temporal lobes. In contrast, magnetic resonance imaging, EEG, and CT detected abnormalities in only 9%, 7%, and 5% of patients, respectively. Kant et al. concluded that SPECT was more sensitive than any of the other techniques in revealing cerebral lesions after head injury and that these lesions themselves were responsible for causing at least some of the persistent postconcussional symptoms.

However, none of these studies distinguished between the effects of postconcussional symptoms and those of head injury *per se*. MacFlynn et al. (1984) found that the changes they observed were maximal in those patients (12 in all) who had suffered vomiting, vertigo, or diplopia at the time of their injury. Nevertheless, Kant et al. (1997) found that the results of SPECT were not related to current neuropsychiatric symptoms.

## A postconcussional "syndrome"?

In the 1960s, Miller's (1961a, 1966) pronouncements encouraged the belief that the persistence of postconcussional symptoms after minor closed head injury was only psychogenic in nature. Nevertheless, the evidence described in the previous section indicates that such a conclusion would be inadequate. Rather, modern opinion is that the postconcussional syndrome represents a long-term neurotic reaction to the short-term organic effects of a closed head injury (Binder, 1986, 1997; Elia, 1974; Evans, 1987; Gronwall & Wrightson, 1974; Long & Novack, 1986; Minderhoud et al., 1980; Rutherford et al., 1977).

However, many authors have been led to question whether it is really appropriate to refer to the condition of persistent postconcussional symptoms as a clinical "syndrome". Symonds (1940) considered that it was convenient to do so because the symptoms of headache, giddiness, and "nervous instability" did very often occur together (see also Brenner et al., 1944; Friedman et al., 1945). Lewin (1970) argued that the individual symptoms that were supposed to be characteristic of the postconcussional syndrome had distinct aetiologies and should be assessed and treated separately from each other.

On the basis of a detailed statistical analysis of postconcussional symptoms, Lidvall et al. (1974) considered that the symptom picture during the later phase of recovery was polymorphous and varied over time in an irregular manner, although anxiety appeared to constitute the nucleus of that picture. Similarly, Rutherford et al. (1977, 1979) suggested that the various individual symptoms might recur over an indefinite period, but that they constituted part of the normal pattern of recovery from a closed head injury and did not deserve to be regarded as a specific clinical syndrome.

Minderhoud et al. (1980) classified postconcussional symptoms on an a priori basis into three syndromes reflecting mental sequelae, sensory sequelae, and somatic sequelae. These syndromes showed different patterns of correlations with biographical and clinical characteristics of the patients. Finally, a diagnostic category of "postconcussional disorder" was proposed for inclusion in DSM-IV, but this proposal was rejected (American Psychiatric Association, 1994, pp. 704–706; for discussion, see Anderson, 1996).

One should also consider whether the relevant symptoms are in any way peculiar to the aftermath of concussional head injury. The specific set of symptoms that appears during the early phase of recovery does appear to be characteristic of closed head injury and a direct result of cerebral trauma. However, the persistence of these symptoms beyond the initial post-traumatic period does not seem to be dependent upon the actual occurrence of concussion (Elia, 1974). Several writers pointed out that exactly the same symptoms may occur in other clinical conditions, such as injuries to the back, the neck, or the hand (Dencker, 1958; Jacobson, 1969; Lidvall et al., 1974; Mayou, 1995). There is in fact a very similar debate about the "whiplash syndrome" associated with neck injuries in rear-end car collisions (Schrader, Obelienien et al., 1996; see commentary by Bjørgen, 1996; de Mol & Heijer, 1996; and Freeman & Croft, 1996; and see reply by Schrader, Bovim, & Sand, 1996).

Lewis (1942, p. 610) noted that the postconcussional syndrome was "apt to occur in much the same person as develops a psychiatric condition in other circumstances without any brain injury at all". The evidence suggests that it is less useful to regard persistent postconcussional symptoms as a distinct clinical syndrome than as more indefinite characteristics of a post-traumatic neurosis (see Lidvall et al., 1974; Long & Webb, 1983). Reference was made earlier to Miller's (1961a, 1961b) notion that the postconcussional syndrome was merely a special case of "accident neurosis" that happened to follow injuries to the head. However, even this concept was criticised as being of little clinical value (Gruneberg, 1970).

It was later supplanted by the notion of a "post-traumatic stress disorder" (American Psychiatric Association, 1980). This condition typically involves emotional episodes of overwhelming fearfulness, anxiety, rage, or helplessness, contrasting with a lack of interest and initiative regarding everyday matters. Such patients may tend to complain of sleep disturbance, memory impairment, and a difficulty in concentrating, and they may also show exaggerated startle responses and a generalised hyperalertness (Peterson, 1986). The symptoms of this disorder emerge during the course of recovery from any form of trauma, regardless of whether the victim has sustained a head injury.

Nevertheless, in the intervening years, this notion has become more rigorously defined, and it is summarised in DSM-IV (American Psychiatric Association, 1994, p. 424) in the following way:

> The essential feature of Posttraumatic Stress Disorder is the development of characteristic symptoms following exposure to an extreme traumatic stressor involving direct personal experience of an event that involves actual or threatened death or serious injury, or other threat to one's physical integrity; or witnessing an event that involves death, injury, or a threat to the physical integrity of another person; or learning about unexpected or violent death, serious harm, or threat of death or injury experienced by a family member or other close associate. … The person's response to the event must involve intense fear, helplessness, or horror. … The characteristic symptoms resulting from the exposure to the extreme trauma include persistent reexperiencing of the traumatic event …, persistent avoidance of stimuli associated with the trauma and numbing of general responsiveness …, and persistent symptoms of increased arousal. … The full symptom picture must be present for more than 1 month …, and the disturbance must cause clinically significant distress or impairment in social, occupational, or other important areas of functioning. …

Essentially these criteria have been adopted by courts in both Britain and the United States. McMillan (1996) described 10 patients (taken from 312 cases of head injury referred for neuropsychological assessment or rehabilitation) who exhibited post-traumatic stress disorder on such conventional criteria.

Nevertheless, this account fails to explain why the early organic aspects of closed head injury should have psychogenic consequences in some patients but not in others. Goldstein (1942, 1952) argued that "neurotic" symptoms following head injury reflected not merely actual damage to the brain, but also the organism's efforts to cope with the resulting deficits while attempting to meet the demands of the environment (cf. Tooth, 1947). Hillbom (1960) stressed that chronic compensatory effort of this sort would be more likely among patients with relatively mild head injuries, because the disabilities of those with more severe head injuries would be immediately apparent, and there would be little or no social pressure upon such patients to resume their former responsibilities.

A similar account was offered by Gronwall and Wrightson (1974) based on their finding of reduced information-processing capacity in patients with minor closed head injury. Consistent with this account, it was noted by Rimel et al. (1981) that the difficulties that head-injured patients experienced in coping with cognitive deficits were the source of considerable stress and tended to exacerbate postconcussional symptoms in the acute phase. Subsequently, van Zomeren et al. (1984) elaborated the idea that persistent postconcussional symptoms reflected a coping response to the demands of everyday life in the light of a reduction in information-processing capacity (see also van Zomeren & van den Burg, 1985). Long and Novack (1986) concluded that the potential for the development and persistence of postconcussional symptoms would exist whenever the environmental demands made upon the head-injured patient exceeded the residual cognitive capacities that were available for dealing effectively with those demands.

## PERSONALITY DISORDERS

A variety of other affective disturbances that may result from a closed head injury have been described in the literature. The early investigation by Meyer (1904) distinguished between two major varieties of post-traumatic disorder. First, a patient might remain in the state of "partial consciousness or actual delirium" after awakening from coma. Second, the patient might make a good recovery but subsequently develop "secondary traumatic insanity" in any of a wide variety of forms. Meyer estimated that "traumatic insanity" was responsible for about 1% of all admissions to psychiatric hospitals, and his own case material indicated that it was more likely in cases of severe concussion and in cases with skull fracture.

In a subsequent report, Schilder (1934) described broader changes in consciousness and mood that were characteristic of the acute phase of recovery among 35 severely injured patients. He commented (p. 186) that "emotional disturbances and changes towards schizoid, psychopathic and epileptoid trends may be the final outcome of the organic disturbance". Persistent psychiatric disturbances following closed head injury are potentially the most serious sequelae for both relatives and prospective employers. Yet, as Newcombe and Artiola i Fortuny (1979) pointed out, they are perhaps the least well understood.

There have indeed been few major developments in the field since an authoritative and influential review was published by Lishman (1973), who considered four main categories of post-traumatic psychiatric disorder: intellectual impairment; change of personality and temperament; psychotic illness; and neurotic disability. With regard to the first of these, he felt that organic brain damage was undoubtedly the principal aetiological factor, but he emphasised that cognitive performance might be impaired by reduced motivation or by disturbances of affect. Other researchers have similarly argued that the cognitive impairment shown by patients with head injury may at least be partly attributable to depression (Daniel, 1987). Conversely, however, apparent changes in mood, motivation, or personality in head-injured patients might well be secondary to persistent cognitive failures in everyday life that would result from the executive dysfunction described in Chapter 5.

### Personality change

Steadman and Graham (1970) found that 42 out of 415 patients with head injuries complained of personality change when they were interviewed five years after their accidents, and this was supported in 35 cases by the testimony of a relative. There was a positive relationship between the incidence of personality change and the severity of the original head injury as measured by the duration of PTA. This would explain why an earlier study involving relatively minor cases of closed head injury had identified personality change in just 3.5% of a series of 200 patients (Adler,

1945). Conversely, personality change is far more likely in cases of severe closed head injury.

Thomsen (1974) described 50 such patients on average 30 months after head injuries, which in many instances had given rise to coma lasting several weeks. At interview, the relatives of 84% of the patients complained of changes in personality, often marked by irritability, hot temper, lack of spontaneity, restlessness, emotional regression, emotional lability, and stubbornness. These changes were still evident in 65% of cases when 40 patients out of the original sample were followed up between 10 and 15 years after their accidents (Thomsen, 1984). Other studies confirmed the high incidence and the persistence of personality change following severe head injury (Livingston & Livingston, 1985; Roberts, 1976, 1979, pp. 57–62); Timming et al., 1982; Weddell, Oddy, & Jenkins, 1980).

The pattern of disturbance in such cases is often typical of the clinical picture associated with lesions of the frontal lobes, involving impaired social judgement, euphoria, and disinhibition (e.g. Brown et al., 1981). Rutter (1981, p. 1541) cautioned that "even in studies of adults with localized injuries there is far from a one-to-one association between these disinhibited behaviors and frontal lobe lesions". Similarly, Stuss and Benson (1984, p. 21) concluded that "the concept of frontal lobe personality alteration remains vague".

Nevertheless, this is an interesting notion in the light of the effects of closed head injury on executive functioning, which, as I mentioned in the previous chapter, have also been associated with damage to the frontal lobes. Malkmus (1983, p. 1953) speculated that behavioural disturbances following closed head injury were "directly related to impaired cognitive function and the individual's attempts to function in an environment beyond his processing capacity". This notion is very similar to the account that was offered by van Zomeren et al. (1984) in the case of the postconcussional syndrome, but the aetiology is linked more specifically to "internal structuring mechanisms" and not simply to information-processing capacity.

In children, especially in those who have sustained very severe head injuries, disinhibited behaviours may take the form of outbursts of temper, disobedience, and hyperactivity (Brink et al., 1970), which given the poor judgement of head-injured patients tends to increase the risk of subsequent injury (Barin, Hanchett, Jacob, & Scott, 1985). However, similar behaviours may have occurred in children with moderate head injuries before their accidents (Bijur, Haslum, & Golding, 1990; Brown et al., 1981; Oddy, 1984b). Among adults, this can take the form of hypersexuality, which poses further problems for remediation (Elliott & Biever, 1996; Price, 1987).

Thomsen (1974) observed that the emotional lability of patients with severe head injury tended to lead their relatives to exclude them from social situations. As a result, the main problem for 60% of the patients in her sample was loneliness. Thomsen noted (p. 182): "Most patients had lost contact with premorbid friends and they had very few possibilities of establishing new contacts, because they spent nearly all [their] time at home." Social isolation was also noted in 37% of a sample of 27 severely injured patients studied by Levin, Grossman, et al. (1979).

An early report by Hooper, McGregor, and Nathan (1945) had been concerned with adult head-injured patients who regularly showed outbursts of explosive and uncontrollable rage. Similar disturbances were described in subsequent research (e.g. Fahy, Irving, & Millac, 1967; Panting & Merry, 1972; Roberts, 1979; Thomsen, 1984). Roberts noted (p. 57) that in many cases it was their aggression rather than their dementia, euphoria, disinhibition, or apathy which was the principal cause of domestic misery and which in some cases had led to their commitment to long-term psychiatric institutions. Gans (1983) argued that rage should be differentiated from feelings of hatred, which he claimed were an intrinsic part of the process of recovery and rehabilitation from a disabling condition. For autobiographical accounts of this condition, see LaBaw (1997) and Linge (1997).

## Psychiatric disorders

Meyer (1904) emphasised that it might often be difficult to decide whether post-traumatic psychiatric symptoms were to be attributed to the trauma itself or to the "mental shock" and its consequences. As mentioned earlier, Ruesch et al. (1945) administered the MMPI to 128 head-injured patients, and they argued (p. 539) that "the post-traumatic personality is more dependent on the pre-traumatic personality than on factors related to the injury". Although the MMPI was originally devised for use with psychiatric patients, recent research has indicated that it contains clusters of items which are sensitive to the cognitive, somatic, and behavioural aspects of dysfunction in head-injured patients (Hamilton, Finlayson, & Alfano, 1995).

Several writers have argued that post-traumatic disorders do not conform to conventional patterns of psychiatric illness (Kozol, 1946; Meyer, 1904; Newcombe, 1982). However, under the heading of "post-traumatic neuroses", Lishman (1973, p. 314) included:

> depressive reactions, anxiety states often with phobic symptomatology, neurasthenic reactions with fatigue, irritability and sensitivity to noise; cases of conversion hysteria and of obsessional neurosis; and, most common of all, a variety of somatic complaints, including headache and dizziness, which may become the subject of anxious introspection and hypochondriacal concern.

Jorge, Robinson, Arndt, Forrester, et al. (1993), and Jorge, Robinson, Arndt, Starkstein, et al. (1993b) pointed out that patients were depressed while in hospital but were no longer depressed at a three-month follow-up. This transient condition was associated with left dorsolateral frontal or left basal ganglia lesions. Other patients developed major depression at a later stage of recovery; this was not linked to any particular lesion site and seemed more likely to be mediated by psychosocial factors.

Lishman (1973) also noted cases of schizophrenia following severe head injury, and he concluded that this was at least in some instances the direct result of organic damage. A similar conclusion had been reached by de Morsier (1973). There is even at least one report of Capgras' syndrome following head injury in a patient with no previous history of psychiatric disorder (Weston & Whitlock, 1971): this state is marked by the delusion that one's close relatives and friends have been replaced by imposters of identical physical appearance.

Shaffer, Chadwick, and Rutter (1975) studied psychiatric outcomes in 98 children at least two years after a unilateral compound depressed fracture of the skull that was associated with a dural tear and visible damage to the underlying cortex. There was no relationship between the presence of psychiatric disorder and the child's age at injury, the locus of the skull fracture, or the severity of the injury measured by duration of coma. Nevertheless, the incidence of psychiatric disorder was high (62%), and Shaffer et al. found that it was significantly related to a number of adverse social and family variables: a broken or unhappy marriage between the parents, contact with two or more social agencies, psychiatric disorder on the part of the mother or father, and having four or more siblings.

In his follow-up study of 291 patients with severe head injuries, Roberts (1979, pp. 62–65) identified just nine cases of "schizophreniform psychosis". All of these cases had been well before their accidents and none had a family history of schizophrenia. Roberts observed that many other patients had experienced paranoid delusional symptoms either transiently during the initial period of post-traumatic confusion or else more persistently during the first year or so following the injury (see also Lewin et al., 1979).

Finally, Thomsen (1984) also identified eight cases of "post-traumatic psychosis" among 40 patients who had sustained very severe closed head injury, including one schizophreniform patient. White, Armstrong, and Rowan (1987) described a patient who developed a paranoid condition nearly four years after he had sustained a minor closed head injury. Since the patient's delusions centred around his preoccupation with the litigation that was in progress, White et al. coined the expression "compensation psychosis" to describe his condition.

## Premorbid personality

Negative social behaviour following closed head injury may of course reflect the patient's premorbid personality rather than organic brain damage (Hayden & Hart, 1986; Jennett, 1984; Miller & Stern, 1965). In the study of 117 head-injured twins reported by Dencker (1958, 1960), 9 monozygotic twins and 11 dizygotic twins were said (either by themselves or their close relatives) to have undergone a change in personality following the head injury. Even so, the monozygotic twins still closely resembled their co-twins, and in 15 of the 16 cases in which there was evidence on the patient's pretraumatic personality it appeared that any "change" actually predated the head injury.

Black, Blumer, Wellner, and Walker (1971) presented findings from a consecutive series of 105 head-injured children of up to 14 years of age. Although there was a considerable increase in the incidence of behavioural disorders such as eating problems, hyperkinesis, and impaired attention, the reports of their parents and guardians suggested that one-third of the children had suffered from at least one of these symptoms before their injury. Nevertheless, roughly 20% of the children who had shown no such symptoms previously became symptomatic after their injury, and the same proportion of children with premorbid behavioural problems showed symptoms that were different in kind or degree after their injury.

Further evidence on this matter was obtained by Levin and Grossman (1978) from 70 patients recovering from closed head injuries of varying degrees of severity who had no history of psychiatric illness. Those patients who had been conscious on their admission to hospital and who had shown no neurological deficits produced little sign of any behavioural disturbance except in terms of somatic concern and anxiety. More severely injured patients showed a distinct pattern of behavioural sequelae that was characterised by cognitive disorganisation, motor retardation, emotional withdrawal, and blunted affect. The degree of behavioural disturbance shown by individual patients was positively related to the duration of coma, the incidence of hemiplegia, and aphasia, and the incidence of abnormalities on electroencephalography and CT. Levin, Grossman, et al. (1979) found a similar pattern of disturbance in 27 severely injured patients more than one year after their accidents.

Brown et al. (1981) conducted a comparative investigation of three groups of children: 28 had suffered "severe" head injuries, resulting in PTA lasting for at least seven days, 29 had suffered "mild" head injuries, resulting in PTA lasting for less than seven days, and 28 had suffered orthopaedic injuries not involving the head. In order to obtain an assessment of these children's behaviour before the injury, interviews were carried out with their parents as soon as possible after the accident, on the assumption that they would not yet know how the children would be affected. The children who had sustained severe head injuries were very similar to the orthopaedic control patients in terms of their previous behaviour; however, within four months of their accidents they showed a substantial increase in their level of behavioural disturbance, and this was still apparent at a follow-up assessment carried out two years later.

In contrast, the children who had sustained mild head injuries manifested a premorbid rate of behavioural disturbance that was markedly higher than that of the orthopaedic control patients, but which showed no increase as a result of the accident. In other words, children with mild head injuries seemed to be behaviourally different before their accidents, but the head injuries did not themselves appear to increase the risk of subsequent psychiatric disorder (see also Bijur et al., 1990). Nevertheless, severe head injuries did appear to exert a causal influence upon personality and social behaviour, and this followed a "dose-response" relationship insofar as the incidence of post-traumatic behavioural disturbance was correlated with the severity of the injury as measured by the duration of PTA (see also Max et al., 1999; Rutter, 1981).

In short, some psychiatric disturbances manifested after closed head injury are merely manifestations of pre-existing behavioural disorders, whereas others are genuinely the result of organic damage incurred as a direct result of the injury. Malkmus (1983) argued that the latter might be related to and mediated by aspects of impaired cognitive function. This kind of analysis serves to integrate current understanding of the cognitive and behavioural consequences of closed head injury, and it directs the attention of professionals concerned with the treatment of behavioural disorders in head-injured patients towards their concomitant neuropsychological deficits.

## FAMILY RELATIONSHIPS

### The burden on relatives

During the 1950s, it was demonstrated that prompt treatment of respiratory insufficiency could substantially reduce the level of mortality following severe head injury. In reporting this finding, Maciver, Lassman, Thomson, and McLeod (1958) claimed that the prospects for the survivors were relatively good. However, London (1967, p. 469) argued that this obscured the "crushing magnitude" of the burden that permanently disabled survivors imposed on their close relatives by virtue of changes in their moods and behaviour. In a study of severely injured children, Brink et al. (1970, p. 570) also noted that "the aggressive, impulsive, and sometimes destructive behavior exhibited by our patients was very often more difficult for the families to manage than the residual physical disability".

This impression was born out by the results of interviews carried out by Thomsen (1974) with relatives of 50 patients between 12 and 70 months after the latter had sustained severe closed head injuries. As Thomsen (1984, p. 264) commented, "while lack of social contact ... was the greatest subjective burden to the patients, changes in personality and emotion represented the severest problem to the families" (see also Lewin et al., 1979). Jennett (1976d, p. 597) pointed out that it was this combination of mental impairment with physical handicap that made brain damage so devastating in its consequences, and so different from the "heroic and happy survival" of mentally intact patients which typified spinal paralysis (see also Florian, Katz, & Lahav, 1989).

Oddy et al. (1978b) asked close relatives (usually parents or spouses) to describe 49 patients with severe head injury on a check list including personality changes and somatic, cognitive, and psychiatric symptoms. The symptoms that were mentioned most frequently by the relatives were "trouble remembering things", "becomes tired very easily", "often impatient", "often loses temper", and "often irritable". The patients and the relatives gave broadly similar accounts of the symptoms experienced, although there were some marked discrepancies in individual cases which Oddy et al. took (p. 615) to "underline the hazards of accepting the patient's report as definitive".

The relatives in this study also received a detailed interview and a depression questionnaire within one month of the accident and at roughly six and twelve months afterwards (Humphrey & Oddy, 1978; Oddy, Humphrey, & Uttley, 1978a; see also Oddy, 1984a). The results indicated that there was overt disturbance in roughly 25% of the patients' families, whether measured by the depression scale or the relatives' reports. The level of reported stress was highest during the first month following the head injury and appeared to reach a plateau between six and twelve months later. More than half of the physical illnesses that were reported by the relatives could be regarded as stress-related, including asthma, migraine, and duodenal ulcer.

Not surprisingly, family relationships appeared to be significantly poorer among patients who had suffered adverse personality changes (Oddy & Humphrey, 1980; see also Weddell et al., 1980). The frequency of arguments and disagreements and of problems in communication increased markedly between six and twelve months after the injury. As in the study by Thomsen (1974), these difficulties were more apparent between the married patients and their partners than between the single patients and their parents (see also Livingston, Brooks, & Bond, 1985a).

A similar investigation was carried out by Brooks and Aughton (1979b) in the case of relatives of 35 patients with severe blunt head injuries. When seen roughly six months after the head injury, the most frequently reported items of burden proved to be related to the patient's mental impairment, and more specifically to changes in the level of irritability, slowness, tiredness, and tension or anxiety; conversely, the least frequently cited items of objective burden were concerned with physical and sensory change. The items of objective burden that best predicted the relatives' perceived subjective burden were the patient's childish behaviour, loss of interest, change in sex life, depression, and tension or anxiety.

McKinlay et al. (1981) interviewed close relatives of 55 patients with severe closed head injury at three, six, and twelve months after their accidents. Once again, the symptoms in the patients most frequently reported as problems by their relatives were emotional changes, memory impairment, and subjective changes such as slowness and tiredness. There was no change in the amount of stress reported in terms of the perceived subjective burden across the three sessions, although there was a tendency for emotional difficulties to be reported in the patients more frequently at the later sessions. It was suggested that the latter might be consequences of the injury that had not been acknowledged during the earlier phase of recovery or else the patients' reactions to a developing awareness of disability.

The relatives in this study were also asked to complete an adjective checklist containing 18 analogue scales that were labelled with pairs of bipolar adjectives (e.g. "talkative—quiet") chosen to reflect the sorts of changes in personality and behaviour that follow severe head injuries. At each session the relative completed the checklist, first, with regard to the patient's personality before the closed head injury and, second, with regard to the present time. The results were reported by Brooks and McKinlay (1983). Not surprisingly, the ratings produced by the relatives on the current and retrospective checklists showed significant changes in the anticipated direction on many of the constituent scales. These were mainly confined to those cases where the relatives judged that there had indeed been some change in the patients' overall personality, though even in the cases where there was no such change the patients were reported to be significantly more quick-tempered, irritable, lifeless, and listless by the 12-month session. Brooks and McKinlay suggested that the latter were characteristics of all head-injured patients rather than specific features of those who had suffered personality change.

Brooks, Campsie, et al. (1986a) carried out a five-year follow-up study involving 42 of their original sample of head-injured patients. The symptoms that were reported as problems by their relatives were broadly the same as those that had been reported at the 12-month assessment. Two items (irritability and tiredness) showed marginal reductions in the intervening period, but two other items (personality change and threats of violence) showed marked increases. The perceived burden showed a significant increase in this period, although once again this was primarily associated with mental and behavioural changes in the patients. Brooks et al. concluded that for the relatives the situation had deteriorated markedly over the five-year period.

A detailed assessment of the psychiatric and social impact of severe head injury upon the patient's female relatives was carried out by Livingston et al. (1985a; Livingston, Brooks, & Bond, 1985b). The relatives produced higher scores on both the General Health Questionnaire (Goldberg, 1978) and the Leeds Anxiety Scale (Snaith, Bridge, & Hamilton, 1976) that persisted throughout the first year. Indeed, on both measures 30–40% of these relatives produced scores that were within the clinical "caseness" range at each of the follow-up sessions. However, no such pattern was demonstrated on the Leeds Depression Scale or the somatic complaints or depression subscales of the General Health Questionnaire.

The relatives in this study also reported a much higher incidence of problems on a formal questionnaire concerned with the perceived burden of living with the patient, and this if anything manifested a slight increase throughout the year. On a Social Adjustment Scale (Weissman, Prusoff, Thompson, Harding, & Myers, 1978), the relatives showed lower subjective levels of functioning within their marital and familial roles. In other words, they rated themselves as being less well adjusted in their social relationships in the family home, whereas their relationships within their extended family, at work, and in their social and leisure activies were largely unaffected. Their scores on global social adjustment became significantly worse between the three-month and six-month assessments and remained poor for the remainder of the year.

Livingston (1987) carried out a regression analysis to determine the biographical characteristics of the relatives of severely head-injured patients, which predicted various measures of psychosocial functioning. The most important determinant of the latter was found to be the relatives' previous experience of illness, as determined from their psychiatric and physical health records. Taken together, these findings led Livingston (pp. 37–38) to suggest a two-stage model of psychosocial breakdown in the families of head-injured patients, based upon accounts of individual vulnerability towards other psychiatric conditions: "Firstly, relatives are 'sensitized' by previous illness experience themselves. Secondly, a maladaptive coping strategy is provoked by the current life stress of the head injury patient's symptoms display."

Johnson and Balleny (1996) compared the reports given by nursing staff about patients with severe head injuries during their acute care with the reports given by relatives of such patients after their discharge. Only 31% of the patients were reported to present behaviour problems by hospital care staff, but the relatives of 82% of the patients reported behavioural change (and in 73% of these cases this was reported as causing practical problems). In particular, aggression and irritability were reported much more often at home than in hospital and more often in patients who had sustained head injuries more than 18 months ago than in those who had sustained injuries within the previous 18 months. In short, the severity of behavioural disturbance tended to increase after the patients' discharge from hospital and to increase further over the next three years.

Wood and Yurdakul (1997) examined the implications of this burden for personal relationships in a heterogeneous sample of patients who had been living with a partner for at least one year before sustaining a head injury. Nearly half of these patients reported that they had become divorced or separated from their partners during the five to eight years after their injury. This outcome was not clearly related to the severity of the injury according to the duration of post-traumatic amnesia, but the probability of divorce or separation was markedly greater in those patients who had had to be admitted to a specialist rehabilitation unit. Wood and Yurdakul concluded that the risk of the breakdown of an existing relationship was substantially increased when a head injury led to functional deficits and behavioural alterations.

## Discrepancies between patients' and relatives' reports

A fundamental problem in evaluating the reports given by the relatives of head-injured patients is that they may differ in important respects from the patients' own accounts. This was first noted in a six-year follow-up study by Fahy et al. (1967) involving patients who had undergone surgical treatment of severe head injury. These researchers carried out standard psychiatric interviews with patients in their own homes in the presence of "suitable informants" (p. 477):

> There were interesting discrepancies between disability as recounted by relatives and as perceived by the patients themselves. Spontaneous complaints by the patients were rare, and motor disabilities were lightly dismissed by patients and relatives alike. Witnessing a standard interview, however, often provoked informants to supply details of abnormal behaviour which would otherwise have

been missed because of lack of insight in demented survivors. Sensible of their difficulties in the fields of intellect, memory, and speech, patients seldom acknowledged temperamental changes, which in turn distressed their families most.

Thomsen (1974) also noted that patients with severe head injuries seldom seemed to be aware of the changes in their personality that were a major problem for their families.

McKinlay and Brooks (1984) addressed this issue in a more systematic fashion by comparing the subjective complaints of 55 patients assessed six months after severe closed head injury with the accounts of their close relatives as described in previous publications from this research group (i.e. Brooks & Aughton, 1979b; Brooks & McKinlay, 1983; McKinlay et al., 1981). They reported a relatively high agreement between the patients' and the relatives' accounts with regard to the incidence of sensory or motor impairment, only a moderate level of agreement with regard to the incidence of cognitive impairment, and very poor agreement with regard to the incidence of emotional and behavioural changes. In particular, there was agreement in only 60% of these cases as to whether or not the patient had become more bad tempered and in only 52% of the cases as to whether or not the patient had become more anxious since the injury. As in the earlier studies by Fahy et al. (1967) and Thomsen (1974), instances of disagreement over emotional and behavioural changes tended predominantly to arise from patients failing to admit to changes that were reported by their relatives (see also Hendryx, 1989; Schalén, Hansson, Nordström, & Nordström, 1994; Sherer et al., 1998).

Obviously, in such cases the patients' reports and their relatives' reports cannot both be accurate. In the passage quoted above, Fahy et al. (1967) ascribed these discrepancies to a lack of insight amongst demented survivors, and the account given by Thomsen (1974) appeared to extend this explanation to a lack of awareness of personality changes. McKinlay and Brooks (1984) noted that this left open the question whether the putative lack of insight was to be attributed to cognitive deficits or to some other mechanism. To explore this possibility further, McKinlay and Brooks compared the number of aspects of behaviour for which each of their patients denied a change which had been reported by a relative with their scores on a variety of psychometric tests. They found no consistent pattern of correlations and concluded (p. 92) that "where patients deny problems which relatives report them to have (i.e., when patients 'lack insight'), this is not related to cognitive deficit".

The alternative possibility is that the perceptions and reports of the relatives of head-injured patients are coloured in a systematic way, perhaps as a coping response to the stress of caring for a disabled and characterologically altered member of the family. It was noted earlier that stress in relatives of head-injured patients was linked to post-traumatic changes in personality (see Lezak, 1978; McKinlay et al., 1981; Oddy et al., 1978a; Rosenbaum & Najenson, 1976). It was also suggested that relatives' stress levels tend to be especially pronounced in those cases where the patients deny problems that their relatives report them to have (e.g. Fahy et al., 1967; Thomsen, 1974). Nevertheless, McKinlay and Brooks (1984) advocated caution in postulating a direct causal link between the reported sequelae of head injury and the degree of family disruption, and they suggested that the levels of stress experienced by the relatives of head-injured patients might be modulated by certain personality characteristics (for instance, emotional stability) that led them to cope more or less easily with their altered situation.

To evaluate this notion, McKinlay and Brooks administered the Eysenck Personality Questionnaire (Eysenck & Eysenck, 1975) to the relatives of the 55 severely head-injured patients in their investigation. They found that the relatives' scores on the Neuroticism scale of this inventory were significantly correlated both with their subjective reports of changes in the head-injured patient (especially of emotional and behavioural changes) and their perceived stress. They took this to mean that the psychosocial outcome was dependent on a complex set of interrelationships rather than a single causal connection.

## OVERVIEW

In addition to subjective complaints of poor memory and concentration, the initial period of recovery following closed head injury is associated with reports of headache, dizziness, fatigue, anxiety, and irritability. These symptoms subside within a matter of days or weeks in many patients, whereas in others they persist beyond the immediate post-traumatic period. This "postconcussional syndrome" may occur both following minor head injuries and following severe head injuries, but it may be more common in patients with a premorbid neurotic personality. This condition also affects both patients who are involved in litigation arising out of their injuries and those who have no possibility of making claims for compensation, but seems to be more common in those who blame their employers or a large impersonal organisation for their accidents.

Persistent postconcussional symptoms may be associated with poorer performance on psychometric testing (although this is obviously under the strategic control of the patients themselves), and they may result from an unsympathetic attitude on the part of doctors. Such a condition probably represents a long-term neurotic reaction to the short-term organic consequences of head injury. From a cognitive point of view it can be seen as a coping response to the impact of a reduction in central information-processing capacity on the demands of daily life. However, studies using brain imaging have shown that patients with persistent postconcussional symptoms have significant residual brain damage, and the possibility remains that this damage itself is responsible for their symptoms.

Apart from intellectual impairment, the main types of post-traumatic psychiatric disturbance are personality changes, psychotic illnesses, and neurotic disability. Personality changes are more common in patients who have suffered severe head injury. Indeed, behavioural disorders following minor head injury may simply reflect the patients' premorbid personality. Post-traumatic personality changes are often reminiscent of the pattern of disturbance that is commonly associated with lesions of the frontal lobes, and have been attributed to a disruption of internal cognitive structure. They involve impaired social judgement, euphoria, and disinhibition, but in extreme cases may include outbursts of uncontrollable rage. Psychoses and neuroses are less common following closed head injury; they do not conform to conventional patterns of psychopathology and may occur in patients with no history of psychiatric illness. Such conditions impose a very severe burden upon the families of head-injured patients, although the relatives' descriptions of the patients' behaviour will not necessarily tally with the accounts of the patients' themselves. These discrepancies are attributable sometimes to a lack of insight on the patients' part and sometimes to the relatives' stress in caring for a disabled and characterologically altered member of the family.

CHAPTER SEVEN

# Outcome, recovery, and rehabilitation

The preceding chapters have been concerned with the short-term impact of closed head injury upon psychological functioning, both during the period of the patient's hospitalisation and following his or her discharge into the community. This chapter is concerned with the patient's subsequent progress, with the likely nature of the long-term outcome, the recovery processes that lead to that outcome, and the scope for facilitating those processes by means of formal rehabilitative intervention.

## MEASURES OF OUTCOME

### Mortality

As a measure of the outcome of closed head injury, death might seem relatively unproblematic. However, Jennett and Bond (1975) emphasised that it might be difficult to agree on the criteria for specifically attributing the causal responsibility to the head injury itself. Those patients who fail to survive closed head injury have often sustained other major traumatic lesions, and they may well go on to develop extracranial complications or fatal systemic disease that is complicated by coma (e.g. Kotwica & Brzezinski, 1990). Most deaths following head injury occur within the first two or three days, and the vast majority of these can be ascribed to the primary brain damage. However, extracranial lesions and complications have an increasing importance after this time and may be responsible for 40% of all deaths occurring during and after the third week; acute renal insufficiency and bronchopulmonary infections seem to be especially important secondary causes of death following closed head injury (Bricolo et al., 1980; Carlsson et al., 1968;

Jennett & Teasdale, 1981, p. 41; Marshall et al., 1991; Pazzaglia, Frank, Frank, & Gaist, 1975).

A number of studies have shown that mortality following severe head injury is inversely related to the patient's score on the Glasgow Coma Scale (GCS) during the first 24 hours after the accident and directly related to the subsequent duration of coma (Alexandre et al., 1983; Bowers & Marshall, 1980; Bricolo et al., 1980; Gennarelli, Spielman, et al., 1982; Gennarelli et al., 1994; Marshall, Becker, et al., 1983). It was noted in Chapter 1 that the total score on the GCS during the early phase of recovery from severe closed head injury was largely a function of the patient's motor responses, and it is therefore unsurprising that the latter element is the best predictor of mortality (Makela, Frankowski, Gildenberg, Grossman, & Wagner, 1982; Mamelak, Pitts, & Damron, 1996).

Some studies have found an increased risk of mortality among patients in whom intracranial mass lesions had been visualised by means of angiography or computerised tomography (CT) (e.g. Bricolo et al., 1980; Gennarelli et al., 1982a; Pazzaglia et al., 1975). Nevertheless, severely injured patients with normal CT scans still show a high mortality rate (Snoek et al., 1979), suggesting that CT may often fail to detect life-threatening cerebral lesions (as noted in Chapter 2). The risk of mortality also seems to be increased in those head-injured patients who produce abnormal electroencephalograms or oculomotor responses suggestive of damage to the mesencephalon (or midbrain) in the early stages of recovery (Alexandre et al., 1983; Mamelak et al., 1996).

Finally, the mortality rate is higher among older patients (e.g. Bricolo et al., 1980; Heiden et al., 1983; Heiskanen & Sipponen, 1970; Jennett, 1976c; Jennett et al., 1976; Mamelak et al., 1996; Pazzaglia et al., 1975; Teasdale, Skene, et al., 1979). Carlsson et al. (1968) found that this trend could be attributed entirely to the occurrence of extracranial complications rather than to primary cerebral injury, except in the case of children aged up to 10 years, whose mortality rate was only half that of older patients.

## Vegetative state

Jennett and Plum (1972, p. 734) observed that some patients with severe head injuries never regain recognisable mental functioning, but

> recover from sleep-like coma in that they have periods of wakefulness when their eyes are open and move; their responsiveness is limited to primitive postural and reflex movements of the limbs, and they never speak. Such patients are best described as in a persistent vegetative state.

Graham et al. (1983) studied 28 patients with fatal head injury who had survived for at least a month after their accidents in a vegetative state together with seven patients who had been assessed as severely disabled. Apart from cerebral contusions, the most common findings at post-mortem were diffuse axonal injury and extensive destruction of nerve cells due to hypoxia. In three cases the hypoxic brain damage was severe and diffuse, akin to that seen in resuscitation following cardiac arrest or status epilepticus (see Jennett & Teasdale, 1981, pp. 39, 85–86).

Within the first three months following a closed head injury, there is limited scope for improvement from this condition. In a prospective study of 213 severely injured patients conducted by Heiden et al. (1983), 16% were in a vegetative state when assessed one month after their accidents. More than a quarter of these patients were found to be conscious (although severely disabled) when followed up 11 months later. On the other hand, more than half had died during the intervening interval. In a subsequent study based in four different countries, Braakman, Jennett, and Minderhoud (1988) followed 140 patients who were in a vegetative state one month after their accidents. When seen 11 months later, 10 patients were judged to have recovered or to be only moderately disabled; all were aged less than 40 and had regained consciousness within three months of their accidents.

The overall proportion of patients with severe closed head injuries who survive in a vegetative state beyond the first three months appears to be less than 5% (e.g. Alexandre et al., 1983; Bowers & Marshall, 1980; Braakman et al., 1988; Bricolo et al., 1980; Bruce et al., 1978; Gennarelli, Spielman, et al., 1982; Heiden et al., 1983; Heiskanen & Sipponen, 1970; Mamelak et al., 1996; Rimel & Jane, 1983; Roberts, 1979, p. 33). Such patients rarely survive more than 10 years after the injury (see Higashi et al., 1977; Roberts, 1979, pp. 41, 151). This may be more likely in the case of patients who have enlarged ventricles on CT scans (Timming et al., 1982).

Braakman et al. (1988) found that they could predict an unfavourable outcome (death or vegetative state) only in a small number of comatose patients, and even here they could not distinguish those who would die from those who would remain in a vegetative state. However, as was mentioned in Chapter 2, Kampfl et al. (1998) found that the presence of lesions of the corpus callosum and the dorsolateral brainstem according to MRI were important in predicting persistence of a vegetative state. Nevertheless, in recent years, it has been increasingly argued that this should not be described as a "persistent" vegetative state, still less as a "permanent" vegetative state, since this confuses a diagnosis with a prognosis (American Congress of Rehabilitation Medicine, 1995; Andrews, 1996).

Considerable public and professional interest has been expressed in the notion that programmes of intense sensory stimulation might help the recovery of such patients. Malkmus (1983, p. 1954) explained the rationale for this approach by saying that it "provides an organized presentation of heightened sensory input to prevent further sensory deprivation, to encourage responsiveness to external input, and to monitor and to assess cognitive status". The empirical justification for such programmes comes from investigations of the effects of environmental enrichment in normal animals and in those with brain lesions (Stein, Brailowsky, & Will, 1995, pp. 126–129).

Nevertheless, Hayden and Hart (1986, p. 206) argued that there was no evidence that these programmes of "sensory bombardment" had any beneficial effect on the survival of comatose patients, and they concluded (p. 206) that "the medical community would do well to treat sensory bombardment programs with a healthy skepticism". They also noted that Luria, Naydin, Tsvetkova, and Vinarskaya (1969, p. 370) had specifically advised that patients with closed head injury "should be protected against strong and excessively strong stimuli" during the acute phase of recovery so as to facilitate the gradual reactivation of temporarily inhibited nerve cells.

Although a number of studies have suggested that certain kinds of stimulation have beneficial consequences with regard to the speed and likelihood with which brain-damaged patients emerge from a prolonged vegetative state, these studies suffer from a variety of methodological problems (Andrews, 1992). Wilson, Powell, Brock, and Thwaites (1996) assessed the responses to sensory stimulation in 24 patients in a vegetative state following head injury. Stimulation led to statistically significant changes in behaviour, especially if it involved the presentation of familiar stimuli to each of the senses in turn. These changes (an increase in the likelihood of eye opening and spontaneous body movements, and a decrease in the likelihood of reflexive movements with the eyes closed) represented enhanced arousal. Nevertheless, there was no significant difference in these responses between the patients who subsequently emerged from a vegetative state and those who did not. A recent Working Party on the Management of the Vegetative State concluded that there was still only very limited evidence as to the long-term benefits of sensory stimulation programmes (Andrews, 1996).

## Neurological outcome

Most closed head injuries are not fatal, and it was noted earlier that most deaths that are attributable to closed head injury occur within the first few days. It follows that most head-injured patients who survive this period will subsequently have a normal life expectancy, and that with regard to the outcome of treatment for these patients "success should be measured less by the fact of survival and more by the quality of survival" (Jennett & Bond, 1975, p. 481).

London (1967) considered that insufficient prominence had been given to the plight of those victims of head injury who suffered severe and permanent disablement. He estimated (p. 462) that head injuries were giving rise to 1000 new "lamebrains" in the United Kingdom each year, roughly half of whom would never work again. This figure is of course cumulative over the years, and subsequent reports suggested that the *prevalence* of chronic disability following closed head injury (that is, the total number of permanently disabled survivors) was between 100 and 150 patients per 100,000 population or between 55,000 and 80,000 patients across the United Kingdom as a whole (Aitken et al., 1982; Bryden, 1989).

Motor impairment is the most conspicuous form of residual disability. Brink et al. (1970) studied the motor function of 46 children with severe head injuries, and found that 93% of the sample manifested degrees of spasticity (defined as hyperactive deep tendon stretch reflexes and increased resistance to passive movement). In a prospective study of 150 adult survivors of severe head injury, Jennett, Snoek, Bond, and Brooks (1981) found that the most frequent neurological sequelae were hemiparesis (paralysis of one side of the body), dysphasia, cranial nerve palsy, post-traumatic epilepsy, and ataxia, although no disability was detected in 26% of the sample. Schalén et al. (1994) identified a range of neurophysical deficits in 147 patients five to eight years after severe head injury, although coordination difficulties were the most common residual sign.

Lewin et al. (1979) conducted a follow-up study of 291 patients of all ages between 10 and 24 years after they had sustained head injury involving post-traumatic amnesia (PTA) lasting at least one week. They argued that patients showed different patterns of neural disability that seemed to reflect different clinical syndromes with distinct though overlapping underlying pathologies (see also Roberts, 1979, chap. 5). Finally, Lewin et al. showed that long-term disability could be predicted in most cases from the age at injury, the worst state of neural disability after injury, and the duration of PTA. The use of the worst state of neural disability is, however, rather at variance with Teasdale and Jennett's (1976) suggestion that one should assess the patient's best level of clinical function during the first 24 hours after the onset of coma (see Chapter 1).

Evans et al. (1976) had also shown that the severity of residual handicap was a direct function of both the duration of unconsciousness and that of PTA. Livingston and Livingston (1985) found that the overall incidence of neurological signs was significantly greater among patients with severe head injuries (defined by a GCS score of 8 or less on admission and a PTA lasting longer than 48 hours) than in patients with mild head injuries. Any improvement in the former group was confined to the first six months after their accidents, whereas the latter group showed virtually no residual signs three months after injury.

Timming et al. (1982) studied 28 victims of very severe head injury who had received CT and undergone an in-hospital rehabilitation programme. Most of the patients who had normal CT scans or small ventricles (consistent with brain swelling) had attained independence in daily activities within 13 weeks, as had about half of those with focal lesions (consistent with intracranial haematomas). However, none of the patients with enlarged ventricles (consistent with diffuse axonal injury) had attained independence in walking or self-care. Overall ratings of independence were related to the duration of coma, the presence of skull fracture (those with a fracture having the *better* outcome), and the occurrence of post-traumatic epilepsy.

Thomsen (1984) described long-term residual disabilities in 40 patients who had sustained very severe head injuries. When they were initially assessed on average 4.5 months after their accidents, all of these patients showed at least some signs of motor impairment. Three-quarters still showed such signs at a follow-up examination on average 30 months after their accident. At a second follow-up examination 10–15 years after their accidents, there was little change in the patients' status. There was however some change in their independence, and Thomsen argued (p. 267) that, "though the patient with very severe head trauma may remain disabled, improvement in psychosocial functions can continue for several years".

## The Glasgow Outcome Scale

Jennett and Bond (1975) argued that the measurement of outcome in cases of severe brain damage should take into account the degree of permanent disablement that required continuing social support. They offered the following scheme, which became known as the Glasgow Outcome Scale (GOS) (pp. 482–483):

> (1) *Death.*—This might seem to require no further definition, but agreement must be reached on what conditions should be met before ascribing death to brain damage. …
> (2) *Persistent vegetative state.*—This is the least ambiguous term to describe patients who remain unresponsive and speechless for weeks or months until death after acute brain damage. …
> (3) *Severe disability (conscious but disabled).*—This is used to describe patients who are dependent for daily support by reason of mental or physical disability, usually a combination of both. …
> (4) *Moderate disability (disabled but independent).*—Such patients can travel by public transport and can work in a sheltered environment, and are therefore independent in so far as daily life is concerned. …
> (5) *Good recovery.*—This implies resumption of normal life even though there may be minor neurological and psychological deficits.

Jennett and Bond reported that the GOS was already in use and had shown good consistency between different observers.

Jennett et al. (1981) examined the interobserver reliability of the GOS more formally in the case of 150 patients seen six months and (in 122 cases) twelve months after severe head injuries. At both sessions there was agreement between two independent judges in more than 95% of the patients. However, Jennett et al. also pointed out that the original GOS would be insensitive to degrees of improvement occurring within one of its categories, and they therefore divided the categories corresponding to severe, moderate, and good recovery into better and worse levels of outcome.

Maas, Braakman, Schouten, Minderhoud, and van Zomeren (1983) found that disagreement between judges was relatively common on the original GOS, and that it was more frequent on the extended GOS and when assessments were based upon patient records rather than direct clinical examination. They argued that accurate predictions of the quality of survival would be difficult to attain unless assessors developed a common frame of reference. Nevertheless, Brooks, Hosie et al. (1986) found that, in assessing 51 patients with severe head injuries, two experienced users of the GOS were agreed to within one outcome category in 100% of cases on the original GOS and in 92% of cases on the extended GOS. Most cases of disagreement were not substantial and had to do with the use of the "moderate disability" category. Among survivors of severe head injury, poor ratings on the GOS are related to the persistence of neurological sequelae, clinically assessed personality changes, and impaired performance on formal cognitive tests (Brooks, Hosie, et al., 1986; Jennett et al., 1981).

An important question is whether patients who have survived a closed head injury continue to improve indefinitely or whether there is a point during the process of recovery at which the final outcome is established. With regard to the GOS, Teasdale and Jennett (1976) suggested that the outcome became stable at six months in most survivors of head injury. Subsequent research confirmed that only a small number of head-injured patients exhibit a change of category on the GOS more than six months after their accidents (Bond & Brooks, 1976; Choi et al., 1994; Heiden et al., 1983; Jennett et al., 1981; Jennett, Teasdale, et al., 1977).

Jennett and his colleagues explored the possibility of predicting the category on the GOS to which a patient was assigned six months after suffering a severe head injury on the basis of clinical features determined within the first week of the accident. This was achieved by a collaborative programme that eventually included 1000 patients who had spent at least six hours in coma following their accidents (Jennett, 1976b, 1976c; Jennett et al., 1975, 1976, 1981; Jennett, Teasdale, et al., 1977, 1979). Six months later 49% of the patients were dead, 3% were vegetative, 10% were severely disabled, 17% were moderately disabled, and 22% had made a good recovery. Thus, although nearly half of all severe head injuries are fatal, nearly half the patients who regain consciousness make a good recovery in terms of living independently (cf. Bond, 1986).

The GOS was designed to complement the GCS, in order to provide the basis for a predictive system (Jennett & Bond, 1975). The central finding from this collaborative investigation was that a patient's category on the GOS six months after a severe head injury showed a strong negative association with the depth of coma noted during the immediate period of hospitalisation on the GCS. This has been replicated in similar studies in the United States (Bowers & Marshall, 1980; Bruce et al., 1978; Gennarelli, Spielman, et al., 1982; Heiden et al., 1983; Jaggi, Obrist, Gennarelli, & Langfitt, 1990; Levin, Gary, et al., 1990; Marshall et al., 1991) and extended to patients with minor or moderate head injuries (Levin, Amparo, et al., 1987; Temkin et al., 1995) and to patients with coma resulting from nontraumatic causes (Levy et al., 1981).

In addition, the subsequent outcome seems to be positively related to the rate of improvement on the GCS during the first few days of hospitalisation (Jennett et al., 1975a) and negatively related to the overall duration of coma (Bricolo et al., 1980; Jennett, 1976c; Levin & Eisenberg, 1986; Marshall et al., 1991; Ruijs et al., 1993). The quality of the outcome is also negatively correlated:

1. with age, such that a poor outcome is more likely in older patients (Bricolo et al., 1980; Heiden et al., 1983; Jaggi et al., 1990; Jennett & Teasdale, 1981, p. 321; Jennett et al., 1976; Jennett, Teasdale, et al., 1979; Marshall et al., 1991; Teasdale, Skene, Spiegelhalter, & Murray, 1982);
2. with the duration of PTA (Brooks, Hosie, et al., 1986; Jennett et al., 1981; Jennett & Teasdale, 1981, p. 326; Levin & Eisenberg, 1986; Levin, O'Donnell, & Grossman, 1979; Livingston et al., 1985b; Ruijs et al., 1993);
3. with disturbances of spontaneous eye movements and the pupillary, oculocephalic and oculovestibular reflexes (Heiden et al., 1983; Jennett, 1976c; Jennett et al., 1976; Marshall et al., 1991);
4. with the presence of focal lesions such as intracranial haematomas (Bricolo et al., 1980; Gennarelli, Spielman, et al., 1982; Jennett et al., 1976; Marshall et al., 1991; Snoek et al., 1979; Williams et al., 1990; but cf. Levin, Grossman, et al., 1979);
5. with elevated intracranial pressure and a depressed cerebral metabolic rate for oxygen during the immediate post-traumatic phase (Jaggi et al., 1990); and
6. with the depth of lesions in the brain according to MRI, as predicted by the model of Ommaya and Gennarelli (1974, 1976) that was discussed in Chapter 2 (Levin, Mendelsohn, et al., 1997; Levin, Williams, et al., 1988).

However, autonomic abnormalities affecting respiration, blood pressure and circulation, and body temperature, the cause of the head injury, the lateralisation of damage to one cerebral hemisphere, and extracranial injuries seem to have little influence on the final outcome when other factors are statistically controlled (Jennett, Teasdale, et al., 1979).

The approach adopted by Jennett and his colleagues was to devise a statistical model by which newly occurring cases of head injury could be compared with the existing data bank to predict the likely outcome on the basis of certain combinations of critical clinical features (Jennett et al., 1975a). The predictive system was to be based solely upon clinical data, because it was intended for use in situations where no laboratory investigations or computer facilities were available (Jennett, 1976c). Even so, over 300 items of data were available for each patient, though in most cases where an outcome could be predicted with 97% confidence this could be achieved on the basis of only 17 items of data, of which the most important were the depth of coma according to the GCS, the motor response pattern, the pattern of eye movements (both spontaneous and reflex), the pupil reactions to light, and the patient's age (Jennett, Teasdale, et al., 1979).

The particular model used by Jennett and his colleagues was the Bayesian discriminant method, which assumes that the various prognostic factors are statistically independent of one another (Jennett, 1976b; Jennett, Teasdale, et al., 1979). An alternative model based on logistic regression analysis was described by Stablein, Miller, Choi, and Becker (1980), and this appeared to be equally successful in predicting the outcome of severe head injury on the basis of early clinical data (see also Mamelak et al., 1996; Marshall et al., 1991).

This methodology aimed to provide clinicians with a basis for making rational decisions about the management of head-injured patients and in particular with a way of testing whether new forms of treatment improved the subsequent outcome (Jennett, 1976b; Teasdale & Jennett, 1976). It might also be of value in allocating limited resources and in counselling the families of head-injured patients. Indeed, the availability of predictions concerning the subsequent outcome does affect the management of head-injured patients (Murray et al., 1993). It would appear, however, that many patients who achieve a "good" outcome on the GOS suffer from persistent major disabilities, and that the GOS is insufficiently differentiated for either neuropsychological assessment or rehabilitation planning (Tate, Lulham, Broe, Strettles, & Pfaff, 1989, discussed later).

## Return to work

The GOS was intended to provide a measure of a patient's "social reintegration" (Jennett & Bond, 1975, p. 481) in addition to his or her recovery in purely neurological terms, and Jennett (1976a, p. 653) stated explicitly that the GOS was designed to enable surviving patients to be classified "according to the overall social outcome". However, the traditional indicator of social recovery following closed head injury has been the patient's capacity for resuming normal employment (see Russell, 1934; Symonds, 1928, 1942; Symonds & Russell, 1943).

Humphrey and Oddy (1980; Oddy et al., 1978) noted that this was a crucial concern for most head-injured patients, psychologically if not financially, especially in the case of the young adults who were most likely to be involved as the victims of closed head injury. It might be expected that a patient's earning capacity would prove to be a useful index of outcome. Nevertheless, Miller and Stern (1965) found that this was contaminated by differential increases in earnings amongst different occupations during the follow-up period, and they concluded that the *nature* of the patient's subsequent employment was a more reliable guide to functional recovery.

A large number of studies have considered a wide variety of possible predictors of return to work after closed head injury in the civilian population (e.g. Bishara, Partridge, Godfrey, & Knight, 1992; Brooks, McKinlay, Symington, Beattie, & Campsie, 1987; Bruckner & Randle, 1972; Carlsson et al., 1968; Denny-Brown, 1945a; Gilchrist & Wilkinson, 1979; Guthkelch, 1980; Heiskanen & Sipponen, 1970; Levin, Grossman, et al., 1979; Lewin et al., 1979; McKinlay et al., 1983; McMordie, Barker, & Paolo, 1990; Oddy & Humphrey, 1980; Rimel et al., 1981; Steadman & Graham, 1970; Temkin et al., 1995; van Zomeren & van den Burg, 1985; Weddell, Oddy, & Jenkins, 1980; Wrightson & Gronwall, 1981). Humphrey and Oddy (1980) concluded from a review of many of these studies that, apart from the severity of the injury as measured by the duration of coma or of PTA, occupational resettlement after head injury was influenced by the age of the patient, his or her previous personality and occupational level, and the occurrence of post-traumatic personality changes, but that much less importance attached to gross physical handicap or specific disabilities. There is some evidence that return to work tends to be later after industrial accidents (Guthkelch, 1980) or traffic accidents (Wrightson & Gronwall, 1981), although the time taken to return to work does not seem to depend on whether or not the patient is pursuing a claim for financial compensation (McKinlay et al., 1983).

Ponsford, Olver, Curran, and Ng (1995) used a discriminant function analysis to try to predict return to work in patients two years after they had sustained severe head injuries. The key variables appeared to be age, the GCS score on acute admission, and the residual level of disability. The duration of PTA also seemed to be important, but it was not included in the analysis because it was very highly correlated with residual disability. Indeed, PTA duration was more highly correlated with employment status than the GCS score, which by itself explained less than 7% of the variation in employment status two years after injury.

In two different sets of patients, Ponsford et al. (1995) found that the three chosen variables correctly predicted employment status in 74% and 68% of cases. This is far better than chance, but it also implies that other factors were operating. Possible contributory factors in those patients who were employed but who were predicted to be unemployed included (p. 18) "employer support, with availability of alternative duties, and determination and adaptability on the part of the injured individual". Possible contributory factors in those patients who were unemployed but who were predicted to be employed included (p. 18) "pre-existing personality or social problems, the presence of multiple trauma, behaviour problems, lack of employer support, availability of financial support from a spouse, or other intervening social circumstances".

Johnson (1998) followed up 62 patients with very severe head injuries over a period of 10 years. He found that 42% had re-established themselves in employment, a further 20% showed an irregular pattern of work, and the remainder had made little or no attempt to work at all. There had been few changes in employment status after the first two years following the injury. In particular, the settlement of compensation claims typically had not led to an improvement in employment status (cf. Chapter 6); indeed, in some cases it seemed to have led to a decline.

Johnson (1998) found that long-term employment status was linked to the severity of the original injury measured by the duration of PTA but was largely unrelated to the patients' age. However, the most important determinant of long-term employment status seemed to be the provision of help in occupational resettlement both before and after they returned to work. Johnson concluded that patients who have sustained severe head injuries needed to have a gradual and supported return to work if successful and stable re-employment were to be achieved.

Generally speaking, residual neurological deficits are not important determinants of occupational resettlement after head injury. Evans (1989) suggested that post-traumatic epilepsy had a "devastating" effect on whether patients were able to resume their previous or equivalent employment. However, this conclusion was based on patients who had been in military service. Haltiner, Temkin, Winn, and Dikmen (1996) confirmed that patients with post-traumatic epilepsy had poorer GOS scores and were less likely to have returned to work than other patients when seen one year after their injuries, but this could be explained entirely by the former patients' longer coma duration. Haltiner et al. concluded that these poorer outcomes reflected the effects of the brain injuries that had caused the seizures rather than the effect of the seizures themselves.

Another possible exception is the loss of the sense of smell (anosmia). Although this disorder would reasonably be expected to follow sphenoidal injury (due to shearing of the afferent fibres), it may also be associated with orbitofrontal damage contiguous to the site of the olfactory bulbs, and its incidence seems to vary with the duration of PTA (see e.g. Guthkelch, 1980). Varney (1988) described 40 patients with total anosmia as the result of closed head injury, almost all of whom had had major employment problems despite having been medically cleared for work and despite having no significant cognitive, motor, or sensory deficits. Interviews carried out with their relatives and employers revealed subtle forms of psychosocial dysfunction in the areas of planning, decision making, and judgement of the sort associated with lesions of the frontal lobes (cf. Lezak, 1982; Stuss & Benson, 1984). Similar results were obtained by Martzke, Swan, and Varney (1991) in 20 patients with relatively minor head injuries.

Occupational resettlement is related to a number of other measures of outcome following closed head injury, including the outcome category achieved on the GOS (Levin, Grossman, et al., 1979), the persistence of postconcussional symptoms (Brenner, 1944; Friedman et al., 1945; Guthkelch, 1980), and disturbances of cognition, memory, and personality (Evans, 1989; Kunishio et al., 1993; McMordie et al., 1990; Weddell et al., 1980). In a prospective study of 538 patients who had sustained minor head injuries, Rimel et al. (1981) found that 34% of those who had been gainfully employed before their accidents were still unemployed three months afterwards; this was attributed to subtle organic deficits of attention, concentration, memory, or judgement and to the emotional stress involved in coping with these problems.

In victims of severe head injury, Brooks et al. (1987) found that the relatives of patients who had returned to work within seven years of an injury reported fewer residual deficits in memory and communication than the relatives of those who had not, and these reports were confirmed in terms of the patients' scores on objective psychometric tests. A multiple regression analysis demonstrated that patients' occupational status was predicted by their scores on the Logical Memory subtest of the Wechsler Memory Scale (WMS) and on a paced auditory serial addition task (PASAT). One problem is that performance on the latter task is correlated with scores on the National Adult Reading Test (NART) and the Wechsler Adult Intelligence Scale (WAIS), and thus in predicting occupational recovery the PASAT may be a proxy for general intelligence (see Crawford, Obansawin, & Allan, 1998).

Indeed, Humphrey and Oddy (1980) pointed out that the occupational resettlement of head-injured patients would depend on factors such as intelligence, education, and professional training because of the range of personal and cognitive skills that these entail, but this is not a peculiarity of victims of head injuries. Dresser et al. (1973) reported the main results of a 15-year follow-up study of 864 head-injured veterans from the Korean War (roughly one-quarter of whom had sustained blunt head wounds), together with 121 controls drawn from the same units. Individuals in *both* groups who on their induction had obtained low scores on the Armed Forces Qualification Test were more likely to be unemployed at the follow-up assessment.

Similar considerations may apply in the case of patients' ages and the nature of their original employment as possible predictors of occupational resettlement. In fact, Ponsford et al. (1995) found that returning to work was less likely in the case of patients aged 40 or older, although it appeared to be unrelated to the level of skill in their previous employment. Moreover, the likelihood that head-injured patients will return to work obviously depends on local socioeconomic circumstances and unemployment levels (Baddeley, Meade, & Newcombe, 1980; Jennett & Bond, 1975).

Another issue is that few researchers have evaluated whether head-injured patients return to their actual previous employment. Highly specialised careers may be dependent upon very specific abilities that can be disrupted by even very subtle deficits, and it may be easier to take up apparently equivalent but less demanding forms of employment. Out of 32 patients who were counted as having "returned to work" two years after severe head injuries, Ponsford et al. (1995) found that only sixteen had returned to their previous position on a full-time basis; four had taken a full-time position with their previous employer but with alternative duties, five had taken a full-time position with a different employer, one had returned to his previous position but on a part-time basis, and six had taken up alternative forms of employment on a part-time basis.

Equally, very few researchers have tried to evaluate the continued employability of head-injured patients. Olver, Ponsford, and Curran (1996) found that many patients who were in education or employment two years after sustaining moderate or severe head injuries were unemployed when seen again three years later. However, as Barth et al. (1983) pointed out, it is hard to draw causal inferences from such findings without access to detailed information on the patients' premorbid employability.

A more fundamental problem is that strictly speaking the criterion of returning to work should only be used in assessing the recovery of patients who have previously been in gainful employment. Brooks et al. (1987) found that 14% of employable individuals who sustained a severe closed head injury in the west of Scotland had in fact been unemployed at the time. Apart from the fact that the notion of *return* to work is in principle inappropriate in such cases, it is highly improbable that their prospects for occupational resettlement would be the same as those of patients who were previously in employment. Similarly, even in patients who had been working when they sustained head injuries, Temkin et al. (1995) found that the best predictor of whether they would be working one year afterwards was whether they had held their previous jobs for at least six months.

Moreover, this criterion of recovery is of even less value in the case of children, those who are near or in retirement, and those who devote themselves to housekeeping or the care of dependants (Baddeley et al., 1980). Steadman and Graham (1970) suggested that recovery from head injury among housewives could be judged against their ability to perform their former routine of housework, whereas children could be judged against previous school performance. Heiskanen and Kaste (1974, p. 13) concluded that "children who remain unconscious for two weeks or more will only rarely be able to manage well at school". Ruijs et al. (1993) found that these academic difficulties were linked to abnormal evoked potentials during the immediate period of recovery. In fact, Kinsella et al. (1997) found that children who had sustained severe head injury and who showed persistent deficits were likely to require special educational placement.

## Social outcome

Until the mid-1970s researchers devoted very little attention to broader aspects of recovery following closed head injury, and the few references to social outcome were apparently based merely upon clinical impression (see e.g. Hpay, 1971). Two studies were published in which patients with severe closed head injuries were classified at follow-up according to the degree of social independence or reintegration (Lundholm, Jepsen, & Thornval, 1975; Pazzaglia et al., 1975); these found that the quality of survival was much poorer among older patients, but was not related to the duration of coma.

Bond (1975) sought to quantify the outcome of severe brain damage in terms of its impact upon a patient's daily life. Many different scales of "activities of daily living" have been devised by geriatric specialists to assess social independence in terms of basic functions of self-care. Instruments of this sort show continuing improvement during the first year of recovery following severe head injury (Livingston & Livingston, 1985). While they may be useful in planning community support for older patients following closed head injury (Wilson, Pentland, Currie, & Miller, 1987), they are often considered to be too restricted for evaluating recovery in young head-injured adults (e.g. Jennett, 1984; Jennett et al., 1981).

Instead, Bond (1975) constructed three separate rating scales for the assessment of physical disability, mental handicap, and social reintegration among patients with

TABLE 7.1

Scales for the assessment of severe brain damage

| |
|---|
| *Neurophysical scale* |
| Motor deficit |
| Sensory deficit |
| Aphasia |
| Ataxia |
| Cranial nerves |
| Physical deficits |
| *Mental scale* |
| 1. Intellect |
| (a) Memory |
| (b) Distractability |
| 2. Personality |
| (a) Apathy to euphoria |
| (b) Irritability to aggression |
| 3. Mental symptoms |
| (a) Free anxiety |
| (b) Phobic anxiety |
| (c) Obsessional symptoms |
| (d) Hysterical symptoms |
| (e) Depressive symptoms |
| *Social scale* |
| 1. Work |
| 2. Family cohesion |
| 3. Leisure |
| 4. Criminality |
| 5. Sexual activity |
| 6.Alcohol consumption |

From Bond, M.R. (1975), Assessment of the psychological outcome after severe head injury. *In outcome of severe damage to the central nervous system* (Ciba Foundation Symposium No. 34, new series). Amsterdam: Elsevier/Excerpta Medica. Copyright 1975 by Ciba Foundation. Reprinted with permission.

severe head injury. The components of these subscales are shown in Table 7.1. Relevant data were obtained from a standard clinical interview and were supplemented by information from a close relative or friend. The procedures for scoring individual patients are contained in an Appendix to Bond's report; these yield ratings increasing from zero on each scale reflecting the degree of disability or impairment relative to the patient's premorbid state. These scales were then evaluated in a pilot study involving 56 patients examined between three months and more than two years after head injuries which had given rise to a PTA lasting longer than 24 hours (see also Bond, 1976).

The overall ratings of physical and mental disability were found to be significantly correlated with the ratings of social disability, but not with each other. Bond (1975, p. 147) explained this by suggesting that "the neurological scale is primarily a measure of focal brain damage whereas the aspects of mental function assessed are probably affected more by diffuse brain dysfunction". Nevertheless, he noted that the overall degree of physical disability was specifically associated with the degree of memory impairment and a loss of work capacity; that the overall degree of mental disability was associated with a loss of work capacity, leisure pursuits, and family cohesion; and that the overall degree of social impairment was associated with disorders of memory and personality but not with symptoms of mental illness.

Additional results from this study were presented by Bond and Brooks (1976) relating scores on the three scales to the time after injury when the assessment had been conducted. There was no sign of any improvement on the neurophysical scale between patients tested six months and two years after their accidents, which was taken to suggest that "the greater part of recovery must have taken place within six months of injury" (p. 130). The mental and social scales showed modest improvements beyond six months of the injury, but in neither case was the trend statistically significant.

Weddell et al. (1980) used Bond's neurophysical scale as part of the clinical assessment of 44 young adults admitted to a rehabilitation centre after very severe head injury. These patients demonstrated a substantial improvement on this scale between six months and two years after the injury, although only eight were totally free from neurophysical deficits at the time of the latter examination. Poor neurophysical status was correlated with a number of aspects of social recovery according to interviews with the patients' relatives, including a failure to resume work, an increased dependency on the family, and a tendency to participate more in activities with parents. However, there was no significant association with overall frequency of social contact or with the relatives' assessment of memory impairment or personality change.

A more elaborated scale, the Glasgow Assessment Schedule (GAS), was devised by Livingston and Livingston (1985) for use in clinical and research settings where longer-term management and rehabilitation of head-injured patients was envisaged. It focused upon the practical implications of particular forms of impairment rather than their aetiology, and is based on clinical examination, self-report measures, and simple objective tests. It yields a comprehensive assessment of neurophysical signs, subjective complaints, personality change, cognitive functioning, activities of daily living, and occupational status. In evaluative studies, the GAS was found to demonstrate acceptable interrater reliability, a high level of discrimination between cases of mild and severe head injury, and a strong association with patients' global ratings on the GOS. Nevertheless, the GAS may not provide an adequate coverage of post-traumatic complaints, especially those relating to fatigability, slowness of thinking, depressive symptoms, anxiety, and flattening of affect ("Psychosocial Outcome", 1986).

Tate et al. (1989) devised a more detailed assessment of psychosocial outcome, the Lidcombe Psychosocial Disability Scale. Each patient was assigned a score of between 1 and 3 by a social worker and a community nurse in each of three areas of functioning: vocational and avocational pursuits; significant interpersonal relationships; and independent living. Those who achieved the minimum score of

3 were classified as having good reintegration; those scoring between 4 and 6 were classified as having substantially limited reintegration; and those scoring between 7 and 9 were classified as having poor reintegration.

When the scale was applied to 87 patients with severe head injuries from a consecutive series of admissions to a regional rehabilitation unit, Tate et al. (1989) found that the proportions in these three categories were 24%, 43%, and 33%, respectively. The scale showed a highly significant concordance with the GOS, and in particular all 16 patients who were assessed as having a severe disability on the GOS were rated as having poor social reintegration.

Nevertheless, more than half of the 45 patients who were assessed as having made a "good" recovery on the GOS were rated as having substantially limited integration; only 18 of these patients were in full-time employment, and most of these had a drop in occupational status or experienced difficulties with their work skills. Moreover, exactly half of the 26 patients who were assessed as having "moderate disability" on the GOS were rated as having poor reintegration; most of these patients required supported and supervised living arrangements, and most exhibited difficulties in forming interpersonal relationships. Tate et al. (1989) suggested that their scale provided a more accurate picture of their patients' daily lives and a better basis for planning future rehabilitative efforts.

## RECOVERY OF FUNCTION

### Subjective reports

A fundamental problem in measuring psychosocial recovery following closed head injury is the paucity of objective measures of psychological function that are sensitive indicators of mental processing and at the same time valid predictors of the ability to cope with the problems of daily life. As Baddeley et al. (1980) observed, this means that information regarding the quality of outcome must come in the first instance from the reports of head-injured patients and their relatives.

Oddy et al. (1978b) constructed a check list of 37 items that related to personality changes and somatic, sensory, cognitive, and psychiatric symptoms. This was administered to 48 patients roughly six months after they had received head injuries leading to a period of PTA lasting longer than 24 hours. In each case the check list was also completed by a close relative (normally the patient's parent or spouse) with reference to the patient's current condition. The duration of PTA was positively related to the number of reported symptoms, and the patients and relatives produced similar distributions of symptom frequency. In both, cognitive and personality changes were predominant, and the most commonly reported symptom was "trouble remembering things". Similar results were obtained by Levin, Grossman, et al. (1979) and by Thomsen (1984).

Kapur and Pearson (1983) devised a Memory Symptoms Test on the basis of the everyday memory difficulties that had been previously reported by a large heterogeneous group of patients with established cerebral pathology. This test was then administered to 14 head-injured patients in whom the duration of PTA had varied from a few minutes to a year during a routine assessment carried out between seven and sixty months after their injuries. The test took the form of a questionnaire in which the patient was to indicate whether his or her memory was unimpaired, slightly impaired, or very much impaired in 10 different functions compared with its capacity before the head injury. For nine of these patients the test was also completed by a close relative or acquaintance with regard to the patient's current condition. The correlation coefficient between the patients' reports and the relatives' reports was substantial and highly significant ($r = 0.92$). However, for neither the patients' reports nor the relatives' reports was there any sign of a relationship between memory symptoms and the patient's performance on tests of memory function.

Sunderland et al. (1983) compared the everyday memory performance of 32 patients with severe closed head injuries interviewed between two and eight years after their accidents and that of a control group of orthopaedic patients with no history of head injury. The patients were given a questionnaire in which they reported the frequency with which they suffered from each of 35 different types of memory failure; they were then asked to keep a daily check list for seven consecutive days, indicating which of these memory failures they had experienced during each day. Both tasks were also carried out by a close relative living in daily contact with the patient with reference to the patient's recent condition.

There was reasonable consistency among the four measures, and three showed a higher incidence of memory failures in the patients with closed head injuries than in the orthopaedic controls. However, the responses given to the patients' questionnaire did not differ between the two groups and failed to correlate with objective performance on a battery of memory tests. In contrast, the relatives' questionnaire did correlate with the patients' objective memory performance and showed the anticipated pattern of a higher frequency of memory failures amongst the head-injured patients than amongst the controls.

Sunderland, Harris, and Gleave (1984) devised a new questionnaire containing 27 items, which was based on those items that had most clearly discriminated between the head-injured and control patients in their first study. This was used in a postal survey of 78 patients between 18 months and six years after they had sustained a severe closed head injury (defined by a PTA lasting longer than 24 hours) and a comparison group of 78 patients with minor closed head injury (in whom the maximum duration of PTA was 10 minutes). A second version of the questionnaire was to be completed by a close friend or relative with reference to the patient's recent condition. The mean number of memory failures reported by the patients with minor head injury was similar to that generated by members of a large subject panel, and it was concluded that patients with minor head injuries did not differ from normal subjects in the incidence of memory failures in everyday life.

The patients with severe head injuries did not differ from those with minor head injuries in terms of the reported frequency of memory failures, but the relatives reported a higher incidence of memory failures among the severely injured patients. There was however no difference between the patients with "very severe" injuries (in whom the duration of PTA was longer than seven days) and those with "severe" injuries (in whom the duration of PTA was between one and seven days) in either their own or their relatives' reports of memory failures. Finally, 21 of the severely injured cases for whom there was clinical evidence of major lesions produced a significantly higher incidence of memory failures than the remaining cases on the relatives' questionnaires but not on their own questionnaires.

The findings of the two latter studies suggest that self-reports have little validity as measures of memory failure, perhaps because forgetful patients tend to forget their own memory lapses. Somewhat more promising results were obtained by Bennett-Levy (1984) using a similar Subjective Memory Questionnaire in which subjects rated their memories on a 5-point scale with regard to 43 everyday situations (Bennett-Levy & Powell, 1980). This study compared 39 severely head-injured patients with 32 orthopaedic controls: the patients in whom PTA had lasted for between one and three weeks rated their own memories if anything more favourably than did the control group, whereas significantly poorer ratings were given by the patients in whom PTA had lasted for more than three weeks.

Moreover, although the findings described by Sunderland and his colleagues indicate that the reports of a close observer (e.g. a relative) may be of some clinical value, these may well be biased by how easily different classes of memory failure can be observed. As Sunderland, Harris, and Baddeley (1984) noted, deficits in aspects of verbal behaviour will be immediately obvious in everyday conversation, whereas failures in face recognition will only be apparent if patients comment on them or behave inappropriately towards individuals whom they should recognise. Nevertheless, under constant test conditions the reports of close observers may be useful in monitoring both the progress of spontaneous recovery and the effectiveness of rehabilitative interventions, and to this end Wilson (1984; 1987a, p. 101) reported that the check list devised by Sunderland et al. (1983) had been successfully adapted for use by the therapists at a rehabilitation centre.

Brooks, Campsie, et al. (1986) asked the relatives of 42 patients with severe closed head injury to report on changes that were apparent in the patient one and five years after the injury. Apart from reports of continuing personality change, the most frequent symptoms were concerned with slowness, memory, irritability, and bad temper. Increases were noted in reports of concentration and memory problems, particularly in terms of the patient forgetting what he or she was doing in the middle of an action sequence, repeating or double checking actions, or losing track of what he or she was saying. One reason for such increases may be that impairments of memory become more significant once patients have returned to work. However, the incidence of these problems at the five-year assessment did not show a significant correlation with the severity of the head injury according to the duration of PTA.

Hendryx (1989) administered a questionnaire to 20 patients who had sustained a head injury between one and seven-and-a-half years earlier but who had made either a good or a moderate recovery according to the GOS. They were asked to quantify the perceived change in each of 15 symptoms in comparison with their pre-injury state. In the case of 13 patients, similar ratings were made about the patient by a close family member. Finally, 20 control subjects were asked to rate changes in themselves over the past five years. The head-injured patients reported greater physical, emotional, and cognitive changes than the control subjects, implying that these were not simply due to the passage of time. The patients also reported that cognitive changes were more pronounced than emotional ones, but the family members regarded all three kinds of changes as equally significant. Indeed, the relatives judged emotional changes to be more pronounced than did the patients themselves. Hendryx suggested that relatives might be less able to recognise the cognitive limitations of head-injured patients than the emotional frustrations to which they gave rise.

Allen and Ruff (1990) obtained self-ratings from 56 head-injured patients with regard to sensorimotor function, attention, arithmetic, language, learning and remembering, and logical thinking. In each case, respondents reported the extent to which different activities were a strength or problem. Allen and Ruff then administered objective tests chosen to assess the same aspects of cognition functioning. Half of the patients had sustained severe head injuries, and the remainder had sustained mild or moderate head injuries. Also, half of the patients were tested up to one year following injury; the remainder were tested more than one year following injury.

In comparison with the self-ratings and test performance of normal controls, the patients with severe head injury tended to overestimate their performance in sensorimotor function and attention, whereas the patients with mild or moderate injuries tended to underestimate their performance, particularly in the areas of sensorimotor function, language, and reasoning. Whereas the control group demonstrated significant correlations between self-ratings and performance in the areas of language, learning and remembering, and reasoning, the corresponding relationships tended to be weaker in the head-injured patients. This supports the view that self-reports are not valid measures of cognitive function following closed head injury.

## Memory function

Situations that demand learning and remembering are clearly a source of concern for head-injured patients and their relatives. Nevertheless, the question arises whether these subjective complaints of persistent memory impairment are confirmed by the results of objective testing.

In the case of minor closed head injury, the empirical research that was described in Chapter 4 suggested that patients suffer an impairment of memory function that persists beyond the period of PTA, but which is a purely transient phenomenon that resolves during the weeks and months after the injury. Evidence on the long-term consequences of minor closed head injury was obtained in a study by Dencker and Löfving (1958), who compared 28 head-injured monozygotic twins with the uninjured co-twins as controls. From a clinical point of view, the former group were an unselected sample of head-injured patients, and the duration of PTA had exceeded 24 hours in only four cases (Dencker, 1958). When the twins were tested on average 10 years after the accidents, the head-injured patients showed no sign of any impairment on tests of digit span, serial learning, and the retention of narrative. Of course, the failure of this or other research to detect permanent psychological dysfunction might be attributed to an insensitivity on the part of the tests or procedures that were used. Nevertheless, these results are entirely consistent with the view that observable deficits in learning and remembering consequent upon minor closed head injury are largely transient in nature (see also Binder, Rohling, & Larrabee, 1997).

This optimistic picture needs to be qualified in a number of ways. First, it was noted in Chapter 4 that the failure to find a statistically significant impairment in an entire group of head-injured patients does not rule out the possibility that one or more individuals within such a group exhibit persistent and clinically significant deficits. Second, the fact that many patients with minor head injuries achieve normal performance in neuropsychological tests does not rule out the possibility that they are impaired in everyday life (see Martzke et al., 1991). Such deficits may be apparent in more naturalistic instruments such as the Rivermead Behavioural Memory Test. Third, lapses of memory in daily life may be secondary to deficits in executive function of the sort that were discussed in Chapter 5. In the next section, it will be noted that a proportion of patients with minor head injuries appear to have persistent cognitive deficits that give rise to difficulties in returning to work.

Nevertheless, other research described in Chapter 4 indicated that a severe closed head injury gives rise to a more global and persistent impairment of memory function. There is some evidence of improvement in performance on repeated testing (e.g., Groher, 1977; Lezak, 1979), but if comparisons are made between patients tested at different follow-up intervals there is usually no sign that the impairment becomes less pronounced with the passage of time (e.g. Brooks, 1972, 1974a, 1974b, 1975, 1976; Levin et al., 1976b; Sunderland et al., 1983; cf. Parker & Serrats, 1976). This apparent lack of improvement can often be ascribed to a need to delay the testing of the most severely injured patients, and it does not therefore necessarily indicate a lack of spontaneous recovery (cf. Levin and Eisenberg, 1979a). Nevertheless, the impairment in question can be readily demonstrated in psychometric testing one or more years after the original accident (Levin , Gary, et al., 1990; Max et al., 1999; Norrman & Svahn, 1961; Sunderland et al., 1983; Thomsen, 1984).

The magnitude of this impairment varies directly with the severity of the head injury, as measured by the duration of coma or PTA (Dailey, 1956; Norrman & Svahn, 1961; Parker & Serrats, 1976; Temkin et al., 1995). Indeed, Bennett-Levy (1984) compared 29 patients between two and five years after they had sustained a severe head injury with 32 orthopaedic cases, and he found that significant deficits on memory tasks were confined to patients in whom PTA had lasted for longer than three weeks. He suggested that a "threshold" of brain damage in terms of PTA operated at about three weeks.

Wilson et al. (1988) tested 25 patients between 5 and 18 months after a head injury that had necessitated their transfer to a regional neurosurgical unit. Impaired performance on the Logical Memory and Associate Learning subtests of the WMS was significantly associated with depth of lesions and ventricular enlargement according to recently conducted MRI scans, but there was no relationship with the findings of MRI scans conducted within 21 days of the original injury. Whether impairment is linked to intracranial hypertension during the acute phase is similarly unclear (Levin, Gary, et al., 1990; Uzzell, Dolinskas, & Wiser, 1990).

Levin, Grossman, et al. (1979) compared 27 severely head-injured patients with 50 intact control subjects in terms of their recall of a word list using the selective reminding procedure. Both the incidence and the magnitude of impairment were related to the quality of recovery according to the GOS. Other researchers have confirmed that the memory performance of severely head-injured patients is related to their recovery on the GOS, mainly because of the poor performance of the patients who are classified as severely disabled (Brooks, Hosie, et al., 1986; Clifton et al., 1993; Jennett et al., 1981). Prigatano et al. (1984) found that those severely head-injured patients who returned to gainful employment or study were significantly different from those who did not in their Memory Quotients on the WMS, and especially in terms of their performance on the Visual Reproduction and Associate Learning subtests. These results suggest that memory skills may be important determinants of occupational resettlement.

## Cognitive function

The empirical research reviewed in Chapter 5 suggested that a minor closed head injury gives rise to a transient and relatively slight impairment of cognitive function. Indeed, the clinical literature is fairly consistent in suggesting that performance returns to broadly normal levels during the month or so after a minor head injury (see Binder et al., 1997).

In their long-term follow-up study of head-injured identical twins and their uninjured co-twins, Dencker and Löfving (1958) found statistically significant deficits on tests of mirror drawing, sorting, and tachistoscopic figure/ground discrimination, and also on a paced choice reaction-time task. However, these effects were fairly small in magnitude, and they were not regarded as being of any practical importance; in particular, as Dencker (1960, p. 571) later observed, "they seemed to make no difference to the occupation the twins chose and did not handicap them in their work".

Nevertheless, more recent work has indicated that a significant proportion of patients with minor head injury may encounter problems in returning to work

(Rimel et al., 1981). This does appear to be linked to persistent cognitive impairment (Barth et al., 1983). In particular, Gentilini et al. (1989) found that patients with mild head injury (defined as a loss of consciousness lasting less than 20 minutes) exhibited significantly slower response latencies in visual search and choice reaction-time tasks three months after their accidents.

Be that as it may, other research has identified a more sustantial, persistent, and global impairment of cognitive functioning among those patients who have sustained severe closed head injury (e.g. Klonoff, Low, & Clark, 1977; Levin, Gary, et al., 1990; Norrman & Svahn, 1961; but cf. Chadwick, Rutter, Shaffer, & Shrout, 1981). This impairment is more apparent in patients whose recovery is poor according to the GOS (Brooks, Hosie, et al., 1986; Clifton et al., 1993; Jennett et al., 1981), but it can be detected even in those who have apparently made a good recovery (Conzen et al., 1992; Stuss et al., 1985). Some early studies suggested that it was the most important indicator of problems with social and vocational rehabilitation (Heiskanen & Sipponen, 1970; Lundholm et al., 1975; cf. Najenson et al., 1975). It is apparent not only in formal psychometric testing but also in a delayed P-300 component of the evoked potential, which is normally interpreted as an index of cognitive efficiency (Campbell et al., 1990). Experimental analyses have identified the response-selection stage of information processing as the primary locus of this impairment (Murray et al., 1992; Shum et al., 1990, 1994).

The magnitude of the cognitive impairment following severe head injury appears to be directly related to the duration of coma (Klonoff et al., 1977; Temkin et al., 1995; van Zomeren & Deelman, 1976; Zwaagstra et al., 1996; but cf. Lundholm et al., 1975). Using a four-choice visual reaction-time task, Van Zomeren and Deelman (1978) found that patients who had been unconscious for seven days or less performed within the normal range by the end of the first year. However, the patients who had been unconscious for longer than seven days showed a persistent deficit on this task, although they showed a slight continuing improvement that extended through the second and third year following injury. Similarly, Klonoff et al. (1977) found that children with severe head injuries continued to improve on the Halstead–Reitan battery even up to five years after their accidents. Nevertheless, these data were obtained using serial assessment of the same subjects, and such improvements may have been merely the result of practice (cf. van Zomeren, 1981, pp. 64–67). Livingston and Livingston (1985) found that significant improvement using serial assessment on a simple battery of cognitive tests was confined to the first six months following severe head injury.

In this regard the results of a study by Miller (1980) of a group of eight patients with severe head injury are especially interesting. These patients demonstrated a substantial impairment on a timed psychomotor task (the Minnesota Spatial Relations Test). However, they then received daily practice sessions on the task, which led to an impressive increase in the level of performance and good transfer to alternative versions of the same task. Nevertheless, Sunderland et al. (1983) found that the performance of severely injured patients tested on a four-choice reaction-time task between two and eight years after their accidents was significantly better than that of other severely injured patients assessed between two and eight months after their accidents (and, indeed, was not significantly different from that of orthopaedic control patients). This finding suggests that there is continuing scope for recovery of cognitive function after severe head injury.

In the study mentioned earlier by Bennett-Levy (1984), 39 patients with severe closed head injury were assessed between two and five years after their accidents and were asked to carry out a timed test of information processing that involved cancelling the largest number in each of a series of rows. Once again, the patients in whom PTA had lasted for more than three weeks were significantly impaired in comparison with a control group of 32 orthopaedic cases, but the patients in whom PTA had lasted for between one and three weeks showed no sign of any impairment on this task. This was taken to confirm the concept of a "threshold" of brain damage that corresponded roughly to a period of PTA lasting three weeks. Neither group of patients showed a deficit on unpaced tests of nonverbal skills, which suggested that a reduced speed of information processing was a salient feature of the long-term sequelae of severe closed head injury.

## Intellectual function

Research on the effects of closed head injury that has used standardised intelligence tests has yielded similar conclusions to those obtained with other cognitive tasks. In particular, patients who have sustained minor closed head injury typically show no persistent impairment of intelligence (e.g. Barth et al., 1983; Bijur et al., 1990, 1995; Binder et al., 1997; Dencker and Löfving, 1958; Rimel et al., 1981). Patients who have sustained severe closed head injury often do show such an impairment (Alexandre, Colombo, Rubini, & Benedetti, 1980; Alexandre et al., 1983; Klonoff et al., 1977; Levin, Grossman, et al., 1979; Max et al., 1999), but some studies failed to confirm this (Norrman & Svahn, 1961; Shaffer et al., 1975; Sunderland et al., 1983). This led some commentators to doubt the sensitivity of psychometric tests as measures of cognitive dysfunction (Baddeley et al., 1980; Barth et al., 1983; Miller, 1979).

The magnitude of this intellectual impairment is directly related to the duration of coma (Chadwick, Rutter, Thompson, & Shaffer, 1981; Dailey, 1956; Johnston & Mellits, 1980; Klonoff et al., 1977; Temkin et al., 1995; but cf. Levin, Grossman, et al., 1979), and to the depth of coma on admission according to the GCS (Alexandre et al., 1983; Temkin et al., 1995; cf. Brooks et al., 1980). Indeed, in research with severely head-injured children Levin and Eisenberg (1979a, 1979b) found that any persistent intellectual deficit was essentially confined to patients who had been in coma for more than 24 hours. In a 27-month follow-up study of 48 head-injured children, Chadwick, Rutter, Brown, Shaffer, and Traub (1981) found that the duration of PTA was related to the likelihood of subsequent impairment on the Wechsler Intelligence Scale for Children (WISC). This "dose-response" effect of the severity of the head injury upon intellectual function was taken to provide evidence for the idea that the resulting intellectual disabilities were due to brain damage (see also Rutter, 1981). Unfortunately, it must be added that many other investigators have failed to find any significant relationship between the impairment of head-injured patients on standard psychometric tests and the duration of PTA (e.g. Alexandre et al., 1983; Brooks et al., 1980; Klonoff et al., 1977; Mandleberg, 1976; Mandleberg & Brooks, 1975; Smith, 1974; cf. Bond, 1975, 1976).

In this regard, it should also be remembered that head-injured patients show a characteristically poor premorbid academic attainment (Haas et al., 1987; Rutter et al., 1980); one should not therefore assume that such patients would match the general population in terms of their long-term post-traumatic level of intellectual function. Be that as it may, research involving the serial assessment of severely head-injured patients has shown that Verbal IQ returns to normal levels before Performance IQ (Chadwick, Rutter, Brown, Shaffer, & Traub, 1981; Chadwick, Rutter, Shaffer, & Shrout, 1981b; Mandleberg, 1976; Mandleberg & Brooks, 1975; see also Mandleberg, 1975), although Bond and Brooks (1976) found very similar rates of recovery between the Mill Hill Vocabulary Test and the Progressive Matrices Test, and Levin, Gary, et al. (1990) found no significant impairment on the Block Design subtest of the Wechsler Adult Intelligence Scale—Revised (WAIS-R) in 120 patients tested one year after severe head injury.

Earlier in this chapter, a study by Wilson et al. (1988) was mentioned, which compared the results of early and late MRI scans with neuropsychological test performance at follow-up. They found that depth of lesions and ventricular enlargement according to recently conducted MRI scans were more strongly associated with impairment on the Performance subtests of the WAIS than with impairment on the Verbal subtests. They speculated that deeper lesions might be associated with slower information processing on timed tests. Once again, however, there was no significant relationship between performance on any of these subtests and the findings of MRI scans conducted within 21 days of the original injury.

Finally, some researchers have considered the relationship between intellectual impairment and other aspects of the outcome following closed head injury. Some studies have found significant relationships between the residual intellectual function after closed head injury and the patient's rating on the GOS, largely because of a particularly pronounced deficit in patients who are rated as "severely disabled" (Brooks, Hosie, et al., 1986; Jennett et al., 1981; Levin, Grossman, et al., 1979). Prigatano et al. (1984) found no difference in Full Scale IQ between severely head-injured patients who did and did not return to gainful employment or study, but out of a variety of psychometric tests the most powerful in discriminating between the two groups was the Digit Symbol subtest from the WAIS.

## Language function

The research literature that was reviewed in Chapter 5 concerning language disorders in the immediate period after a closed head injury indicated that classical aphasia was a relatively rare consequence. Acute disturbances of comprehension and repetition may result from damage to the left temporal lobe (Heilman et al., 1971; Thomsen, 1976), but often show rapid recovery (e.g. Arseni et al., 1970; Stone, Lopes, & Moody, 1978), and the prognosis for traumatic aphasia is considered to be much better than for language deficits resulting from other causes, such as vascular disease (Alajouanine, Castaigne, Lhermitte, Escourolle, & de Ribaucourt, 1957). Levin, Grossman, et al. (1979) found that any obvious and persistent impairments of comprehension and conversational speech were confined to those patients who were rated as severely disabled on the GOS.

Nevertheless, subclinical disturbances of language function and of communication in general are much more common, especially in patients who have sustained severe head injuries. As Milton and Wertz (1986) observed, the persistent cognitive and communicative problems of these patients have a potentially devastating impact upon their everyday activities. Moreover, even those patients who seem to have recovered their language skills to a high level of functional ability may show more subtle forms of communicative deficits on careful testing (see e.g. Liles, Coelho, Duffy, & Zalagens, 1989).

In studying recovery from severe head injury in 46 children, Brink et al. (1970, p. 567) remarked that "the relearning of intelligible speech paralleled the recovery of motor function". Najenson et al. (1978) made a similar observation regarding nine patients with prolonged traumatic coma, even though in some patients neither communicative function nor locomotor function exhibited any recovery at all until five to seven months after the injury. However, Najenson et al. noted that, paradoxically, it was the motor aspect of speech impairment that showed the slowest and least complete recovery. Brooks, Campsie, et al. (1986) confirmed that dysarthria was a common outcome of severe head injury and one that showed little sign of restitution even over the course of five years after the injury. The other predominant form of residual language disturbance after closed head injury is in the area of word finding; Levin (1981) noted that such an impairment could be demonstrated by appropriate formal testing even in those patients who had fairly intact spontaneous speech (see also Schalén et al., 1994).

Thomsen (1984) presented a long-term follow-up of 40 patients with severe head injury. When re-examined 10–15 years later, only four patients presented with aphasic symptoms, all of whom had sustained focal lesions in the left hemisphere. In contrast to this, dysarthria remained a serious problem, and at the follow-up was still evident in all 15 of the patients who had been dysarthric at the initial examination. In addition, many patients, regardless of whether or not they had originally been regarded as "aphasic", showed some residual problems in their spontaneous speech (p. 263): "Subnormal rate of speaking, impaired word finding and sporadic verbal paraphasia of the semantic type, frequent pauses, the use of many set phrases, and perseveration on words and sentences were common."

In their seven-year follow-up study of 134 cases of severe head injury, Brooks et al. (1987) found that communication deficits were significant predictors of a failure to return to work. In particular, 34% of the patients who had been previously employable were said by relatives to have difficulty in carrying on a conversation, and 31% were said to have difficulty in understanding a conversation; either problem seemed to preclude any gainful employment. Nevertheless, Brooks et al. (p. 17) suggested that these problems were not the result of any single specific impairment such as dysphasia or dyslexia, but were "rather subtle and multifactorial" and reflected a wide range of deficits including attentional difficulties, slowness in thinking, and memory problems.

## Social interaction

It was noted earlier in this chapter that some of the measures of outcome following closed head injury were supposed to reflect the degree to which a patient had achieved satisfactory social reintegration, but some studies have considered this aspect of recovery directly.

Thomsen (1974) interviewed the 50 patients in her study on average 30 months following their accidents, and found that their main problem was a lack of social contact. Similarly, in the study by Levin, Grossman, et al. (1979), 10 out of the 27 patients had been socially active young adults before sustaining a severe head injury, but when they were followed up on average 12 months afterwards had withdrawn to solitary activities (such as listening to music and watching television) and tended to avoid group situations. Thomsen (1984) subsequently followed up 40 of her patients between 10 and 15 years after their original injury, and she found that a loss of social contact remained the patients' most disabling handicap in their daily life.

Oddy et al. (1978b) interviewed the close relatives of 50 patients about the social activities of the latter during the month before they had sustained a severe closed head injury and during the two months preceding a follow-up assessment six months after the injury. Although 19 (or 38%) of these patients showed some reduction in their leisure activities, this was attributed to the interruption in their normal routine rather than to brain injury, since a similar reduction was observed in a control group of 30 patients who had sustained traumatic limb fractures. Neither group showed any significant reduction in their overall amount of social contact.

Nevertheless, the patients who had suffered very severe closed head injuries (as evidenced by a PTA lasting longer than seven days) did show a significant fall in the number of their close friends, in their amount of contact with close friends, and in the number of visits exchanged with their friends; in some patients the latter had led to social isolation. Moreover, single patients within this subgroup had tended to become more dependent upon their parents. Because the control patients had not become socially isolated either through physical disability or through absence from work, Oddy et al. (1978b) concluded that the social problems of the patients with very severe head injuries were a reflection of personality changes such as restlessness, irritability, and impatience.

Oddy and Humphrey (1980) followed up these patients at 12 and 24 months after their injury. Half of the head-injured patients continued to engage in fewer leisure activities than before their accidents, but this seemed to be the result of a lack of motivation rather than of any appreciable physical disability. These patients reported fewer social excursions, and those with very severe head injuries continued to receive fewer social visits, although by the 24-month follow-up they no longer had fewer close friends than before their accidents and their family relationships also appeared to have returned to normal. Similar results were obtained by Weddell et al. (1980). (In fact, as will be noted towards the end of this section, problems in initiating social interactions often have more to do with executive dysfunction than with motivational factors.)

In their study of 147 patients seen four to eight years after severe head injury, Schalén et al. (1994) found that 28% had symptom scores on a check list that indicated a need for psychiatric treatment. Relatively few patients reported problems to do with working relationships, but roughly 40% reported problems in personal and social relationships, especially in terms of an abnormal dependence upon their families or partners. Ratings of their overall quality of life given by close relatives varied with the patients' scores on all three of the assessment scales devised by Bond (1975), although the mental and social scales showed stronger relationships than the neurophysical scale.

In Chapter 5, I pointed out that head-injured patients are liable to show persistent problems in the cohesion, coherence, and structure of their discourse, as well as in initiating and sustaining topics in conversation (Coelho, 1995). This in turn will affect the quality of their social interactions such that their communicative partners will find their interactions less interesting or rewarding (Bond & Godfrey, 1997). At the same time, head-injured patients may also be impaired in aspects of social cognition that are crucial to maintaining interpersonal relationships, and this is likely to exacerbate their problems in daily social functioning (see Ponsford, Sloan, & Snow, 1995, chap. 5; Van Horn, Levine, & Curtis, 1992).

These points were illustrated in an investigation by Marsh and Knight (1991) involving 18 patients who had suffered severe head injuries more than 18 months previously, plus 18 controls. Independent judges rated the social skills of each participant in two structured interactions with a close friend or relative and in informal conversation with a stranger. The head-injured patients were given lower ratings than the control subjects in all three social situations, particularly in terms of their use of language and the quality of their speech delivery. Marsh and Knight concluded that the reduced social skills of head-injured patients reflected (in part, at least) deficits in language use and that the latter might be due to disruption of the executive control system responsible for organising cognitive activities.

Mazaux et al. (1997) examined in some detail the extent to which social activities were affected five years after head injury and the extent to which the impairment might be associated with neuropsychological deficits. They found that severely injured patients were more likely to be unemployed and were more likely to have difficulties when shopping, using public transport, and carrying out administrative or financial management tasks. This loss of employability and social autonomy appeared to be caused by persistent deficits in both executive functions and speed of information processing.

Max et al. (1999) tested children between the ages of five and fourteen roughly two years after they had sustained either severe or minor head injuries. They found that intellectual function was negatively associated with novel psychiatric disorders in the children themselves and with psychiatric disorders in one or more of their immediate family members. However, Max et al. were uncertain as to the direction of the causal relationship. On the one hand, they suggested that cognitive rehabilitation and educational adaptations might help to prevent psychiatric dysfunction in head-injured children. On the other hand, they suggested that psychiatric treatment for head-injured children and their family members might improve the cognitive outcome.

## THE PROCESS OF RECOVERY

### Age and recovery

It is often assumed that the long-term effects of brain damage tend to increase with the age of the individual to whom that damage has occurred, reflecting the relative resilience or "plasticity" of the young brain as opposed to the relative vulnerability of the elderly brain. According to Schneider (1979), Teuber attributed the principle that "It is better to have your brain lesion early" to the work of Kennard (1938). It should be noted that very similar notions had been entertained by 19th-century investigators, that Kennard was concerned only with the restitution of motor function following ablation of major areas of the cerebral cortex, and that she herself certainly did not regard this as an invariant rule (see Finger, 1991). It is true that experimental research with infrahuman species has demonstrated that identical lesions may have quite different consequences when sustained earlier rather than later in life. However, Schneider's own observations on lesions of the optic tract in the hamster showed that in detail the nature of these changes depends on the specific site of damage and the specific function that is under consideration.

Russell (1934, p. 139) suggested that "the most important single factor which influences the ultimate prognosis in a case of head injury is the age of the patient". This conclusion was based on observations obtained from an unselected sample of 200 patients admitted to hospital following head injury. When they were classified into successive age groups, the proportion of patients with postconcussional symptoms persisting more than two months after their discharge increased continuously from 46% in the case of those aged 10–20 years to 100% in the case of those of over 50 years of age, although 66% of children aged up to 10 years also suffered from such symptoms. More recent research has tended to find nonsignificant increases in the incidence of persistent postconcussional symptoms with advancing age (Rutherford et al., 1977, 1979).

However, in evaluating the consequences of closed head injury, there are at least four considerations that militate against the possibility of making meaningful comparisons across different age groups of patients (see Kapur, 1988, p. 108). First, as was pointed out in Chapter 1, closed head injuries are much more common among young adults, so that unselected samples of head-injured patients may include relatively few individuals from the extremes of the age range. A second problem is that the sorts of accidents that give rise to closed head injury may be quite different in different age groups (see also Chapter 1). A third difficulty is that staff working in accident and emergency departments may differentiate among the three groups in terms of the criteria for admission. Finally, it is possible that individuals in different age groups have different pathophysiological responses to closed head injury or else different levels of susceptibility to complications.

## Head injuries in children

In neurophysical terms, most children who are admitted to hospital after closed head injury appear to make a good recovery (Gaidolfi & Vignolo, 1980; Klonoff et al., 1977). However, such an assessment may well tend to obscure serious residual difficulties (Miner, Fletcher, & Ewing-Cobbs, 1986). Indeed, the research literature suggests that head-injured children show persistent deficits of memory and cognition that are qualitatively similar to those shown by head-injured adults (see Ewing-Cobbs, Levin, & Fletcher, 1998; Levin, High, et al., 1988; Max et al., 1999).

Indeed, precisely because brain damage tends to impair the learning of new information, Rutter (1981) argued that its effects in young children might well be expected to be disproportionately severe, simply because they had more new learning still to do and less accumulated knowledge and fewer established skills on which to rely. As a result, "cognitive tasks may have a different meaning at different ages" (p. 1539). Hence, even mild learning deficits may cumulatively lead to poor academic achievement in later years, or else they may only become evident in intellectually demanding tasks.

To illustrate this point, it has often been assumed that children who sustain mild head injuries subsequently exhibit relatively normal levels of educational attainment (see e.g. Bijur, Haslum, & Golding, 1990, 1995). However, the situation is not entirely clear, especially in the case of children who sustain head injuries before they begin compulsory education (Gronwall, Wrightson, & McGinn, 1997). Wrightson, McGinn, and Gronwall (1995) identified children who had sustained a head injury between the ages of two-and-a-half and four-and-a-half that had not been severe enough to warrant their admission to hospital for observation. At follow-up, these children were impaired on a test of visual closure involving the identification of objects embedded in pictures. Moreover, during their first year of formal schooling aged five to six, these children were more likely to have difficulties with reading than a group of children with injuries elsewhere.

Levin and Eisenberg (1979a) administered a neuropsychological battery to 22 children between 6 and 12 years of age and 42 adolescents between 13 and 18 years of age, and in each case compared the results with data from normal individuals of the same ages. Memory deficits tended to be more common among the children, but other types of impairment were rather more frequent among the adolescents; however, in no case was the relationship between age and impairment statistically significant. Levin and Eisenberg (1979b) found a nonsignificant trend for children to be more impaired than adolescents, but they also made a specific observation that the incidence of post-traumatic aphasia appeared to be somewhat lower in children and in adolescents than in adults. They took this to be consistent with Hécaen's (1976) notion that the child's brain has greater potential for functional reorganisation among the regions that subserve language. The latter idea is also supported by the results of the study by Chadwick, Rutter, Thompson, and Shaffer (1981) that were described in Chapter 5.

Levin, Eisenberg et al. (1982) suggested that the supposed greater neural plasticity of the young brain might well facilitate the reorganisation of cognitive function following focal lesions, but that it would confer no particular advantage in recovery from the sort of diffuse insult that was typically produced by severe closed head injury. They compared 30 head-injured children (aged between 2 and 12 years at the time of injury) with 30 head-injured adolescents (aged between 13 and 19 years) in terms of verbal recall using the selective reminding procedure, continuous visual recognition memory for familiar objects, and intellectual functioning according to the age-appropriate Wechsler intelligence scale. In each age group, half of the patients had sustained severe head injuries (defined by a GCS score on admission of 8 or less), whereas half had sustained minor head injuries (defined by a GCS score on admission of more than 8).

At a follow-up assessment several months or years after their accidents, the severely injured patients in both age groups performed worse on all three tests than those with minor injuries, but there was no suggestion of any greater residual impairment among the adolescents. Indeed, when compared with age-matched normal controls, the children were somewhat more likely to show persistent memory impairments. Moreover, of the severely injured children, five had a Verbal IQ of less than 80, and six had a Performance IQ of less than 80, whereas none of the adolescents showed any subnormal intellectual functioning in this sense. Although the two age groups had been matched in terms of their GCS scores, Levin, Eisenberg, et al. (1982) suggested that their adolescent patients might if anything be expected to have suffered more severe injuries than the children in their study because of their more frequent involvement in high-speed vehicular accidents. They concluded (p. 672) that their findings "provide no evidence that the young brain confers an advantage with respect to the development and restitution of higher functions after traumatic brain injury". Analogous results using a range of cognitive tasks were found by Levin et al. (1993) when comparing head-injured children aged 6–10 with those aged 11–16, and other research has confirmed the idea that the sequelae of head injuries are more pronounced in younger children than in older children or adolescents (see Taylor & Alden, 1997, for review).

## Mechanisms of recovery

The discussion so far has described recovery following closed head injury as if it were a unitary process, and this is certainly implicit in the exponential model of the relationship between objective performance and the time since the injury. Nevertheless, it is nowadays generally agreed that there are two different types of mechanism underlying the process of recovery from brain damage (Bond, 1986; Cronholm, 1972).

First, there are a number of mechanisms of primary recovery that operate at a neuronal level from the instant that the injury has occurred. Their effects are manifested in the neurological outcome and especially in the recovery of motor function (Bond, 1979). Clinical findings suggest that in these terms recovery is complete or else reaches a plateau within six months of a closed head injury (e.g. Livingston & Livingston, 1985). However, recent physiological evidence indicates that regenerative processes may continue over a much longer period (Stein, 1998).

Second, the possibility of improvement beyond this six-month period depends upon the patient's adaptation to residual deficits and the development of compensatory strategies (Humphrey & Oddy, 1980; Jennett & Bond, 1975). These in turn demand the patient's awareness of the nature and extent of his or her disability, and hence they begin with the restitution of full consciousness at the end of the period of PTA (see Bond, 1979; Bond & Brooks, 1976). The literature that was reviewed earlier in this chapter suggests that the processes of spontaneous recovery of higher cognitive functions and the establishment of changes in personality and in social behaviour also occur predominantly within the first six months following a closed head injury (Bond, 1979), but the key to rehabilitative endeavours is that such processes may persist for much longer.

Until relatively recently, the effects of brain damage were discussed solely in terms of the direct morphological changes to nerve cells, and it was widely assumed that cells within the central nervous system lacked any capacity for regeneration. On this assumption recovery must consist in a process of relearning, involving the development of other neural pathways. This can take the form either of vicarious functioning of undamaged neural tissue, in which some region of the brain takes on a function for which it previously had no responsibility; or of behavioural substitution, in which undamaged systems retain their original function but are also deployed in the service of novel goals (see Rutter, 1981).

However, the possibility of recovery at a purely physiological level is indicated by the findings of magnetic resonance imaging (MRI) in head-injured patients. As mentioned in Chapter 2, MRI can indicate lesions of the grey and white matter of the brain in greater quantity and of larger volume than are visualised by means of CT scans. These lesions generally resolve within one to three months; moreover, they do not in themselves appear to demand any changes in the clinical management of head-injured patients, although they may be related to the persistence and nature of cognitive sequelae (Levin, Amparo, et al., 1987).

There are a number of short-term processes that promote the recovery of neuronal function in the immediate period after a head injury, including the replenishment of neurotransmitters and the restoration of cell membrane potential, in addition to the reversal of complications such as vascular constriction and brain swelling (Rutter, 1981; Teasdale & Mendelow, 1984). It is however clear that lesions of the brain may have longer-term implications of both a positive and a negative sort. Schoenfeld and Hamilton (1977) argued that these secondary changes may be more significant in terms of their effects upon behaviour than the primary damage itself.

In particular, it would appear that there is considerable potential for structural reorganisation within the brain as the result of both regenerative growth and sprouting involving both damaged and intact neurones. Damage to the nervous system can also lead to a heightened sensitivity of deafferented tissue and the "unmasking" of functional activity that is normally suppressed or inhibited in intact organisms. Nevertheless, in principle, these changes could be beneficial, detrimental, or of no consequence to the functioning organism (see Stein, 1998; Stein et al., 1995, pp. 46–62).

Von Monakow (1914/1969) postulated the idea of *diaschisis*, which was assumed to constitute a transient and reversible form of "shock" that could affect neurones far removed from the site of damage when they were deprived of afferent input. Pavlov and many other Soviet psychologists speculated that this inhibitory process served to protect intact areas of the brain, concussion being seen as a prime example (see Luria et al., 1969, p. 370). Schoenfeld and Hamilton (1977) argued that diaschisis lacked an adequate operational definition, and initial experimental tests of the notion proved unsuccessful. However, studies using brain imaging confirmed the existence of diaschisis following strokes (Hausen, Lachmann, & Nagler, 1997; Heiss et al., 1983; Infeld, Davis, Lichtenstein, Mitchell, & Hopper, 1995), except that it exerts both inhibitive and disinhibitive effects upon neural activity (Andrews, 1991; see Stein, 1998, for discussion).

The possibility of adaptation and compensation obviously depends upon the nature of the patients' residual deficits, but also upon the quality of the interactions between the patients and the individuals who are responsible for their continuing care and rehabilitation. The latter are themselves vulnerable to emotional changes that may in turn influence the patients' recovery (Bond,

1986; McKinlay & Brooks, 1984). At this level recovery following closed head injury is both a psychosocial process and a neurophysiological one. The coping strategies, successful or otherwise, that patients and their families adopt in such circumstances will depend on their cognitive, emotional, and motivational resources and on the amount and quality of the support that they receive (Barth et al., 1983; Newcombe, 1982).

## REHABILITATION

Traditional approaches to the treatment of head-injured patients tended to emphasise the need for conservative management. However, experiences during the Second World War brought about a marked change in clinical attitudes in favour of more active forms of rehabilitation such as occupational therapy, physiotherapy, and intellectual and recreational pursuits (Lewis, 1942; Symonds, 1942; see also Relander, Troupp, & Björkesten, 1972).

Nevertheless, rehabilitative efforts were focused almost exclusively upon the remediation of physical deficits with the primary aim of facilitating the patient's return to gainful employment; indeed, it was often assumed that very little could be done to promote the restoration of cognitive and behavioural functioning (see Bigler, 1987; Bond, 1975). Weddell et al. (1980) speculated that such an emphasis might have been reinforced by head-injured patients themselves and by their relatives since physical deficits were more easily recognised and accepted. For similar reasons, resources tended to be aimed towards severely disabled patients, despite the fact that those with moderate disability were more numerous and more likely to benefit from early active rehabilitation (Aitken et al., 1982).

During the 1970s, however, a number of factors encouraged a growing awareness of the need for a deeper understanding of the broader aspects of recovery from closed head injury. First, it became apparent that even occupational resettlement depended upon residual cognitive and behavioural deficits as well as upon physical recovery. Second, residual deficits of this nature were seen to be of even greater significance in determining general social recovery, and hence to constitute a fundamental obstacle to rehabilitation. Third, clinical neuropsychologists began to take a more active professional interest in questions of treatment and rehabilitation as opposed to observation and assessment (see Brooks, 1979; Oddy & Humphrey, 1980). As a result, in recent years there has been a trend towards the view that the effective rehabilitation of head-injured patients demands an interdisciplinary approach that integrates traditional forms of treatment with cognitive retraining and behaviour modification, as well as counselling for both the patients and their relatives (see e.g. Bond, 1979; Christensen, Pinner, Moller Pedersen, Teasdale, & Trexler, 1992; Cohen & Titonis, 1985; Eames & Wood, 1989; Evans, 1981; Livingston, 1986; Malkmus, 1983; Najenson et al., 1978; Sohlberg & Mateer, 1989).

## Counselling and psychotherapy

Treatment that goes beyond conventional forms of rehabilitation would seem to be most apposite in dealing with persistent postconcussional symptoms. As Long and Novack (1986) noted, how these symptoms should be treated does not depend critically upon whether or not they define a clinical syndrome. Moreover, whether or not one accepts that any such syndrome is entirely an iatrogenic disease (i.e. one resulting from an unsupportive attitude on the part of the patient's doctor: see Chapter 6), it is obvious that the clinician's attitude may be of major importance in determining whether the patient is able to resolve any psychic conflict that results from the trauma of a closed head injury.

Russell (1934) emphasised the importance of "simple reassurance" in ensuring the disappearance of postconcussional symptoms, though Lewis (1942, p. 613) argued that "direct psychological treatment" would sometimes be called for, and Symonds (1942, p. 605) went so far as to suggest that psychotherapy "has a place in the treatment of every case of this kind". In a similar manner Björkesten (1971) argued that the postconcussional syndrome could be reduced by active mobilisation, by appropriate psychotherapy, and by good encouragement regarding the eventual prognosis, whereas Martin (1974, p. 117) suggested that "adequate initial treatment of the syndrome, sympathy, recognition of its reality and reassurance that it is only temporary will usually prevent the appearance of a neurosis" (see also Wrightson & Gronwall, 1981). Conversely, the genesis of postconcussional symptoms and other psychosocial problems in patients with closed head injury tends to be attributed to the lack of provision for counselling and follow-up services (e.g. Jennett, 1975b; McMillan & Glucksman, 1987; Newcombe et al., 1994).

Minderhoud et al. (1980) compared 352 patients with cerebral concussion who received no systematic treatment during the period of their hospitalisation and 180 patients who received a strict programme of treatment that involved information, explanation, and encouragement. With the exception of those of over 60 years of age, the latter patients reported fewer postconcussional symptoms both three weeks and six months after their head injuries, and in particular were less likely to complain of irritability, loss of memory, and loss of concentration. These findings were taken to support the hypothesis that postconcussional sequelae start from an organic basis but that the persistence of symptoms following minor head injury is caused by psychogenic and especially by iatrogenic factors.

As was mentioned in the previous chapter, Gronwall and Wrightson (1974) hypothesised that persistent postconcussional symptoms represented a neurotic reaction to a subtle yet transient impairment of information-processing capacity in the absence of adequate information and support from medical staff. They concluded that the effective management of patients with closed head injury depended not merely upon a supportive attitude on the part of their physicians, but also upon the monitoring and assessment of cognitive functioning throughout the period of recovery in order to ensure that the intellectual demands involved in returning to work did not exceed a patient's available information-processing capacity.

During the course of a single year, Gronwall and Wrightson (1974) monitored 80 head-injured patients in this manner. Five patients were identified as being "at risk" for the development of a postconcussional syndrome on the basis of the delayed recovery of performance on the PASAT. They were "guided to eventual complete recovery" (p. 608) by means of a formal rehabilitation programme aimed at gradually building up tolerance to fatigue and at developing the abilities to work at speed, to tolerate noise, and to ignore distraction (see also Gronwall, 1977). This was a somewhat ambitious project that involved a full-time research fellow, two part-time occupational therapists and two part-time physiotherapists; however, Gronwall and Wrightson considered that the expenditure represented by these resources was not excessive.

Just as Gronwall and Wrightson (1974) used the PASAT to monitor the recovery of cognitive functioning in adult patients returning to gainful employment, Levin and Eisenberg (1979a, p. 401) observed that in the recovery of children following closed head injury "the degree of improvement over time in verbal learning and memory using the selective reminding test provides an indication of the patient's readiness to cope with the mnemonic demands of schoolwork". Subsequently, Malkmus (1983) and Long and Novack (1986) advocated a similar approach to rehabilitation, based on matching the information-processing demands of environmental tasks to the patient's cognitive capabilities at each stage of recovery.

Nowadays, more intensive rehabilitation programmes tend to incorporate psychotherapeutic interventions that are specifically intended to develop in head-injured patients "increased awareness and acceptance of the injury and residual deficits" and "an understanding of their particular emotional and motivational disturbances and their personal reactions to the injury" (Prigatano et al., 1984, p. 507; see also Prigatano et al., 1986, chaps. 5 & 6). Nevertheless, Hayden and Hart (1986) considered that full-blown psychodynamically orientated psychotherapy was typically not appropriate for dealing with head-injured patients because they often lacked the necessary level of abstraction and needed much more structure than was provided by psychodynamic methods (see also Oddy, 1993).

## Cognitive retraining

Cognitive deficits are ubiquitous in head-injured patients, and it was thus hardly surprising that they became a major focus of attention when researchers and professional workers came to reconsider the goals of rehabilitation following closed head injury. This was also encouraged by concomitant theoretical developments in the field of cognitive psychology during the 1970s. Cognitive retraining tackles the direct remediation of deficits in higher intellectual functions by providing practice on tasks that exercise the defective skills or that encourage the development of new cognitive strategies (Hayden & Hart, 1986). As Cicerone and Tupper (1986) explained, the treatment of a word-finding impairment might proceed through repetitive vocabulary-link exercises, the use of visual imagery as an aid to word retrieval, or the development of circumlocutory strategies. To take a somewhat different example, head-injured patients might be given systematic training on Gronwall and Wrightson's (1974) PASAT or other tasks relying upon executive function in an attempt to enhance their central processing capacity (see Newcombe, 1982; Sohlberg & Mateer, 1989).

In everyday life, cognitive dysfunction leads to a failure to respond adequately or appropriately to the demands of one's immediate environment. In an institutional setting, the remediation of cognitive dysfunction can also be encouraged by increasing the amount of structure that is afforded by that external environment, both social and physical. This goal can be achieved by eliminating (or, at least, reducing) sources of ambiguity and by ensuring that the environment contains prompts which elicit appropriate forms of behaviour. For instance, Hayden and Hart (1986) recommended that professional staff should use verbal cues that elicit particular cognitive or behavioural strategies (or "scripts") designed to cope with problematic situations. Such an approach obviously requires the collaboration of all of the staff concerned (Malkmus, 1983). However, it also suffers from the limitation that explicit structure is unlikely to be encountered in daily life, and so techniques of this sort will be of little practical benefit unless patients can also be trained to generate their own internal cues.

Generally speaking, cognitive remediation in brain-damaged patients is based upon the notion of behavioural substitution described earlier in this chapter: that is, the assumption that undamaged systems within the brain can be deployed towards different goals (Rutter, 1981). Cicerone and Tupper (1986) observed that this is an essentially subversive approach to rehabilitation because it implicitly contradicts the concept of "deficit testing" in neuropsychological assessment: the latter assumes a uniform level of competence within the intact individual that constitutes a single benchmark against which to evaluate intellectual impairment in brain-damaged patients (see e.g. Lezak, 1984). Cognitive remediation instead assumes that the potential for recovery and retraining in brain-damaged patients varies from one cognitive function to another, and that the same behavioural goal can be achieved by deploying different functional systems or by taking different routes through the same system. The scope for rehabilitation therefore depends more upon the complexity of the tasks confronting the patient and upon his or her executive control of alternative strategies than upon any single overall measure of attainment (see Ylivsaker & Szekeres, 1998).

Cognitive retraining methods are often considered to be useful ways of encouraging the rehabilitation of head-injured patients, though controlled studies demonstrating their clinical efficacy have mostly been carried out with stroke patients in whom brain damage may well be more circumscribed (Hayden & Hart, 1986). Prigatano et al. (1984) evaluated the benefits of a neuropsychological rehabilitation programme that included intensive cognitive retraining of selected residual deficits and psychotherapeutic intervention in addition to traditional rehabilitation (see also Prigatano et al., 1986, chaps. 6 & 7). An experimental group of 18 patients with closed head injury was compared with 17 matched control patients (who only received traditional rehabilitation) in terms of their IQs on the Wechsler Adult Intelligence Scale before and after a six-month period. The two groups were very similar in terms of their baseline scores, which were clearly impaired in the case of Performance IQ but not in the case of Verbal IQ. After cognitive retraining there was a significant difference between the groups in terms of their mean Performance IQs that was mainly attributable to the Block Design subtest. Unfortunately, the magnitude of this difference was less than four points when corrected for the patients' baseline scores. Moreover, many of the control patients had specifically declined to participate in the intensive neuropsychological rehabilitation programme; consequently, these findings might simply have resulted from subject selection artefacts (Schacter & Glisky, 1986).

## Memory retraining and remediation

Much of the work on cognitive remediation following closed head injury has been concerned specifically with memory impairment. Apart from being the most apparent form of residual dysfunction, this has an obvious impact on academic attainment in children and young people and on learning capacity in general, and it tends to constrain the effectiveness of other forms of rehabilitation (such as social skills training) that depend upon adequate mnemonic and cognitive functioning (McGuire & Sylvester, 1987). Harris (1984) classified methods for improving memory into four broad categories: physical treatments (i.e. drugs); external devices; repetitive practice; and mnemonic strategies. The use of drugs seems to be of little practical value in alleviating memory disorders, but Harris and Sunderland (1981) found that the three remaining categories were widely used in British rehabilitation units.

External aids include both devices for storing information (such as notepads) and devices for cueing action (such as alarm cooking timers and shopping lists). Harris (1978) found that such devices were widely used by intact individuals in everyday life, and he argued that they warranted further investigation. More recently, electronic aids such as personal organisers have become widely available. The few published case studies suggest that brain-damaged patients require special forms of training and prompting if they are to use such devices effectively (e.g. Sandler & Harris, 1991).

Many of the latest devices require a considerable amount of learning and may therefore not be useful for people with reduced cognitive capacity (Herrmann, Yoder, Wells, & Raybeck, 1996). However, Kapur (1995) discussed the potential role of simpler devices in rehabilitation, and he argued that they could yield an appropriate means of overcoming everyday memory difficulties. Under this heading, Schacter and Glisky (1986) mentioned structured environments that reduce or eliminate the need for remembering, such as a kitchen in which the contents of cupboards are labelled, and in principle there is a wide variety of environmental manipulations that could be employed (Collerton, 1993).

Repetitive practice involves the continual administration of memory games (such as Kim's game) or conventional laboratory tasks. Harris and Sunderland (1981, p. 208) commented that its widespread use "is apparently based on the assumption that memory responds like a 'mental muscle', and that exercising it on one task will strengthen it for use on other tasks". Schacter and Glisky (1986) reported that they had met similar ideas in informal discussions with professional rehabilitation workers in North America. Harris and Sunderland argued that repetitive practice might be rewarding for head-injured patients and that it might conceivably promote neural regeneration, but they acknowledged that there was little evidence that it was of any practical benefit for either normal or impaired memory.

In the study mentioned earlier, Prigatano et al. (1984, 1986, chap. 7) found that cognitive retraining in head-injured patients led to a statistically significant improvement in terms of their Memory Quotients according to the WMS, though not in terms of their performance on any of the constituent subtests. Quite apart from the problem of possible subject selection artefacts, Schacter and Glisky (1986) pointed out that the improvement in question corresponded to a net increase of one item per patient on each subtest as the result of roughly 625 hours of training. They concluded that repetitive drill or practice did not produce general improvements in memory function. Subsequent research has produced no evidence to contradict this (Collerton, 1993).

From a psychological point of view, the most interesting category of rehabilitative intervention is training in the use of particular mnemonic strategies. Instructions to use imagery mnemonics in particular are well known to produce substantial improvements in laboratory experiments with normal subjects, and during the 1970s there were a great many attempts to adapt these techniques for use with neurological patients (see Richardson, Cermak, Blackford, & O'Connor, 1987). There is some evidence that imagery mnemonics might help to alleviate memory impairment following severe head injury, but patients appear to have considerable difficulty in transferring such strategies to learning situations in everyday life (Crosson & Buenning, 1984; Crovitz, Harvey, & Horn, 1979; Glasgow, Zeiss, Barrera, & Lewinsohn, 1977). In common with other patients with acquired memory disorders, they do not seem to be able to continue to use these strategies in the absence of explicit instructions or prompting, or to generalise their use to learning tasks and situations other than the ones used for training; instead they revert to the use of external memory aids (Richardson et al., 1987; Schacter & Glisky, 1986).

There has been little or no research on the use of verbal mnemonics and other devices in the case of head-injured patients, but similar considerations are likely to apply. Cicerone and Tupper (1986) argued that the ability to maintain and transfer cognitive strategies depended upon higher executive function and the patient's awareness and knowledge of how and when such strategies might be employed (see also Richardson et al., 1987). Even if the latter "metacognitive" skills were imparted to patients with closed head injury, deficits of higher executive function of the sort discussed in Chapter 5 would still constrain the efficacy of mnemonic training. Freeman, Mittenberg, Dicowden, and Bat-Ami (1992) employed a retraining programme based on both executive and compensatory strategies. This led to a significant improvement on the part of six head-injured patients in their ability to remember the content of short narratives, and Freeman et al. suggested that this would also serve to enhance the patients' self-esteem and feelings of efficacy in everyday situations.

A number of researchers have claimed that microcomputers have an important role to play in cognitive rehabilitation (e.g. Newcombe, 1982). Kerner and Acker (1985) tested 12 patients with closed head injury on a battery of memory tests at least three months after their accidents, and found highly significant gains in performance as the result of a memory retraining programme that was delivered by a microcomputer in 12 sessions over the course of 30 days. The patients also seemed to have more positive feelings about themselves as well as enhanced motivation for academic and vocational pursuits, and some continued to use the computer voluntarily beyond the end of the study. The contents of the programme were not described in detail, but they seem to have included repetitive practice on a memory-span task and also training in the use of mental imagery and simple stories as mediating devices in verbal learning tasks (cf. Gianutsos & Grynbaum, 1983). However, Schacter and Glisky (1986) argued that there no evidence that computerised programmes differed from cognitive retraining presented by other means in their effects, or that such programmes had any generalised effect on memory function.

Niemann, Ruff, and Baser (1990) evaluated the efficacy of two retraining programmes concerned with attention and memory, respectively. In both cases, patients with severe head injuries received repetitive practice with detailed feedback on relevant tasks. Patients in the attention retraining programme improved more than patients in the memory retraining programme on four measures of attention and especially on the Trail Making Test. However, the reverse pattern was not found in the case of four measures of memory, and there was no evidence that either form of retraining carried over to other neuropsychological tests. In subsequent research, Ruff et al. (1994) found that attention retraining and memory retraining led to small but statistically significant improvements on measures of attention and memory as well as ratings of everyday behaviour made by close friends or family members, but not on patients' self-ratings.

In a similar study, Middleton, Lambert, and Seggar (1991) compared a programme concerned with attention and memory and a programme concerned with reasoning and logical thinking. These programmes were administered to 36 brain-damaged patients, the majority of whom were cases of closed head injury. Both of the programmes led to significant improvements in performance both on tests of attention and memory and on tests of reasoning and logical thinking. There was no evidence of selective effects of either programme, and no attempt was made to evaluate whether these improvements generalised to other kinds of test.

Chen, Thomas, Glueckauf, and Bracy (1997) reviewed earlier attempts to evaluated computer-assisted cognitive retraining in head-injured patients, and concluded that there was a dearth of well-controlled studies. Because of the ethical issue involved in withholding rehabilitation from a control group with similar injuries, Chen et al. argued that the effects of computer-based retraining should be compared with those of traditional therapy methods. They found that severely head-injured patients exposed to a computer-based programme covering four areas of cognition (attention, spatial orientation, memory, and problem solving) showed significant improvements in all four areas, but only to the same extent as a control group exposed to more traditional methods such as speech therapy and occupational therapy.

## Behaviour modification

Newcombe, Brooks, and Baddeley (1980) observed that personality changes and behavioural disorders often constituted serious barriers to effective rehabilitation in head-injured patients; this seemed to be associated with the patients' impaired ability to monitor their own behaviour as a result of damage to the frontal lobes (cf. Deaton, 1987; Luria, 1963). They suggested that behaviour therapy was likely to be the most useful technique in treating these severe behavioural disorders, although at the time it was only just beginning to be systematically exploited in the treatment of brain-damaged patients. Nowadays, rehabilitation of patients with severe head injuries typically involves a combination of cognitive remediation and behavioural techniques (Brooks, 1984).

Behaviour therapy is the process of modifying undesirable behaviour by means of operant conditioning, in which the probability of a specific response being repeatedly emitted in the context of a particular stimulus is affected by the consequences of the individual's behaviour. This can be used to increase the likelihood of desirable behaviour through reward or positive reinforcement, to reduce the likelihood of undesirable behaviour through punishment or negative reinforcement, and also to shape existing forms of behaviour into more complex or appropriate ones (Goldstein, 1993). An operant analysis is most often applied to social behaviour, but it is also applicable to cognitive behaviours such as attention, insight, and memory, as well as speech and motor deficits (McGlynn, 1990).

Eames and Wood (1985b) carried out an evaluation of behaviour therapy in the case of 24 severely damaged patients of whom 12 had suffered closed head injury. Since the major impact of the patients' behaviour disorders had been to make them unacceptable in conventional settings devoted either to rehabilitation or to continuing care, the effect of therapy was defined in terms of a scale of possible placements from self care in patients' own homes to institutionalisation in a psychiatric, psychogeriatric, or mental handicap hospital. The patients' carers also completed rating scales that were concerned with changes in behaviour and "activities of daily living". Three-quarters of the patients demonstrated an improvement in the overall outcome, and more than half were discharged to their own homes. This was broadly maintained at a follow-up assessment between six months and three years later. A similar impression was given by the assessment of activities of daily living, which in 10 patients approached normal achievement in five out of the seven areas examined at the follow-up session.

Eames and Wood (1985b, p. 618) considered that a high proportion of severely damaged individuals "could achieve dramatic and lasting improvements in behaviour and (thanks to consequent accessibility to rehabilitative interventions) in personal and social independence". They also emphasised that these improvements had been achieved in spite of long delays between brain injury and the beginning of rehabilitation; indeed, the average interval between the injury and admission to the rehabilitation unit was 45 months. Eames and Wood interpreted their findings as being inconsistent with the notion that any improvement in the outcome was to be expected during the first two or three years following closed head injury. They concluded (p. 618) "that, even years after injury, persistent and comprehensive rehabilitation can achieve changes significant enough to make worthwhile improvements in the quality of life".

Finally, Eames and Wood (1985a) noted that problems in monitoring and controlling behaviour should be tackled by means of behaviour therapy with groups of patients together, not least because many of these problems were in the area of social behaviour. Deaton (1987) claimed that interventions of this nature provided peer support, feedback, and social modelling, and might therefore be particularly appropriate for head-injured children and adolescents who might be seeking acceptance from their peer group. Deaton argued that behaviour modification could serve to increase adaptive skills such as eating or socialising that were often important to the development of a patient's self-esteem and independence. She also suggested that a carefully structured environment might circumvent problems in behaviour modification that resulted from cognitive deficits, memory impairment, and poor self-monitoring skills.

## Support for families

Livingston et al. (1985a) noted that the relatives of patients with severe head injury themselves showed a significant level of psychiatric morbidity (see Chapter 6). The occurrence of such problems varied with the level of the patients' subjective complaints but not with the severity of the injury, which entailed that it could not be predicted in individual families at the time of the patients' initial hospitalisation. Livingston et al. (p. 876) concluded that "these findings suggest the need for comprehensive rehabilitation of head injury patients and their relatives". It has also been suggested that good family relationships tend to facilitate successful rehabilitation (Oddy & Humphrey, 1980); whereas Jennett (1975b, p. 270) considered that "prophylactic and ongoing psychosocial counselling of the patient and the family" might influence the outcome of closed head injury more significantly than physical rehabilitation. Quine, Pierce, and Lyle (1988) even suggested that relatives could be recruited as lay-therapists in the task of rehabilitating of head-injured patients (see also Oddy, 1993), although they did acknowledge that this burden would tend to fall upon female relatives who had other family responsibilities.

Bond (1979) recommended that while head-injured patients were still in coma their relatives should receive individual counselling with regard to the likely course of recovery to prevent them from developing unrealistic expectations. Complaints from relatives concerning a lack of information from medical staff about the patient's condition and prognosis seem to be fairly common (e.g. Oddy et al., 1978a), but it is really unclear to what extent such complaints are justified. Thomsen (1974) found that they came exclusively from working-class families, which she interpreted as evidence for a genuine problem in doctor–patient communication.

Junqué, Bruna, and Mataró (1997) carried out a postal survey of family members of patients who had sustained moderate or severe head injuries between one and twenty-four years previously. In two-thirds of all cases, the relatives still expressed a need for information about the consequences of head injury. This was more likely if the family members perceived behavioural and affective changes on the part of the patients. Junqué et al. inferred that the expressed need for information was actually due to the resulting psychological distress. Others regard complaints concerning a lack of information as expressions of anger towards professional staff, perhaps arising out of unresolved denial during earlier stages of recovery (e.g. Levin, Benton, & Grossman, 1982, p. 209).

Once head-injured patients exhibit relative independence in basic functions of self-care, they tend to be discharged to their homes, even if they exhibit severe physical or mental deficits (Livingston et al., 1985a; Timming et al., 1982). Continuing support for relatives is clearly important at this juncture, but it is generally agreed that this should go well beyond general advice and include more constructive and dynamic forms of treatment such as family therapy, group therapy, and psychotherapy (Aitken et al., 1982; Andrews, 1996; Bond, 1979; Lewin et al., 1979; McGuire & Sylvester, 1987; Ponsford, Sloan, & Snow, 1995, chap. 9; Rosenbaum, Lipsitz, Abraham, & Najenson, 1978). Hendryx (1989) and Florian, Katz, and Lahav (1989) stressed the importance of focusing rehabilitative counselling and other support services on the entire family as a system.

Hayden and Hart (1986) argued that models of grief and bereavement provided a useful perspective from which to view the difficulties encountered by the families of patients after severe head injury, namely, as resulting from the inevitable disruption of the normal grieving process by the uncertainty concerning the precise nature of the loss and the challenge of maintaining a relationship with the "lost" individual. More recently, Martin (1994) endorsed a bereavement model as useful in enabling family members to adjust to "loss without death". Moreover, especially in the absence of adequate rehabilitation facilities, families of head-injured patients must rely on voluntary self-help and support groups such as those organised in the United Kingdom by Headway, the National Head Injuries Association, and in the United States by the National Head Injury Foundation.

## OVERVIEW

Most deaths attributable to closed head injury occur within the first few days as the result of primary brain damage. Mortality rates are higher in older victims as the result of extracranial complications, but the picture is unclear in the case of children. A relatively small number of severely injured patients may survive for up to several years in a vegetative state for which any effective rehabilitation has yet to be discovered. In other cases, the quality of survival can be judged in terms of the neurophysical outcome, occupational resettlement, or social outcome; the GOS provides a convenient way of categorising patients in terms of their social dependence or independence.

Recovery of function can be measured in terms of subjective complaints or in terms of objective performance, but in either case the most obvious long-term deficits among patients with severe head injury are in the areas of memory, cognition, and communication. These have obvious implications for these patients' ability to cope with situations at work, at school, or in public life more generally, which demand skilled and efficient learning, thinking, and social skills. Substantial restitution of these functions usually takes place during the first six months, but the rate of improvement gradually slows, and there may be relatively little change after the first year. In contrast, after a minor head injury, performance usually returns to broadly normal levels during the first month or so, although a small proportion of patients show persistent deficits that interfere with their return to work.

There is a good deal of evidence that the effects of closed head injury are rather more pronounced in older patients than in young adults, confirming that the elderly brain is more vulnerable to brain damage. However, there is no unambiguous evidence that children are any less susceptible to functional impairment after closed head injury than adults by virtue of the supposed plasticity of the young brain. The mechanisms underlying recovery of function are still poorly understood but involve both neural regeneration and behavioural adaptation.

Effective rehabilitation following closed head injury depends upon an interdisciplinary approach combining occupational therapy, physiotherapy, medical management, counselling, psychotherapy, cognitive retraining, and behaviour modification. Counselling is an important means of dealing with postconcussional symptoms, especially when it is informed by continuing neuropsychological assessment; however, persistent cognitive deficits may militate against the use of psychoanalytically based methods. Cognitive retraining is usually based upon the use of repetitive practice or alternative strategies, but neither technique seems to be of much value in everyday life and patients may rely more on external aids or structured environments. Nevertheless, some success has been reported in the use of microcomputers with head-injured patients and in the use of partial cueing techniques to teach particular domains of knowledge. Formal programmes of behaviour therapy can lead to substantial and persistent improvements in patients' daily activities which may well be a prerequisite for attempting any other forms of rehabilitative intervention.

Finally, it is now widely recognised that patients' families should be involved in such intervention not simply because they can promote successful rehabilitation, but because family members may themselves exhibit a significant degree of psychiatric morbidity. Individual counselling needs to begin even during the period of coma, whereas continuing support for the relatives and carers (including family therapy and psychotherapy) needs to be available after the patients are discharged to their homes.

# References

Adams, H., & Graham, D.I. (1972). The pathology of blunt head injuries. In M. Critchley, J.L. O'Leary, & B. Jennett (Eds.), *Scientific foundations of neurology* (pp. 478–491). London: Heinemann.

Adams, J.H. (1988). The autopsy in fatal non-missile head injuries. In C.L. Berry (Ed.), *Current topics in pathology: Vol. 76. Neuropathology* (pp. 1–22). Berlin: Springer-Verlag.

Adams, J.H., Doyle, D., Ford, I., Graham, D.I., McGee, M., & McLellan, D.R. (1989a). Brain damage in fatal non-missile head injury in relation to age and type of injury. *Scottish Medical Journal*, *34*, 399–401.

Adams, J.H., Doyle, D., Ford, I., Gennarelli, T.A., Graham, D.I., & McLellan, D.R. (1989b). Diffuse axonal injury in head injury: Definition, diagnosis and grading. *Histopathology*, *15*, 49–59.

Adams, J.H., Doyle, D., Graham, D.I., Lawrence, A.E., & McLellan, D.R. (1984). Diffuse axonal injury in head injuries caused by a fall. *Lancet*, *2*, 1420–1422.

Adams, J.H., Doyle, D., Graham, D.I., Lawrence, A.E., & McLellan, D.R. (1986a). Deep intracerebral (basal ganglia) haematomas in fatal non-missile head injury in man. *Journal of Neurology, Neurosurgery, and Psychiatry*, *49*, 1039–1043.

Adams, J.H., Doyle, D., Graham, D.I., Lawrence, A.E., & McLellan, D.R. (1986b). Gliding contusions in nonmissile head injury in humans. *Archives of Pathology and Laboratory Medicine*, *110*, 485–488.

Adams, J.H., Doyle, D., Graham, D.I., Lawrence, A.E., McLellan, D.R., Gennarelli, T.A., Pastusko, M., & Sakamoto, T. (1985). The contusion index: A reappraisal in human and experimental non-missile head injury. *Neuropathology and Applied Neurobiology*, *11*, 299–308.

Adams, J.H., & Graham, D.I. (1976). The relationship between ventricular fluid pressure and the neuropathology of raised intracranial pressure. *Neuropathology and Applied Neurobiology*, *2*, 323–332.

Adams, J.H., Graham, D.I., & Gennarelli, T.A. (1982). Neuropathology of acceleration-induced head injury in the subhuman primate. In R.G. Grossman & P.L. Gildenberg (Eds.), *Head injury: Basic and clinical aspects* (pp. 141–150). New York: Raven Press.

Adams, J.H., Graham, D.I., & Gennarelli, T.A. (1983). Head injury in man and experimental animals: Neuropathology. *Acta Neurochirurgica*, (Suppl. 32), 15–30.

Adams, J.H., Graham, D.I., Murray, L.S., & Scott, G. (1982). Diffuse axonal injury due to nonmissile head injury in humans: An analysis of 45 cases. *Annals of Neurology*, *12*, 557–563.

Adams, J.H., Graham, D.I., Scott, G., Parker, L.S., & Doyle, D. (1980). Brain damage in fatal non-missile head injury. *Journal of Clinical Pathology*, *33*, 1132–1145.

Adams, J.H., Mitchell, D.E., Graham, D.I., & Doyle, D. (1977). Diffuse brain damage of immediate impact type: Its relationship to "primary brain-stem damage" in head injury. *Brain*, *100*, 489–502.

Adams, J.H., Scott, G., Parker, L.S., Graham, D.I., & Doyle, D. (1980). The contusion index: A quantitative approach to cerebral contusions in head injury. *Neuropathology and Applied Neurobiology*, *6*, 319–324.

Adler, A. (1945). Mental symptoms following head injury: A statistical analysis of two hundred cases. *Archives of Neurology and Psychiatry*, *53*, 34–43.

Aitken, C., Baddeley, A., Bond, M.R., Brocklehurst, J.C., Brooks, D.N., Hewer, R.L., Jennett, B., London, P., Meade, T., Newcombe, F., Shaw, D.A., Smith, M., & James, D.R. (1982). Research aspects of rehabilitation after acute brain damage in adults. *Lancet*, *2*, 1034–1036.

Akbarova, N.A. (1972). [Aspects of memory dysfunction in patients with closed cranio–cerebral trauma of mild and moderate severity]. *Zhurnal Nevropatologii i Psikhiatrii*, *72*, 1641–1646.

Akbarova, N.A. (1972). Osobennosti narusheniia pamiati u bol'nykh s zakrytoi cherepno-mozgovoi travmoi srednei i legkoi stepeni [Aspects of memory dysfunction in patients with closed cranio-cerebral trauma of mild and moderate severity]. *Zhurnal Nevropatologii i Psikhiatrii*, *72*, 1641–1646.

Alajouanine, T., Castaigne, P., Lhermitte, F., Escourolle, R., & de Ribaucourt, B. (1957). Étude de 43 cas d'aphasie post-traumatique: Confrontation anatomo-clinique et aspects évolutifs [Study of 43 cases of post-traumatic aphasia: Anatomo-clinical comparison and prognostic aspects]. *Éncephale*, *46*, 1–45.

Albert, M.L., Silverberg, R., Reches, A., & Berman, M. (1976). Cerebral dominance for consciousness. *Archives of Neurology*, *33*, 453–454.

Alexandre, A., Colombo, F., Nertempi, P., & Benedetti, A. (1983). Cognitive outcome and early indices of severity of head injury. *Journal of Neurosurgery*, *59*, 751–761.

Alexandre, A., Colombo, F., Rubini, L., & Benedetti, A. (1980). Evaluation of sleep EEG alterations during posttraumatic coma in order to predict cognitive defects. In W. Grote, M. Brock, H.-E. Clar, M. Klinger, & H.-E. Nau (Eds.), *Advances in Neurosurgery, Vol. 8, Surgery of cervical myelopathy: Infantile hydrocephalus—Long-term results* (pp. 374–380). Berlin: Springer-Verlag.

Alexandre, A., Nertempi, P., Farinello, C., & Rubini, L. (1979). Recognition memory alterations after severe head injury: Preliminary results in a series of 50 patients. *Journal of the Neurosurgical Sciences, 23,* 201–206.

Allen, C.C., & Ruff, R.M. (1990). Self-rating versus neuropsychological performance of moderate versus severe head-injured patients. *Brain Injury*, *4*, 7–17.

American Congress of Rehabilitation Medicine. (1995). Recommendations for use of uniform nomenclature pertinent to patients with severe alterations in consciousness. *Archives of Physical Medicine and Rehabilitation*, *76*, 205–209.

American Psychiatric Association. (1980). *Diagnostic and statistical manual of mental disorders* (3rd ed.). Washington, DC: American Psychiatric Association.

American Psychiatric Association. (1994). *Diagnostic and statistical manual of mental disorders* (4th ed.). Washington, DC: American Psychiatric Association.

American Psychological Association. (1994). *Publication manual of the American Psychological Association* (4th ed.). Washington, DC: American Psychological Association.

Anderson, C.V., Bigler, E.D., & Blatter, D.D. (1995). Frontal lobe lesions, diffuse damage, and neuropsychological functioning in traumatic brain-injured patients. *Journal of Clinical and Experimental Neuropsychology*, *17*, 900–908.

Anderson, D.W., Kalsbeek, W.D., & Hartwell, T.D. (1980). The National Head and Spinal Cord Injury Survey: Design and methodology. *Journal of Neurosurgery*, *53*, S11–S18.

Anderson, S.D. (1996). Postconcussional disorder and loss of consciousness. *Bulletin of the American Academy of Psychiatry and Law*, *24*, 493–504.

Andrews, K. (1992). Managing the persistent vegetative state. *British Medical Journal*, *305*, 486–487.

Andrews, K. (1996). International Working Party on the Management of the Vegetative State: Summary report. *Brain Injury*, *10*, 797–806.

Andrews, R.J. (1991). Transhemispheric diaschisis: A review and comment. *Stroke*, *22*, 943–949.

Annegers, J.F., Grabow, J.D., Kurland, L.T., & Laws, E.R., Jr. (1980). The incidence, causes, and secular trends of head trauma in Olmsted County, Minnesota, 1935–1974. *Neurology*, *30*, 912–919.

Arseni, C., Constantinovici, A., Iliescu, D., Dobrotá, I., & Gagea, A. (1970). Considerations on posttraumatic aphasia in peace time. *Psychiatria Neurologia Neurochirurgia*, *73*, 105–112.

Artiola i Fortuny, L., Briggs, M., Newcombe, F., Ratcliff, G., & Thomas, C. (1980). Measuring the duration of post traumatic amnesia. *Journal of Neurology, Neurosurgery, and Psychiatry*, *43*, 377–379.

Ashton, S.J., Pedder, J.B., & Mackay, G.M. (1977). *Pedestrian injuries and the car exterior.* Paper presented at the Society of Automotive Engineers' International Automotive Engineering Congress and Exposition, Detroit, MI.

Ashwal, S., & Holshouser, B.A. (1997). New neuroimaging techniques and their potential role in patients with acute brain injury. *Journal of Head Trauma Rehabilitation*, *12*(4), 13–35.

Atkinson, L., Cyr, J.J., Doxey, N.C.S., & Vigna, C.M. (1989). Generalizability of WAIS-R factor structure within and between populations. *Journal of Clinical Psychology*, *45*, 124–129.

Atkinson, R.C., & Shiffrin, R.M. (1968). Human memory: A proposed system and its control processes. In K.W. Spence & J.T. Spence, (Eds.), *The psychology of learning and motivation: Advances in research and theory* (Vol. 2, pp. 89–195). New York: Academic Press.

Autti, T., Sipilä, L., Autti, H., & Salonen, O. (1997). Brain lesions in players of contact sports. *Lancet*, *349*, 1144.

Azouvi, P., Jokic, C., Van Der Linden, M., Marlier, N., & Bussel, B. (1996). Working memory and supervisory control after severe closed-head injury: A study of dual task performance and random generation. *Journal of Clinical and Experimental Neuropsychology*, *18*, 317–337.

Babcock, H. (1930). An experiment in the measurement of mental deterioration. *Archives of Psychology*, Whole No. 117.

Baddeley, A. (1997). *Human memory: Theory and practice* (Rev. ed.). Hove, UK: Psychology Press.

Baddeley, A., & Della Sala, S. (1996). Working memory and executive control. *Philosophical Transactions of the Royal Society of London B*, *351*, 1397–1404.

Baddeley, A., Della Sala, S., Papagno, C., & Spinnler, H. (1997). Dual-task performance in dysexecutive and nondysexecutive patients with a frontal lesion. *Neuropsychology*, *11*, 198–194.

Baddeley, A., Meade, T., & Newcombe, F. (1980). Design problems in research on rehabilitation after brain damage. *International Rehabilitation Medicine, 2,* 138–142.

Baddeley, A., & Wilson, B. (1985). Phonological coding and short-term memory in patients without speech. *Journal of Memory and Language*, *24*, 490–502.

Baddeley, A.D. (1986) *Working memory*. Oxford, UK: Oxford University Press.

Baddeley, A.D., & Hitch, G.J. (1974). Working memory. In G.H. Bower (Ed.), *The psychology of learning and motivation: Advances in research and theory* (Vol. 8, pp. 47–89). New York: Academic Press.

Bakay, L., & Glasauer, F.E. (1980). *Head injury*. Boston: Little, Brown.

Baker, S.P., Fowler, C., Li, G., Warner, M., & Dannenberg, A.L. (1994). Head injuries incurred by children and young adults during informal recreation. *American Journal of Public Health, 84*, 649–652.

Barber, H.M. (1973). Horse-play: Survey of accidents with horses. *British Medical Journal, 3*, 532–534.

Barin, J.J., Hanchett, J.M., Jacob, W.L., & Scott, M.B. (1985). Counseling the head injured patient. In M. Ylvisaker (Ed.), *Head injury rehabilitation: Children and adolescents* (pp. 361–379). San Diego, CA: College-Hill Press. London: Taylor & Francis.

Barona, A., Reynolds, C.R., & Chastain, R. (1984). A demographically based index of premorbid intelligence for the WAIS-R. *Journal of Consulting and Clinical Psychology, 52*, 885–887.

Barth, J.T., Alves, W.M., Ryan, T.V., Macciocchi, S.N., Rimel, R.W., Jane, J.A., & Nelson, W.E. (1989). Mild head injury in sports: Neuropsychological sequelae and recovery of function. In H.S. Levin, H.M. Eisenberg, & A.L. Benton (Eds.), *Mild head injury* (pp. 257–275). New York: Oxford University Press.

Barth, J.T., Macciocchi, S.N., Giordani, B., Rimel, R., Jane, J.A., & Boll, T.J. (1983). Neuropsychological sequelae of minor head injury. *Neurosurgery, 13*, 529–533.

Beck, N.C., Tucker, D., Frank, R., Parker, J., Lake, R., Thomas, S., Lichty, W., Horwitz, E., Horwitz, B., & Merritt, F. (1989). The latent factor structure of the WAIS-R: A factor analysis of individual item responses. *Journal of Clinical Psychology, 45*, 281–293.

Becker, B. (1975). Intellectual changes after closed head injury. *Journal of Clinical Psychology, 31*, 307–309.

Behrman, S. (1977). Migraine as a sequela of blunt head injury. *Injury, 9*, 74–76.

Bennett-Levy, J., & Powell, G.E. (1980). The Subjective Memory Questionnaire (SMQ): An investigation into the self-reporting of "real-life" memory skills. *British Journal of Social and Clinical Psychology, 19*, 177–188.

Bennett-Levy, J.M. (1984). Long-term effects of severe closed head injury on memory: Evidence from a consecutive series of young adults. *Acta Neurologica Scandinavica, 70*, 285–298.

Benson, D.F., & Geschwind, N. (1967). Shrinking retrograde amnesia. *Journal of Neurology, Neurosurgery, and Psychiatry, 30*, 539–544.

Benson, D.F., Gardner, H., & Meadows, J.C. (1976). Reduplicative paramnesia. *Neurology, 26*, 147–151.

Benson, V., & Marano, M.A. (1994). *Current estimates from the National Health Interview Survey, 1993* (Vital and health statistics, Series 10, No. 190: DHHS Publication No. PHS 95–1518). Washington, DC: US Government Printing Office.

Benton, A. L. (1967). Problems of test construction in the field of aphasia. *Cortex, 3,* 32–58.

Benton, A.L. (1968). Differential behavioral effects in frontal lobe disease. *Neuropsychologia, 6*, 53–60.

Benton, A.L. (1969). Development of a multilingual aphasia battery: Progress and problems. *Journal of the Neurological Sciences, 9*, 39–48.

Benton, A.L., Van Allen, M.W., & Fogel, M.L. (1964). Temporal orientation in cerebral disease. *Journal of Nervous and Mental Disease, 139*, 110–119.

Bigler, E.D. (1987). Acquired cerebral trauma: Behavioral, neuropsychiatric, psychoeducational assessment and cognitive retraining issues. *Journal of Learning Disabilities, 20*, 579–580.

Bigler, E.D., Johnson, S.C., Anderson, C.V., Blatter, D.D., Gale, S.D., Russo, A.A., Ryser, D.K., Macnamara, S.E., Bailey, B.J., Hopkins, R.O., & Abildskov, T.J. (1996). Traumatic brain injury and memory: The role of hippocampal atrophy. *Neuropsychology, 10*, 333–342.

Bijur, P.E., Haslum, M., & Golding, J. (1990). Cognitive and behavioral sequelae of mild head injury in children. *Pediatrics*, *86*, 337–344.

Bijur, P.E., Haslum, M., & Golding, J. (1995). Cognitive outcomes of multiple mild head injuries in children. *Journal of Developmental and Behavioral Pediatrics*, *17*, 143–148.

Binder, L.M. (1986). Persisting symptoms after mild head injury: A review of the postconcussive syndrome. *Journal of Clinical and Experimental Neuropsychology*, *8*, 323–346.

Binder, L.M. (1997). A review of mild head trauma: Pt. II. Clinical implications. *Journal of Clinical and Experimental Neuropsychology*, *19*, 432–457.

Binder, L.M., & Rohling, M.L. (1996). Money matters: A meta-analytic review of the effects of financial incentives on recovery after closed head injury. *American Journal of Psychiatry*, *153*, 5–8.

Binder, L.M., Rohling, M.L., & Larrabee, G.J. (1997). A review of mild head trauma: Pt. I. Meta-analytic review of neuropsychological studies. *Journal of Clinical and Experimental Neuropsychology*, *19*, 421–431.

Bishara, S.N., Partridge, F.M., Godfrey, H.P.D., & Knight, R.G. (1992). Post-traumatic amnesia and Glasgow Coma Scale related to outcome in survivors in a consecutive series of patients with severe closed head injury. *Brain Injury*, *6*, 373–380.

Bjørgen, I.A. (1996). Late whiplash syndrome. *Lancet*, *348*, 124.

Björkesten, G. af (1971). Summary. In *Head injuries: Proceedings of an international symposium* (pp. 341–342). Edinburgh, UK: Churchill Livingstone.

Black, F.W. (1973). Cognitive and memory performance in subjects with brain damage secondary to penetrating missile wounds and closed head injury. *Journal of Clinical Psychology*, *29*, 441–442.

Black, P., Blumer, D., Wellner, A.M., & Walker, A.E. (1971). The head-injured child: Time-course of recovery, with implications for rehabilitation. In *Head injuries: Proceedings of an international symposium* (pp. 131–137). Edinburgh, UK: Churchill Livingstone.

Blomert, D.M., & Sisler, G.C. (1974). The measurement of retrograde post-traumatic amnesia. *Canadian Psychiatric Association Journal*, *19*, 185–192.

Blumbergs, P.C., Scott, G., Manavis, J., Wainright, H., Simpson, D.A., & McLean, A.J. (1995). Topography of axonal injury as defined by amyloid precursor protein and the sector scoring method in mild and severe closed head injury. *Journal of Neurotrauma*, *12*, 565–572.

Bohnen, N., Jolles, J., & Twijnstra, A. (1992). Neuropsychological deficits in patients with persistent symptoms six months after mild head injury. *Neurosurgery*, *30*, 692–696.

Bohnen, N.I., Jolles, J., Twijnstra, A., Mellink, R., & Wijnen, G. (1995). Late neurobehavioural symtoms after mild head injury. *Brain Injury*, *9*, 27–33.

Boller, F.C., Albert, M.L., LeMay, M., & Kertesz, A. (1972). Enlargement of the Sylvian aqueduct: A sequel of head injuries. *Journal of Neurology, Neurosurgery, and Psychiatry*, *35*, 463–467.

Bond, F., & Godfrey, H.P.D. (1997). Conversation with traumatically brain-injured individuals: A controlled study of behavioural changes and their impact. *Brain Injury*, *11*, 319–329.

Bond, M.R. (1975). Assessment of the psychosocial outcome after severe head injury. In *Outcome of severe damage to the central nervous system* (Ciba Foundation Symposium No. 34, new series, pp. 141–157). Amsterdam: Elsevier/Excerpta Medica/North-Holland.

Bond, M.R. (1976). Assessment of the psychosocial outcome of severe head injury. *Acta Neurochirurgica*, *34*, 57–70.

Bond, M.R. (1979). The stages of recovery from severe head injury with special reference to late outcome. *International Rehabilitation Medicine*, *1*, 155–159.

Bond, M.R. (1986). Neurobehavioral sequelae of closed head injury. In I. Grant & K.M. Adams (Eds.), *Neuropsychological assessment of neuropsychiatric disorders* (pp. 347–373). New York: Oxford University Press.

Bond, M.R., & Brooks, D.N. (1976). Understanding the process of recovery as a basis for the investigation of rehabilitation for the brain injured. *Scandinavian Journal of Rehabilitation Medicine*, *8*, 127–133.

Bouma, G.J., & Muizelaar, J.P. (1995). Cerebral blood flow in severe clinical head injury. *New Horizons*, *3*, 384–394.

Bowden, S.C., Dodds, B., Whelan, G., Long, C., Dudgeon, P., Ritter, A., & Clifford, C. (1997). Confirmatory factor analysis of the Wechsler Memory Scale-Revised in a sample of clients with alcohol dependency. *Journal of Clinical and Experimental Neuropsychology*, *19*, 755–762.

Bowers, S.A., & Marshall, L.F. (1980). Outcome in 200 consecutive cases of severe head injury treated in San Diego County: A prospective analysis. *Neurosurgery*, *6*, 237–242.

Braakman, R., Avezaat, C.J.J., Maas, A.I.R., Roel, M., & Schouten, H.J.A. (1977). Inter observer agreement in the assessment of the motor response of the Glasgow "coma" scale. *Clinical Neurology and Neurosurgery*, *80*, 100–106.

Braakman, R., Jennett, W.B., & Minderhoud, J.M. (1988). Prognosis of the posttraumatic vegetative state. *Acta Neurochirurgica*, *95*, 49–52.

Brenner, C., Friedman, A.P., Merritt, H.H., & Denny-Brown, D.E. (1944). Post-traumatic headache. *Journal of Neurosurgery*, *1*, 379–391.

Bricolo, A., Turazzi, S., & Feriotti, G. (1980). Prolonged posttraumatic unconsciousness: Therapeutic assets and liabilities. *Journal of Neurosurgery*, *52*, 625–634.

Brierley, J.B. (1976). Cerebral hypoxia. In W. Blackwood & J.A.N. Corsellis (Eds.), *Greenfield's neuropathology* (3rd ed., pp. 43–85). London: Edward Arnold.

Brink, J.D., Garrett, A.L., Hale, W.R., Woo-Sam, J., & Nickel, V.L. (1970). Recovery of motor and intellectual function in children sustaining severe head injuries. *Developmental Medicine and Child Neurology*, *12*, 565–571.

Broadbent, D.E. (1958). *Perception and communication*. Oxford, UK: Pergamon.

Brock, S. (1960). General considerations in injuries of the brain and spinal cord and their coverings. In S. Brock (Ed.), *Injuries of the Brain and Spinal Cord and Their Coverings* (4th ed., pp. 1–22). London: Cassell.

Brookes, M., MacMillan, R., Cully, S., Anderson, E., Murray, S., Mendelow, A.D., & Jennett, B. (1990). Head injuries in accident and emergency departments: How different are children from adults? *Journal of Epidemiology and Community Health*, *44*, 147–151.

Brooks, D.N. (1972). Memory and head injury. *Journal of Nervous and Mental Disease*, *155*, 350–355.

Brooks, D.N. (1974a). Recognition memory after head injury: A signal detection analysis. *Cortex*, *11*, 224–230.

Brooks, D.N. (1974b). Recognition memory, and head injury. *Journal of Neurology, Neurosurgery, and Psychiatry*, *37*, 794–801.

Brooks, D.N. (1975). Long and short term memory in head injured patients. *Cortex*, *11*, 329–340.

Brooks, D.N. (1976). Wechsler Memory Scale performance and its relationship to brain damage after severe closed head injury. *Journal of Neurology, Neurosurgery, and Psychiatry*, *39*, 593–601.

Brooks, D.N. (1979). Psychological deficits after severe blunt head injury: Their significance and rehabilitation. In D.J. Oborne, M.M. Gruneberg, & J.R. Eiser (Eds.), *Research in psychology and medicine: Vol. II. Social Aspects: Attitudes, Communication, Care and Training* (pp. 469–476). London: Academic Press.

Brooks, N. (1984). Cognitive deficits after head injury. In N. Brooks (Ed.), *Closed head injury: Psychological, social, and family consequences* (pp. 44–73). Oxford, UK: Oxford University Press.

Brooks, D.N., & Aughton, M.E. (1979a). Cognitive recovery during the first year after severe blunt head injury. *International Rehabilitation Medicine, 1*, 166–172.

Brooks, D.N., & Aughton, M.E. (1979b). Psychological consequences of blunt head injury. *International Rehabilitation Medicine, 1*, 160–165.

Brooks, D.N., Aughton, M.E., Bond, M.R., Jones, P., & Rizvi, S. (1980). Cognitive sequelae in relationship to early indices of severity of brain damage after severe blunt head injury. *Journal of Neurology, Neurosurgery, and Psychiatry, 43*, 529–534.

Brooks, D.N., Deelman, B.G., van Zomeren, A.H., van Dongen, H., van Harskamp, F., & Aughton, M.E. (1984). Problems in measuring cognitive recovery after acute brain injury. *Journal of Clinical Neuropsychology, 6*, 71–85.

Brooks, D.N., Hosie, J., Bond, M.R., Jennett, B., & Aughton, M. (1986). Cognitive sequelae of severe head injury in relation to the Glasgow Outcome Scale. *Journal of Neurology, Neurosurgery, and Psychiatry, 49*, 549–553.

Brooks, D.N., & McKinlay, W. (1983). Personality and behavioural change after severe blunt head injury: A relative's view. *Journal of Neurology, Neurosurgery, and Psychiatry, 46*, 336–344.

Brooks, N., Campsie, L., Symington, C., Beattie, A., & McKinlay, W. (1986a). The five year outcome of severe blunt head injury: A relative's view. *Journal of Neurology, Neurosurgery, and Psychiatry, 49*, 764–770.

Brooks, N., McKinlay, W., Symington, C., Beattie, A., & Campsie, L. (1987). Return to work within the first seven years of severe head injury. *Brain Injury, 1*, 5–19.

Brown, G., Chadwick, O., Shaffer, D., Rutter, M., & Traub, M. (1981). A prospective study of children with head injuries in adulthood: III. Psychiatric sequelae. *Psychological Medicine, 11*, 63–78.

Bruce, D.A., Alavi, A., Bilaniuk, L., Dolinskas, C., Obrist, W., & Uzzell, B. (1981). Diffuse cerebral swelling following head injuries in children: The syndrome of "malignant brain edema". *Journal of Neurosurgery, 54*, 170–178.

Bruce, D.A., Schut, L., Bruno, L.A., Wood, J.H., & Sutton, L.N. (1978). Outcome following severe head injuries in children. *Journal of Neurosurgery, 48*, 679–688.

Bruckner, F.E., & Randle, A.P.H. (1972). Return to work after severe head injuries. *Rheumatology and Physical Medicine, 11*, 344–348.

Bryden, J. (1989). How many head-injured? The epidemiology of post head injury disability. In R.L. Wood & P. Eames (Eds.), *Models of brain injury rehabilitation* (pp. 17–27). London: Chapman & Hall.

Buschke, H. (1973). Selective reminding for analysis of memory and learning. *Journal of Verbal Learning and Verbal Behavior, 12*, 543–550.

Buschke, H., & Fuld, P. (1974). Evaluating storage, retention, and retrieval in disordered memory and learning. *Neurology, 24*, 1019–1025.

Caffey, J. (1972). On the theory and practice of shaking infants: Its potential residual effects of permanent brain damage and mental retardation. *American Journal of Diseases of Children, 124*, 161–169.

Caffey, J. (1974). The whiplash shaken infant syndrome: Manual shaking by the extremities with whiplash-induced intracranial and intraocular bleedings, linked with residual permanent brain damage and mental retardation. *Pediatrics, 54*, 396–403.

Caine, E.D., Ebert, M.H., & Weingartner, H. (1977). An outline for the analysis of dementia: The memory disorder of Huntingtons disease. *Neurology, 27*, 1087–1092.

Campbell, K.B., Suffield, J.B., & Deacon, D.L. (1990). Electrophysiological assessment of cognitive disorder in closed head–injured outpatients. In P. M. Rossini & F. Mauguière (Eds.), *New trends and advanced techniques in clinical neurophysiology* (Electroencephalography and clinical neurophysiology, Suppl. 41, pp. 202–215). Amsterdam: Elsevier.

Canavan, A.G.M., Dunn, G., & McMillan, T.M. (1986). Principal components of the WAIS-R. *British Journal of Clinical Psychology*, *25*, 81–85.

Carlsson, C.-A., von Essen, C., & Löfgren, J. (1968). Factors affecting the clinical course of patients with severe head injuries. *Journal of Neurosurgery*, *29*, 242–251.

Carty, H., & Ratcliffe, J. (1995). The shaken infant syndrome. *British Medical Journal*, *310*, 344–345.

Caveness, W.F. (1979). Incidence of craniocerebral trauma in the United States in 1976 with trend from 1970 to 1975. *Advances in Neurology*, *22*, 1–3.

Chadwick, O. (1985). Psychological sequelae of head injury in children. *Developmental Medicine and Child Neurology*, *27*, 72–75.

Chadwick, O., Rutter, M., Brown, G., Shaffer, D., & Traub, M. (1981). A prospective study of children with head injuries: II. Cognitive sequelae. *Psychological Medicine*, *11*, 49–61.

Chadwick, O., Rutter, M., Shaffer, D., & Shrout, P.E. (1981). A prospective study of children with head injuries: IV. Specific cognitive deficits. *Journal of Clinical Neuropsychology*, *3*, 101–120.

Chadwick, O., Rutter, M., Thompson, J., & Shaffer, D. (1981). Intellectual performance and reading skills after localized head injury in childhood. *Journal of Child Psychology and Psychiatry*, *22*, 117–139.

Champion, H.R., Copes, W.S., Sacco, W.J., Lawnick, M.M., Bain, L.W., Gann, D.S., Gennarelli, T., Mackenzie, E., & Schwaitzberg, S. (1990). A new characterization of injury severity. *Journal of Trauma*, *30*, 539–546.

Champion, H.R., Sacco, W.J., Copes, W.S., Gann, D.S., Gennarelli, T.A., & Flanagan, M.E. (1989). A revision of the Trauma Score. *Journal of Trauma*, *29*, 623–629.

Chapman, S.B., Culhane, K.A., Levin, H.S., Harward, H., Mendelsohn, D., Ewing-Cobbs, L., Fletcher, J.M., & Bruce, D. (1992). Narrative discourse after closed head injury in children and adolescents. *Brain and Language*, *43*, 42–65.

Chen, S.H.A., Thomas, J.D., Glueckauf, R.L., & Bracy, O.L. (1997). The effectiveness of computer-assisted cognitive rehabilitation for persons with traumatic brain injury. *Brain Injury*, *11*, 197–209.

Choi, S.C., Barnes, T.Y., Bullock, R., Germanson, T.A., Marmarou, A., & Young, H.F. (1994). Temporal profile of outcomes in severe head injury. *Journal of Neurosurgery*, *81*, 169–173.

Christensen, A.-L., Pinner, E.M., Moller Pedersen, P., Teasdale, T.W., & Trexler, L.E. (1992). Psychosocial outcome following individualized neuropsychological rehabilitation of brain damage. *Acta Neurologica Scandinavica*, *85*, 32–38.

Church, J. (Ed.). (1997). *Social trends 27: 1997 edition*. London: Her Majesty's Stationery Office.

Cicerone, K.D., & Tupper, D.E. (1986). Cognitive assessment in the neuropsychological treatment of head-injured adults. In B.P. Uzzell & Y. Gross (Eds.), *Clinical neuropsychology of intervention* (pp. 59–83). Boston: Martinus Nijhoff.

Clifton, G.L., Grossman, R.G., Makela, M.E., Miner, M.E., Handel, S., & Sadhu, V. (1980). Neurological course and correlated computerized tomography findings after severe closed head injury. *Journal of Neurosurgery*, *52*, 611–624.

Clifton, G.L., Kreutzer, J.S., Choi, S.C., Devany, C.W., Eisenberg, H.M., Foulkes, M.A., Jane, J.A., Marmarou, A., & Marshall, L.F. (1993). Relationship between Glasgow Outcome Scale and neuropsychological measures after brain injury. *Neurosurgery*, *33*, 34–39.

Coelho, C.A. (1995). Discourse production deficits following traumatic brain injury: A critical review of the recent literature. *Aphasiology*, *9*, 409–429.

Coelho, C.A., Liles, B.Z., & Duffy, R.J. (1995). Impairments of discourse abilities and executive functions in traumatically brain-injured adults. *Brain Injury*, *9*, 471–477.

Cohen, S.B., & Titonis, J. (1985). Head injury rehabilitation: Management issues. In M. Ylvisaker (Ed.), *Head injury rehabilitation: Children and adolescents* (pp. 429–443). London: Taylor & Francis.

Cole, E. M. (1945). Intellectual impairment in head injury. In *Research publications of the association for research in nervous and mental disease: Vol. 24. Trauma of the central nervous system* (pp. 473–479). Baltimore: Williams & Wilkins.

Collerton, D. (1993). Memory disorders. In R. Greenwood, M.P. Barnes, T.M. McMillan, & C.D. Ward (Eds.), *Neurological rehabilitation* (pp. 363–375). Edinburgh. UK: Churchill Livingstone.

Conkey, R.C. (1938). Psychological changes associated with head injuries. *Archives of Psychology, 33*(Whole No. 232).

Conzen, M., Ebel, H., Swart, E., Skreczek, W., Dette, M., & Oppel, F. (1992). Long-term neuropsychological outcome after severe head injury with good recovery. *Brain Injury, 6*, 45–52.

Cook, J.B. (1969). The effects of minor head injuries sustained in sport and the postconcussional syndrome. In A.E. Walker, W.F. Caveness, & M. Critchley (Eds.), *The late effects of head injury* (pp. 408–413). Springfield, IL: Thomas.

Cook, J.B. (1972). The post-concussional syndrome and factors influencing recovery after minor head injury admitted to hospital. *Scandinavian Journal of Rehabilitation Medicine, 4*, 27–30.

Cooper, K., Tabaddor, K., Hauser, W., Shulman, K., Feiner, C., & Factor, P. (1983). The epidemiology of head injury in the Bronx. *Neuroepidemiology, 2*, 70–88.

Cooper, P.R. (1982a). Epidemiology of head injury. In P.R. Cooper (Ed.), *Head injury* (pp. 1–14). Baltimore: Williams & Wilkins.

Cooper, P.R. (1982b). Post-traumatic intracranial mass lesions. In P.R. Cooper (Ed.), *Head injury* (pp. 185–232). Baltimore: Williams & Wilkins.

Cope, D.N. (1987). Combined head and spinal cord injury. In M.E. Miner & K.A. Wagner (Eds.), *Neurotrauma: Treatment, rehabilitation, and related issues, No. 2* (pp. 99–102). Boston: Butterworths.

Corkin, S., Cohen, N.J., Sullivan, E.V., Clegg, R.A., Rosen, T.J., & Ackerman, R.H. (1985). Analyses of global memory impairments of different etiologies. *Annals of the New York Academy of Sciences, 444*, 10–40.

Corrigan, J.D., & Hinkeldey, N.S. (1987). Comparison of intelligence and memory in patients with diffuse and focal injury. *Psychological Reports, 60*, 899–906.

Corrigan, J.D., Mysiw, W.J., Gribble, M.W., & Chock, S.K.L. (1992). Agitation, cognition and attention during post-traumatic amnesia. *Brain Injury, 6*, 155–160.

Courville, C.B. (1942). Coup-contrecoup mechanism of craniocerebral injuries: Some observations. *Archives of Surgery, 45*, 19–43.

Courville, C.B. (1950). *Pathology of the central nervous system* (3rd ed.). Mountain View, CA: Pacific Press Publishing.

Crawford, J.R. (1992). Current and premorbid intelligence measures in neuropsychological assessment. In J.R. Crawford & D.M. Parker (Eds.), *A handbook of neuropsychological assessment* (pp. 21–49). Hove, UK: Lawrence Erlbaum Associates Ltd.

Crawford, J.R., & Allan, K.M. (1997). Estimating premorbid WAIS-R IQ with demographic variables: Regression equations derived from a UK sample. *Clinical Neuropsychologist, 11*, 192–197.

Crawford, J.R., Allan, K.M., Stephen, D.W., Parker, D.M., & Besson, J.A.O. (1989). The Wechsler Adult Intelligence Scale—Revised (WAIS-R): Factor structure in a UK sample. *Personality and Individual Differences, 10*, 1209–1212.

Crawford, J.R., Johnson, D.A., Mychalkiw, B., & Moore, J.W. (1997). WAIS-R performance following closed-head injury: A comparison of the clinical utility of summary IQs, factor scores, and subtest scatter indices. *Clinical Neuropsychologist*, *11*, 345–355.

Crawford, J.R., Obansawin, M.C., & Allan, K.M. (1998). PASAT and components of WAIS-R performance: Convergent and discriminant validity. *Neuropsychological Rehabilitation*, *8*, 255–272.

Crawford, J.R., Parker, D.M., & Besson, J.A.O. (1988). Estimation of premorbid intelligence in organic conditions. *British Journal of Psychiatry*, *153,* 178–181.

Crompton, M.R. (1971). Hypothalamic lesions following closed head injury. *Brain*, *94*, 165–172.

Cronholm, B. (1972). Evaluation of mental disturbances after head injury. *Scandinavian Journal of Rehabilitation Medicine*, *4*, 35–38.

Crosson, B., & Buenning, W. (1984). An individualized memory retraining program after closed-head injury: A single-case study. *Journal of Clinical Neuropsychology*, *6*, 287–301.

Crosson, B., Novack, T.A., Trenerry, M.R., & Craig, P.L. (1988). California Verbal Learning Test (CVLT) performance in severely head-injured and neurologically normal adult males. *Journal of Clinical and Experimental Neuropsychology*, *10*, 754–768.

Crovitz, H.F., Harvey, M.T., & Horn, R.W. (1979). Problems in the acquisition of imagery mnemonics: Three brain-damaged cases. *Cortex*, *15*, 225–234.

Crovitz, H.F., Horn, R.W., & Daniel, W.F. (1983). Inter-relationships among retrograde amnesia, post-traumatic amnesia, and time since head injury: A retrospective study. *Cortex*, *19*, 407–412.

Cullum, C.M., & Bigler, E.D. (1985). Late effects of hematoma on brain morphology and memory in closed head injury. *International Journal of Neuroscience*, *28*, 279–283.

Cyr, J.J., & Brooker, B.H. (1984). Use of appropriate formulas for selecting WAIS-R short forms. *Journal of Consulting and Clinical Psychology*, *52*, 903–905.

Dahlstrom, W.G., Welsh, G.S., & Dahlstrom, L.E. (1972). *An MMPI handbook: Vol. 1. Clinical interpretation*. Minneapolis, MN: University of Minnesota Press.

Dailey, C.A. (1956). Psychologic findings five years after head injury. *Journal of Clinical Psychology*, *12*, 349–352.

Daniel, M.S. (1987). Memory and depression following brain injury. *Dissertation Abstracts International*, *47*, 3514B.

Davidoff, G., Morris, J., Roth, E., & Bleiberg, J. (1985). Closed head injury in spinal cord injured patients: Retrospective study of loss of consciousness and post-traumatic amnesia. *Archives of Physical Medicine and Rehabilitation*, *66*, 41–43.

Davidoff, G., Roth, E., Morris, J., & Bleiberg, J. (1987). Evaluation of closed head injury and cognitive deficits in patients with traumatic spinal cord injury. In M.E. Miner & K.A. Wagner (Eds.), *Neurotrauma: Treatment, rehabilitation, and related issues, No. 2* (pp. 127–135). Boston: Butterworths.

Deary, I.J., Langan, S.J., Hepburn, D.A., & Frier, B.M. (1991). Which abilities does the PASAT measure? *Personality and Individual Differences*, *12*, 983–987.

Deaton, A.V. (1987). Behavioral change strategies for children and adolescents with severe brain injury. *Journal of Learning Disabilities*, *20*, 581–589.

De Mol, B.A., & Heijer, T. (1996). Late whiplash syndrome. *Lancet*, *348*, 124–125.

De Morsier, G. (1973). Les hallucinations survenant après les traumatismes cranio-cérébraux: La schizophrénie traumatique. [Hallucinations following cranio-cerebral traumatism: Traumatic schizophrenia]. *Annales médico-psychologiques*, *130*, 183–194.

Dencker, S.J. (1958). A follow-up study of 128 closed head injuries in twins using co–twins as controls. *Acta Psychiatrica et Neurologica Scandinavica, 33*(Suppl. 123).

Dencker, S.J. (1960). Closed head injury in twins: Neurologic, psychometric, and psychiatric follow-up study of consecutive cases, using co-twins as controls. *Archives of General Psychiatry, 2*, 569–575.

Dencker, S.J., & Löfving, B. (1958). A psychometric study of identical twins discordant for closed head injury. *Acta Psychiatrica et Neurologica Scandinavica, 33*(Suppl. 122).

Denny-Brown, D. (1945a). Disability arising from closed head injury. *Journal of the American Medical Association, 127*, 429–436.

Denny-Brown, D. (1945b). Intellectual deterioration resulting from head injury. In *Research publications of the association for research in nervous and mental disease: Vol. 24, Trauma of the central nervous system* (pp. 467–472). Baltimore: Williams & Wilkins.

Denny-Brown, D.E., & Russell, W.R. (1941). Experimental cerebral concussion. *Brain, 64*, 93–164.

Department of Health. (1993). *Hospital episode statistics: Vol. 1. Finished consultant episodes by diagnosis, operation and speciality. England: Financial year 1989–90*. London: Author.

Deparment of Health. (1994a). *Hospital episode statistics. England: Financial year 1988–89*. London: Author.

Department of Health. (1994b). *Hospital episode statistics: Vol. 1. Finished consultant episodes by diagnosis, operation and speciality. England: Financial year 1990–91*. London: Author.

Department of Health. (1994c). *Hospital episode statistics: Vol. 1. Finished consultant episodes by diagnosis, operation and speciality. England: Financial year 1991–92*. London: Author.

Department of Health. (1994d). *Hospital episode statistics: Vol. 1. Finished consultant episodes by diagnosis, operation and speciality. England: Financial year 1992–93*. London: Author.

Department of Health. (1995). *Hospital episode statistics: Vol. 1. Finished consultant episodes by diagnosis and operative procedure; injury/poisoning by external causes. England: Financial year 1993–94*. London: Author.

Department of Health (1996). *Hospital episode statistics: Vol. 1. Finished consultant episodes by diagnosis and operative procedure; injury/poisoning by external causes. England: Financial year 1994–95*. London: Author.

De Renzi, E., & Vignolo, L.A. (1962). The Token Test: A sensitive test to detect receptive disturbances in aphasics. *Brain, 85*, 665–678.

Deshpande, S.A., Millis, S.R., Reeder, K.P., Fuerst, D., & Ricker, J.H. (1996). Verbal learning subtypes in traumatic brain injury. *Journal of Clinical and Experimental Neuropsychology, 18*, 836–842.

Dikmen, S., & Reitan, R.M. (1976). Psychological deficits and recovery of functions after head injury. *Transactions of the American Neurological Association, 101*, 72–77.

Dikmen, S., & Reitan, R.M. (1977). Emotional sequelae of head injury. *Annals of Neurology, 2*, 492–494.

Dikmen, S., Reitan, R.M., & Temkin, N.R. (1983). Neuropsychological recovery in head injury. *Archives of Neurology, 40*, 333–338.

Dixon, K.C. (1962). The amnesia of cerebral concussion. *Lancet, 2*, 1359–1360.

Dowler, R.N., Harrington, D.L., Haaland, K.Y., Swanda, R.M., Fee, F., & Fiedler, K. (1997). Profiles of cognitive functioning in chronic spinal injury and the role of moderating variables. *Journal of the International Neuropsychological Society, 3*, 464–472.

Dresser, A.C., Meirowsky, A.M., Weiss, G.H., McNeel, M.L., Simon, G.A., & Caveness, W.F. (1973). Gainful employment following head injury. *Archives of Neurology, 29*, 111–116.

Duhaime, A.-C., Gennarelli, T.A., Thibault, L.E., Bruce, D.A., Margulies, S.S., & Wiser, R. (1987). The shaken baby syndrome: A clinical, pathological, and biomechanical study. *Journal of Neurosurgery, 66*, 409–415.

Dunn, J., & Brooks, D.N. (1974). Memory and post traumatic amnesia. *IRCS (Research on Neurology and Neurosurgery; Psychiatry and Clinical Psychology; Psychology), 2*, 1497.

Dye, O.A., Milby, J.B., & Saxon, S.A. (1979). Effects of early neurological problems following head trauma on subsequent neuropsychological performance. *Acta Neurologica Scandinavica, 59*, 10–14.

Eames, P., & Wood, R. (1985a). Rehabilitation after severe brain injury: A special-unit approach to behaviour disorders. *International Rehabilitation Medicine, 7*, 130–133.

Eames, P., & Wood, R. (1985). Rehabilitation after severe brain injury: A follow-up study of a behaviour modification approach. *Journal of Neurology, Neurosurgery, and Psychiatry, 48*, 613–619.

Eames, P., & Wood, R.L. (1989). The structure and content of a head injury rehabilitation service. In R.L. Wood & P. Eames (Eds.), *Models of brain injury rehabilitation* (pp. 31–47). London: Chapman & Hall.

Eden, K., & Turner, J.W.A. (1941). Loss of consciousness in different types of head injury. *Proceedings of the Royal Society of Medicine, 34*, 685–691.

Edna, T.-H., & Cappelen, J. (1987). Late postconcussional symptoms in traumatic head injury: An analysis of frequency and risk factors. *Acta Neurochirurgica, 86*, 12–17.

Eisenberg, H.M., & Weiner, R.L. (1987). Input variables: How information from the acute injury can be used to characterize groups of patients for studies of outcome. In H.S. Levin, J. Grafman, & H. M. Eisenberg (Eds.), *Neurobehavioral recovery from head injury* (pp. 13–29). New York: Oxford University Press.

Elia, J. (1974). Cranial injuries and the post concussion syndrome. *Medical Trial Techniques Quarterly, 21*, 127–161.

Elliott, M.L., & Biever, L.S. (1996). Head injury and sexual dysfunction. *Brain Injury, 10*, 703–717.

Enderson, B.L., Reath, D.B., Meadors, J., Dallas, W., DeBoo, J.M., & Maull, K.I. (1990). The tertiary trauma study: A prospective study of missed injury. *Journal of Trauma, 30*, 666–670.

Englander, J., Hall, K., Stimpson, T., & Chaffin, S. (1992). Mild traumatic brain injury in an insured population: Subjective complaints and return to employment. *Brain Injury, 6*, 161–166.

English, T.C. (1904). The after-effects of head injuries: Lecture II. *Lancet, 1*, 559–563.

Esselman, P.C., & Uomoto, J.M. (1995). Classification of the spectrum of mild traumatic brain injury. *Brain Injury, 9*, 417–424.

Evans, C. (1989). Long-term follow-up. In R.L. Wood & P. Eames (Eds.), *Models of brain injury rehabilitation* (pp. 183–204). London: Chapman & Hall.

Evans, C.D. (Ed.). (1981). *Rehabilitation after severe head injury.* Edinburgh, UK: Churchill Livingstone.

Evans, C.D., Bull, C.P.I., Devonport, M.J., Hall, P.M., Jones, J., Middleton, F.R.I., Russell, G., Stichbury, J.C., & Whitehead, B. (1976). Rehabilitation of the brain-damaged survivor. *Injury, 8*, 80–97.

Evans, R.W. (1987). Postconcussive syndrome: An overview. *Texas Medicine, 83*, 49–53.

Ewert, J., Levin, H.S., Watson, M.G., & Kalisky, Z. (1989). Procedural memory during posttraumatic amnesia in survivors of severe closed head injury: Implications for rehabilitation. *Archives of Neurology, 46*, 911–916.

Ewing-Cobbs, L., Levin, H.S., & Fletcher, J.M. (1998). In M. Ylvisaker (Ed.), *Traumatic brain injury rehabilitation: Children and adolescents* (2nd ed., pp. 11–26). Boston: Butterworth-Heinemann.

Ewing-Cobbs, L., Levin, H.S., Fletcher, J.M., Miner, M.E., & Eisenberg, H.M. (1990). The Children's Orientation and Amnesia Test: Relationship to severity of acute head injury and to recovery of memory. *Neurosurgery, 27*, 683–691.

Eysenck, H.J., & Eysenck, S.B.G. (1975). *Eysenck Personality Questionnaire.* London: Hodder & Stoughton.

Eysenck, M.W. (1979). Anxiety, learning, and memory: A reconceptualization. *Journal of Research in Personality*, *13*, 365–385.

Eysenck, M.W. (1982). *Attention and arousal: Cognition and performance.* Berlin: Springer-Verlag.

Fahy, T.J., Irving, M.H., & Millac, P. (1967). Severe head injuries: A six-year follow-up. *Lancet*, *2*, 475–479.

Ferguson, G.A., & Takane, Y. (1989). *Statistical analysis in psychology and education* (6th ed.). New York: McGraw-Hill.

Field, J.H. (1976). *Epidemiology of head injuries in England and Wales.* London: Her Majesty's Stationery Office.

Fife, D. (1987). Head injury with and without hospital admission: Comparisons of incidence and short-term disability. *American Journal of Public Health*, *77*, 810–812.

Finger, S. (1991). Brain damage, development, and behavior: Early findings. *Developmental Neuropsychology*, *7*, 261–274.

Fisher, C.M. (1966). Concussion amnesia. *Neurology*, *16*, 826–830.

Florian, V., Katz, S., & Lahav, V. (1989). Impact of traumatic brain damage on family dynamics and functioning: A review. *Brain Injury*, *3*, 219–233.

Flynn, J.R. (1984). The mean IQ of Americans: Massive gains 1932 to 1978. *Psychological Bulletin*, *95*, 29–51.

Forrester, G., Encel, J., & Geffen, F. (1994). Measuring post-traumatic amnesia (PTA): An historical review. *Brain Injury*, *8*, 175–184.

Foster, J.B., Leiguarda, R., & Tilley, P.J.B. (1976). Brain damage in National Hunt jockeys. *Lancet*, *1*, 981–983.

Frankowski, R.F. (1986). Descriptive epidemiologic studies of head injury in the United States: 1974–1984. In L.G. Peterson & G.J. O'Shanick (Eds.), *Advances in psychosomatic medicine, Vol. 16*: *Psychiatric aspects of trauma* (pp. 153–172). Basel, Switzerland: Karger.

Frazee, J.G. (1986). Head trauma. *Emergency Medicine Clinics of North America*, *4*, 859–874.

Freeman, M.D., & Croft, A.C. (1996). Late whiplash syndrome. *Lancet*, *348*, 125.

Freeman, M.R., Mittenberg, W., Dicowden, M., & Bat-Ami, M. (1992). Executive and compensatory memory retraining in traumatic brain injury. *Brain Injury*, *6*, 65–70.

Friedman, A.P., Brenner, C., & Denny-Brown, D. (1945). Post-traumatic vertigo and dizziness. *Journal of Neurosurgery*, *2*, 36–46.

Gaidolfi, E., & Vignolo, L.A. (1980). Closed head injuries of school-age children: Neuropsychological sequelae in early adulthood. *Italian Journal of Neurological Sciences*, *2*, 65–73.

Galbraith, S., Murray, W.R., Patel, A.R., & Knill-Jones, R. (1976). The relationship between alcohol and head injury and its effect on the conscious level. *British Journal of Surgery*, *63*, 128–130.

Gandy, S.E., Snow, R.B., Zimmerman, R.D., & Deck, M.D.F. (1984). Cranial nuclear magnetic resonance imaging in head trauma. *Annals of Neurology*, *16*, 254–257.

Gans, J.S. (1983). Hate in the rehabilitation setting. *Archives of Physical Medicine and Rehabilitation*, *64*, 176–179.

Gass, C.S., & Apple, C. (1997). Cognitive complaints in closed-head injury: Relationship to memory test performance and emotional disturbance. *Journal of Clinical and Experimental Neuropsychology*, *19*, 290–299.

Gennarelli, T.A. (1983). Head injury in man and experimental animals: Clinical aspects. *Acta Neurochirurgica*, (Suppl. 32), 1–13.

Gennarelli, T.A. (1996). The spectrum of traumatic axonal injury. *Neuropathology and Applied Neurobiology*, *22*, 509-513.

Gennarelli, T.A., Champion, H.R., Copes, W.S., & Sacco, W.J. (1994). Comparison of mortality, morbidity, and severity of 59,713 head injured patients with 114,447 patients with extracranial injuries. *Journal of Trauma*, *37*, 962–968.

Gennarelli, T.A., Champion, H.R., Sacco, W.J., Copes, W.S., & Alves, W.M. (1989). Mortality of patients with head injury and extracranial injury treated in trauma centers. *Journal of Trauma*, *29*, 1193–1202.

Gennarelli, T.A., Spielman, G.M., Langfitt, T.W., Gildenberg, P.L., Harrington, T., Jane, J.A., Marshall, L.F., Miller, J.D., & Pitts, L.H. (1982). Influence of the type of intracranial lesion on outcome from severe head injury: A multicenter study using a new classification system. *Journal of Neurosurgery*, *56*, 26–32.

Gennarelli, T.A., Thibault, L.E., Adams, J.H., Graham, D.I., Thompson, C.J., & Marcincin, R.P. (1982). Difffuse axonal injury and traumatic coma in the primate. *Annals of Neurology*, *12*, 564–574.

Gentilini, M., Nichelli, P., & Schoenhuber, R. (1989). Assessment of attention in mild head injury. In H.S. Levin, H.M. Eisenberg, & A.L. Benton (Eds.), *Mild head injury* (pp. 163–175). New York: Oxford University Press.

Gentilini, M., Nichelli, P., Schoenhuber, R., Bortolotti, P., Tonelli, L., Falasca, A., & Merli, G.A. (1985). Neuropsychological evaluation of mild head injury. *Journal of Neurology, Neurosurgery, and Psychiatry*, *48*, 137–140.

Gentleman, S.M., Roberts, G.W., Gennarelli, T.A., Maxwell, W.L., Adams, J.H., Kerr, S., & Graham, D.I. (1995). Axonal injury: A universal consequence of fatal closed head injury? *Acta Neuropathologica*, *89*, 537–543.

Geschwind, N. (1971). Aphasia. *New England Journal of Medicine*, *284*, 654–656.

Gianutsos, R., & Grynbaum, B.B. (1983). Helping brain-injured people to contend with hidden cognitive deficits. *International Rehabilitation Medicine*, *5*, 37–40.

Gilchrist, E., & Wilkinson, M. (1979). Some factors determining prognosis in young people with severe head injuries. *Archives of Neurology*, *36*, 355–359.

Glasgow, R.E., Zeiss, R.A., Barrera, M., Jr., & Lewinsohn, P.M. (1977). Case studies on remediating memory deficits in brain-damaged individuals. *Journal of Clinical Psychology*, *33*, 1049–1054.

Goldberg, D. (1978). *Manual of the General Health Questionnaire*. Windsor, UK: NFER Publishing.

Goldberg, E., Antin, S.P., Bilder, R.M.,Jr., Gerstman, L.J., Hughes, J.E.O., & Mattis, S. (1981). Retrograde amnesia: Possible role of mesencephalic reticular activation in long-term memory. *Science*, *213*, 1392–1394.

Goldstein, K. (1936). The problem of the meaning of words based upon observation of aphasic patients. *Journal of Psychology*, *2*, 301–316.

Goldstein, K. (1942). *Aftereffects of brain injuries in war: Their evaluation and treatment. The application of psychologic methods in the clinic*. London: Heinemann.

Goldstein, K. (1943). Brain concussion: Evaluation of the after effects by special tests. *Diseases of the Nervous System*, *4*, 325–334.

Goldstein, K. (1952). The effect of brain damage on the personality. *Psychiatry*, *15*, 245–260.

Goldstein, L. (1993). Behaviour problems. In R. Greenwood, M. P. Barnes, T. M. McMillan, & C. D. Ward (Eds.), *Neurological rehabilitation* (pp. 389–401). Edinburgh, UK: Churchill Livingstone.

Goodglass, H., & Kaplan, E. (1972). *The assessment of aphasia and related disorders*. New York: Lea & Febiger.

Gordon, W.A., Brown, M., Sliwinski, M., Hibbard, M.R., Patti, N., Weiss, M.J., Kalinsky, R., & Sheerer, M. (1998). The enigma of "hidden" traumatic brain injury. *Journal of Head Trauma Rehabilitation*, *13*(6), 39–56.

Gosch, H.H., Gooding, E., & Schneider, R.C. (1970). The lexan calvarium for the study of cerebral responses to acute trauma. *Journal of Trauma, 10*, 370–376.

Graf, P., & Schacter, D.L. (1985). Implicit and explicit memory for new associations in normal and amnesic subjects. *Journal of Experimental Psychology: Learning, Memory, and Cognition, 2*, 501–518.

Graf, P., Squire, L.R., & Mandler, G. (1984). The information that amnesic patients do not forget. *Journal of Experimental Psychology: Learning, Memory, and Cognition, 10*, 164–178.

Graham, D.I. (1985). The pathology of brain ischaemia and possibilities for therapeutic intervention. *British Journal of Anaesthesia, 57*, 3–17.

Graham, D.I., Adams, J.H., & Doyle, D. (1978). Ischaemic brain damage in fatal non–missile head injuries. *Journal of the Neurological Sciences, 39*, 213–234.

Graham, D.I., Adams, J.H., & Gennarelli, T.A. (1988). Mechanisms of non-penetrating head injury. In R. F. Bond (Ed.), *Progress in clinical and biological research, Vol. 264: . Perspectives in shock research.* (pp. 159–168). New York: Liss.

Graham, D.I., Clark, J.C., Adams, J.H., & Gennarelli, T.A. (1992). Diffuse axonal injury caused by assault. *Journal of Clinical Pathology, 45*, 840–841.

Graham, D.I., Ford, I., Adams, J.H., Doyle, D., Lawrence, A.E., McLellan, D.R., & Ng, H. K. (1989). Fatal head injury in children. *Journal of Clinical Pathology, 42*, 18–22.

Graham, D.I., Ford, I., Adams, J.H., Doyle, D., Teasdale, G.M., Lawrence, A.E., & McLellan, D.R. (1989). Ischaemic brain damage is still common in fatal non-missile head injury. *Journal of Neurology, Neurosurgery, and Psychiatry, 52*, 346–350.

Graham, D.I., Lawrence, A.E., Adams, J.H., Doyle, D., & McLellan, D.R. (1987). Brain damage in non-missile head injury secondary to high intracranial pressure. *Neuropathology and Applied Neurobiology, 13*, 209–217.

Graham, D.I., Lawrence, A.E., Adams, J.H., Doyle, D., & McLellan, D.R. (1988). Brain damage in fatal non-missile head injury without high intracranial pressure. *Journal of Clinical Pathology, 41*, 34–37.

Graham, D.I., McLellan, D., Adams, J.H., Doyle, D., Kerr, A., & Murray, L.S. (1983). The neuropathology of the vegetative state and severe disability after non-missile head injury. *Acta Neurochirurgica*, (Suppl. 32), 65–67.

Grattan, E., & Hobbs, J.A. (1978). *Injuries to occupants of heavy goods vehicles* (TRRL Laboratory Report 854). Crowthorne, UK: Transport and Road Research Laboratory.

Grattan, E., & Hobbs, J.A. (1980). *Permanent disability in road traffic accident casualties* (TRRL Laboratory Report 924). Crowthorne, UK: Transport and Road Research Laboratory.

Grattan, E., Hobbs, J.A., & Keigan, M.E. (1976, September). *Anatomical sites and severities of injury in unprotected road users.* Paper presented to the 3rd international conference of the International Research Committee on the Biokinetics of Impacts, Amsterdam.

Graves, E.J. (1991a). *Detailed diagnoses and procedures, National Hospital Discharge Survey, 1988.* (Vital and Health Statistics, Series 13, No. 107). Washington, DC: US Government Printing Office.

Graves, E.J. (1991b). *Detailed diagnoses and procedures, National Hospital Discharge Survey, 1989.* (Vital and Health Statistics, Series 13, No. 108). Washington, DC: US Government Printing Office.

Graves, E.J. (1992). *Detailed diagnoses and procedures, National Hospital Discharge Survey, 1990.* (Vital and Health Statistics, Series 13, No. 113). Washington, DC: US Government Printing Office.

Graves, E.J. (1994a). *Detailed diagnoses and procedures, National Hospital Discharge Survey, 1991.* (Vital and Health Statistics, Series 13, No. 115). Washington, DC: US Government Printing Office.

Graves, E.J. (1994b). *Detailed diagnoses and procedures, National Hospital Discharge Survey, 1992.* (Vital and Health Statistics, Series 13, No. 118). Washington, DC: US Government Printing Office.

Graves, E.J. (1995). *Detailed diagnoses and procedures, National Hospital Discharge Survey, 1993.* (Vital and Health Statistics, Series 13, No. 122). Washington, DC: US Government Printing Office.

Graves, E.J., & Gillum, B.S. (1997). *Detailed diagnoses and procedures, National Hospital Discharge Survey, 1995* (Vital and health statistics, Series 13, No. 130: DHHS Publication No. PHS 98–1791). Washington, DC: US Government Printing Office.

Graves, E.J., & Gillum, B.S. (1997a). *Detailed diagnoses and procedures, National Hospital Discharge Survey, 1994* (Vital and Health Statistics, Series 13, No. 127). Washington, DC: US Government Printing Office.

Greenwood, R. (1997). Value of recording duration of post–traumatic amnesia. *Lancet, 349,* 1041–1042.

Greiffenstein, M.F., Baker, W.J., & Gola, T. (1996). Motor dysfunction profiles in traumatic brain injury and postconcussion syndrome. *Journal of the International Neuropsychological Society, 2,* 477–485.

Groher, M. (1977). Language and memory disorders following closed head trauma. *Journal of Speech and Hearing Research, 20,* 212–223.

Gronwall, D., & Wrightson, P. (1974). Delayed recovery of intellectual function after minor head injury. *Lancet, 2,* 605–609.

Gronwall, D., & Wrightson, P (1975). Cumulative effect of concussion. *Lancet, 2,* 995–997.

Gronwall, D., & Wrightson, P. (1980). Duration of post-traumatic amnesia after mild head injury. *Journal of Clinical Neuropsychology, 2,* 51–60.

Gronwall, D., & Wrightson, P. (1981). Memory and information processing capacity after closed head injury. *Journal of Neurology, Neurosurgery, and Psychiatry, 44,* 889–895.

Gronwall, D., Wrightson, P., & McGinn, V. (1997). Effect of mild head injury during the preschool years. *Journal of the International Neuropsychological Society, 3,* 592–597.

Gronwall, D.M.A. (1976). Performance changes during recovery from closed head injury. *Proceedings of the Australian Association of Neurologists, 13,* 143–147.

Gronwall, D.M.A. (1977). Paced auditory serial-addition task: A measure of recovery from concussion. *Perceptual and Motor Skills, 44,* 367–373.

Gronwall, D.M.A., & Sampson, H. (1974). *The psychological effects of concussion.* Auckland, New Zealand: Auckland University Press/Oxford University Press.

Group of Neurosurgeons. (1984). Guidelines for initial management after head injury in adults. *British Medical Journal, 288,* 983–985.

Gruneberg, R. (1970). The concept of accident neurosis. *Injury, 1,* 209–212.

Gurdjian, E.S., & Gurdjian, E.S. (1975). Re-evaluation of the biomechanics of blunt impact injury of the head. *Surgery, Gynecology, and Obstetrics, 140,* 845–850.

Gurdjian, E.S., & Gurdjian, E.S. (1978). Acute head injuries. *Surgery, Gynecology, and Obstetrics, 146,* 805–820.

Guthkelch, A.N. (1980). Posttraumatic amnesia, post-concussional symptoms and accident neurosis. *European Neurology, 19,* 91–102.

Haas, J.F., Cope, D.N., & Hall, K. (1987). Premorbid prevalence of poor academic performance in severe head injury. *Journal of Neurology, Neurosurgery, and Psychiatry, 50,* 52–56.

Hagen, C. (1984). Language disorders in head trauma. In A.L. Holland (Ed.), *Language disorders in adults: Recent advances* (pp. 245–281). San Diego, CA: College-Hill Press.

Haines, D.E. (1991). On the question of a subdural space. *Anatomical Record, 230,* 3–21.

Hall, K.M., Cope, D.N., & Wilmot, C.B. (1987). Occult head injury in spinal cord injury: Relationship to premorbid history and learning self-care. In M.E. Miner & K.A. Wagner (Eds.), *Neurotrauma: Treatment, rehabilitation, and related issues, No. 2* (pp. 113–125). Boston: Butterworths.

Halpern, H., Darley, F.L., & Brown, J.R. (1973). Differential language and neurologic characteristics in cerebral involvement. *Journal of Speech and Hearing Disorders, 38*, 162–173.

Halstead, W.C. (1947). *Brain and intelligence: A quantitative study of the frontal lobes.* Chicago: University of Chicago Press.

Haltiner, A.M., Temkin, N.R., Winn, H.R., & Dikmen, S.S. (1996). The impact of posttraumatic seizures on 1-year neuropsychological and psychosocial outcome of head injury. *Journal of the International Neuropsychological Society, 2*, 494–504.

Hamilton, J.M., Finlayson, M.A.J., & Alfano, D.P. (1995). Dimensions of neurobehavioural dysfunction: Cross-validation using a head-injured sample. *Brain Injury, 9*, 479–485.

Han, J.S., Kaufman, B., Alfridi, R.J., Yeung, H.N., Benson, J.E., Haaga, J.R., El Yousef, S.J., Clampitt, M.E., Bonstelle, C.T., & Huss, R. (1984). Head trauma evaluated by magnetic resonance and computed tomography: A comparison. *Radiology, 150*, 71–77.

Hannay, H.J., & James, C.M. (1981). Simulation of a memory deficit on the Continuous Recognition Memory Test. *Perceptual and Motor Skills, 53*, 51–58.

Hannay, H.J., & Levin, H.S. (1985). Selective reminding test: An examination of the equivalence of four forms. *Journal of Clinical and Experimental Neuropsychology, 7*, 251–263.

Hannay, H.J., & Levin, H.S. (1988). Visual continuous recognition memory in normal and closed-head-injured adolescents. *Journal of Clinical and Experimental Neuropsychology, 11*, 444–460.

Hannay, H.J., Levin, H.S., & Grossman, R.G. (1979). Impaired recognition memory after head injury. *Cortex, 15*, 269–283.

Hannay, H.J., Levin, H.S., & Kay, M. (1982). Tachistoscopic visual perception after closed head injury. *Journal of Clinical Neuropsychology, 4*, 117–129.

Hardman, J.M. (1979). The pathology of traumatic brain injuries. *Advances in Neurology, 22*, 15–50.

Harris, J.E. (1978). External memory aids. In M. Gruneberg, P.E. Morris, & R.N. Sykes (Eds.), *Practical aspects of memory* (pp. 172–179). London: Academic Press.

Harris, J. (1984). Methods of improving memory. In B.A. Wilson & N. Moffat (Eds.), *Clinical management of memory problems* (pp. 46–62). London: Croom Helm.

Harris, J.E., & Sunderland, A. (1981). A brief survey of the management of memory disorders in rehabilitation units in Britain. *International Rehabilitation Medicine, 3*, 206–209.

Hartley, L.L. (1995). *Cognitive-communicative abilities following brain injury: A functional approach.* San Diego, CA: Singular Publishing Group.

Hartley, L.L., & Jensen, P.J. (1991). Narrative and procedural discourse after closed head injury. *Brain Injury, 5*, 267–285.

Hausen, H.S., Lachmann, E.A., & Nagler, W. (1997). Cerebral diaschisis following cerebellar hemorrhage. *Archives of Physical Medicine and Rehabilitation, 78*, 546–549.

Hawthorne, V.M. (1978). Epidemiology of head injuries. *Scottish Medical Journal, 23*, 92.

Hayden, M.E., & Hart, T. (1986). Rehabilitation of cognitive and behavioral dysfunction in head injury. In L.G. Peterson & G.J. O'Shanick (Eds.), *Advances in psychosomatic medicine: Psychiatric aspects of trauma.Vol. 16*, (pp. 194–229). Basel, Switzerland: Karger.

Hécaen, H. (1976). Acquired aphasia in children and the ontogenesis of hemispheric functional specialization. *Brain and Language, 3*, 114–134.

Heiden, J.S., Small, R., Caton, W., Weiss, M., & Kurze, T. (1983). Severe head injury: Clinical assessment and outcome. *Physical Therapy, 63*, 1946–1951.

Heilman, K.M., Safran, A., & Geschwind, N. (1971). Closed head trauma and aphasia. *Journal of Neurology, Neurosurgery, and Psychiatry, 34*, 265–269.

Heiskanen, O., & Kaste, M. (1974). Late prognosis of severe brain injury in children. *Developmental Medicine and Child Neurology, 16*, 11–14.

Heiskanen, O., & Sipponen, P. (1970). Prognosis of severe brain injury. *Acta Neurologica Scandinavica, 46*, 343–348.

Heiss, W.D., Ilsen, H.W., Wagner, R., Pawlik, G., Wienhard, K., & Eriksson, L. (1983). Decreased glucose metabolism in functionally inactivated brain regions in ischemic stroke and its alteration by activating drugs. In J.S. Meyer, H. Lechner, M. Reivich, & E.O. Ott (Eds.), *Proceedings of the World Federation of Neurology 11th International Salzburg Conference: Cerebral vascular disease.* (pp. 162–167). Amsterdam: Excerpta Medica.

Hendrick, E.B., Harwood-Hash, D.C.F., & Hudson, A.R. (1964). Head injuries in children: A survey of 4465 consecutive cases at the Hospital for Sick Children, Toronto, Canada. *Clinical Neurosurgery, 11*, 46–65.

Hendryx, P.M. (1989). Psychosocial changes perceived by closed-head-injured adults and their families. *Archives of Physical Medicine and Rehabilitation, 70*, 526–530.

Herrmann, D., Yoder, C.Y., Wells, J., & Raybeck, D. (1996). Portable electronic scheduling/reminding devices. *Cognitive Technology, 1*, 36–44.

Hick, W.E. (1952). On the rate of gain of information. *Quarterly Journal of Experimental Psychology, 4*, 11–26.

Higashi, K., Sakata, Y., Hatano, M., Abiko, S., Ihara, K., Katayama, S., Wakuta, Y., Okamura, T., Ueda, H., Zenke, M., & Aoki, H. (1977). Epidemiological studies on patients with a persistent vegetative state. *Journal of Neurology, Neurosurgery, and Psychiatry, 40*, 876–885.

Hill, J.F. (1979). Blunt injury with particular reference to recent terrorist bombing incidents. *Annals of the Royal College of Surgeons of England, 61*, 4–11.

Hillbom, E. (1960). After-effects of brain-injuries: Research on the symptoms causing invalidism of persons in Finland having sustained brain-injuries during the wars of 1939–1940 and 1941–1944. *Acta Psychiatrica et Neurologica Scandinavica, 35*(Suppl. 142).

Hinton-Bayre, A.D., Geffen, G., & McFarland, K. (1997). Mild head injury and speed of information processing: A prospective study of professional rugby league players. *Journal of Clinical and Experimental Neuropsychology, 19*, 275–289.

Hirsch, A.E., & Ommaya, A.K. (1972). Head injury caused by underwater explosion of a firecracker: Case report. *Journal of Neurosurgery, 37*, 95–99.

Hjern, B., & Nylander, I. (1964). Acute head injuries in children: Traumatology, therapy and prognosis. *Acta Pediatrica,* (Suppl. 152).

Hobbs, C.A. (1981). *Car occupant injury patterns and mechanisms* (TRRL Scientific Report No. 648). Crowthorne, UK: Transport and Road Research Laboratory.

Hodges, W.F., & Spielberger, C.D. (1969). Digit-span: An indicant of trait or state anxiety? *Journal of Consulting and Clinical Psychology, 33*, 430–434.

Holbourn, A.H.S. (1943). Mechanics of head injuries. *Lancet, 2*, 438–441.

Holbourn, A.H.S. (1945). The mechanics of brain injuries. *British Medical Bulletin, 3*, 147–149.

Holland, A.L. (1982). When is aphasia aphasia? The problem of closed head injury. In R.H. Brookshire (Ed.), *Clinical aphasiology: Proceedings of the conference 1982* (pp. 345–349). Minneapolis, MN: BRK Publishers.

Hooper, R.S., McGregor, J.M., & Nathan, P.W. (1945). Explosive rage following head injury. *Journal of Mental Science, 91*, 458–471.

Horowitz, I., Costeff, H., Sadan, N., Abraham, E., Geyer, S., & Najenson, T. (1983). Childhood head injuries in Israel: Epidemiology and outcome. *International Rehabilitation Medicine, 5*, 32–36.

Hpay, H. (1971). Psycho-social effects of severe head injury. In *Head injuries: Proceedings of an international symposium* (pp. 110–119). Edinburgh, UK: Churchill Livingstone.

Hughes, M., & Cohen, W.A. (1993). Radiographic evaluation. In P.R. Cooper (Ed.), *Head injury* (3rd ed., pp. 65–89). Baltimore: Williams & Wilkins.

Humphrey, M., & Oddy, M. (1978). The social costs of head injuries. *New Society*, *45*, 452–454.

Humphrey, M., & Oddy, M. (1980). Return to work after head injury: A review of post-war studies. *Injury*, *12*, 107–114.

Hunkin, N.M., Parkin, A.J., Bradley, V.A., Burrows, E.H., Aldrich, F.K., Jansari, A., & Burdon-Cooper, C. (1995). Focal retrograde amnesia following closed head injury: A case study and theoretical account. *Neuropsychologia*, *33*, 509–523.

Infeld, B., Davis, S.M., Lichtenstein, M., Mitchell, P.J., & Hopper, J.L. (1995). Crossed cerebellar diaschisis and brain recovery after stroke. *Stroke*, *26*, 90–95.

Iverson, G.L., & Franzen, M.D. (1994). The Recognition Memory Test, Digit Span, and Knox Cube Test as markers of malingered memory impairment. *Assessment*, *1*, 323–334.

Jacobson, S.A. (1969). Mechanisms of the sequelae of minor craniocervical trauma. In A.E. Walker, W.F. Caveness, & M. Critchley (Eds.), *The late effects of head injury* (pp. 35–45). Springfield, IL: Thomas.

Jagger, J., Levine, J., Jane, J., & Rimel, R. (1984). Epidemiologic features of head injury in a predominantly rural population. *Journal of Trauma*, *24*, 40–44.

Jaggi, J. L., Obrist, W.D., Gennarelli, T.A., & Langfitt, T.W. (1990). Relationship of early cerebral blood flow and metabolism to outcome in acute head injury. *Journal of Neurosurgery*, *72*, 176–182.

Jamieson, K.G. (1971). *A first notebook of head injury* (2nd ed.). London: Butterworths.

Jamieson, K.G., & Yelland, J.D.N. (1968). Extradural hematoma: Report of 167 cases. *Journal of Neurosurgery*, *29*, 13–23.

Jamieson, K.G., & Yelland, J.D.N. (1972). Traumatic intracerebral hematoma: Report of 63 surgically treated cases. *Journal of Neurosurgery*, *37*, 528–532.

Jane, J.A., Rimel, R.W., Pobereskin, L.H., Tyson, G.W., Steward, O., & Gennarelli, T.A. (1982). Outcome and pathology of head injury. In R.G. Grossman & P.L. Gildenberg (Eds.), *Head injury: Basic and clinical aspects* (pp. 229–237). New York: Raven Press.

Jane, J.A., Steward, O., & Gennarelli, T. (1985). Axonal degeneration induced by experimental noninvasive minor head injury. *Journal of Neurosurgery*, *62*, 96–100.

Jenkins, A., Teasdale, G., Hadley, M.D.M., Macpherson, P., & Rowan J.O. (1986). Brain lesions detected by magnetic resonance imaging in mild and severe head injuries. *Lancet*, *2*, 445–446.

Jennett, B. (1969). Early traumatic epilepsy: Definition and identity. *Lancet*, *1*, 1023–1025.

Jennett, B. (1972). Head injuries in children. *Developmental Medicine and Child Neurology*, *14*, 137–147.

Jennett, B. (1973). Epilepsy after non-missile head injuries. *Scottish Medical Journal*, *18*, 8–13.

Jennett, B. (1974). Early traumatic epilepsy: Incidence and significance after nonmissile injuries. *Archives of Neurology*, *30*, 394–398.

Jennett, B. (1975a). Epilepsy and acute traumatic intracranial haematoma. *Journal of Neurology, Neurosurgery, and Psychiatry*, *38*, 378–381.

Jennett, B. (1975b). Who cares for head injuries? *British Medical Journal*, *3*, 267–270.

Jennett, B. (1976a). Assessment of the severity of head injury. *Journal of Neurology, Neurosurgery, and Psychiatry*, *39*, 647–655.

Jennett, B. (1976b). Predicting outcome after head injury. *Proceedings of the Royal Society of Medicine*, *69*, 140–141.

Jennett, B. (1976c). Prognosis of severe head injury. In R.L. McLaurin (Ed.), *Head injuries: Proceedings of the second Chicago symposium on neural trauma* (pp. 45–47). New York: Grune & Stratton.

Jennett, B. (1976d). Resource allocation for the severely brain damaged. *Archives of Neurology, 33*, 595–597.

Jennett, B. (1979). Defining brain damage after head injury. *Journal of the Royal College of Physicians of London, 13*, 197–200.

Jennett, B. (1984). The measurement of outcome. In N. Brooks (Ed.), *Closed head injury: Psychological, social, and family consequences* (pp. 37–43). Oxford, UK: Oxford University Press.

Jennett, B. (1989). Some international comparisons. In H.S. Levin, H.M. Eisenberg, & A. L. Benton (Eds.), *Mild head injury* (pp. 23–34). New York: Oxford University Press.

Jennett, B. (1996). Epidemiology of head injury. *Journal of Neurology, Neurosurgery, and Psychiatry, 60*, 362–369.

Jennett, B., & Bond, M. (1975). Assessment of outcome after severe brain damage. *Lancet, 1*, 480–484.

Jennett, B., & Carlin, J. (1978). Preventable mortality and morbidity after head injury. *Injury, 10*, 31–39.

Jennett, B., & Galbraith, S. (1983). *An introduction to neurosurgery* (4th ed.). London: Heinemann.

Jennett, W.B., & Lewin, W. (1960). Traumatic epilepsy after closed head injuries. *Journal of Neurology, Neurosurgery, and Psychiatry, 23*, 295–301.

Jennett, B., & MacMillan, R. (1981). Epidemiology of head injury. *British Medical Journal, 282*, 101–104.

Jennett, B., Miller, J.D., & Braakman, R. (1974). Epilepsy after nonmissile depressed skull fracture. *Journal of Neurosurgery, 41*, 208–216.

Jennett, B., Murray, A., Carlin, J., McKean, M., MacMillan, R., & Strang, I. (1979). Head injuries in three Scottish neurosurgical units: Scottish Head Injury Management Study. *British Medical Journal, 2*, 955–958.

Jennett, B., Murray, A., MacMillan, R., Macfarlane, J., Bentley, C., Strang, I., & Hawthorne, V. (1977). Head injuries in Scottish hospitals: Scottish Head Injury Management Study. *Lancet, 2*, 696–698.

Jennett, B., & Plum, F. (1972). Persistent vegetative state after brain damage: A syndrome in search of a name. *Lancet, 1*, 734–737.

Jennett, B., Snoek, J., Bond, M.R., & Brooks, N. (1981). Disability after severe head injury: Observations on the use of the Glasgow Outcome Scale. *Journal of Neurology, Neurosurgery, and Psychiatry, 44*, 285–293.

Jennett, B., & Teasdale, G. (1977). Aspects of coma after severe head injury. *Lancet, 1*, 878–881.

Jennett, B., & Teasdale, G. (1981). *Management of head injuries*. Philadelphia: Davis.

Jennett, B., Teasdale, G., Braakman, R., Minderhoud, J., Heiden, J., & Kurze, T. (1979). Prognosis of patients with severe head injury. *Neurosurgery, 4*, 283–289.

Jennett, B., Teasdale, G., Braakman, R., Minderhoud, J., & Knill-Jones, R. (1976). Predicting outcome in individual patients after severe head injury. *Lancet, 1*, 1031–1034.

Jennett, B., Teasdale, G., Galbraith, S., Pickard, J., Grant, H., Braakman, R., Avezaat, C., Maas, A., Minderhoud, J., Vecht, C.J., Heiden, J., Small, R., Caton, W., & Kurze, T. (1977). Severe head injuries in three countries. *Journal of Neurology, Neurosurgery, and Psychiatry, 40*, 291–298.

Jennett, B., Teasdale, G., & Knill-Jones, R. (1975b). Prognosis after severe head injury. In *Outcome of severe damage to the central nervous system* (Ciba Foundation Symposium No. 34, new series, pp. 309–324). Amsterdam: Elsevier/Excerpta Medica/North-Holland.

Jennett, B., Teasdale, G.M., & Knill-Jones, R.P. (1975a). Predicting outcome after head injury. *Journal of the Royal College of Physicians of London, 9*, 231–237.

Jennett, B., Teather, D., & Bennie, S. (1973). Epilepsy after head injury: Residual risk after varying fit-free intervals since injury. *Lancet, 2,* 652–653.

Johnson, R. (1998). How do people get back to work after severe head injury? A 10 year follow-up study. *Neuropsychological Rehabilitation*, *8*, 61–79.

Johnson, R., & Balleny, H. (1996). Behaviour problems after brain injury: Incidence and need for treatment. *Clinical Rehabilitation*, *10*, 173–181.

Johnston, R.B., & Mellits, E.D. (1980). Pediatric coma: Prognosis and outcome. *Developmental Medicine and Child Neurology*, *22*, 3–12.

Jones-Gotman, M., & Milner, B. (1977). Design fluency: The invention of nonsense drawings after focal cortical lesions. *Neuropsychologia*, *15*, 653–674.

Jordan, F.M., Ozanne, A.E., & Murdoch, B.E. (1988). Long-term speech and language disorders subsequent to closed head injury in children. *Brain Injury*, *2*, 179–185.

Jordan, F.M., Ozanne, A.E., & Murdoch, B.E. (1990). Performance of closed head-injured children on a naming task. *Brain Injury*, *4*, 27–32.

Jordan, S.E., Green, G.A., Galanty, H.L., Mandelbaum, B.R., & Jabour, B.A. (1996). Acute and chronic brain injury in United States National Team soccer players. *American Journal of Sports Medicine*, *24*, 205–210.

Jorge, R.E., Robinson, R.G., Arndt, S.V., Forrester, A.W., Geisler, F., & Starkstein, S.E. (1993). Comparison between acute- and delayed-onset depression following traumatic brain injury. *Journal of Neuropsychiatry and Clinical Neurosciences*, *5*, 43–49.

Jorge, R.E., Robinson, R.G., Arndt, S.V., Starkstein, S.E., Forrester, A.W., & Geisler, F. (1993). Depression following traumatic brain injury: A 1 year longitudinal study. *Journal of Affective Disorders*, *27*, 233–243.

Junqué, C., Bruna, O., & Mataró, M. (1997). Information needs of the traumatic brain injury patient's family members regarding the consequences of the injury and associated perception of physical, cognitive, emotional and quality of life changes. *Brain Injury*, *11*, 251–258.

Kalisky, Z., Goldman, A.M., Morrison, D.P., & Von Laufen, A. (1987). Comparison of results with CT scanning and magnetic resonance imaging of brain-injured patients undergoing rehabilitation. In M.E. Miner & K.A. Wagner (Eds.), *Neurotrauma: Treatment, rehabilitation, and related issues, No. 2* (pp. 89–97). Boston: Butterworths.

Kalsbeek, W.D., McLaurin, R.L., Harris, B.S.H., III, & Miller, J.D. (1980). The National Head and Spinal Cord Injury Survey: Major findings. *Journal of Neurosurgery*, *53*, S19–S31.

Kampfl, A., Schmutzhard, E., Franz, G., Pfausler, B., Haring, H.-P., Ulmer, H., Felber, S., Golaszewski, S., & Aichner, F. (1998). Prediction of recovery from post-traumatic vegetative state with cerebral magnetic-resonance imaging. *Lancet*, *351*, 1763–1767.

Kant, R., Smith-Seemiller, L., Isaac, G., & Duffy, J. (1997). Tc-HMPAO SPECT in persistent post-concussion syndrome after mild head injury: Comparison with MRI/CT. *Brain Injury*, *11*, 115–124.

Kapur, N. (1988). *Memory disorders in clinical practice*. London: Butterworths.

Kapur, N. (1995). Memory aids in the rehabilitation of memory disordered patients. In A.D. Baddeley, B.A. Wilson, & F.N. Watts (Eds.), *Handbook of memory disorders* (pp. 533–556). Chichester, UK: Wiley.

Kapur, N. (1997). Autobiographical amnesia and temporal lobe pathology. In A. J. Parkin (Ed.), *Case studies in the neuropsychology of memory* (pp. 37–62). Hove, UK: Psychology Press.

Kapur, N., & Pearson, D. (1983). Memory symptoms and memory performance of neurological patients. *British Journal of Psychology*, *74*, 409–415.

Kay, D.W.K., Kerr, T.A., & Lassman, L.P. (1971). Brain trauma and the postconcussional syndrome. *Lancet*, *2*, 1052–1055.

Kear-Colwell, J.J., & Heller, M. (1980). The Wechsler Memory Scale and closed head injury. *Journal of Clinical Psychology*, *36*, 782–787.

Kelly, R. (1975). The post-traumatic syndrome: An iatrogenic disease. *Forensic Science*, *6*, 17–24.

Kennard, M.A. (1938). Reorganization of motor function in the cerebral cortex of monkeys deprived of motor and premotor areas in infancy. *Journal of Neurophysiology*, *1*, 477–496.

Kerner, M.J., & Acker, M. (1985). Computer delivery of memory retraining with head injured patients. *Cognitive Rehabilitation*, *3*(6), 26–31.

Kerr, C. (1995). Dysnomia following traumatic brain injury: An information-processing approach to assessment. *Brain Injury*, *9*, 777–796.

Kerr, T. A., Kay, D. W. K., & Lassman, L. P. (1971). Characteristics of patients, type of accident, and mortality in a consecutive series of head injuries admitted to a neurosurgical unit. *British Journal of Preventive and Social Medicine, 25,* 179–185.

King, N.S., Crawford, S., Wenden, F.J., Moss, N.E.G., Wade, D.T., & Caldwell, F.E. (1997). Measurement of post-traumatic amnesia: How reliable is it? *Journal of Neurology, Neurosurgery, and Psychiatry*, *62*, 38–42.

Kinsella, G.J., Prior, M., Sawyer, M., Ong, B., Murtagh, D., Eisenmajer, R., Bryan, D., Anderson, V., & Klug, G. (1997). Predictors and indicators of academic outcome in children 2 years following traumatic brain injury. *Journal of the International Neuropsychological Society*, *3*, 608–616.

Klauber, M., Barrett-Connor, E., Marshall, L., & Bowers, S. (1978). The epidemiology of head injury: A prospective study of an entire community—San Diego County, California. *American Journal of Epidemiology*, *113*, 500–509.

Kline, N.A. (1979). Reversal of post-traumatic amnesia with lithium. *Psychosomatics*, *20*, 363–364.

Klonoff, H. (1971). Head injuries in children: Predisposing factors, accident conditions, accident proneness, and sequelae. *American Journal of Public Health*, *61*, 2405–2417.

Klonoff, H., Low, M.D., & Clark, C. (1977). Head injuries in children: A prospective five year follow-up. *Journal of Neurology, Neurosurgery, and Psychiatry*, *40*, 1211–1219.

Klonoff, H., & Paris, R. (1974). Immediate, short-term and residual effects of acute head injuries in children: Neuropsychological and neurological correlates. In R. Reitan & L.A. Davison (Eds.), *Clinical neuropsychology: Current status and applications* (pp. 179–210). Washington, DC: Winston.

Klonoff, H., & Thompson, G.B. (1969). Epidemiology of head injuries in adults: A pilot study. *Canadian Medical Association Journal*, *100*, 235–241.

Kløve, H., & Cleeland, C.S. (1972). The relationship of neuropsychological impairment to other indices of severity of head injury. *Scandinavian Journal of Rehabilitation Medicine*, *4*, 55–60.

Kollevold, T. (1976). Immediate and early cerebral seizures after head injuries: Pt. I. *Journal of the Oslo City Hospitals*, *26*, 99–114.

Kollevold, T. (1978). Immediate and early cerebral seizures after head injuries: Pt. III. *Journal of the Oslo City Hospitals*, *28*, 77–86.

Kollevold, T. (1979). Immediate and early cerebral seizures after head injuries: Pt. IV. *Journal of the Oslo City Hospitals*, *29*, 35–47.

Kopaniky, D.R., & Wagner, K.A. (1987). Incidence of combined head and spinal cord injury and potential for errors in diagnosis. In M.E. Miner & K.A. Wagner (Eds.), *Neurotrauma: Treatment, rehabilitation, and related issues, No. 2* (pp. 103–112). Boston: Butterworths.

Kotapka, M.J., Gennarelli, T.A., Graham, D.I., Adams, J.H., Thibault, L.E., Ross, D.T., & Ford, I. (1991). Selective vulnerability of hippocampal neurons in acceleration–induced experimental head injury. *Journal of Neurotrauma*, *8*, 247–258.

Kotapka, M.J., Graham, D.I., Adams, J.H., & Gennarelli, T.A. (1992). Hippocampal pathology in fatal non-missile human head injury. *Acta Neuropathologica*, *83*, 530–534.

Kotapka, M.J., Graham, D.I., Adams, J.H., & Gennarelli, T.A. (1994). Hippocampal pathology in fatal human head injury without high intracranial pressure. *Journal of Neurotrauma*, *11*, 317–324.

Kotwica, Z., & Brzezinski, J. (1990). Head injuries complicated by chest trauma: A review of 50 consecutive patients. *Acta Neurochirurgica*, *103*, 109–111.

Kozol, H.L. (1945). Pretraumatic personality and psychiatric sequelae of head injury: I. Categorical pretraumatic personality status correlated with general psychiatric reaction to head injury based on analysis of two hundred cases. *Archives of Neurology and Psychiatry*, *53*, 358–364.

Kozol, H.L. (1946). Pretraumatic personality and psychiatric sequelae of head injury: II. Correlation of multiple, specific factors in the pretraumatic personality and psychiatric reaction to head injury, based on analysis of one hundred and one cases. *Archives ofNeurology and Psychiatry*, *56*, 245–275.

Kraus, J.F. (1978). Epidemologic features of head and spinal cord injury. *Advances in Neurology*, *19*, 261–278.

Kraus, J.F. (1980). Injury to the head and spinal cord: The epidemiological relevance of the medical literature published from 1960 to 1978. *Journal of Neurosurgery*, *53*, S3–S10.

Kraus, J.F. (1993). Epidemiology of head injury. In P.R. Cooper (Ed.), *Head injury* (3rd ed., pp. 1–25). Baltimore: Williams & Wilkins.

Kraus, J.F., Black, M.A., Hessol, N., Ley, P., Rokaw, W., Sullivan, C., Bowers, S., Knowlton, S., & Marshall, L. (1984). The incidence of acute brain injury and serious impairment in a defined population. *American Journal of Epidemiology*, *119*, 186–201.

Kraus, J.F., & Nourjah, P. (1989). The epidemiology of mild head injury. In H.S. Levin, H.M. Eisenberg, & A.L. Benton (Eds.), *Mild head injury* (pp. 8–22). New York: Oxford University Press.

Kunishio, K., Matsumoto, Y., Kawada, S., Miyoshi, Y., Matsuhisa, T., Moriyama, E., Norikane, H., & Tanaka, R. (1993). Neuropsychological outcome and social recovery of head-injured patients. *Neurologia Medico-Chirurgica*, *33*, 824–829.

LaBaw, W.L. (1997). Thirty-five months of recovery from trauma, a subjective report: Closed brain injury. In N. Kapur (Ed.), *Injured brains of medical minds: Views from within* (pp. 298–305). Oxford, UK: Oxford University Press.

Lampert, P.W., & Hardman, J.M. (1984). Morphological changes in brains of boxers. *Journal of the American Medical Association*, *251*, 2676–2679.

Lancon, J.A., Haines, D.E., & Parent, A.D. (1998). Anatomy of the shaken baby syndrome. *Anatomical Record (New Anatomist)*, *253*, 13–18.

Landesman, S., & Cooper, P.R. (1982). Infectious complications of head injury. In P.R. Cooper (Ed.), *Head injury* (pp. 343–362). Baltimore: Williams & Wilkins.

Landy, P.J. (1968). The post-traumatic syndrome in closed head injuries accident neurosis. *Proceedings of the Australian Association of Neurologists*, *5*, 463–466.

Larrabee, G.J. (1987). Further cautions in interpretation of comparisons between the WAIS-R and the Wechsler Memory Scale. *Journal of Clinical and Experimental Neuropsychology*, *9*, 456–460.

Lee, K.F., Wagner, L.K., & Kopaniky, D.R. (1987). Protective effect of facial fractures on closed head injuries. In M.E. Miner & K.A. Wagner (Eds.), *Neurotrauma: Treatment, rehabilitation, and related issues, No. 2* (pp. 15–29). Boston: Butterworths.

Leventhal, B.L., & Midelfort, H.B. (1986). The physical abuse of children: A hurt greater than pain. In L.G. Peterson & G.J. O'Shanick (Eds.), *Advances in Psychosomatic Medicine: Psychiatric aspects of trauma Vol. 16*. (pp. 48–83). Basel, Switzerland: Karger.

Levin, H.S. (1981). Aphasia in closed head injury. In M. T. Sarno (Ed.), *Acquired aphasia* (pp. 427–463). New York: Academic Press.

Levin, H.S., Amparo, E., Eisenberg, H.M., Williams, D.H., High, W.M., Jr., McArdle, C.B., & Weiner, R.L. (1987). Magnetic resonance imaging and computerized tomography in relation to the neurobehavioral sequelae of mild and moderate head injuries. *Journal of Neurosurgery*, *66*, 706–713.

Levin, H.S., Benton, A.L., & Grossman, R.G. (1982) *Neurobehavioral consequences of closed head injury*. New York: Oxford University Press.

Levin, H.S., Culhane, K.A., Mendelsohn, D., Lilly, M.A., Bruce, D., Fletcher, J.M., Chapman, S.B., Harward, H., & Eisenberg, H.M. (1993). Cognition in relation to magnetic resonance imaging in head-injured children and adolescents. *Archives of Neurology*, *50*, 897–905.

Levin, H.S., & Eisenberg, H.M. (1979a). Neuropsychological impairment after closed head injury in children and adolescents. *Journal of Pediatric Psychology*, *4*, 389–402.

Levin, H.S., & Eisenberg, H.M. (1979b). Neuropsychological outcome of closed head injury in children and adolescents. *Child's Brain*, *5*, 281–292.

Levin, H.S., & Eisenberg, H.M. (1986). The relative durations of coma and posttraumatic amnesia after severe nonmissile head injury: Findings from the pilot phase of the National Traumatic Coma Data Bank. In M.E. Miner & K.A. Wagner (Eds.), *Neurotrauma: Treatment, rehabilitation, and related issues, No. 1* (pp. 89–97). Boston: Butterworths.

Levin, H.S., Eisenberg, H.M., Gary, H.E., Marmarou, A., Foulkes, M.A., Jane, J.A., Marshall, L.F., & Portman, S.M. (1991). Intracranial hypertension in relation to memory functioning during the first year after severe head injury. *Neurosurgery*, *28*, 196–200.

Levin, H.S., Eisenberg, H.M., Wigg, N.R., & Kobayashi, K. (1982). Memory and intellectual ability after head injury in children and adolescents. *Neurosurgery*, *11*, 668–673.

Levin, H.S., Gary, H.E., Jr., & Eisenberg, H.M. (1989). Duration of impaired consciousness in relation to side of lesion after severe head injury. *Lancet*, *1*, 1001–1003.

Levin, H.S., Gary, H.E., Eisenberg, H.M., Ruff, R.M., Barth, J.T., Kreutzer, J., High, W.M., Jr., Portman, S., Foulkes, M.A., Jane, J.A., Marmarou, A., & Marshall, L.F. (1990). Neurobehavioral outcome 1 year after severe head injury: Experience of the Traumatic Coma Data Bank. *Journal of Neurosurgery*, *73*, 699–709.

Levin, H.S., Gary, H.E., Jr., High, W.M., Jr., Mattis, S., Ruff, R.M., Eisenberg, H.M., Marshall, L.F., & Tabaddor, K. (1987). Minor head injury and the postconcussional syndrome: Methodological issues in outcome studies. In H.S. Levin, J. Grafman, & H.M. Eisenberg (Eds.), *Neurobehavioral recovery from head injury* (pp. 262–275). New York: Oxford University Press.

Levin, H.S., & Goldstein, F.C. (1986). Organization of verbal memory after severe closed-head injury. *Journal of Clinical and Experimental Neuropsychology*, *8*, 643–656.

Levin, H.S., & Grossman, R.G. (1978). Behavioral sequelae of closed head injury: A quantitative study. *Archives of Neurology*, *35*, 720–727.

Levin, H.S., Grossman, R.G., & Kelly, P.J. (1976a). Aphasic disorder in patients with closed head injury. *Journal of Neurology, Neurosurgery, and Psychiatry*, *39*, 1062–1070.

Levin, H.S., Grossman, R.G., & Kelly, P.J. (1976b). Short-term recognition memory in relation to severity of head injury. *Cortex*, *12*, 175–182.

Levin, H.S., Grossman, R.G., & Kelly, P.J. (1977a). Assessment of long-term memory in brain-damaged patients. *Journal of Consulting and Clinical Psychology*, *45*, 684–688.

Levin, H.S., Grossman, R.G., & Kelly, P.J. (1977b). Impairment of facial recognition after closed head injuries of varying severity. *Cortex*, *13*, 119–130.

Levin, H.S., Grossman, R.G., Rose, J.E., & Teasdale, G. (1979). Long-term neuropsychological outcome of closed head injury. *Journal of Neurosurgery*, *50*, 412–422.

Levin, H.S., Grossman, R.G., Sarwar, M., & Meyers, C.A. (1981). Linguistic recovery after closed head injury. *Brain and Language*, *12*, 360–374.

Levin, H.S., Handel, S.F., Goldman, A.M., Eisenberg, H.M., & Guinto, F.C., Jr. (1985). Magnetic resonance imaging after "diffuse" nonmissile head injury: A neurobehavioral study. *Archives of Neurology*, *42*, 963–968.

Levin, H.S., High, W.M., Jr., Ewing-Cobbs, L., Fletcher, J.M., Eisenberg, H.M., Miner, M.E., & Goldstein, F.C. (1988). Memory functioning during the first year after closed head injury in children and adolescents. *Neurosurgery*, *22*, 1043–1052.

Levin, H.S., High, W.M., Meyers, C.A., von Laufen, A., Hayden, M.E., & Eisenberg, H.M. (1985). Impairment of remote memory after closed head injury. *Journal of Neurology, Neurosurgery, and Psychiatry*, *48*, 556–563.

Levin, H.S., Kalisky, Z., Handel, S.F., Goldman, A.M., Eisenberg, H.M., Morrison, D., & Von Laufen, A. (1985). Magnetic resonance imaging in relation to the sequelae and rehabilitation of diffuse closed head injury: Preliminary findings. *Seminars in Neurology*, *5*, 221–232.

Levin, H.S., Mattis, S., Ruff, R.M., Eisenberg, H.M., Marshall, L.F., Tabaddor, K., High, W.M., Jr., & Frankowski, R.F. (1987). Neurobehavioral outcome following minor head injury: A three-center study. *Journal of Neurosurgery*, *66*, 234–243.

Levin, H.S., Mendelsohn, D., Lilly, M.A., Fletcher, J.M., Culhane, K.A., Chapman, S.B., Harward, J., Kusnerik, L., Bruce, D., & Eisenberg, H.M. (1994). Tower of London performance in relation to magnetic resonance imaging following closed head injury in children. *Neuropsychology*, *8*, 171–179.

Levin, H.S., Mendelsohn, D., Lilly, M.A., Yeakley, J., Song, J., Scheibel, R.S., Harward, H., Fletcher, J. M., Kufera, J.A., Davidson, K.C., & Bruce, D. (1997). Magnetic resonance imaging in relation to functional outcome of pediatric closed head injury: A test of the Ommaya–Gennarelli model. *Neurosurgery*, *40*, 432–441.

Levin, H.S., Meyers, C.A., Grossman, R.G., & Sarwar, M. (1981). Ventricular enlargement after closed head injury. *Archives of Neurology*, *38*, 623–629.

Levin, H.S., O'Donnell, V.M., & Grossman, R.G. (1979). The Galveston Orientation and Amnesia Test: A practical scale to assess cognition after head injury. *Journal of Nervous and Mental Disease*, *167*, 675–684.

Levin, H.S., Papanicolaou, A., & Eisenberg, H.M. (1984). Observations on amnesia after nonmissile head injury. In L. R. Squire & N. Butters (Eds.), *Neuropsychology of memory* (pp. 247–257). New York: Guilford Press.

Levin, H.S., & Peters, B.H. (1976). Neuropsychological testing following head injuries: Prosopagnosia without visual field defect. *Diseases of the Nervous System*, *37*, 68–71.

Levin, H.S., Song, J., Scheibel, R.S., Fletcher, J.M., Harward, H., Lilly, M., & Goldstein, F. (1997). Concept formation and problem-solving following closed head injury in children. *Journal of the International Neuropsychological Society*, *3*, 598–607.

Levin, H.S., Williams, D., Crofford, M.J., High, W.M., Jr., Eisenberg, H.M., Amparo, E.G., Guinto, F.C., Jr., Kalisky, Z., Handel, S.F., & Goodman, A.M. (1988). Relationship of depth of brain lesions to consciousness and outcome after closed head injury. *Journal of Neurosurgery*, *69*, 861–866.

Levin, H.S., Williams, D.H., Valastro, M., Eisenberg, H.M., Crofford, M.J., & Handel, S.F. (1990). Corpus callosal atrophy following closed head injury: Detection with magnetic resonance imaging. *Journal of Neurosurgery*, *73*, 77–81.

Levy, D.E., Bates, D., Caronna, J.J., Cartlidge, N.E.F., Knill-Jones, R.P., Lapinski, R.H., Singer, B.H., Shaw, D.A., & Plum, F. (1981). Prognosis in nontraumatic coma. *Annals of Internal Medicine*, *94*, 293–301.

Levy, P. (1968). Short-form tests: A methodological review. *Psychological Bulletin*, *69*, 410–416.

Lewin, W. (1970). Rehabilitation needs of the brain-damaged patient. *Proceedings of the Royal Society of Medicine*, *63*, 8–12.

Lewin, W., Marshall, T.F. de C., & Roberts, A.H. (1979). Long-term outcome after severe head injury. *British Medical Journal*, *2*, 1533–1538.

Lewis, A. (1942). Discussion on differential diagnosis and treatment of post-contusional states. *Proceedings of the Royal Society of Medicine*, *35*, 607–614.

Lezak, M.D. (1978). Living with the characterologically altered brain injured patient. *Journal of Clinical Psychiatry*, *39*, 592–598.

Lezak, M.D. (1979). Recovery of memory and learning functions following traumatic brain injury. *Cortex*, *15*, 63–72.

Lezak, M.D. (1982). The problem of assessing executive functions. *International Journal of Psychology*, *17*, 281–297.

Lezak, M.D. (1984). An individualized approach to neuropsychological assessment. In P.E. Logue & J.M. Schear (Eds.), *Clinical neuropsychology: A multidisciplinary approach* (pp. 29–49). Springfield, IL: Thomas.

Lidvall, H.F., Linderoth, B., & Norlin, B. (1974). Causes of the post-concussional syndrome. *Acta Neurologica Scandinavica, 50*(Suppl. 56).

Liebert, R.M., & Morris, L.W. (1967). Cognitive and emotional components of test anxiety: A distinction and some initial data. *Psychological Reports*, *20*, 975–978.

Liles, B.Z., Coelho, C.A., Duffy, R.J., & Zalagens, M.R. (1989). Effects of elicitation procedures on the narratives of normal and closed head-injured adults. *Journal of Speech and Hearing Disorders*, *54*, 356–366.

Lindenberg, R., & Freytag, E. (1960). The mechanism of cerebral contusions. *Archives of Pathology and Laboratory Medicine*, *69*, 440–469.

Lindenberg, R., & Freytag, E. (1969). Morphology of brain lesions from blunt trauma in early infancy. *Archives of Pathology*, *87*, 298–305.

Lindsay, K.W., McLatchie, G., & Jennett, B. (1980). Serious head injury in sport. *British Medical Journal*, *281*, 789–791.

Linge, F.R. (1997). What does it feel like to be brain damaged? In N. Kapur (Ed.), *Injured brains of medical minds: Views from within* (pp. 317–324). Oxford, UK: Oxford University Press.

Lishman, W.A. (1968). Brain damage in relation to psychiatric disability after head injury. *British Journal of Psychiatry*, *114*, 373–410.

Lishman, W.A. (1973). The psychiatric sequelae of head injury: A review. *Psychological Medicine*, *3*, 304–318.

Livingston, M.G. (1986). Assessment of need for coordinated approach in families with victims of head injury. *British Medical Journal*, *293*, 742–744.

Livingston, M.G. (1987). Head injury: The relatives' response. *Brain Injury*, *1*, 33–39.

Livingston, M.G., Brooks, D.N., & Bond, M.R. (1985a). Patient outcome in the year following severe head injury and relatives' psychiatric and social functioning. *Journal of Neurology, Neurosurgery, and Psychiatry*, *48*, 876–881.

Livingston, M.G., Brooks, D.N., & Bond, M.R. (1985b). Three months after severe head injury: Psychiatric and social impact on relatives. *Journal of Neurology, Neurosurgery, and Psychiatry*, *48*, 870–875.

Livingston, M.G., & Livingston, H.M. (1985). The Glasgow Assessment Schedule: Clinical and research assessment of head injury outcome. *International Rehabilitation Medicine*, *7*, 145–149.

Logie, R.H. (1995). *Visuo-spatial working memory*. Hove: UK: Lawrence Erlbaum Associates Ltd.

London, P.S. (1967). Some observations on the course of events after severe injury of the head. *Annals of the Royal College of Surgeons of England*, *41*, 460–479.

Long, C.J., & Novack, T.A. (1986). Postconcussion symptoms after head trauma: Interpretation and treatment. *Southern Medical Journal*, *79*, 728–732.

Long, C.S., & Webb, W.L., Jr. (1983). Psychological sequelae of head trauma. *Psychiatric Medicine*, *1*, 35–77.

Longoni, A.M., Richardson, J.T.E., & Aiello, A. (1993). Articulatory rehearsal and phonological storage in working memory. *Memory and Cognition*, *21*, 11–22.

Loring, D.W., & Papanicolaou, A.C. (1987). Memory assessment in neuropsychology: Theoretical considerations and practical utility. *Journal of Clinical and Experimental Neuropsychology*, *9*, 340–358.

Lundholm, J., Jepsen, B.N., & Thornval, G. (1975). The late neurological, psychological, and social aspects of severe traumatic coma. *Scandinavian Journal of Rehabilitation Medicine*, *7*, 97–100.

Luria, A.R. (1963). *Restoration of function after brain injury.* Oxford, UK: Pergamon.

Luria, A.R., Naydin, V.L., Tsvetkova, L.S., & Vinarskaya, E.N. (1969). Restoration of higher cortical function following local brain damage. In P.J. Vinken & G.W. Bruyn (Eds.), *Handbook of clinical neurology: Vol. 3. Disorders of higher nervous activity* (pp. 368–433). Amsterdam: North-Holland.

Lynch, S., & Yarnell, P.R. (1973). Retrograde amnesia: Delayed forgetting after concussion. *American Journal of Psychology*, *86*, 643–645.

Maas, A.I.R., Braakman, R., Schouten, H.J.A., Minderhoud, J.M., & van Zomeren, A.H. (1983). Agreement between physicians on assessment of outcome following severe head injury. *Journal of Neurosurgery*, *58*, 321–325.

MacFlynn, G., Montgomery, E.A., Fenton, G.W., & Rutherford, W. (1984). Measurement of reaction time following minor head injury. *Journal of Neurology, Neurosurgery, and Psychiatry*, *47*, 1326–1331.

Maciver, I.N., Lassman, L.P., Thomson, C.W., & McLeod, I. (1958). Treatment of severe head injuries. *Lancet*, *2*, 544–550.

Macpherson, B.C.M., Macpherson, P., & Jennett, B. (1990). CT evidence of intracranial contusion and haematoma in relation to the presence, site and type of skull fracture. *Clinical Radiology*, *42*, 321–326.

Macpherson, P., & Graham, D.I. (1978). Correlations between angiographic findings and the ischaemia of head injury. *Journal of Neurology, Neurosurgery, and Psychiatry*, *41*, 122–127.

Macpherson, P., Jennett, B., & Anderson, E. (1990). CT scanning and surgical treatment of 1551 head injured patients admitted to a regional neurosurgical unit. *Clinical Radiology*, *42*, 85–87.

Makela, M.E., Frankowski, R., Gildenberg, P.L., Grossman, R.G., & Wagner, K.A. (1982). Comparison of head injury outcome rates at two adjacent hospitals. In R.G. Grossman & P. L. Gildenberg (Eds.), *Head injury: Basic and clinical aspects* (pp. 203–212). New York: Raven Press.

Malkmus, D. (1983). Integrating cognitive strategies into the physical therapy setting. *Physical Therapy*, *63*, 1952–1959.

Mamelak, A.N., Pitts, L.H., & Damron, S. (1996). Predicting survival from head trauma 24 hours after injury: A practical method with therapeutic implications. *Journal of Trauma: Injury, Infection, and Critical Care*, *41*, 91–99.

Mandleberg, I.A. (1975). Cognitive recovery after severe head injury: 2. Wechsler Adult Intelligence Scale during post-traumatic amnesia. *Journal of Neurology, Neurosurgery, and Psychiatry*, *38*, 1127–1132.

Mandleberg, I.A. (1976). Cognitive recovery after severe head injury: 3. WAIS Verbal and Performance IQs as a function of post-traumatic amnesia duration and time from injury. *Journal of Neurology, Neurosurgery, and Psychiatry, 39,* 1001–1007.

Mandleberg, I.A., & Brooks, D.N. (1975). Cognitive recovery after severe head injury: 1. Serial testing on the Wechsler Adult Intelligence Scale. *Journal of Neurology, Neurosurgery, and Psychiatry*, *38*, 1121–1126.

Manly, T., & Robertson, I.H. (1997). Sustained attention and the frontal lobes. In P. Rabbitt (Ed.), *Methodology of frontal and executive function* (pp. 135–153). Hove, UK: Psychology Press.

Marschark, M., & Hunt, R.R. (1989). A re-examination of the role of imagery in learning and memory. *Journal of Experimental Psychology: Learning, Memory, and Cognition, 15*, 710–720.

Marschark, M., Richman, C.L., Yuille, J.C., & Hunt, R.R. (1987). The role of imagery in memory: On shared and distinctive information. *Psychological Bulletin, 102*, 28–41.

Marschark, M., & Surian, L. (1989). Why does imagery improve memory? *European Journal of Cognitive Psychology, 1*, 251–263.

Marsh, N.V., & Knight, R.G. (1991). Behavioral assessment of social competence following severe head injury. *Journal of Clinical and Experimental Neuropsychology, 13*, 729–740.

Marshall, L.F., Becker, D.P., Bowers, S.A., Cayard, C., Eisenberg, H., Gross, C.R., Grossman, R.G., Jane, J.A., Kunitz, S.C., Rimel, R., Tabaddor, K., & Warren, J. (1983). The National Traumatic Coma Data Bank: Pt. I. Design, purpose, goals, and results. *Journal of Neurosurgery, 59*, 276–284.

Marshall, L.F., & Bowers, S.A. (1985). Outcome prediction in severe head injury. In R.H. Wilkins & S.S. Rengachary (Eds.), *Neurosurgery* (pp. 1605–1608). New York: McGraw-Hill.

Marshall, L.F., Gautille, T., Klauber, M.R., Eisenberg, H.M., Jane, J.A., Luerssen, T.G., Marmarou, A., & Foulkes, M.A. (1991). The outcome of severe closed head injury. *Journal of Neurosurgery, 75*, S28–S36.

Marshall, L.F., Toole, B.M., & Bowers, S.A. (1983). The National Traumatic Coma Data Bank: Pt. 2. Patients who talk and deteriorate: Implications for treatment. *Journal of Neurosurgery, 59*, 285–288.

Martin, G. (1974). *A manual of head injuries in general surgery*. London: Heinemann.

Martin, K.M. (1994). Loss without death: A dilemma for the head-injured patient's family. *Journal of Neurosurgical Nursing, 26*, 134–139.

Martzke, J.S., Swan, C.S., & Varney, N.R. (1991). Posttraumatic anomsia and orbital frontal damage: Neuropsychological and neuropsychiatric correlates. *Neuropsychology, 5*, 213–225.

Mattson, A.J., & Levin, H.S. (1990). Frontal lobe dysfunction following closed head injury: A review of the literature. *Journal of Nervous and Mental Disease, 178*, 282–291.

Matz, P.G., & Pitts, L. (1997). Monitoring in traumatic brain injury. *Clinical Neurosurgery, 44*, 267–294.

Max, J.E., Roberts, M.A., Koele, S.L., Lindgren, S.D., Robin, D.A., Arndt, S., Smith, W.L., Jr., & Sato, Y. (1999). Cognitive outcome in children and adolescents following severe traumatic brain injury: Influence of psychosocial, psychiatric, and injury-related variables. *Journal of the International Neuropsychological Society, 5*, 58–68.

Maxwell, A.E. (1960). Obtaining factor scores on the Wechsler Adult Intelligence Scale. *Journal of Mental Science, 106*, 1060–1062.

Maxwell, E. (1957). Validities of abbreviated WAIS scales. *Journal of Consulting Psychology, 21*, 121–126.

Maxwell, W.L., Kansagra, A.M., Graham, D.I., Adams, J.H., & Gennarelli, T.A. (1988). Freeze-fracture studies of reactive myelinated nerve fibres after diffuse axonal injury. *Acta Neuropathologica, 76*, 395–406.

Maxwell, W.L., Watt, C., Graham, D.I., & Gennarelli, T.A. (1993). Ultrastructural evidence of axonal shearing as a result of lateral acceleration of the head in non-human primates. *Acta Neuropathologica, 86*, 136–144.

Mayes, A.R. (1995). The assessment of memory disorders. In A.D. Baddeley, B.A. Wilson, & F.N. Watts (Eds.), *Handbook of memory disorders* (pp. 367–391). Chichester, UK: Wiley.

Mayou, R. (1995). Medico-legal aspects of road traffic accidents. *Journal of Psychosomatic Research, 39*, 789–798.

Mazaux, J.M., Masson, F., Levin, H.S., Alaoui, P., Maurette, P., & Barat, M. (1997). Long-term neuropsychological outcome and loss of social autonomy after traumatic brain injury. *Archives of Physical Medicine and Rehabilitation*, *78*, 1316–1320.

McGlynn, S.M. (1990). Behavioral approaches to neuropsychological rehabilitation. *Psychological Bulletin*, *108*, 420–441.

McGuire, T.L., & Sylvester, C.E. (1987). Neuropsychiatric evaluation and treatment of children with head injury. *Journal of Learning Disabilities*, *20*, 590–595.

McKinlay, W.W., & Brooks, D.N. (1984). Methodological problems in assessing psychosocial recovery following severe head injury. *Journal of Clinical Neuropsychology*, *6*, 87–99.

McKinlay, W.W., Brooks, D.N., & Bond, M.R. (1983). Post-concussional symptoms, financial compensation and outcome of severe blunt head injury. *Journal of Neurology, Neurosurgery, and Psychiatry*, *46*, 1084–1091.

McKinlay, W.W., Brooks, D.N., Bond, M.R., Martinage, D.P., & Marshall, M.M. (1981). The short-term outcome of severe blunt head injury as reported by relatives of the injured persons. *Journal of Neurology, Neurosurgery, and Psychiatry*, *44*, 527–533.

McLatchie, G., Brooks, N., Galbraith, S., Hutchison, J.S.F., Wilson, L., Melville, I., & Teasdale, E. (1987). Clinical neurological examination, neuropsychology, electroencephalography and computed tomographic head scanning in active amateur boxers. *Journal of Neurology, Neurosurgery, and Psychiatry*, *50*, 96–99.

McLean, A., Jr., Temkin, N.R., Dikmen, S., & Wyler, A.R. (1983). The behavioral sequelae of head injury. *Journal of Clinical Neuropsychology*, *5*, 361–376.

McLean, A.J. (1995). Brain injury without head impact? *Journal of Neurotrauma*, *12*, 621–625.

McMillan, T.M. (1996). Post-traumatic stress disorder following minor and severe closed head injury: 10 single cases. *Brain Injury*, *10*, 749–758.

McMillan, T.M., & Glucksman, E.E. (1987). The neuropsychology of moderate head injury. *Journal of Neurology, Neurosurgery, and Psychiatry*, *50*, 393–397.

McMordie, W.R., Barker, S.L., & Paolo, T.M. (1990). Return to work (RTW) after head injury. *Brain Injury*, *4*, 57–69.

Mearns, J., & Lees-Haley, P.R. (1993). Discriminating neuropsychological sequelae of head injury from alcohol-abuse-induced deficits: A review and analysis. *Journal of Clinical Psychology*, *49*, 714–720.

Medical Disability Society. (1988). *Report of the Working Party on the Management of Traumatic Brain Injury*. London: Development Trust for the Young Disabled on behalf of the Medical Disability Society.

Merskey, H., & Woodforde, J.M. (1972). Psychiatric sequelae of minor head injury. *Brain*, *95*, 521–528.

Messick, S. (1965). The impact of negative affect on cognition and personality. In S.S. Tomkins & C.E. Izard (Eds.), *Affect, cognition, and personality: Empirical studies* (pp. 98–128). New York: Springer.

Meyer, A. (1904). The anatomical facts and clinical varieties of traumatic insanity. *American Journal of Insanity*, *60*, 373–441.

Middleton, D.K., Lambert, M.J., & Seggar, L.B. (1991). Neuropsychological rehabilitation: Microcomputer-assisted treatment of brain-injured adults. *Perceptual and Motor Skills*, *72*, 527–530.

Milberg, W.P., Hebben, N., & Kaplan, E. (1986). The Boston Process Approach to neuropsychological assessment. In I. Grant & K.H. Adams (Eds.), *Neuropsychological assessment of neuropsychiatric disorders* (pp. 65–86). New York: Oxford University Press.

Miller, E. (1970). Simple and choice reaction time following severe head injury. *Cortex*, *6*, 121–127.

Miller, E. (1979). The long-term consequences of head injury: A discussion of the evidence with special reference to the preparation of legal reports. *British Journal of Social and Clinical Psychology*, *18*, 87–98.

Miller, E. (1980). The training characteristics of severely head-injured patients: A preliminary study. *Journal of Neurology, Neurosurgery, and Psychiatry*, *43*, 525–528.

Miller, E., & Cruzat, A. (1981). A note on the effects of irrelevant information on task performance after mild and severe head injury. *British Journal of Clinical Psychology*, *20*, 69–70.

Miller, H. (1961a). Accident neurosis: Lecture I. *British Medical Journal*, *1*, 919–925.

Miller, H. (1961b). Accident neurosis: Lecture II. *British Medical Journal*, *1*, 992–998.

Miller, H. (1966). Mental after-effects of head injury. *Proceedings of the Royal Society of Medicine*, *59*, 257–261.

Miller, H., & Cartlidge, N. (1972). Simulation and malingering after injuries to the brain and spinal cord. *Lancet*, *1*, 580–585.

Miller, H., & Stern, G. (1965). The long-term prognosis of severe head injury. *Lancet*, *1*, 225–229.

Miller, J.D., & Jennett, W.B. (1968). Complications of depressed skull fracture. *Lancet*, *2*, 991–995.

Milos, R. (1975). Hypnotic exploration of amnesia after cerebral injuries. *International Journal of Clinical and Experimental Hypnosis*, *23*, 103–110.

Milton, S.B., & Wertz, R.T. (1986). Management of persisting communication deficits in patients with traumatic brain injury. In B.P. Uzzell & Y. Gross (Eds.), *Clinical neuropsychology of intervention* (pp. 223–256). Boston: Martinus Nijhoff.

Minderhoud, J.M., Boelens, M.E.M., Huizenga, J., & Saan, R.J. (1980). Treatment of minor head injuries. *Clinical Neurology and Neurosurgery*, *82*, 127–140.

Miner, M.E., Fletcher, J.M., & Ewing-Cobbs, L. (1986). Recovery versus outcome after head injury in children. In M.E. Miner & K.A. Wagner (Eds.), *Neurotrauma: Treatment, rehabilitation, and related issues, No. 1* (pp. 233–240). Boston: Butterworths.

Mitchell, D.E., & Adams, J.H. (1973). Primary focal impact damage to the brainstem in blunt head injuries: Does it exist? *Lancet*, *2*, 215–218.

Mittl, R.L., Jr., Grossman, R.I., Hiehle, J.F., Jr., Hurst, R.W., Kauder, D.R., Gennarelli, T.A., & Alburger, G.W. (1994). Prevalence of MR evidence of diffuse axonal injury in patients with mild head injury and normal head CT findings. *American Journal of Neuroradiology*, *15*, 1583–1589.

Montgomery, A., Fenton, G.W., & McClelland, R.J. (1984). Delayed brainstem conduction time in post-concussional syndrome. *Lancet*, *1*, 1011.

Moore, B.E., & Ruesch, J. (1944). Prolonged disturbances of consciousness following head injury. *New England Journal of Medicine*, *230*, 445–452.

Morris, L.W., & Liebert, R.M. (1970). Relationship of cognitive and emotional components of test anxiety to physiological arousal and academic performance. *Journal of Consulting and Clinical Psychology*, *35*, 332–337.

Murdoch, B.E., & Theodoros, D.G. (1999). Dysarthria following traumatic brain injury. In S. McDonald, L. Togher, & C. Code (Eds.), *Traumatic brain injury and communication disorders* (pp. 211–233). Hove, UK: Psychology Press.

Murray, L.S., Teasdale, G.M., Murray, G.D., Jennett, B., Miller, J.D., Pickard, J.D., Shaw, M.D.M., Achilles, J., Bailey, S., Jones, P., Kelly, D., & Lacey, J. (1993). Does prediction of outcome alter patient management? *Lancet*, *341*, 1487–1491.

Murray, R., Shum, D., & McFarland, K. (1992). Attentional deficits in head-injured children: An information processing analysis. *Brain and Cognition*, *18*, 99–115.

Najenson, T., Groswasser, Z., Stern, M., Schechter, I., Daviv, C., Berghaus, N., & Mendelson, L. (1975). Prognostic factors in rehabilitation after severe head injury. *Scandinavian Journal of Rehabilitation Medicine*, *7*, 101–105.

Najenson, T., Sazbon, L., Fiselzon, J., Becker, E., & Schechter, I. (1978). Recovery of communicative functions after prolonged traumatic coma. *Scandinavian Journal of Rehabilitation Medicine*, *10*, 15–21.

National Center for Health Statistics. (1984). *Multiple causes of death in the United States* (Monthly Vital Statistics Report, Vol. 32, No. 10, Suppl. 2: DHHS Publication No. PHS 84–1120). Washington, DC: US Government Printing Office.

National Center for Health Statistics. (1996). *Vital statistics of the United States, 1992: Vol. II. Mortality, Pt. A* (DHHS Publication No. PHS 96–1101). Washington, DC: US Government Printing Office.

Nelson, H.E. (1976). A modified card sorting test sensitive to frontal lobe defects. *Cortex*, *12*, 313–324.

Nelson, H.E. (1982). *National Adult Reading Test (NART): Test manual*. Windsor, UK: NFER-Nelson.

Nelson, H.E., & McKenna, P. (1975). The use of current reading ability in the assessment of dementia. *British Journal of Social and Clinical Psychology*, *14*, 259–267.

Nelson, H.E., & O'Connell, A. (1978). Dementia: The estimation of premorbid intelligence levels using the New Adult Reading Test. *Cortex*, *14*, 234–244.

Nevin, N.C. (1967). Neuropathological changes in the white matter following head injury. *Journal of Neuropathology and Experimental Neurology*, *26*, 77–84.

Newberg, A.B., & Alavi, A. (1996). Neuroimaging in patients with traumatic brain injury. *Journal of Head Trauma Rehabilitation*, *11*(6), 65–79.

Newcombe, F. (1982). The psychological consequences of closed head injury: Assessment and rehabilitation. *Injury*, *14*, 111–136.

Newcombe, F., & Artiola i Fortuny, L. (1979). Problems and perspectives in the evaluation of psychological deficits after cerebral lesions. *International Rehabilitation Medicine*, *1*, 182–192.

Newcombe, F., Brooks, N., & Baddeley, A. (1980). Rehabilitation after brain damage: An overview. *International Rehabilitation Medicine*, *2*, 133–137.

Newcombe, F., Rabbitt, P., & Briggs, M. (1994). Minor head injury: Pathophysiological or iatrogenic sequelae? *Journal of Neurology, Neurosurgery, and Psychiatry*, *57*, 709–716.

Niemann, H., Ruff, R.M., & Baser, C.A. (1990). Computer-assisted attention retraining in head-injured individuals: A controlled efficacy study of an outpatient program. *Journal of Consulting and Clinical Psychology*, *58*, 811–817.

Nies, K.J., & Sweet, J.J. (1994). Neuropsychological assessment and malingering: A critical review of past and present strategies. *Archives of Clinical Neuropsychology*, *9*, 501–552.

Norman, D.A., & Shallice, T. (1986). *Attention to action: Willed and automatic control of behavior*. In R.J. Davidson, G.E. Schwarts, & D. Shapiro (Eds.), *Consciousness and self-regulation: Advances in research and theory* (Vol. 4, pp. 1–18). New York: Plenum Press. (Original work published 1982).

Norrman, B., & Svahn, K. (1961). A follow-up study of severe brain injuries. *Acta Psychiatrica Scandinavica*, *37*, 236–264.

Noseworthy, J.H., Miller, J., Murray, T.J., & Regan, D. (1981). Auditory brainstem responses in postconcussion syndrome. *Archives of Neurology*, *38*, 275–278.

Oddy, M. (1984a). Head injury and social adjustment. In N. Brooks (Ed.), *Closed head injury: Psychological, social, and family consequences* (pp. 108–122). Oxford, UK: Oxford University Press.

Oddy, M. (1984b). Head injury during childhood: The psychological implications. In N. Brooks (Ed.), *Closed head injury: Psychological, social, and family consequences* (pp. 179–194). Oxford, UK: Oxford University Press.

Oddy, M. (1993). Psychosocial consequences of brain injury. In R. Greenwood, M.P. Barnes, T.M. McMillan, & C.D. Ward (Eds.), *Neurological rehabilitation* (pp. 423–433). Edinburgh, UK: Churchill Livingstone.

Oddy, M., & Humphrey, M. (1980). Social recovery during the year following severe head injury. *Journal of Neurology, Neurosurgery, and Psychiatry, 43*, 798–802.

Oddy, M., Humphrey, M., & Uttley, D. (1978a). Stresses upon the relatives of head-injured patients. *British Journal of Psychiatry, 133*, 507–513.

Oddy, M., Humphrey, M., & Uttley, D. (1978b). Subjective impairment and social recovery after closed head injury. *Journal of Neurology, Neurosurgery, and Psychiatry, 41*, 611–616.

Office for National Statistics (1996). *Mortality statistics: Cause* (Series DH2, No. 21). London: Her Majesty's Stationery Office.

Office for National Statistics (1997). *Mortality statistics: Cause* (Series DH2, No. 22). London: Her Majesty's Stationery Office.

Office for National Statistics (1998). *Mortality statistics: Cause* (Series DH2, No. 23). London: Her Majesty's Stationery Office.

Office of Population Censuses and Surveys. (1989). *Mortality statistics 1987: Cause* (Series DH2, No. 14). London: Her Majesty's Stationery Office.

Office of Population Censuses and Surveys. (1990). *Mortality statistics 1987: Cause* (Series DH2, No. 15). London: Her Majesty's Stationery Office.

Office of Population Censuses and Surveys. (1991a). *Mortality statistics 1987: Cause* (Series DH2, No. 16). London: Her Majesty's Stationery Office.

Office of Population Censuses and Surveys. (1991b). *Mortality statistics 1987: Cause* (Series DH2, No. 17). London: Her Majesty's Stationery Office.

Office of Population Censuses and Surveys. (1993a). *Mortality statistics 1987: Cause* (Series DH2, No. 18). London: Her Majesty's Stationery Office.

Office of Population Censuses and Surveys. (1993b). *Mortality statistics 1987: Cause* (Series DH2, No. 19). London: Her Majesty's Stationery Office.

Oliveros, J.C., Jandali, M.K., Timsit-Berthier, M., Remy, R., Benghezal, A., Audibert, A., & Moeglen, J.M. (1978). Vasopressin in amnesia. *Lancet, 1*, 41–42.

Olver, J.H., Ponsford, J.L., & Curran, C.A. (1996). Outcome following traumatic brain injury: A comparison between 2 and 5 years after injury. *Brain Injury, 10*, 841–848.

Ommaya, A.K., Faas, F., & Yarnell, P. (1968). Whiplash injury and brain damage: An experimental study. *Journal of the American Medical Association, 204*, 285–289.

Ommaya, A.K., Geller, A., & Parsons, L.C. (1971). The effect of experimental head injury on one-trial learning in rats. *International Journal of Neuroscience, 1*, 371-378.

Ommaya, A.K., & Gennarelli, T.A. (1974). Cerebral concussion and traumatic unconsciousness: Correlation of experimental and clinical observations on blunt head injuries. *Brain, 97*, 633–654.

Ommaya, A.K., & Gennarelli, T.A. (1976). A physiopathologic basis for noninvasive diagnosis and prognosis of head injury severity. In R.L. McLaurin (Ed.), *Head injuries: Proceedings of the second Chicago symposium on neural trauma* (pp. 49–75). New York: Grune & Stratton.

Ommaya, A.K., Grubb, R.L., Jr., & Naumann, R.A. (1971). Coup and contrecoup injury: Observations on the mechanics of visible brain injuries in the rhesus monkey. *Journal of Neurosurgery, 35*, 503–516.

Ommaya, A.K., & Yarnell, P. (1969). Subdural haematoma after whiplash injury. *Lancet, 2*, 237–239.

Oppenheimer, D.R. (1968). Microscopic lesions in the brain following head injury. *Journal of Neurology, Neurosurgery, and Psychiatry, 31*, 299–306.

Orne, M.T., Soskis, D.A., Dinges, D.F., & Orne, E.C. (1984). Hypnotically induced testimony. In G.L. Wells & E.F. Loftus (Eds.), *Eyewitness testimony: Psychological perspectives* (pp. 171–213). Cambridge, UK: Cambridge University Press.

Overgaard, J., Christensen, S., Hvid-Hansen, O., Haase, J., Land, A. -M., Hein, O., Pedersen, K.K., & Tweed, W.A. (1973). Prognosis after head injury based on early clinical examination. *Lancet, 2*, 631–635.

Paivio, A. (1971). *Imagery and verbal processes*. New York: Holt, Rinehart, & Winston.

Panting, A., & Merry, P. (1972). The long-term rehabilitation of severe head injuries with particular reference to the need for social and medical support for the patient's family. *Rehabilitation, 38*, 33–37.

Papanicolaou, A.C., Levin, H.S., Eisenberg, H.M., Moore, B.D., Goethe, K.E., & High, W.M., Jr. (1984). Evoked potential correlates of posttraumatic amnesia after closed head injury. *Neurosurgery, 14*, 676–678.

Parker, S.A., & Serrats, A.F. (1976). Memory recovery after traumatic coma. *Acta Neurochirurgica, 34*, 71–77.

Parkinson, D. (1977). Concussion. *Mayo Clinic Proceedings, 52*, 492–496.

Payne-Johnson, J.C. (1986). Evaluation of communication competence in patients with closed head injury. *Journal of Communication Disorders, 19*, 237–249.

Pazzaglia, P., Frank, G., Frank, F., & Gaist, G. (1975). Clinical course and prognosis of acute post-traumatic coma. *Journal of Neurology, Neurosurgery, and Psychiatry, 38*, 149–154.

Perrone, N. (1972). Biomechanical problems related to vehicle impact. In Y.C. Fung, N. Perrone, & M. Anliker (Eds.), *Biomechanics: Its foundations and objectives* (pp. 567–583). Englewood Cliffs, NJ: Prentice-Hall.

Peterson, L.G. (1986). Acute response to trauma. In L.G. Peterson & G.J. O'Shanick (Eds.), *Advances in Psychosomatic Medicine: Vol. 16. Psychiatric aspects of trauma.* (pp. 84–92). Basel, Switzerland: Karger.

Ponsford, J., & Kinsella, G. (1992). Attentional deficits following closed-head injury. *Journal of Clinical and Experimental Neuropsychology, 14*, 822–838.

Ponsford, J., Sloan, S., & Snow, P. (1995). *Traumatic brain injury: Rehabilitation for everyday adaptive living*. Hove, UK: Lawrence Erlbaum Associates Ltd.

Ponsford, J.L., Olver, J.H., Curran, C., & Ng, K. (1995). Prediction of employment status 2 years after traumatic brain injury. *Brain Injury, 9*, 11–20.

Pressley, M., Borkowski, J.G., & Johnson, C.J. (1987). The development of good strategy use: Imagery and related mnemonic strategies. In M.A. McDaniel & M. Pressley (Eds.), *Imagery and related mnemonic processes: Theories, individual differences, and applications* (pp. 274–297). New York: Springer-Verlag.

Price, D.J.E., & Murray, A. (1972). The influence of hypoxia and hypotension on recovery from head injury. *Injury, 3*, 218–224.

Price, J.R. (1987). Sexuality following traumatic brain injury. In M.E. Miner & K.A. Wagner (Eds.), *Neurotrauma: Treatment, rehabilitation, and related issues, No. 2* (pp. 173–180). Boston: Butterworths.

Prifitera, A., & Barley, W.D. (1985). Cautions in interpretation of comparisons between the WAIS-R and the Wechsler Memory Scale. *Journal of Consulting and Clinical Psychology, 53*, 564–565.

Prigatano, G.P. (1978). Wechsler Memory Scale: A selective review of the literature. *Journal of Clinical Psychology, 34*, 816–832.

Prigatano, G.P., Fordyce, D.J., Zeiner, H.K., Roueche, J.R., Pepping, M., & Wood, B.C. (1984). Neuropsychological rehabilitation after closed head injury in young adults. *Journal of Neurology, Neurosurgery, and Psychiatry*, *47*, 505–513.

Prigatano, G.P., Fordyce, D.J., Zeiner, H.K., Roueche, J.R., Pepping, M., & Wood, B.C. (1986). *Neuropsychological rehabilitation after brain injury*. Baltimore: Johns Hopkins University Press.

Pritchard, W.S. (1981). Psychophysiology of P300. *Psychological Bulletin*, *89*, 506–540.

Psychosocial outcome of head injury [Editorial]. (1986). *Lancet*, *1*, 1361–1362.

Public Health Service, Health Care Financing Administration. (1980). *ICD-9-CM: International classification of diseases, 9th revision, clinical modification: Vol. 1. Diseases: Tabular list* (2nd ed.) (DHHS Publication No. PHS 80–1260). Washington, DC: US Government Printing Office.

Pudenz, R.H., & Shelden, C.H. (1946). The lucite calvarium—a method for direct observation of the brain: II. Cranial trauma and brain movement. *Journal of Neurosurgery*, *3*, 487–505.

Quine, S., Pierce, J.P., & Lyle, D.M. (1988). Relatives as lay-therapists for the severely head-injured. *Brain Injury*, *2*, 139–149.

Raginsky, B.B. (1969). Hypnotic recall of aircrash cause. *International Journal of Clinical and Experimental Hypnosis*, *17*, 1–19.

Raven, J.C. (1960). *Guide to the Standard Progressive Matrices*. London: Lewis.

Raven, J.C. (1962). *Extended guide to the Mill Hill Vocabulary Scales*. London: Lewis.

Registrar General for Scotland. (1996). *Annual Report 1995*. Edinburgh, UK: General Register Office for Scotland.

Reilly, E.L., Kelley, J.T., & Faillace, L.A. (1986). Role of alcohol use and abuse in trauma. In L.G. Peterson & G.J. O'Shanick (Eds.), *Advances in Psychosomatic Medicine: Vol. 16. Psychiatric aspects of trauma.* (pp. 17–30). Basel, Switzerland: Karger.

Reilly, P L., Adams, J.H., Graham, D.I., & Jennett, B. (1975). Patients with head injury who talk and die. *Lancet*, *2*, 375–377.

Reitan, R.M. (1966). A research program on the psychological effects of brain lesions in human beings. In N. R. Ellis (Ed.), *International review of research in mental retardation* (Vol. 1, pp. 153–218). New York: Academic Press.

Reitan, R.M. (1986). Theoretical and methodological bases of the Halstead-Reitan Neuropsychological Test Battery. In I. Grant & K.M. Adams (Eds.), *Neuropsychological assessment of neuropsychiatric disorders* (pp. 3–30). New York: Oxford University Press.

Reitan, R.M., & Davison, L.A. (Eds.). (1974). *Clinical neuropsychology: Current status and applications*. Washington, DC: Winston.

Relander, M., Troupp, H., & Björkesten, G. af (1972). Controlled trial of treatment for cerebral concussion. *British Medical Journal*, *4*, 777–779.

Reynell, W.R. (1944). A psychometric method of determining intellectual loss following head injury. *Journal of Mental Science*, *90*, 710–719.

Reynolds, C.R., & Gutkin, T.B. (1979). Predicting the premorbid intellectual status of children using demographic data. *Clinical Neuropsychology*, *1*(2), 36–38.

Ribot, T. (1882). *Diseases of memory: An essay in the positive psychology*. New York: Appleton.

Richardson, F.C., O'Neil, H.F., Jr., Whitmore, S., & Judd, W. A. (1977). Factor analysis of the test anxiety scale and evidence concerning the components of test anxiety. *Journal of Consulting and Clinical Psychology*, *45*, 704–705.

Richardson, J.T.E. (1979). Mental imagery, human memory, and the effects of closed head injury. *British Journal of Social and Clinical Psychology*, *18*, 319–327.

Richardson, J.T.E. (1982). Memory disorders. In A. Burton (Ed.), *The pathology and psychology of cognition* (pp. 48–77). London: Methuen.

Richardson, J.T.E. (1984). Developing the theory of working memory. *Memory and Cognition, 12*, 71–83.

Richardson, J.T.E. (1987). Social class limitations on the efficacy of imagery mnemonic instructions. *British Journal of Psychology, 78*, 65–77.

Richardson, J.T.E. (1991). Imagery and the brain. In C. Cornoldi & M.A. McDaniel (Eds.), *Imagery and cognition* (pp. 1–45). New York: Springer-Verlag.

Richardson, J.T.E. (1994). Continuous recognition memory tests: Are the assumptions of the theory of signal detection really met? *Journal of Clinical and Experimental Neuropsychology, 16*, 482–486.

Richardson, J.T.E. (1996). Evolving issues in working memory. In J.T.E. Richardson, R.W. Engle, L. Hasher, R.H. Logie, E.R. Stoltzfus, & R.T. Zacks, *Working memory and human cognition* (pp. 120–154). New York: Oxford University Press.

Richardson, J.T.E., & Barry, C. (1985). The effects of minor closed head injury upon human memory: Further evidence on the role of mental imagery. *Cognitive Neuropsychology, 2*, 149–168.

Richardson, J.T.E., Cermak, L.S., Blackford, S.P., & O'Connor, M. (1987). The efficacy of imagery mnemonics following brain damage. In M.A. McDaniel & M. Pressley (Eds.), *Imagery and related mnemonic processes: Theories, individual differences, and applications* (pp. 303–328). New York: Springer-Verlag.

Richardson, J.T.E., & Snape, W. (1984). The effects of closed head injury upon human memory: An experimental analysis. *Cognitive Neuropsychology, 1*, 217–331.

Rimel, R.W., Giordani, B., Barth, J.T., Boll, T.J., & Jane, J.A. (1981). Disability caused by minor head injury. *Neurosurgery, 9*, 221–228.

Rimel, R.W., & Jane, J.A. (1983). Characteristics of the head–injured patients. In M. Rosenthal, E.R. Griffith, M.R. Bond, & J.D. Miller (Eds.), *Rehabilitation of the head injured adult* (pp. 9–21). Philadelphia: Davis.

Roberts, A.H. (1969). *Brain damage in boxers: A study of the prevalence of traumatic encephalopathy among ex-professional boxers*. London: Pitman.

Roberts, A.H. (1976). Long-term prognosis of severe accidental head injury. *Proceedings of the Royal Society of Medicine, 69*, 137–140.

Roberts, A. H. (1979). *Severe accidental head injury: An assessment of long-term prognosis*. London: Macmillan.

Robertson, I.H., Manly, T., Andrade, J., Baddeley, B.T., & Yiend, J. (1997). "Oops!": Performance correlates of everyday attentional failures in traumatic brain injured and normal subjects. *Neuropsychologia, 35*, 747–758.

Rose, J., Valtonen, S., & Jennett, B. (1977). Avoidable factors contributing to death after head injury. *British Medical Journal, 2*, 615–618.

Rosenbaum, M., Lipsitz, N., Abraham, J., & Najenson, T. (1978). A description of an intensive treatment project for the rehabilitation of severely brain-injured soldiers. *Scandinavian Journal of Rehabilitation Medicine, 10*, 1–6.

Rosenbaum, M., & Najenson, T. (1976). Changes in life patterns and symptoms of low mood as reported by wives of severely brain-injured soldiers. *Journal of Consulting and Clinical Psychology, 44*, 881–888.

Roth, D.L., Conboy, T.J., Reeder, K.P., & Boll, T.J. (1990). Confirmatory factor analysis of the Wechsler Memory Scale-Revised in a sample of head-injured patients. *Journal of Clinical and Experimental Neuropsychology, 12*, 834–842.

Roth, D.L., Hughes, C.W., Monkowski, P.G., & Crosson, B. (1984). Investigation of validity of WAIS-R short forms for patients suspected to have brain impairment. *Journal of Consulting and Clinical Psychology, 52*, 722–723.

Rowbotham, G.F., Maciver, I.N., Dickson, J., & Bousfield, M.E. (1954). Analysis of 1,400 cases of acute injury to the head. *British Medical Journal, 1*, 726–730.

Rubens, A.B., Geschwind, N., Mahowald, M.W., & Mastri, A. (1977). Posttraumatic cerebral hemispheric disconnection syndrome. *Archives of Neurology, 34*, 750–755.

Ruesch, J. (1944a). Dark adaptation, negative after images, tachistoscopic examinations and reaction time in head injuries. *Journal of Neurosurgery, 1*, 243–251.

Ruesch, J. (1944b). Intellectual impairment in head injuries. *American Journal of Psychiatry, 100*, 480–496.

Ruesch, J., Harris, R.E., & Bowman, K.M. (1945). Pre- and post-traumatic personality in head injuries. In *Research Publications of the Association for Research in Nervous and Mental Disease: Vol. 24. Trauma of the central nervous system.* (pp. 507–544). Baltimore: Williams & Wilkins.

Ruesch, J., & Moore, B.E. (1943). Measurement of intellectual functions in the acute stage of head injury. *Archives of Neurology and Psychiatry, 50*, 165–170.

Ruff, R., Mahaffey, R., Engel, J., Farrow, C., Cox, D., & Karzmark, P. (1994). Efficacy study of THINKable in the attention and memory retraining of traumatically head-injured patients. *Brain Injury, 8*, 3–14.

Ruijs, M.B.M., Keyser, A., Gabreëls, F.J.M., & Notermans, S.L.H. (1993). Somatosensory evoked potentials and cognitive sequelae in children with closed head–injury. *Neuropediatrics, 24*, 307–312.

Rune, V. (1970). Acute head injuries in children: A retrospective, epidemiologic, and electroencephalographic study on primary school children in Umea. *Acta Paediatrica Scandinavica, 209*, 3–12.

Russell, E.W. (1975). A multiple scoring method for the assessment of complex memory functions. *Journal of Consulting and Clinical Psychology, 43*, 800–809.

Russell, G. (1981). Educational therapy. In C.D. Evans (Ed.), *Rehabilitation after severe head injury* (pp. 76–90). Edinburgh, UK: Churchill Livingstone.

Russell, I.F. (1986). Comparison of wakefulness with two anaesthetic regimens: Total i.v. v. balanced anaesthesia. *British Journal of Anaesthesia, 58*, 965–968.

Russell, W.R. (1932). Cerebral involvement in head injury: A study based on the examination of two hundred cases. *Brain, 55*, 549–603.

Russell, W.R. (1934). The after-effects of head injury. *Edinburgh Medical Journal, 41*, 129–144.

Russell, W.R. (1935). Amnesia following head injuries. *Lancet, 2*, 762–763.

Russell, W.R. (1951). Disability caused by brain wounds: A review of 1,166 cases. *Journal of Neurology, Neurosurgery, and Psychiatry, 14*, 35–39.

Russell, W.R. (1960). Injury to cranial nerves and optic chiasm. In S. Brock (Ed.), *Injuries of the brain and spinal cord and their coverings* (4th ed., pp. 118–126). London: Cassell.

Russell, W.R. (1971). *The traumatic amnesias.* London: Oxford University Press.

Russell, W.R., & Nathan, P.W. (1946). Traumatic amnesia. *Brain, 69*, 280–300.

Russell, W.R., & Smith, A. (1961). Post-traumatic amnesia in closed head injury. *Archives of Neurology, 5*, 16–29.

Rutherford, W.H. (1989). Postconcussion symptoms: Relationship to acute neurological indices, individual differences, and circumstances of injury. In H.S. Levin, H.M. Eisenberg, & A.L. Benton (Eds.), *Mild head injury* (pp. 217–228). New York: Oxford University Press.

Rutherford, W.H., Greenfield, T., Hayes, H.R.M., & Nelson, J.K. (1985). *The medical effects of seat belt legislation in the United Kingdom* (Department of Health and Social Security, Research Rep. No. 13). London: Her Majesty's Stationery Office.

Rutherford, W. H., Merrett, J. D., & McDonald, J. R. (1977). Sequelae of concussion caused by minor head injuries. *Lancet, 1,* 1–4.

Rutherford, W.H., Merrett, J.D., & McDonald, J.R. (1979). Symptoms at one year following concussion from minor head injuries. *Injury*, *10*, 225–230.

Rutter, M. (1981). Psychological sequelae of brain damage in children. *American Journal of Psychiatry*, *138*, 1533–1544.

Rutter, M., Chadwick, O., Shaffer, D., & Brown, G. (1980). A prospective study of children with head injuries: I. Design and methods. *Psychological Medicine*, *10*, 633–645.

Sahgal, A. (1984). A critique of the vasopressin-memory hypothesis. *Psychopharmacology*, *83*, 215–228.

Salazar, A.M., Grafman, J.H., Vance, S.C., Weingartner, H., Dillon, J. D., & Ludlow, C. (1986). Consciousness and amnesia after penetrating head injury: Neurology and anatomy. *Neurology*, *36*, 178–187.

Sampson, H. (1956). Pacing and performance on a serial addition task. *Canadian Journal of Psychology*, *10*, 219–225.

Sampson, H. (1961). Effects of practice on paced performance. *Australian Journal of Psychology*, *13*, 185–194.

Sandler, A B., & Harris, J.L. (1991). Use of external memory aids with a head-injured patient. *American Journal of Occupational Therapy*, *46*, 163–166.

Sarno, M.T. (1980). The nature of verbal impairment after closed head injury. *Journal of Nervous and Mental Disease*, *168*, 685–692.

Schacter, D.L. (1987). Implicit expressions of memory in organic amnesia: Learning of new facts and associations. *Human Neurobiology*, *6*, 107–118.

Schacter, D.L., & Crovitz, H.F. (1977). Memory function after closed head injury: A review of the quantitative research. *Cortex*, *13*, 150–176.

Schacter, D.L., & Glisky, E.L. (1986). Memory remediation: Restoration, alleviation, and the acquisition of domain-specific knowledge. In B.P. Uzzell & Y. Gross (Eds.), *Clinical neuropsychology of intervention* (pp. 257–282). Boston: Martinus Nijhoff.

Schalén, W., Hansson, L., Nordström, G., & Nordström, C.-H. (1994). Psychosocial outcome 5–8 years after severe traumatic brain lesions and the impact of rehabilitation services. *Brain Injury*, *8*, 49–64.

Schilder, P. (1934). Psychic disturbances after head injuries. *American Journal of Psychiatry*, *91*, 155–188.

Schmitter-Edgecombe, M., & Kibby, M.K. (1998). Visual selective attention after severe closed head injury. *Journal of the International Neuropsychological Society*, *4*, 144–159.

Schneider, G.E. (1979). Is it really better to have your brain lesion early? A revision of the "Kennard Principle". *Neuropsychologia*, *17*, 557–583.

Schoenfeld, T.A., & Hamilton, L.W. (1977). Secondary brain changes following lesions: A new paradigm for lesion experimentation. *Physiology and Behavior*, *18*, 951–967.

Schrader, H., Obelieniene, D., Bovim, G., Surkiene, D., Mickeviciene, D., Miseviciene, I., & Sand T. (1996). Natural evolution of late whiplash syndrome outside the medicolegal context. *Lancet*, *347*, 1207–1211.

Schwartz, B. (1967). Hemispheric dominance and consciousness. *Acta Neurologica Scandinavica*, *43*, 513–525.

Schwartz, M.L., Carruth, F., Binns, M.A., Brandys, C., Moulton, R., Snow, W.G., & Stuss, D.T. (1998). The course of post-traumatic amnesia: Three little words. *Canadian Journal of the Neurological Sciences*, *25*, 108–116.

Selecki, B.R., Hoy, R.J., & Ness, P. (1968). Neurotraumatic admissions to a teaching hospital: A retrospective survey: Pt. 2. Head injuries. *Medical Journal of Australia*, *1*, 582–585.

Shaffer, D., Chadwick, O., & Rutter, M. (1975). Psychiatric outcome of localized head injury in children. In *Outcome of severe damage to the central nervous system* (Ciba Foundation Symposium No. 34, new series, pp. 191–213). Amsterdam: Elsevier/Excerpta Medica/North-Holland.

Shallice, T. (1982). Specific impairments of planning. *Philosophical Transactions of the Royal Society of London B, 298*, 199–209.

Shallice, T., & Burgess, P.W. (1991). Deficits in strategy application following frontal lobe damage in man. *Brain, 114*, 727–741.

Shallice, T., Fletcher, P., Frith, C.D., Grasby, P., Frackowiak, R.S.J., & Dolan, R.J. (1994). Brain regions associated with acquisition and retrieval of verbal episodic memory. *Nature, 368*, 633–635.

Shallice, T., & Warrington, E.K. (1970). Independent functioning of verbal memory stores: A neuropsychological study. *Quarterly Journal of Experimental Psychology, 22*, 261–273.

Sharples, P.M., Storey, A., Aynsley-Green, A., & Eyre, J.A. (1990). Causes of fatal childhood accidents involving head injury in Northern region, 1979–86. *British Medical Journal, 301*, 1193–1197.

Sherer, M., Boake, C., Levin, E., Silver, B.V., Ringholz, G., & High, W.M., Jr. (1998). Characteristics of impaired awareness after traumatic brain injury. *Journal of the International Neuropsychological Society, 4*, 380–387.

Shetter, A.G., & Demakas, J.J. (1979). The pathophysiology of concussion: A review. *Advances in Neurology, 22*, 5–14.

Shiffrin, R.M., & Schneider, W. (1977). Controlled and automatic human information processing: II. Perceptual learning, automatic attending, and a general theory. *Psychological Review, 84*, 127–190.

Shimamura, A.P. (1986). Priming effect in amnesia: Evidence for a dissociable memory function. *Quarterly Journal of Experimental Psychology, 38A*, 619–644.

Shores, E.A. (1989). Comparison of the Westmead PTA Scale and Glasgow Coma Scale as predictors of neuropsychological outcome following extremely severe blunt head injury. *Journal of Neurology, Neurosurgery, and Psychiatry, 52*, 126–127.

Shores, E.A., Marosszeky, J.E., Sandanam, J., & Batchelor, J. (1986). Preliminary validation of a clinical scale for measuring the duration of post-traumatic amnesia. *Medical Journal of Australia, 144*, 569–572.

Schrader, H., Bovim, G., & Sand, T. (1996). Late whiplash syndrome: Authors' reply. *Lancet, 348*, 125–126.

Shum, D.H.K., McFarland, K., & Bain, J.D. (1994). Effects of closed-head injury on attentional processes: Generality of Sternberg's additive factor method. *Journal of Clinical and Experimental Neuropsychology, 16*, 547–555.

Shum, D.H.K., McFarland, K., Bain, J.D., & Humphreys, M.S. (1990). Effects of closed-head injury on attentional processes: An information-processing stage analysis. *Journal of Clinical and Experimental Neuropsychology, 12*, 247–264.

Silver, J.R., Morris, W.R., & Otfinowski, J.S. (1980) Associated injuries in patients with spinal injury. *Injury, 12*, 219–224.

Silverstein, A.B. (1982). Two- and four-subtest short forms of the Wechsler Adult Intelligence Scale—Revised. *Journal of Consulting and Clinical Psychology, 50*, 415–418.

Simpson, D.A., Cockington, R.A., Hanieh, A., Raftos, J., & Reilly, P.L. (1991). Head injuries in infants and young children: The value of the Paediatric Coma Scale. *Child's Nervous System, 7*, 183–190.

Sims, A.C.P. (1985). Head injury, neurosis, and accident proneness. *Advances in Psychosomatic Medicine, 13*, 49–70.

Sisler, G., & Penner, H. (1975). Amnesia following severe head injury. *Canadian Psychiatric Association Journal*, *20*, 333–336.

Sitaram, N., Weingartner, H., Caine, E.D., & Gillin, J.C. (1978). Choline: Selective enhancement of serial learning and encoding of low imagery words in man. *Life Sciences*, *22*, 1555–1560.

Skilbeck, C.E., & Woods, R.T. (1980). The factorial structure of the Wechsler Memory Scale: Samples of neurological and psychogeriatric patients. *Journal of Clinical Neuropsychology*, *2*, 293–300.

Smith, A. (1961). Duration of impaired consciousness as an index of severity in closed head injuries: A review. *Diseases of the Nervous System*, *22*, 69–74.

Smith, D.H., Meaney, D.F., Lenkinski, R.E., Alsop, D.C., Grossman, R., Kimura, H., McIntosh, T.K., & Gennarelli, T.A. (1995). New magnetic resonance imaging techniques for the evaluation of traumatic brain injury. *Journal of Neurotrauma*, *12*, 573–577.

Smith, E. (1974). Influence of site of impact on cognitive impairment persisting long after severe closed head injury. *Journal of Neurology, Neurosurgery, and Psychiatry*, *37*, 719–726.

Smith-Seemiller, L., Lovell, M R., Smith, S., Markosian, N., & Townsend, R.N. (1997). Impact of skull fracture on neuropsychological functioning following closed head injury. *Brain Injury*, *11*, 191–196.

Snaith, R.P., Bridge, G.W.K., & Hamilton, M. (1976). The Leeds Scale for the self–assessment of anxiety and depression. *British Journal of Psychiatry*, *128*, 156–165.

Snoek, J., Jennett, B., Adams, J.H., Graham, D.I., & Doyle, D. (1979). Computerised tomography after recent severe head injury in patients without acute intracranial haematoma. *Journal of Neurology, Neurosurgery, and Psychiatry*, *42*, 215–225.

Snow, R.B., Zimmerman, R.D., Gandy, S.E., & Deck, M.D.F. (1986). Comparison of magnetic resonance imaging and computed tomography in the evaluation of head injury. *Neurosurgery*, *18*, 45–52.

Sohlberg, M.M., & Mateer, C.A. (1989). *Introduction to cognitive rehabilitation: Theory and practice.* New York: Guilford Press.

Solomon, G.S., Greene, R.L., Farr, S.P., & Kelly, M.P. (1986). Relationships among Wechsler Intelligence and Memory Scale Quotients in adult closed head injured patients. *Journal of Clinical Psychology*, *42*, 318–323.

Sosin, D.M., Sniezek, J.E., & Waxweiler, R.J. (1995). Trends in death associated with traumatic brain injury, 1979 through 1992. *Journal of the American Medical Association*, *273*, 1778–1780.

Spielberger, C.D. (1966). Theory and research on anxiety. In C.D. Spielberger (Ed.), *Anxiety and behavior* (pp. 3–20). New York: Academic Press.

Spielberger, C.D. (1972). Anxiety as an emotional state. In C.D. Spielberger (Ed.), *Anxiety: Current trends in theory and research* (Vol. 1, pp. 23–49). New York: Academic Press.

Spikman, J.M., van Zomeren, A.H., & Deelman, B.G. (1996). Deficits of attention after closed-head injury: Slowness only? *Journal of Clinical and Experimental Neuropsychology*, *18*, 755–767.

Spreen, O., & Benton, A.L. (1969). *Neurosensory Center Comprehensive Examination for Aphasia: Manual of directions*. Victoria, BC: University of Victoria, Neuropsychology Laboratory.

Spreen, O., & Strauss, E. (1998). *A compendium of neuropsychological tests: Administration, norms, and commentary* (2nd ed.). New York: Oxford University Press.

Squire, L.R., Slater, P.C., & Chace, P.M. (1975). Retrograde amnesia: Temporal gradient in very long term memory following electroconvulsive therapy. *Science*, *187*, 77–79.

Stablein, D.M., Miller, J.D., Choi, S.C., & Becker, D.P. (1980). Statistical methods for determining prognosis in severe head injury. *Neurosurgery*, *6*, 243–248.

Stallings, G., Boake, C., & Sherer, M. (1995). Comparison of the California Verbal Learning Test and the Rey Auditory Verbal Learning Test in head-injured patients. *Journal of Clinical and Experimental Neuropsychology*, *17*, 706–712.

Steadman, J.H., & Graham, J.G. (1970). Head injuries: An analysis and follow-up study. *Proceedings of the Royal Society of Medicine*, *63*, 23–28.

Stein, D.G. (1998). Brain injury and theories of recovery. In L. B. Goldstein (Ed.), *Restorative neurology: Advances in pharmacotherapy for recovery after stroke* (pp. 1–34). Armonk, NY: Futura.

Stein, D.G., Brailowsky, S., & Will, B. (1995). *Brain repair*. New York: Oxford University Press.

Stevens, M.M. (1982). Post concussion syndrome. *Journal of Neurosurgical Nursing*, *14*, 239–244.

Stewart, D.P., Kaylor, J., & Koutanis, E. (1996). Cognitive deficits in presumed minor head-injury patients. *Academic Emergency Medicine*, *3*, 21–26.

Stewart, W., Gordon, B., Selnes, O., Tusa, R., Jankel, W., Zeger, S., Randall, R., & Celentano, D. (1989). A prospective study of amateur boxers: Methodological issues. *Journal of Clinical and Experimental Neuropsychology*, *11*, 22–23.

Stone, J.L., Lopes, J.R., & Moody, R.A. (1978). Fluent aphasia after closed head injury. *Surgical Neurology*, *9*, 27–29.

Stover, S.L., & Zeiger, H.E. (1976). Head injury in children and teenagers: Functional recovery correlated with the duration of coma. *Archives of Physical Medicine and Rehabilitation*, *57*, 201–205.

Strang, I., MacMillan, R., & Jennett, B. (1978). Head injuries in accident and emergency departments at Scottish hospitals. *Injury, 10,* 154–159.

Strauss, I., & Savitsky, N. (1934). Head injury: Neurologic and psychiatric aspects. *Archives of Neurology and Psychiatry*, *31*, 893–955.

Strich, S.J. (1956). Diffuse degeneration of the cerebral white matter in severe dementia following head injury. *Journal of Neurology, Neurosurgery, and Psychiatry*, *19*, 163–185.

Strich, S.J. (1961). Shearing of nerve fibres as a cause of brain damage due to head injury: A pathological study of twenty cases. *Lancet*, *2*, 443–448.

Strich, S.J. (1969). The pathology of brain damage due to blunt head injuries. In A.E. Walker, W.F. Caveness, & M. Critchley (Eds.), *The late effects of head injury* (pp. 501–526). Springfield, IL: Thomas.

Stroop, J.R. (1935). Studies of interference in serial verbal reactions. *Journal of Experimental Psychology*, *18*, 643–662.

Stuss, D.T., & Benson, D.F. (1984). Neuropsychological studies of the frontal lobes. *Psychological Bulletin*, *95*, 3–28.

Stuss, D.T., Ely, P., Hugenholtz, H., Richard, M.T., LaRochelle, S., Poirer, C.A., & Bell, I. (1985). Subtle neuropsychological deficits in patients with good recovery after closed head injury. *Neurosurgery*, *17*, 41–47.

Stuss, D.T., Binns, M.A., Carruth, F.G., Levine, B., Brandys, C.E., Moulton, R.J., Snow, W.G., & Schwartz, M.L. (1999). The acute period of recovery from traumatic brain injury: Posttraumatic amnesia or posttraumatic confusional state? *Journal of Neurosurgery*, *90*, 635–643.

Suhr, J., Tranel, D., Wefel, J., & Barrash, J. (1997). Memory performance after head injury: Contributions of malingering, litigation status, psychological factors, and medication use. *Journal of Clinical and Experimental Neuropsychology*, *19*, 500–514.

Sumner, D. (1964). Post-traumatic anosmia. *Brain*, *87*, 107–120.

Sunderland, A., Harris, J.E., & Baddeley, A.D. (1983). Do laboratory tests predict everyday memory? A neuropsychological study. *Journal of Verbal Learning and Verbal Behavior*, *22*, 341–357.

Sunderland, A., Harris, J.E., & Baddeley, A.D. (1984). Assessing everyday memory after severe head injury. In J.E. Harris & P.E. Morris (Eds.), *Everyday memory, actions and absent-mindedness* (pp. 191–206). London: Academic Press.

Sunderland, A., Harris, J.E., & Gleave, J. (1984). Memory failures in everyday life following severe head injury. *Journal of Clinical Neuropsychology*, *6*, 127–142.

Swann, I.J., MacMillan, R., & Strang, I. (1981). Head injuries at an inner city accident and emergency department. *Injury*, *12*, 274–278.

Symonds, C.P. (1928). Observations on the differential diagnosis and treatment of cerebral states consequent upon head injuries. *British Medical Journal*, *2*, 829–832.

Symonds, C.P. (1937). Mental disorder following head injury. *Proceedings of the Royal Society of Medicine*, *30*, 1081–1094.

Symonds, C.P. (1940). Concussion and contusion of the brain and their sequelae. In S. Brock (Ed.), *Injuries of the skull, brain and spinal cord: Neuro-psychiatric, surgical, and medico–legal aspects* (pp. 69–111). London: Baillière, Tindall & Cox.

Symonds, C.P. (1942). Discussion on the differential diagnosis and treatment of post–contusional states. *Proceedings of the Royal Society of Medicine*, *35*, 601–607.

Symonds, C.P. (1962). Concussion and its sequelae. *Lancet*, *1*, 1–5.

Symonds, C.P. (1966). Disorders of memory. *Brain*, *89*, 625–644.

Symonds, C.P., & Russell, W.R. (1943). Accidental head injuries: Prognosis in Service patients. *Lancet*, *1*, 7–10.

Tarlov, E. (1976). Optimal management of head injuries. *International Anesthesiology Clinics*, *14*, 69–94.

Tate, R.L., Lulham, J.M., Broe, G.A., Strettles, B., & Pfaff, A. (1989). Psychosocial outcome for the survivors of severe blunt head injury: The results from a consecutive series of 100 patients. *Journal of Neurology, Neurosurgery, and Psychiatry*, *52*, 1128–1134.

Taylor, A.R. (1969). The cerebral circulatory disturbance associated with the late effects of head injury: An examination of the underlying pathologic and biochemical changes. In A.E. Walker, W.F. Caveness, & M. Critchley (Eds.), *The late effects of head injury* (pp. 46–54). Springfield, IL: Thomas.

Taylor, A.R., & Bell, T.K. (1966). Slowing of cerebral circulation after concussional head injury. *Lancet*, *2*, 178–180.

Taylor, H.G., & Alden, J. (1997). Age-related differences in outcomes following childhood brain insults: An introduction and overview. *Journal of the International Neuropsychological Society*, *3*, 555–567.

Teasdale, G. (1975). Acute impairment of brain function: 1. Assessing "conscious level". *Nursing Times*, *71*, 914–917.

Teasdale, G., & Jennett, B. (1974). Assessment of coma and impaired consciousness: A practical scale. *Lancet*, *2*, 81–84.

Teasdale, G., & Jennett, B. (1976). Assessment and prognosis of coma after head injury. *Acta Neurochirurgica*, *34*, 45–55.

Teasdale, G., Knill–Jones, R., & Van der Sande, J. (1978). Observer variability in assessing impaired consciousness and coma. *Journal of Neurology, Neurosurgery, and Psychiatry*, *41*, 603–610.

Teasdale, G., & Mendelow, D. (1984). Pathophysiology of head injuries. In N. Brooks (Ed.), *Closed head injury: Psychological, social, and family consequences* (pp. 4–36). Oxford, UK: Oxford University Press.

Teasdale, G., Murray, G., Parker, L., & Jennett, B. (1979). Adding up the Glasgow Coma Score. *Acta Neurochirurgica. (*Suppl. 28), 13–16.

Teasdale, G., Skene, A., Parker, L., & Jennett, B. (1979). Age and outcome of severe head injury. *Acta Neurochirurgica. (*Suppl. *28*), 140–143.

Teasdale, G., Skene, A., Spiegelhalter, D., & Murray, L. (1982). Age, severity, and outcome of head injury. In R.G. Grossman & P.L. Gildenberg (Eds.), *Head injury: Basic and clinical aspects* (pp. 213–220). New York: Raven Press.

Teasdale, G.M., Knill-Jones, R., & Jennett, W.B. (1974). Assessing and recording "conscious level". *Journal of Neurology, Neurosurgery, and Psychiatry*, *37*, 1286.

Teasdale, G.M., Murray, G., Anderson, E., Mendelow, A.D., MacMillan, R., Jennett, B., & Brookes, M. (1990). Risks of acute traumatic intracranial haematoma in children and adults: Implications for managing head injuries. *British Medical Journal*, *300*, 363–367.

Temkin, N.R., Holubkov, R., Machamer, J.E., Winn, H.R., & Dikmen, S.S. (1995). Classification and regression trees (CART) for prediction of function at 1 year following head trauma. *Journal of Neurosurgery*, *82*, 764–771.

Teuber, H.-L. (1969). Neglected aspects of the posttraumatic syndrome. In A.E. Walker, W.F. Caveness, & M. Critchley (Eds.), *The late effects of head injury* (pp. 13–34). Springfield, IL: Thomas.

The best yardstick we have [Editorial]. (1961). *Lancet, 2,* 1445–1446.

Thomsen, I.V. (1974). The patient with severe head injury and his family: A follow-up study of 50 patients. *Scandinavian Journal of Rehabilitation Medicine*, *6*, 180–183.

Thomsen, I.V. (1975). Evaluation and outcome of aphasia in patients with severe closed head trauma. *Journal of Neurology, Neurosurgery, and Psychiatry*, *38*, 713–718.

Thomsen, I.V. (1976). Evaluation and outcome of traumatic aphasia in patients with severe verified focal lesions. *Folia Phoniatrica*, *28*, 362–377.

Thomsen, I.V. (1977). Verbal learning in aphasic and non-aphasic patients with severe head injuries. *Scandinavian Journal of Rehabilitation Medicine*, *9*, 73–77.

Thomsen, I.V. (1984). Late outcome of very severe blunt head trauma: A 10–15 year second follow-up. *Journal of Neurology, Neurosurgery, and Psychiatry*, *47*, 260–268.

Thomsen, I.V., & Skinhøj, E. (1976). Regressive language in severe head injury. *Acta Neurologica Scandinavica*, *54*, 219–226.

Thorson, J. (1974). Pedal cycle accidents: With special reference to the prevention of injuries caused by falls. *Scandinavian Journal of Social Medicine*, *2*, 121–128.

Timming, R., Orrison, W.W., & Mikula, J.A. (1982). Computerized tomography and rehabilitation outcome after severe head trauma. *Archives of Physical Medicine and Rehabilitation*, *63*, 154–159.

Todorow, S., & Heiss, E. (1978). The "fall-asleep-syndrome": A kind of secondary disturbance of consciousness after head injury in children. In R.A. Frowein, O. Wilcke, A. Karimi-Nejad, M. Brock, & M. Klinger (Eds.), *Advances in Neurosurgery: Vol. 5. Head injuries; Tumors of the cerebellar region.* (pp. 102–104). Berlin: Springer-Verlag.

Tooth, G. (1947). On the use of mental tests for the measurement of disability after head injury with a comparison between the results of these tests in patients after head injury and psychoneurotics. *Journal of Neurology, Neurosurgery, and Psychiatry*, *10*, 1–11.

Tranel, D., Anderson, S.W., & Benton, A. (1994). Development of the concept of "executive function" and its relationship to the frontal lobes. In F. Boller & H. Spinnler (Eds.), *Handbook of neuropsychology* (Vol. 9, pp. 125–148). Amsterdam: Elsevier.

Trueblood, W. (1994). Qualitative and quantitative characteristics of malingered and other invalid WAIS-R and clinical memory data. *Journal of Clinical and Experimental Neuropsychology*, *16*, 597–607.

Tulving, E. (1972). Episodic and semantic memory. In E. Tulving & W. Donaldson (Eds.), *Organization of memory* (pp. 381–403). New York: Academic Press.

Turazzi, S., Alexandre, A., & Bricolo, A. (1975). Incidence and significance of clinical signs of brainstem traumatic lesions: Study of 2600 head injured patients. *Journal of Neurosurgical Sciences, 19,* 215–222.

Twum, M., & Parenté, R. (1994). Role of imagery and verbal labeling in the performance of paired associates tasks by persons with closed head injury. *Journal of Clinical and Experimental Neuropsychology, 16*, 630–639.

Tysvaer, A.T. (1992). Head and neck injuries in soccer: Impact of minor trauma. *Sports Medicine, 14*, 200–213.

Uzzell, B.P., Dolinskas, C.A., & Wiser, R.F. (1990). Relation between intracranial pressure, computed tomographic lesion, and neuropsychological outcome. In D.M. Long (Ed.), *Advances in Neurology: Vol. 52. Brain edema: Pathogenesis, imaging, and therapy.* (pp. 269–274). New York: Raven Press.

Uzzell, B.P., Zimmerman, R.A., Dolinskas, C.A., & Obrist, W.D. (1979). Lateralized psychological impairment associated with CT lesions in head injured patients. *Cortex, 15*, 391–401.

Vakil, E., Biederman, Y., Liran, G., Groswasser, Z., & Aberbuch, S. (1994). Head-injured patients and control group: Implicit versus explicit measures of frequency of occurrence. *Journal of Clinical and Experimental Neuropsychology, 16*, 539–546.

Van Horn, K.R., Levine, M.J., & Curtis, C.L. (1992). Developmental levels of social cognition in head-injury patients. *Brain Injury, 6*, 15–28.

Van Zomeren, A.H. (1981). *Reaction time and attention after closed head injury.* Lisse, Switzerland: Swets & Zeitlinger.

Van Zomeren, A.H. (1997, November). *Impairments of attention after severe head injury: Slowness, impaired control, slowness of control?* Paper presented at a meeting of the British Neuropsychological Society, London.

Van Zomeren, A.H., & Brouwer, W.H. (1992). Assessment of attention. In J.R. Crawford, D.M. Parker, & W.W. McKinlay (Eds.), *A handbook of neuropsychological assessment* (pp. 241–266). Hove, UK: Lawrence Erlbaum Associates Ltd.

Van Zomeren, A.H., Brouwer, W.H., & Deelman, B.G. (1984). Attentional deficits: The riddles of selectivity, speed, and alertness. In N. Brooks (Ed.), *Closed head injury: Psychological, social, and family consequences* (pp. 74–107). Oxford, UK: Oxford University Press.

Van Zomeren, A.H., & Deelman, B.G. (1976). Differential effects of simple and choice reaction after closed head injury. *Clinical Neurology and Neurosurgery, 79*, 81–90.

Van Zomeren, A.H., & Deelman, B.G. (1978). Long-term recovery of visual reaction time after closed head injury. *Journal of Neurology, Neurosurgery, and Psychiatry, 41*, 452–457.

Van Zomeren, A.H., & van den Burg, W. (1985). Residual complaints of patients two years after severe head injury. *Journal of Neurology, Neurosurgery, and Psychiatry, 48*, 21–28.

Varney, N.R. (1988). The prognostic significance of anosmia in patients with closed–head trauma. *Journal of Clinical and Experimental Neuropsychology, 10*, 250–254.

Veltman, J.V., Brouwer, W.H., van Zomeren, A.H., & van Wolffelaar, P.C. (1996). Central executive aspects of attention in subacute severe and very severe closed head injury patients: Planning, inhibition, flexibility, and divided attention. *Neuropsychology, 10*, 357–367.

Vigouroux, R.P., Baurand, C., Naquet, R., Chament, J.H., Choux, M., Benayoun, R., Bureau, M., Charpy, J.P., Clamens-Guey, M.J., & Guey, J. (1971). A series of patients with cranio-cerebral injuries studied neurologically, psychometrically, electro-encephalographically, and socially. In *Head injuries: Proceedings of an international symposium* (pp. 335–341). Edinburgh, UK: Churchill Livingstone.

Viktrup, L., Knudsen, G.M., & Hansen, S.H. (1995). Delayed onset of fatal basilar thrombotic embolus after whiplash injury. *Stroke, 26*, 2194–2196.

Von Monakow, C. (1969). Diaschisis (G. Harris, Trans.). In K.H. Pribram (Ed.), *Brain and behaviour: 1. Mood, states and mind. Selected readings* (pp. 27–36). Harmondsworth, UK: Penguin Books. (Original work published 1914)

Von Wowern, F. (1966). Posttraumatic amnesia and confusion as an index of severity in head injury. *Acta Neurologica Scandinavica*, *42*, 373–378.

Wacks, M.R., & Bird, H.A. (1970). Massive gross pulmonary embolism of cerebral tissue following severe head trauma. *Journal of Trauma*, *10*, 344–348.

Waddell, P.A., & Gronwall, D.M.A. (1984). Sensitivity to light and sound following minor head injury. *Acta Neurologica Scandinavica*, *69*, 270–276.

Walsh, K.W. (1978). *Neuropsychology: A clinical approach*. Edinburgh, UK: Churchill Livingstone.

Ward, A.A., Jr. (1966). The physiology of concussion. *Clinical Neurosurgery*, *12*, 95–111.

Warrington, E.K., James, M., & Maciejewski, C. (1986). The WAIS as a lateralizing and localizing diagnostic instrument: A study of 656 patients with unilateral cerebral lesions. *Neuropsychologia*, *24*, 223–229.

Warrington, E.K., Logue, V., & Pratt, R.T.C. (1971). The anatomical localisation of selective impairment of auditory verbal short-term memory. *Neuropsychologia*, *9*, 377–387.

Warrington, E.K., & Shallice, T. (1970). The selective impairment of auditory verbal short-term memory. *Brain*, *92*, 885–896.

Wasterlain, C.G. (1971). Are there two types of post-traumatic retrograde amnesia? *European Neurology*, *5*, 225–228.

Waxweiler, R. J., Thurman, D., Sniezek, J., Sosin, D., & O'Neil, J. (1995). Monitoring the impact of traumatic brain injury: A review and update. *Journal of Neurotrauma, 12,* 509–516.

Wechsler, D. (1941). *The measurement of adult intelligence* (2nd ed.). Baltimore: Williams & Wilkins.

Wechsler, D. (1944). *The measurement of adult intelligence* (3rd ed.). Baltimore: Williams & Wilkins.

Wechsler, D. (1945). A standardized memory scale for clinical use. *Journal of Psychology*, *19*, 87–95.

Wechsler, D. (1949). *Wechsler Intelligence Scale for Children*. New York: Psychological Corporation.

Wechsler, D. (1955). *Wechsler Adult Intelligence Scale*. New York: Psychological Corporation.

Wechsler, D. (1981). *Wechsler Adult Intelligence Scale—Revised*. New York: Psychological Corporation.

Wechsler, D. (1987). *Manual for the Wechsler Memory Scale—Revised*. San Antonio, TX: Psychological Corporation.

Wechsler, D. (1997a). *Wechsler Adult Intelligence Scale (3rd Ed.)*. San Antonio, TX: Psychological Corporation.

Wechsler, D. (1997b). *Wechsler Memory Scale (3rd Ed.)*. San Antonio, TX: Psychological Corporation.

Weddell, R., Oddy, M., & Jenkins, D. (1980). Social adjustment after rehabilitation: A two year follow-up of patients with severe head injury. *Psychological Medicine*, *10*, 257–263.

Weighill, VE. (1983). "Compensation neurosis": A review of the literature. *Journal of Psychosomatic Research*, *27*, 97–104.

Weingartner, H., Caine, E.D., & Ebert, M.H. (1979a). Encoding processing, learning, and recall in Huntington's disease. In T. N. Chase, N. S. Wexler, & A. Barbeau (Eds.), *Advances in Neurology: Vol. 23. Huntington's Disease*. (pp. 215–226). New York: Raven Press.

Weingartner, H., Caine, E.D., & Ebert, M.H. (1979b). Imagery, encoding, and retrieval of information from memory: Some specific encoding-retrieval changes in Huntington's disease. *Journal of Abnormal Psychology*, *88*, 52–58.

Weisberg, L.A. (1979). Computed tomography in the diagnosis of intracranial disease. *Annals of Internal Medicine*, *91*, 87–105.

Weissman, M.M., Prusoff, B.A., Thompson, W.D., Harding, P.S., & Myers, J.K. (1978). Social adjustment by self-report in a community sample and in psychiatric outpatients. *Journal of Nervous and Mental Disease*, *166*, 317–326.

Weston, M.J., & Whitlock, F.A. (1971). The Capgras syndrome following head injury. *British Journal of Psychiatry*, *119*, 25–31.

White, A.C., Armstrong, D., & Rowan, D. (1987). Compensation psychosis. *British Journal of Psychiatry*, *150*, 692–694.

Whitman, S., Coonly-Hoganson, R., & Desai, B. (1984). Comparative head trauma experiences in two socioeconomically different Chicago-area communities: A population study. *American Journal of Epidemiology*, *119*, 186–201.

Whyte, J., Fleming, M., Polansky, M., Cavallucci, C., & Coslett, H.B. (1998). The effects of visual distraction following traumatic brain injury. *Journal of the International Neuropsychological Society*, *4*, 127–136.

Williams, D.H., Levin, H.S., & Eisenberg, H.M. (1990). Mild head injury classification. *Neurosurgery*, *27*, 422–428.

Williams, M. (1969). Traumatic retrograde amnesia and normal forgetting. In G.A. Talland & N.C. Waugh (Eds.), *The pathology of memory* (pp. 75–80). New York: Academic Press.

Williams, M. (1979). *Brain damage and the mind.* Chichester, UK: Wiley.

Williams, M., & Zangwill, O.L. (1952). Memory defects after head injury. *Journal of Neurology, Neurosurgery, and Psychiatry*, *15*, 54–58.

Wilmot, C.B., Cope, N., Hall, K.M., & Acker, M. (1985). Occult head injury: Its incidence in spinal cord injury. *Archives of Physical Medicine and Rehabilitation*, *66*, 227–231.

Wilson, B. (1984). Memory therapy in practice. In B.A. Wilson & N. Moffat (Eds.), *Clinical management of memory problems* (pp. 89–111). London: Croom Helm.

Wilson, B.A. (1987). *Rehabilitation of memory*. New York: Guilford Press.

Wilson, B.A., Baddeley, A., Shiel, A., & Patton, G. (1992). How does post-traumatic amnesia differ from the amnesic syndrome and from chronic memory impairment? *Neuropsychological Rehabilitation*, *2*, 231–243.

Wilson, J.A., Pentland, B., Currie, C.T., & Miller, J.D. (1987). The functional effects of head injury in the elderly. *Brain Injury*, *1*, 183–188.

Wilson, J.T.L., Teasdale, G.M., Hadley, D.M., Wiedmann, K.D., & Lang, D. (1994). Post-traumatic amnesia: Still a valuable yardstick. *Journal of Neurology, Neurosurgery, and Psychiatry*, *57*, 198–201.

Wilson, J.T.L., Wiedmann, K.D., Hadley, D.M., Condon, B., Teasdale, G., & Brooks, D.N. (1988). Early and late magnetic resonance imaging and neuropsychological outcome after head injury. *Journal of Neurology, Neurosurgery, and Psychiatry*, *51*, 391–396.

Wilson, S.L., Powell, G.E., Brock, D., & Thwaites, H. (1996). Vegetative state and responses to sensory stimulation: An analysis of 24 cases. *Brain Injury*, *10*, 807–818.

Windle, W.F., Groat, R.A., & Fox, C.A. (1944). Experimental structural alterations in the brain during and after concussion. *Surgery, Gynecology, and Obstetrics*, *79*, 561–572.

Winogron, H.W., Knights, R.M., & Bawden, H.N. (1984). Neuropsychological deficits following head injury in children. *Journal of Clinical Neuropsychology*, *6*, 269–286.

Witol, A., & Webbe, F. (1994). Neuropsychological deficits associated with soccer play. *Archives of Clinical Neuropsychology, 9*, 204–205. (Abstract)

Wolkowitz, O. M., Tinklenberg, J. R., & Weingartner, H. (1985). A psychopharmacological perspective of cognitive functions: II. Specific pharmacologic agents. *Neuropsychobiology*, *14*, 133–156. (Abstract).

Wood, R.L. (1979). The relationship of brain damage, measured by computerised axial tomography, to quantitative intellectual impairment. In D.J. Oborne, M.M. Gruneberg, & J.R. Eiser (Eds.), *Research in psychology and medicine: Vol. 1. Physical aspects: Pain, stress, diagnosis and organic damage* (pp. 339–346). London: Academic Press.

Wood, R.L., & Yurdakul, L.K. (1997). Change in relationship status following traumatic brain injury. *Brain Injury, 11*, 491–502.

Woodard, J.L. (1993). Confirmatory factory analysis of the Wechsler Memory Scale—Revised in a mixed clinical population. *Journal of Clinical and Experimental Neuropsychology, 15*, 968–973.

Woo-Sam, J., Zimmerman, I.L., Brink, J.D., Uyehara, K., & Miller, A.R. (1970). Socio-economic status and post-trauma intelligence in children with severe head injuries. *Psychological Reports, 27*, 147–153.

World Health Organisation. (1977). *Manual of the international statistical classification of diseases, injuries, and causes of death* (Vol. 1). Geneva: Author. (London: Her Majesty's Stationery Office)

World Health Organisation. (1992). *International statistical classification of diseases and related health problems.* (10th ed., Vol. 1). Geneva: Author.

Wrightson, P., & Gronwall, D. (1981). Time off work and symptoms after minor head injury. *Injury, 12*, 445–454.

Wrightson, P., & Gronwall, D. (1998). Mild head injury in New Zealand: Incidence of injury and persisting symptoms. *New Zealand Medical Journal, 111*, 99–101.

Wrightson, P., McGinn, V., & Gronwall, D. (1995). Mild head injury in preschool children: Evidence that it can be associated with a persisting cognitive defect. *Journal of Neurology, Neurosurgery, and Psychiatry, 59*, 375–380.

Yarnell, P.R., & Lynch, S. (1970). Retrograde memory immediately after concussion. *Lancet, 1*, 863–864.

Yarnell, P.R., & Lynch, S. (1973). The "ding": Amnestic states in football trauma. *Neurology, 23*, 196–197.

Ylvisaker, M., & Szekeres, S.F. (1998). A framework for cognitive rehabilitation. In M. Ylvisaker (Ed.), *Traumatic brain injury rehabilitation: Children and adolescents* (2nd ed., pp. 125–158). Boston: Butterworth-Heinemann.

Zimmerman, R.A., Bilaniuk, L.T., Bruce, D., Dolinskas, C., Obrist, W., & Kuhl, D. (1978). Computed tomography of pediatric head trauma: Acute general cerebral swelling. *Radiology, 126*, 403–408.

Zimmerman, R.A., Bilaniuk, L.T., & Genneralli, T. (1978). Computed tomography of shearing injuries of the cerebral white matter. *Radiology, 127*, 393–396.

Zwaagstra, R., Schmidt, I., & Vanier, M. (1996). Recovery of speed of information processing in closed-head-injury patients. *Journal of Clinical and Experimental Neuropsychology, 18*, 383–393.

Zwimpfer, T.J., Brown, J., Sullivan, I., & Moulton, R.J. (1997). Head injuries due to falls caused by seizures: A group at high risk for traumatic intracranial hematomas. *Journal of Neurosurgery, 86*, 433–437.

# Author index

# Subject index